D0833291

Newnes Pocket DICTIONARY of QUOTATIONS

NEWNES
Pocket
DICTIONARY of QUOTATIONS

Edited by
Jonathan Hunt

NEWNES BOOKS

NEWNES·BOOKS

First published in 1979 by
The Hamlyn Publishing Group Limited
Published in 1983 by Newnes Books,
84–88 The Centre, Feltham, Middlesex, England

Fifth Impression 1984

ISBN 0 600 37420 3

Compiled by
Laurence Urdang Associates Limited,
Aylesbury, Bucks

Printed in Great Britain by
Hazell Watson & Viney Limited,
Member of the BPCC Group,
Aylesbury, Bucks

Introduction

The quotations in this book have been selected primarily for their qualities of succinctness, perception, and wit. Many well-known quotations by major authors have been included, but the main criterion for the inclusion of a quotation has been that it should make an original or colourful observation about life. Such quotations, whether they are from speeches or plays, poetry or prose, are potentially useful to the writer or speaker who is looking for something to illustrate a point and is in need of an apt quotation. They also form an interesting introduction to the life, work, or personality of their authors, as well as providing entertaining reading.

An effort has been made to make this selection widely representative and fully up to date. Foreign quotations are given in English where they are best known in this form or in the original language (with a translation) where that is more familiar. Equal weight has been given to the humorous and the serious so as to reflect all aspects of life from the sternly philosophical to the broadly comical.

The quotations are arranged under their authors' names, which are listed alphabetically with a brief biographical description. Additional information is provided for quotations which are set in a specific context or which refer to a particular person or thing. The names of characters in plays and novels are given wherever such information is useful and references to the sources of quotations have been made as full as possible. Within the entry for each author, quotations are arranged in alphabetical order of sources in the case of novels, plays, poems, and other books, and in chronological order in the case of speeches, broadcasts, etc. In the entry for George Bernard Shaw, for example, quotations from the plays are listed first, then a quotation from a novel, and finally miscellaneous and attributed remarks.

Aylesbury, February 1979

Jonathan Hunt
John Daintith

How to use this book

To assist the reader in finding a particular quotation, each author and each quotation has its own reference number. The author's number forms the first part of the reference number of each quotation by that author. Thus, 'Addison' bears the number '4' and the quotations by Addison are numbered '4.1', '4.2', '4.3', etc.

Each quotation is indexed under a number of key words to enable a fully or half remembered quotation to be traced easily. Key phrases from each quotation are listed in alphabetical order under the appropriate key word, and followed by the reference number of the full form of the quotation in the main text. An additional feature of the index is that some quotations which refer to a particular person or place have been indexed under the appropriate name, even though the name itself does not actually occur in the quotation. Thus 'Oxford' occurs in the index, even though Matthew Arnold does not refer to the 'city with her dreaming spires' by name at that point in his poem *Thyrsis*.

The reader may wish to consult the main section of the book directly in order to discover quotations by a particular author. He can use the index to discover the source of a particular quotation and also as a subject index to find quotations about, for example, 'beauty', 'war', or 'time'. Browsing through both text and index will offer him the pleasures of variety, chance discovery, and the juxtaposition of the contradictory and the unexpected.

Note on the Index

The first part of a reference number refers to a particular author. The second part refers to the appropriate quotation by that author.

Plurals of nouns are indexed separately from the singular. Possessive forms, such as 'man's' or 'God's' will be found under 'man' and 'God'. Third person singular forms of verbs, such as 'makes' or 'hurries' are indexed separately from the plain form of the verb.

Foreign words are printed in italics. Index words which do not occur within a particular quotation are also printed in italics.

Dictionary of Quotations

A

1 Acton, John Emerich Edward Dalberg, 1st Baron (1834-1902), English historian.

1.1
Power tends to corrupt, and absolute power corrupts absolutely. Great men are almost always bad men...There is no worse heresy than that the office sanctifies the holder of it. *Letter to Bishop Mandell Creighton, 5 Apr 1887*

2 Adams, John Quincy (1767-1848), President of the United States.

2.1
Think of your forefathers! Think of your posterity! *Speech, Plymouth, Massachusetts, 22 Dec 1802*

3 Adcock, Sir Frank (1886-1968), English classicist.

3.1
That typically English characteristic for which there is no English name—*esprit de corps.*
Presidential address

4 Addison, Joseph (1672-1719), English essayist and dramatist.

4.1
'Tis not in mortals to command success,
But we'll do more, Sempronius; we'll deserve it. *Cato, I:2*

4.2
The woman that deliberates is lost.
same, IV:1

4.3
When vice prevails, and impious men bear sway,
The post of honour is a private station.
same

4.4
Thus I live in the world rather as a Spectator of mankind, than as one of the species, by which means I have made myself a speculative statesman, soldier, merchant, and artisan, without ever meddling with any practical part of life. *The Spectator, 1 Mar 1711*

4.5
Sunday clears away the rust of the whole week. *same, 9 July 1711*

4.6
[*Sir Roger*] told them, with the air of a man who would not give his judgment rashly, that 'much might be said on both sides'. *same, 20 July 1711*

4.7
A woman seldom asks advice until she has bought her wedding clothes.
same, 4 Sept 1712

4.8
We are always doing something for posterity, but I would fain see posterity do something for us.
same, 20 Aug 1714

4.9
See in what peace a Christian can die.
Last words

5 Ady, Thomas (*c.* 1655), English poet.

5.1
Matthew, Mark, Luke and John,
The bed be blest that I lie on.
A Candle in the Dark

6 Aesop, (*c.* 550 B.C.), Greek fabulist.

6.1
Beware that you do not lose the substance by grasping at the shadow.
Fables, 'The Dog and the Shadow'

6.2
The gods help them that help themselves. *same, 'Hercules and the Waggoner'*

6.3
It is not only fine feathers that make fine birds. *same, 'The Jay and the Peacock'*

6.4
Don't count your chickens before they are hatched. *same, 'The Milkmaid and her Pail'*

7 Agar, Herbert Sebastian (b. 1897), American poet and writer.

7.1
The truth that makes men free is for the most part the truth which men prefer not to hear. *A Time for Greatness*

8 Akins, Zoë (1886-1958), American dramatist.

8.1
The Greeks Had a Word for It.
Title of play

9 Albee, Edward (b. 1928), American dramatist.

9.1
Who's Afraid of Virginia Woolf?
Title of play

9.2
I have a fine sense of the ridiculous, but no sense of humour.
Who's Afraid of Virginia Woolf?, Act I

10 Alcuin, (735-804), English cleric and adviser of Charlemagne.

10.1
Vox populi, vox dei.
The voice of the people is the voice of God. *Letter to Charlemagne*

11 Allainval, Abbé Lénor d' (1700-1753), French dramatist.

11.1
L'embarras des richesses.
A superfluity of good things.
Title of play

12 Ambrose, Saint (340?-397?), Bishop of Milan.

12.1
When in Rome, live as the Romans do: when elsewhere, live as they live elsewhere. *Advice to St. Augustine*

13 Amery, Leopold Stennett (1873-1955), English statesman.

13.1
[*To Neville Chamberlain, quoting Cromwell*] You have sat too long here for any good you have been doing. Depart, I say, and let us have done with you. In the name of God, *go!*
Speech, House of Commons, May 1940

14 Anouilh, Jean (b. 1910), French dramatist.

14.1
The object of art is to give life a shape.
The Rehearsal, I:2

14.2
What fun it would be to be poor, as long as one was *excessively* poor! Anything in excess is most exhilarating. *Ring Round the Moon, Act 2*

15 The Arabian Nights

15.1
Who will change old lamps for new ones? ... new lamps for old ones?
The History of Aladdin

15.2
Open Sesame!
The History of Ali Baba

16 Archimedes, (287-212 B.C.), Greek scientist.

16.1
Give me a firm place to stand, and I will move the earth. *On the Lever*

16.2
Eureka!
I have found it! *Remark on making a discovery*

17 Aristotle, (384-322 B.C.), Greek philosopher and scientist.

17.1
What we have to learn to do, we learn by doing. *Ethics, 2*

17.2
Man is by nature a political animal.
Politics, 1

17.3
Inferiors revolt in order that they may be equal and equals that they may be superior. Such is the state of mind which creates revolutions. *same, 5*

17.4
Plato is dear to me, but dearer still is truth. *Attributed*

18 Armstrong, Neil (b. 1930), American astronaut.

18.1
[*Of his first step onto the moon*] That's one small step for man, one giant leap for mankind. *Remark, 21 July 1969*

19 Arnold, George (1834-1865), American poet and writer.

19.1
The living need charity more than the dead. *The Jolly Old Pedagogue*

20 Arnold, Matthew (1822-1888), English poet and critic.

20.1
The sea is calm to-night,
The tide is full, the moon lies fair
Upon the Straits. *Dover Beach*

20.2
And we are here as on a darkling plain
Swept with confused alarms of struggle and flight,
Where ignorant armies clash by night.
same

20.3
Is it so small a thing
To have enjoy'd the sun,
To have lived light in the spring,
To have loved, to have thought, to have done? *Empedocles on Etna*

20.4
Come, dear children, let us away;
Down and away below.
The Forsaken Merman

20.5
She left lonely for ever
The kings of the sea. *same*

20.6
Who saw life steadily, and saw it whole:
The mellow glory of the Attic stage.
Sonnets to a Friend

20.7
Wandering between two worlds, one dead,
The other powerless to be born.
The Grand Chartreuse

20.8
Go, for they call you, Shepherd, from the hill. *The Scholar Gipsy*

20.9
All the live murmur of a summer's day. *same*

20.10
Before this strange disease of modern life,
With its sick hurry, its divided aims.
same

20.11
Still nursing the unconquerable hope,
Still clutching the inviolable shade.
same

20.12
Others abide our question, Thou art free,
We ask and ask: Thou smilest and art still,
Out-topping knowledge.
Shakespeare

20.13
[*Of Oxford*] that sweet City with her dreaming spires
She needs not June for beauty's heightening. *Thyrsis*

20.14
The pursuit of perfection, then, is the pursuit of sweetness and light.
Culture and Anarchy

20.15
Thus we have got three distinct terms, Barbarians, Philistines, Populace, to denote roughly the three great classes into which our society is divided.
same

20.16
[*Of Oxford*] Home of lost causes, and forsaken beliefs, and unpopular names, and impossible loyalties! *Essays in Criticism, First Series, Preface*

20.17
I am bound by my own definition of criticism: a disinterested endeavour to learn and propagate the best that is known and thought in the world.
same, Functions of Criticism at the Present Time

20.18
Culture, the acquainting ourselves with the best that has been known and said in the world, and thus with the history of the human spirit. *Literature and Dogma, Preface*

21 Arnold, Thomas (1795–1842), English scholar and headmaster.

21.1
What we must look for here is, first, religious and moral principles; secondly, gentlemanly conduct; thirdly, intellectual ability.
Address to the Scholars at Rugby

21.2
My object will be, if possible to form Christian men, for Christian boys I can scarcely hope to make.
Letter on appointment as Headmaster of Rugby, 1828

22 Ashburton, Baron see **Dunning, John**

23 Asquith, Herbert Henry, 1st Earl of Oxford and Asquith (1852–1928), British statesman.

23.1
Wait and see. *In various speeches, 1910*

24 Astor, John Jacob the third (b. 1918), American millionaire.

24.1
A man who has a million dollars is as well off as if he were rich.
Attributed

25 Auden, Wystan Hugh (1907–1973), English poet.

25.1
Let us honour if we can
The vertical man
Though we value none
But the horizontal one.
Epigraph for Poems

25.2
To save your world you asked this man to die:
Would this man, could he see you now, ask why? *Epitaph for an Unknown Soldier*

25.3
To us he is no more a person
Now but a whole climate of opinion.
In Memory of Sigmund Freud

25.4
In the nightmare of the dark
All the dogs of Europe bark,
And the living nations wait,
Each sequestered in its hate.
In Memory of W. B. Yeats

25.5
Intellectual disgrace
Stares from every human face,
And the seas of pity lie
Locked and frozen in each eye.
same

25.6
Lay your sleeping head, my love,
Human on my faithless arm.
Lullaby

25.7
To the man-in-the-street, who, I'm sorry to say
Is a keen observer of life,
The word Intellectual suggests straight away
A man who's untrue to his wife.
Note on Intellectuals

25.8
Our researchers into Public Opinion are content
That he held the proper opinions for the time of year;
When there was peace, he was for peace; when there was war, he went.
The Unknown Citizen

26 Augustine, Saint (354–430), Bishop of Hippo.

26.1
Give me chastity and continence, but not yet. *Confessions, 8*

27 Austen, Jane (1775–1817), English novelist.

27.1
EMMA. One half of the world cannot understand the pleasures of the other.
Emma, Ch. 9

27.2
MR WOODHOUSE. Nobody is healthy in London, nobody can be.
same, Ch. 12

27.3
JOHN KNIGHTLEY. Business, you know, may bring money, but friendship hardly ever does. *same, Ch. 34*

27.4
Let other pens dwell on guilt and misery. *Mansfield Park, Ch. 48*

27.5
CATHERINE MORLAND. But are they all horrid, are you sure they are all horrid?
Northanger Abbey, Ch. 6

27.6
A woman, especially if she have the misfortune of knowing anything, should conceal it as well as she can.
same, Ch. 14

27.7
One does not love a place the less for having suffered in it, unless it has all been suffering, nothing but suffering.
Persuasion, Ch. 20

27.8
It is a truth universally acknowledged, that a single man in possession of a good fortune must be in want of a wife. *Pride and Prejudice, Ch. 1*

27.9
Happiness in marriage is entirely a matter of chance. *same, Ch. 6*

27.10
MR BENNET. For what do we live, but to make sport for our neighbours, and laugh at them in our turn?
same, Ch. 57

27.11
MR DARCY. I have been a selfish being all my life, in practice, though not in principle. *same, Ch. 58*

27.12
What dreadful hot weather we have! It keeps me in a continual state of inelegance. *Letter, 18 Sept 1796*

28 Austin, Alfred (1835–1913), English poet.

28.1
Across the wires the electric message came:
'He is no better, he is much the same.'
On the Illness of the Prince of Wales, attributed

29 Ayer, Sir Alfred Jules (b. 1910), English philosopher.

29.1
No morality can be founded on authority, even if the authority were divine. *Essay on Humanism*

B

30 Bacon, Francis, 1st Baron Verulam (1561–1626), English writer, philosopher and statesman.

30.1
If a man will begin with certainties, he shall end in doubts, but if he will be content to begin with doubts, he shall end in certainties.
The Advancement of Learning, I:5:8

30.2
What is truth? said jesting Pilate, and would not stay for an answer.
Essays, 1, Of Truth

30.3
Men fear death, as children fear to go in the dark; and as that natural fear in children is increased with tales, so is the other. *same, 2, Of Death*

30.4
It is natural to die as to be born; and to a little infant, perhaps, the one is as painful as the other. *same*

30.5
All colours will agree in the dark.
same, 3, Of Unity in Religion

30.6
Revenge is a kind of wild justice; which the more man's nature runs to, the more ought law to weed it out.
same, 4, Of Revenge

30.7
Prosperity doth best discover vice; but adversity doth best discover virtue.
same, 5, Of Adversity

30.8
The joys of parents are secret, and so are their griefs and fears. *same, 7, Of Parents and Children*

30.9
Children sweeten labours, but they make misfortunes more bitter.
same

30.10
He that hath wife and children hath given hostages to fortune; for they are impediments to great enterprises, either of virtue or mischief. *same, 8, Of Marriage and Single Life*

30.11
Wives are young men's mistresses; companions for middle age; and old men's nurses. *same*

30.12
He was reputed one of the wise men, that made answer to the question, when a man should marry? A young man not yet, an elder man not at all.
same, 8, Of Marriage and Single Life

30.13
There is in human nature generally more of the fool than of the wise.
same, 12, Of Boldness

30.14
If the hill will not come to Mahomet, Mahomet will go to the hill. *same*

30.15
In charity there is no excess.
same, 13, Of Goodness, and Goodness of Nature

30.16
If a man be gracious and courteous to strangers, it shews he is a citizen of the world. *same*

30.17
Money is like muck, not good except it be spread. *same, 15, Of Seditions and Troubles*

30.18
The remedy is worse than the disease.
same

30.19
It were better to have no opinion of God at all, than such an opinion as is unworthy of him. *same, 17, Of Superstition*

30.20
Travel, in the younger sort, is a part of education; in the elder, a part of experience. *same, 18, Of Travel*

30.21
It is a miserable state of mind to have few things to desire and many things to fear. *same, 19, Of Empire*

30.22
Nothing destroyeth authority so much as the unequal and untimely interchange of power pressed too far, and relaxed too much. *same*

30.23
Be so true to thyself, as thou be not false to others. *same, 23, Of Wisdom for a Man's Self*

30.24
He that will not apply new remedies must expect new evils: for time is the greatest innovator. *same, 24, Of Innovations*

30.25
To choose time is to save time.
same, 25, Of Dispatch

30.26
Whosoever is delighted in solitude is either a wild beast or a god.
same, 27, Of Friendship

30.27
Cure the disease and kill the patient.
same

30.28
Riches are for spending. *same, 28, Of Expense*

30.29
Age will not be defied. *same, 30, Of Regiment of Health*
30.30
Suspicions amongst thoughts are like bats amongst birds, they ever fly by twilight. *same, 31, Of Suspicion*
30.31
Nature is often hidden, sometimes overcome, seldom extinguished.
same, 38, Of Nature in Men
30.32
A man that is young in years may be old in hours, if he have lost no time.
same, 42, Of Youth and Age
30.33
Virtue is like a rich stone, best plain set *same, 43, Of Beauty*
30.34
There is no excellent beauty that hath not some strangeness in the proportion. *same*
30.35
Houses are built to live in, and not to look on. *same, 45, Of Building*
30.36
God Almighty first planted a garden. And indeed it is the purest of human pleasures. *same, 46, Of Gardens*
30.37
Studies serve for delight, for ornament, and for ability. *same, 50, Of Studies*
30.38
Some books are to be tasted, others to be swallowed, and some few to be chewed and digested. *same*
30.39
Reading maketh a full man; conference a ready man; and writing an exact man. *same*
30.40
Fame is like a river, that beareth up things light and swoln, and drowns things weighty and solid.
same, 53, Of Praise
30.41
Nature, to be commanded, must be obeyed. *Novum Organum*
30.42
I have taken all knowledge to be my province.
Letter to Lord Burleigh, 1592

31 Bacon, Francis (b. 1909), Irish artist.
31.1
How can I take an interest in my work when I don't like it? *Francis Bacon (Sir John Rothenstein)*

32 Bagehot, Walter (1826-1877), English economist and journalist.
32.1
The Times has made many ministries.
The English Constitution, Ch. 1
32.2
It has been said that England invented the phrase, 'Her Majesty's Opposition'. *same, Ch. 2*
32.3
Poverty is an anomaly to rich people. It is very difficult to make out why people who want dinner do not ring the bell. *Literary Studies, 2*

33 Bairnsfather, Charles Bruce (1888-1959), English soldier and cartoonist.
33.1
Well, if you knows of a better 'ole, go to it. *Fragments from France, 1*

34 Baldwin, James Arthur (b. 1924), American writer.

34.1
If the concept of God has any validity or use, it can only be to make us larger, freer, and more loving. If God cannot do this, then it is time we got rid of Him. *The Fire next Time*
34.2
Money, it turned out, was exactly like sex, you thought of nothing else if you didn't have it and thought of other things if you did. *Nobody Knows My Name*
34.3
The future is...black.
Observer 'Sayings of the Week', 25 Aug 1963

35 Baldwin, Stanley (1867-1947), British statesman.
35.1
I would rather be an opportunist and float than go to the bottom with my principles round my neck.
Attributed
35.2
The intelligent are to the intelligentsia what a man is to a gent. *Attributed*

36 Balfour, Arthur James (1848-1930), British statesman and philosopher.
36.1
It is unfortunate, considering that enthusiasm moves the world, that so few enthusiasts can be trusted to speak the truth. *Letter to Mrs Drew, 1918*
36.2
Nothing matters very much, and very few things matter at all. *Attributed*

37 Ball, John (?-1381), English priest and leader of the Peasants' Revolt.
37.1
When Adam delved and Eve span,
Who was then the gentleman?
Text for sermon

38 Bankhead, Tallulah (1903-1968), American actress.
38.1
[*Of the revival of a play by Maeterlinck*] There is less in this than meets the eye. *Remark*
38.2
I'm as pure as the driven slush.
Observer 'Sayings of the Week', 24 Feb 1957

39 Barnum, Phineas Taylor (1810-1891), American showman.
39.1
There's a sucker born every minute.
Attributed

40 Barrie, Sir James Matthew (1860-1937), Scottish novelist and dramatist.
40.1
When the first baby laughed for the first time, the laugh broke into a thousand pieces and they all went skipping about, and that was the beginning of fairies. *Peter Pan, Act 1*
40.2
Every time a child says 'I don't believe in fairies' there is a little fairy somewhere that falls down dead.
same
40.3
One's religion is whatever he is most interested in, and yours is Success.
The Twelve-Pound Look
40.4
You've forgotten the grandest moral attribute of a Scotsman, Maggie, that he'll do nothing which might damage

his career. *What Every Woman Knows, Act 2*

40.5
There are few more impressive sights in the world than a Scotsman on the make. *same*

40.6
I have always found that the man whose second thoughts are good is worth watching. *same, Act 3*

40.7
Never ascribe to an opponent motives meaner than your own.
Rectorial Address, St. Andrews, 3 May 1922

41 Barth, Karl (1886-1968), Swiss theologian.

41.1
Men have never been good, they are not good, they never will be good.
Time, 12 Apr 1954

42 Baruch, Bernard (1870-1965), American financier and public servant.

42.1
The cold war. *Saying*

42.2
I will never be an old man. To me, old age is always fifteen years older than I am. *Observer 'Sayings of the Week', 21 Aug 1955*

43 Bayly, Thomas Haynes (1797-1839), English songwriter.

43.1
Absence makes the heart grow fonder,
Isle of Beauty, Fare thee well!
Isle of Beauty

44 Beatty, David, 1st Earl Beatty (1871-1936), British admiral.

44.1
There's something wrong with our bloody ships today. *Remark during Battle of Jutland, 1916*

45 Beaumont, Francis (1584-1616) and **Fletcher, John** (1579-1625), English dramatists.

45.1
You are no better than you should be.
The Coxcomb, IV:3

45.2
It is always good
When a man has two irons in the fire.
The Faithful Friends, I:2

45.3
Let's meet, and either do, or die.
The Island Princess, II:2

45.4
I'll put a spoke among your wheels.
The Mad Lover, III:6

45.5
Those have most power to hurt us that we love. *The Maid's Tragedy, V:6*

45.6
All your better deeds
Shall be in water writ, but this in marble. *The Nice Valour, V:3*

45.7
I'll have a fling. *Rule a Wife and have a Wife, III:5*

45.8
Kiss till the cow comes home.
Scornful Lady, II:2

45.9
Whistle and she'll come to you.
Wit Without Money, IV:4

46 Beauvoir, Simone Lucie de (b. 1908), French writer.

46.1
One is not born a woman, one becomes one. *The Second Sex, Ch.2*

47 Beckett, Samuel (b. 1906), Irish novelist and dramatist.

47.1
CLOV. Do you believe in the life to come?
HAMM. Mine was always that.
Endgame

47.2
ESTRAGON. Nothing happens, nobody comes, nobody goes, its awful!
Waiting for Godot, Act 1

47.3
VLADIMIR. That passed the time.
ESTRAGON. It would have passed in any case.
VLADIMIR. Yes, but not so rapidly.
same

47.4
ESTRAGON. ... Let's go.
VLADIMIR. We can't.
ESTRAGON. Why not?
VLADIMIR. We're waiting for Godot.
same

47.5
We all are born mad. Some remain so.
same, Act 2

47.6
Habit is a great deadener.
same, Act 3

48 Beckford, William (1759-1844), English writer.

48.1
I am not over-fond of resisting temptation. *Vathek*

49 Becon, Thomas (1512-1567), English cleric.

49.1
For when the wine is in, the wit is out.
Catechism, 375

50 Bee, Bernard Elliott (1823-1861), American Unionist soldier.

50.1
There is Jackson standing like a stone wall. *First Battle of Bull Run, 1861*

51 Beerbohm, Sir Max (1872-1956), English writer and caricaturist.

51.1
Most women are not so young as they are painted. *A Defence of Cosmetics*

51.2
There is always something rather absurd about the past. *'1880'*

51.3
To give an accurate and exhaustive account of that period would need a far less brilliant pen than mine.
same

51.4
The lower one's vitality, the more sensitive one is to great art.
Seven Men, 'Enoch Soames'

51.5
Women who love the same man have a kind of bitter freemasonry.
Zuleika Dobson, Ch.4

51.6
You will find that the woman who is really kind to dogs is always one who has failed to inspire sympathy in men.
same, Ch.6

51.7
Beauty and the lust for learning have yet to be allied. *same, Ch.7*

51.8
You will think me lamentably crude: my experience of life has been drawn from life itself. *same, Ch.7*

51.9
You cannot make a man by standing a sheep on its hind legs. But by standing a flock of sheep in that position you can make a crowd of men.
same, Ch.9

51.10
She was one of the people who say, 'I don't know anything about music really, but I know what I like'.
same, Ch.16

52 Behan, Brendan (1923-1964), Irish writer.
52.1
He was born an Englishman and remained one for years.
The Hostage, Act 1
52.2
I wish I'd been a mixed infant.
same, Act 2
52.3
I am a sociable worker. *same*

53 Behn, Aphra (1640-1689), English writer.
53.1
Love ceases to be a pleasure, when it ceases to be a secret.
The Lover's Watch, Four o'clock
53.2
Faith, Sir, we are here to-day, and gone tomorrow.
The Lucky Chance, 4

54 Bell, Clive (1881-1964), English critic.
54.1
It would follow that 'significant form' was form behind which we catch a sense of ultimate reality. *Art, I:3*
54.2
I will try to account for the degree of my aesthetic emotion. That, I conceive, is the function of the critic.
same, II:3
54.3
Only reason can convince us of those three fundamental truths without a recognition of which there can be no effective liberty: that what we believe is not necessarily true; that what we like is not necessarily good; and that all questions are open.
Civilization

55 Belloc, Hilaire (1870-1953), Anglo-French author.
55.1
Child! do not throw this book about;
Refrain from the unholy pleasure
Of cutting all the pictures out!
Preserve it as your chiefest treasure.
The Bad Child's Book of Beasts, Dedication
55.2
The Chief Defect of Henry King
Was chewing little bits of String.
Cautionary Tales, Henry King
55.3
'Oh, my Friends, be warned by me,
That Breakfast, Dinner, Lunch and Tea
Are all the Human Frame requires...'
With that the Wretched Child expires.
same
55.4
When I am dead, I hope it may be said:
'His sins were scarlet, but his books were read.'
Epigrams, On His Books
55.5
I'm tired of Love: I'm still more tired of Rhyme.
But Money gives me pleasure all the Time. *Fatigue*
55.6
The Microbe is so very small
You cannot make him out at all.
More Beasts for Worse Children, The Microbe

55.7
I always like to associate with a lot of priests because it makes me understand anti-clerical things so well.
Letter to E. S. P. Haynes, 9 Nov. 1909

56 Bennett, Enoch Arnold (1867-1931), English novelist.
56.1
'Ye can call it influenza if ye like,' said Mrs Machin. 'There was no influenza in my young days. We called a cold a cold.' *The Card, Ch.8*
56.2
Being a husband is a whole-time job. That is why so many husbands fail. They cannot give their entire attention to it. *The Title, Act 1*

57 Benson, Arthur Christopher (1862-1925), English writer.
57.1
Land of Hope and Glory, Mother of the Free,
How shall we extol thee, who are born of thee?
Wider still and wider shall thy bounds be set;
God who made thee mighty, make thee mightier yet. *Land of Hope and Glory*

58 Bentham, Jeremy (1748-1832), English writer on jurisprudence and utilitarianism.
58.1
The greatest happiness of the greatest number is the foundation of morals and legislation.
The Commonplace Book

59 Bentley, Edmund Clerihew (1875-1956), English journalist, novelist and versifier.
59.1
When their lordships asked Bacon
How many bribes he had taken
He had at least the grace
To get very red in the face.
Baseless Biography, Bacon
59.2
The Art of Biography
Is different from Geography.
Geography is about Maps,
But Biography is about Chaps.
Biography for Beginners, Introductory Remarks
59.3
Sir Christopher Wren
Said, 'I am going to dine with some men.
If anybody calls
Say I am designing St Paul's.'
same, Sir Christopher Wren
59.4
What I like about Clive
Is that he is no longer alive.
There is a great deal to be said
For being dead. *same, Clive*

60 Betjeman, Sir John (b. 1906), English poet.
60.1
Phone for the fish knives Norman,
As Cook is a little unnerved;
You kiddies have crumpled the serviettes
And I must have things daintily served.
How to get on in Society
60.2
I know what I wanted to ask you;
Is trifle sufficient for sweet? *same*
60.3
Miss J. Hunter Dunn, Miss J. Hunter Dunn,

Furnish'd and burnish'd by Aldershot sun. *A Subaltern's Love song*

61 Bevan, Aneurin (1897-1960), British politician.

61.1
The language of priorities is the religion of Socialism.
Aneurin Bevan (Vincent Brome), Ch.1

61.2
[*Of Churchill*] He is a man suffering from petrified adolescence.
same, Ch.11

61.3
We know what happens to people who stay in the middle of the road. They get run over. *Observer 'Sayings of the Week', 9 Dec 1953*

61.4
I read the newspaper avidly. It is my one form of continuous fiction.
same, 3 Apr 1960

62 The Bible (Authorised Version, 1611)

62.1
In the beginning God created the heaven and the earth.
And the earth was without form, and void. *Genesis, I:1-2*

62.2
And God said, Let there be light: and there was light. *same, I:3*

62.3
So God created man in his own image, in the image of God created he him; male and female created he them.
same, I:27

62.4
For dust thou art, and unto dust shalt thou return. *same, III:19*

62.5
Am I my brother's keeper?
same, IV:9

62.6
His hand will be against every man, and every man's hand against him.
same, XVI:12

62.7
Ye shall eat the fat of the land.
same, XLV:18

62.8
Unstable as water, thou shalt not excel.
same, XLIX:4

62.9
I have been a stranger in a strange land. *Exodus, II:22*

62.10
A land flowing with milk and honey.
same, III:8

62.11
I AM THAT I AM. *same, III:14*

62.12
Let my people go, that they may serve me. *same, VIII:1*

62.13
Thou shalt have no other gods before me. *same, XX:3*

62.14
Thou shalt not make unto thee any graven image. *same, XX:4*

62.15
Thou shalt not take the name of the Lord thy God in vain. *same, XX:7*

62.16
Six days shalt thou labour, and do all thy work:
But the seventh day is the sabbath of the Lord thy God. *same, XX:8-10*

62.17
Honour thy father and thy mother: that thy days may be long unto the land which the Lord thy God giveth thee. *same, XX:12*

62.18
Thou shalt not kill. *same, XX:13*

62.19
Thou shalt not commit adultery. *same, XX:14*

62.20
Thou shalt not steal. *same, XX:15*

62.21
Thou shalt not bear false witness against thy neighbour. *same, XX:16*

62.22
Thou shalt not covet thy neighbour's house, thou shalt not covet thy neighbour's wife, nor his manservant, nor his maidservant, nor his ox, nor his ass, nor any thing that is thy neighbour's. *same, XX:17*

62.23
Thou shalt give life for life,
Eye for eye, tooth for tooth, hand for hand, foot for foot.
same, XXI:23-24

62.24
Thou shalt not suffer a witch to live. *same, XXII:18*

62.25
Let him go for a scapegoat into the wilderness. *Leviticus, XVI:10*

62.26
Thou shalt love thy neighbour as thyself. *same, XIX:18*

62.27
Man doth not live by bread only, but by every word that proceedeth out of the mouth of the Lord doth man live.
Deuteronomy, VIII:3

62.28
For the poor shall never cease out of the land. *same, XV:11*

62.29
He kept him as the apple of his eye. *same, XXXII:10*

62.30
Hewers of wood and drawers of water. *Joshua, IX:21*

62.31
Say now Shibboleth. *Judges, XII:6*

62.32
Out of the eater came forth meat, and out of the strong came forth sweetness. *same, XIV:14*

62.33
Quit yourselves like men. *1 Samuel, IV:9*

62.34
Saul hath slain his thousands, and David his ten thousands. *same, XVIII:7*

62.35
How are the mighty fallen! *2 Samuel, I:19*

62.36
DAVID. [*Of Jonathan*] Thy love to me was wonderful, passing the love of women. *same, I:26*

62.37
A still small voice. *1 Kings, XIX:12*

62.38
Naked came I out of my mother's womb, and naked shall I return thither: the Lord gave, and the Lord hath taken away; blessed be the name of the Lord. *Job, I:21*

62.39
Man that is born of a woman is of few days, and full of trouble. *same, XIV:1*

62.40
I am escaped with the skin of my teeth. *same, XIX:20*

62.41
I know that my redeemer liveth. *same, XIX:25*

62.42
Out of the mouth of babes and sucklings hast thou ordained strength.
Psalms, VIII:2

62.43
What is man, that thou art mindful of him? *same, VIII:4*

62.44
The fool hath said in his heart, There is no God. *same, XIV:1*

62.45
The heavens declare the glory of God; and the firmament sheweth his handywork. *same, XIX:1*

62.46
The Lord is my shepherd, I shall not want. *same, XXIII:1*

62.47
He maketh me to lie down in green pastures: he leadeth me beside the still waters. *same, XXIII:2*

62.48
Yea, though I walk through the valley of the shadow of death, I will fear no evil: for thou art with me, thy rod and thy staff they comfort me.
same, XXIII:4

62.49
Weeping may endure for a night, but joy cometh in the morning.
same, XXX:5

62.50
Into thy hands I commend my spirit.
same, XXXI:6 (Book of Common Prayer version)

62.51
But the meek shall inherit the earth.
same, XXXVII:11

62.52
God is our refuge and strength, a very present help in trouble.
same, XLVI:1

62.53
Oh that I had wings like a dove!
same, LV:6

62.54
For a thousand years in thy sight are but as yesterday when it is past, and as a watch in the night. *same, XC:4*

62.55
The days of our years are threescore years and ten; and if by reason of strength they be fourscore years, yet is their strength labour and sorrow; for it is soon cut off, and we fly away.
same, XC:10

62.56
As for man, his days are as grass: as a flower of the field, so he flourisheth.
same, CIII:15

62.57
They that go down to the sea in ships, that do business in great waters.
same, CVII:23

62.58
The fear of the Lord is the beginning of wisdom. *same, CXI:10*

62.59
The stone which the builders refused is become the head stone of the corner.
same, CXVIII:22

62.60
I will lift up mine eyes unto the hills, from whence cometh my help.
same, CXXI:1

62.61
They that sow in tears shall reap in joy. *same, CXXVI:5*

62.62
By the rivers of Babylon, there we sat down, yea, we wept, when we remembered Zion. *same, CXXXVII:1*

62.63
Put not your trust in princes.
same, CXL:3

62.64
Go to the ant, thou sluggard; consider her ways, and be wise.
Proverbs, VI:6

62.65
For wisdom is better than rubies.
same, VIII:11

62.66
Stolen waters are sweet, and bread eaten in secret is pleasant.
same, IX:17

62.67
A wise son maketh a glad father: but a foolish son is the heaviness of his mother. *same, X:1*

62.68
As a jewel of gold in a swine's snout, so is a fair woman which is without discretion. *same, XI:22*

62.69
Hope deferred maketh the heart sick.
same, XIII:12

62.70
He that spareth his rod hateth his son: but he that loveth him chasteneth him betimes. *same, XIII:24*

62.71
Pride goeth before destruction, and an haughty spirit before a fall.
same, XVI:18

62.72
Wealth maketh many friends.
same, XIX:4

62.73
Even a child is known by his doings.
same, XX:11

62.74
A good name is rather to be chosen than great riches. *same, XXII:1*

62.75
If thine enemy be hungry, give him bread to eat; and if he be thirsty, give him water to drink:
For thou shalt heap coals of fire upon his head, and the Lord shall reward thee. *same, XXV:21-22*

62.76
Whoso diggeth a pit shall fall therein.
same, XXVI:27

62.77
Open rebuke is better than secret love.
same, XXVII:5

62.78
Where there is no vision, the people perish. *same, XXIX:18*

62.79
Vanity of vanities, saith the Preacher, vanity of vanities; all is vanity.
Ecclesiastes, I:2

62.80
There is no new thing under the sun.
same, I:9

62.81
For in much wisdom is much grief: and he that increaseth knowledge increaseth sorrow. *same, I:18*

62.82
To every thing there is a season, and a time to every purpose under the heaven. *same, III:1*

62.83
Be not righteous over much.
same, VII:16

62.84
Cast thy bread upon the waters: for thou shalt find it after many days.
same, XI:1

62.85
Of making many books there is no end; and much study is a weariness of the flesh. *same, XII:12*

62.86
Fear God, and keep his commandments: for this is the whole duty of man. *same, XII:13*

62.87
Let him kiss me with the kisses of his mouth: for thy love is better than wine. *The Song of Solomon, I:2*

62.88
The flowers appear on the earth; the time of the singing of birds is come, and the voice of the turtle is heard in our land. *same, II:12*

62.89
Love is strong as death; jealousy is cruel as the grave. *same, VIII:6*

62.90
Many waters cannot quench love. *same, VIII:7*

62.91
Though your sins be as scarlet, they shall be as white as snow. *Isaiah, I:18*

62.92
They shall beat their swords into plowshares, and their spears into pruning-hooks: nation shall not lift up sword against nation, neither shall they learn war any more. *same, II:4*

62.93
What mean ye that ye beat my people to pieces, and grind the faces of the poor? *same, III:15*

62.94
The people that walked in darkness have seen a great light. *same, IX:2*

62.95
For unto us a child is born, unto us a son is given: and the government shall be upon his shoulder: and his name shall be called Wonderful, Counseller, The mighty God, The everlasting Father, The Prince of Peace. *same, IX:6*

62.96
The wolf also shall dwell with the lamb, and the leopard shall lie down with the kid; and the calf and the young lion and the fatling together; and a little child shall lead them. *same, XI:6*

62.97
Let us eat and drink; for to-morrow we shall die. *same, XXII:13*

62.98
All flesh is grass. *same, XL:6*

62.99
There is no peace, saith the Lord, unto the wicked. *same, XLVIII:22*

62.100
All we like sheep have gone astray. *same, LIII:6*

62.101
He is brought as a lamb to the slaughter. *same, LIII:7*

62.102
Can the Ethiopian change his skin, or the leopard his spots? *Jeremiah, XIII:23*

62.103
Remembering mine affliction and my misery, the wormwood and the gall. *Lamentations, III:19*

62.104
MENE, MENE, TEKEL, UPHARSIN. *Daniel, V:25*

62.105
Thou art weighed in the balances, and art found wanting. *same, V:27*

62.106
The law of the Medes and Persians, which altereth not. *same, VI:12*

62.107
The Ancient of days. *same, VII:13*

62.108
They have sown the wind, and they shall reap the whirlwind. *Hosea, VIII:7*

62.109
Your old men shall dream dreams, your young men shall see visions. *Joel, II:28*

62.110
Give not thy soul unto a woman.
Ecclesiasticus, IX:2

62.111
Forsake not an old friend.
same, IX:10

62.112
All wickedness is but little to the wickedness of a woman.
same, XXV:19

62.113
Let us now praise famous men, and our fathers that begat us.
same, XLIV:1

62.114
Rachel weeping for her children, and would not be comforted, because they are not. *St. Matthew, II:18*

62.115
The voice of one crying in the wilderness. *same, III:3*

62.116
O generation of vipers, who hath warned you to flee from the wrath to come? *same, III:7*

62.117
Man shall not live by bread alone, but by every word that proceedeth out of the mouth of God. *same, IV:4*

62.118
Blessed are the meek: for they shall inherit the earth. *same, V:5*

62.119
Blessed are the pure in heart: for they shall see God. *same, V:8*

62.120
Ye are the salt of the earth: but if the salt have lost his savour, wherewith shall it be salted? *same, V:13*

62.121
An eye for an eye, and a tooth for a tooth. *same, V:38*

62.122
Resist not evil: but whosoever shall smite thee on thy right cheek, turn to him the other also. *same, V:39*

62.123
Love your enemies. *same, V:44*

62.124
He maketh his sun to rise on the evil and on the good, and sendeth rain on the just and on the unjust.
same, V:45

62.125
Let not thy left hand know what thy right hand doeth. *same, VI:3*

62.126
No man can serve two masters.
same, VI:24

62.127
Ye cannot serve God and mammon.
same, VI:28

62.128
Consider the lilies of the field, how they grow; they toil not, neither do they spin. *same, VI:28*

62.129
Sufficient unto the day is the evil thereof. *same, VI:34*

62.130
Judge not, that ye be not judged.
same, VII:1

62.131
Neither cast ye your pearls before swine. *same, VII:6*

62.132
Beware of false prophets, which come to you in sheep's clothing, but inwardly they are ravening wolves.
same, VII:15

62.133
What went ye out into the wilderness to see? A reed shaken with the wind?
same, XI:7

62.134
He that is not with me is against me.
same, XII:30

62.135
One pearl of great price.
same, XIII:46

62.136
A prophet is not without honour, save in his own country. *same, XIII:57*

62.137
If the blind lead the blind, both shall fall into the ditch. *same, XV:14*

62.138
Get thee behind me, Satan.
same, XVI:23

62.139
If thine eye offend thee, pluck it out.
same, XVIII:9

62.140
For many are called, but few are chosen. *same, XXII:14*

62.141
Render therefore unto Caesar the things which are Caesar's; and unto God the things that are God's.
same, XXII:21

62.142
Wars and rumours of wars.
same, XXIV:6

62.143
As a shepherd divideth his sheep from the goats. *same, XXV:32*

62.144
Ye have the poor always with you.
same, XXVI:11

62.145
The spirit indeed is willing, but the flesh is weak. *same, XXVI:41*

62.146
The sabbath was made for man, and not man for the sabbath.
St. Mark, II:27

62.147
If a house be divided against itself, that house cannot stand.
same, III:25

62.148
For what shall it profit a man, if he shall gain the whole world and lose his own soul? *same, VIII:36*

62.149
What therefore God hath joined together, let not man put asunder.
same, X:9

62.150
Suffer the little children to come unto me, and forbid them not: for of such is the kingdom of God. *same, X:14*

62.151
Before the cock crow twice, thou shalt deny me thrice. *same, XIV:30*

62.152
Crucify him. *same, XVI:13*

62.153
Physician, heal thyself.
St. Luke, IV:23

62.154
No man putteth new wine into old bottles. *same, V:37*

62.155
The labourer is worthy of his hire.
same, X:7

62.156
He passed by on the other side.
same, X:31

62.157
Joy shall be in heaven over one sinner that repenteth, more than over ninety and nine just persons, which need no repentance. *same, XV:7*

62.158
The crumbs which fell from the rich man's table. *same, XVI:21*

62.159
Between us and you there is a great gulf fixed. *same, XVI:26*

62.160
Father, forgive them; for they know not what they do. *same, XXIII:34*

62.161
In the beginning was the Word, and the Word was with God, and the Word was God. *St. John, I:1*

62.162
He came unto his own, and his own received him not. *same, I:11*

62.163
The Word was made flesh, and dwelt among us. *same, I:14*

62.164
Ye must be born again. *same, III:7*

62.165
The wind bloweth where it listeth. *same, III:8*

62.166
For God so loved the world, that he gave his only begotten Son, that whosoever believeth in him should not perish, but have everlasting life. *same, III:16*

62.167
He that is without sin among you, let him first cast a stone at her. *same, VIII:7*

62.168
I am the light of the world. *same, VIII:12*

62.169
The good shepherd giveth his life for the sheep. *same, X:11*

62.170
A new commandment I give unto you, That ye love one another. *same, XIII:34*

62.171
Greater love hath no man than this, that a man lay down his life for his friends. *same, XV:13*

62.172
Pilate saith unto him, What is truth? *same, XVIII:38*

62.173
Blessed are they that have not seen, and yet have believed. *same, XX:29*

62.174
It is hard for thee to kick against the pricks. *The Acts of the Apostles, IX:5*

62.175
God is no respecter of persons. *same, X:34*

62.176
In him we live, and move, and have our being. *same, XVII:28*

62.177
It is more blessed to give than to receive. *same, XX:35*

62.178
These, having not the law, are a law unto themselves. *Romans, II:14*

62.179
Death hath no more dominion over him. *same, VI:9*

62.180
The wages of sin is death. *same, VI:23*

62.181
Vengeance is mine; I will repay, saith the Lord. *same, XII:19*

62.182
Be not overcome of evil, but overcome evil with good. *same, XII:21*

62.183
Absent in body, but present in spirit. *1 Corinthians, V:3*

62.184
Know ye not that a little leaven leaveneth the whole lump?
same, V:6

62.185
All things to all men. *same, IX:22*

62.186
When I became a man, I put away childish things. *same, XIII:11*

62.187
Now we see through a glass, darkly; but then face to face. *same, XIII:12*

62.188
And now abideth faith, hope, charity, these three; but the greatest of these is charity. *same, XIII:13*

62.189
O death, where is thy sting? O grave, where is thy victory? *same, XV:55*

62.190
The letter killeth, but the spirit giveth life. *2 Corinthians, III:6*

62.191
For ye suffer fools gladly, seeing ye yourselves are wise. *same, XI:19*

62.192
A thorn in the flesh. *same, XII:7*

62.193
The right hands of fellowship.
Galatians, II:9

62.194
Ye are fallen from grace. *same, V:4*

62.195
Bear ye one another's burdens.
same, VI:2

62.196
Be not deceived; God is not mocked: for whatsoever a man soweth, that shall he also reap. *same, VI:7*

62.197
Work out your own salvation with fear and trembling.
Philippians, II:12

62.198
The peace of God, which passeth all understanding. *same, IV:7*

62.199
Not greedy of filthy lucre.
1 Timothy, III:3

62.200
Drink no longer water, but use a little wine for thy stomach's sake and thine often infirmities. *same, V:23*

62.201
For we brought nothing into this world, and it is certain we can carry nothing out. *same, VI:7*

62.202
The love of money is the root of all evil. *same, VI:10*

62.203
It is appointed unto men once to die, but after this the judgment.
Hebrews, IX:27

62.204
Faith is the substance of things hoped for, the evidence of things not seen.
same, XI:1

62.205
Jesus Christ the same yesterday, and today, and for ever. *same, XIII:8*

62.206
Faith without works is dead.
James, II:20

62.207
All flesh is as grass. *1 Peter, I:24*

62.208
Honour all men. Love the brotherhood. Fear God. Honour the king.
same, II:17

62.209
Charity shall cover the multitude of sins. *same, IV:8*

62.210
God is love. *1 John, IV:8*

62.211
There is no fear in love; but perfect love casteth out fear. *same, IV:18*

62.212
I am Alpha and Omega, the beginning and the ending. *Revelation, I:8*

62.213
Be thou faithful unto death, and I will give thee a crown of life. *same, II:10*

62.214
He shall rule them with a rod of iron. *same, II:27*

62.215
Behold a pale horse: and his name that sat on him was Death, and Hell followed with him. *same, VI:8*

62.216
And when he had opened the seventh seal, there was silence in heaven about the space of half an hour.
same, VIII:1

62.217
The bottomless pit. *same, IX:1*

62.218
And I saw a new heaven and a new earth: for the first heaven and the first earth were passed away; and there was no more sea. *same, XXI:1*

62.219
The holy city, new Jerusalem, coming down from God out of heaven, prepared as a bride adorned for her husband. *same, XXI:2*

62.220
And God shall wipe away all tears from their eyes; and there shall be no more death, neither sorrow, nor crying, neither shall there be any more pain: for the former things are passed away.
same, XXI:4

63 Bierce, Ambrose (1842?-1914), American journalist and humorist.

63.1
Bore, n. A person who talks when you wish him to listen.
The Devil's Dictionary

63.2
Brain, n. An apparatus with which we think that we think. *same*

63.3
Debauchee, n. One who has so earnestly pursued pleasure that he has had the misfortune to overtake it.
same

63.4
Egotist, n. A person of low taste, more interested in himself than in me.
same

63.5
Future, n. That period of time in which our affairs prosper, our friends are true and our happiness is assured. *same*

63.6
Marriage, n. The state or condition of a community consisting of a master, a mistress and two slaves, making in all two. *same*

63.7
Patience, n. A minor form of despair, disguised as a virtue. *same*

63.8
Peace, n. In international affairs, a period of cheating between two periods of fighting. *same*

64 Binyon, Laurence Robert (1869-1943), English poet.

64.1
They shall grow not old, as we that are left grow old:
Age shall not weary them, nor the years condemn.
At the going down of the sun and in the morning
We will remember them.
For the Fallen (1914-1918)

65 Blackstone, Sir William (1723–1780), English jurist.

65.1
The king never dies.
Commentaries on the Laws of England, I:7

65.2
That the king can do no wrong, is a necessary and fundamental principle of the English constitution.
same, III:17

65.3
It is better that ten guilty persons escape than one innocent suffer.
same, IV:27

66 Blair, Eric, see **Orwell, George**

67 Blake, William (1757–1827), English poet, painter and engraver.

67.1
To see a World in a grain of sand,
And a Heaven in a wild flower,
Hold Infinity in the palm of your hand,
And Eternity in an hour.
Auguries of Innocence, 1

67.2
A robin redbreast in a cage
Puts all Heaven in a rage. *same, 5*

67.3
Does the Eagle know what is in the pit
Or wilt thou go ask the Mole?
Can Wisdom be put in a silver rod,
Or love in a golden bowl?
The Book of Thel, Thel's Motto

67.4
He who would do good to another must do it in Minute Particulars.
General Good is the plea of the scoundrel, hypocrite, and flatterer.
Jerusalem, 55

67.5
I care not whether a man is Good or Evil; all that I care
Is whether he is a Wise Man or a Fool. Go! put off Holiness,
And put on Intellect. *same, 91*

67.6
And did those feet in ancient time
Walk upon England's mountains green?
And was the holy lamb of God
On England's pleasant pastures seen?
Milton, Preface

67.7
I will not cease from mental fight,
Nor shall my sword sleep in my hand,
Till we have built Jerusalem
In England's green and pleasant land.
same

67.8
Mock on, mock on, Voltaire, Rousseau;
Mock on, mock on; 'tis all in vain!
You throw the sand against the wind,
And the wind blows it back again.
Mock on, mock on, Voltaire, Rousseau

67.9
Love seeketh not itself to please,
Nor for itself hath any care,
But for another gives its ease,
And builds a Heaven in Hell's despair.
Songs of Experience, The Clod and the Pebble

67.10
Love seeketh only Self to please,
To bind another to its delight,
Joys in another's loss of ease,
And builds a Hell in Heaven's despite.
same

67.11
My mother groan'd, my father wept,
Into the dangerous world I leapt;
Helpless, naked, piping loud,

Like a fiend hid in a cloud.
same, Infant Sorrow

67.12
Tiger! Tiger! burning bright
In the forests of the night,
What immortal hand or eye
Could frame thy fearful symmetry?
same, The Tiger

67.13
Piping down the valleys wild,
Piping songs of pleasant glee,
On a cloud I saw a child. *Songs of Innocence, Introduction*

67.14
'Pipe a song about a Lamb!'
So I piped with merry cheer. *same*

67.15
Little Lamb, who made thee?
Dost thou know who made thee?
same, The Lamb

67.16
To Mercy, Pity, Peace, and Love
All pray in their distress. *same, The Divine Image*

67.17
For Mercy has a human heart,
Pity a human face,
And Love, the human form divine,
And Peace, the human dress. *same*

67.18
'What,' it will be questioned, 'when the sun rises, do you not see a round disc of fire somewhat like a guinea?' 'O no, no, I see an innumerable company of the heavenly host crying, "Holy, Holy, Holy is the Lord God Almighty!"' *Descriptive Catalogue*

67.19
Without Contraries is no progression. Attraction and Repulsion, Reason and Energy, Love and Hate, are necessary to Human existence.
The Marriage of Heaven and Hell

67.20
Energy is Eternal Delight.
same, The Voice of the Devil

67.21
The road of excess leads to the palace of Wisdom. *same, Proverbs of Hell*

67.22
He who desires but acts not, breeds pestilence. *same*

67.23
A fool sees not the same tree that a wise man sees. *same*

67.24
Damn braces. Bless relaxes. *same*

67.25
Exuberance is Beauty. *same*

67.26
If the doors of perception were cleansed everything would appear to man as it is, infinite.
same, A Memorable Fancy

68 Boethius, Anicius Manlius Severinus (c. 475–524), Roman statesman and philosopher.

68.1
In every adversity of fortune, to have been happy is the most unhappy kind of misfortune.
De Consolatione Philosophiae, II:4

69 Borges, Jorge Luis (b. 1899), Argentinian poet, writer and critic.

69.1
I have known uncertainty: a state unknown to the Greeks.
Ficciones, The Babylonian Lottery

69.2
The visible universe was an illusion or, more precisely, a sophism. Mirrors and fatherhood are abominable because they multiply it and extend it.
same, Tlön, Uqbar, Orbis Tertius

70 Borrow, George Henry (1803-1881), English writer.

70.1

Youth will be served, every dog has his day, and mine has been a fine one.

Lavengro, Ch. 92

71 Bosquet, Marshal Pierre (1810-1861), French soldier.

71.1

[*Of the Charge of the Light Brigade at the Battle of Balaclava, 1854*] *C'est magnifique, mais ce n'est pas la guerre.* It is magnificent, but it is not war.

72 Bracken, Brendan (1901-1958), Irish journalist and politician.

72.1

It's a good deed to forget a poor joke.

Observer 'Sayings of the Week', 17 Oct 1943

73 Bradford, John (1510?-1555), English Protestant martyr.

73.1

[*On seeing some criminals being led to execution*] There, but for the grace of God, goes John Bradford. *Remark*

74 Brecht, Bertolt (1898-1956), German dramatist and poet.

74.1

What they could do with round here is a good war. *Mother Courage, Sc.1*

74.2

When he told men to love their neighbour, their bellies were full. Nowadays things are different. *same, Sc.2*

74.3

I don't trust him. We're friends.

same, Sc.3

74.4

The finest plans have always been spoiled by the littleness of those that should carry them out. Even emperors can't do it all by themselves.

same, Sc.6

74.5

A war of which we could say it left nothing to be desired will probably never exist. *same*

74.6

What happens to the hole when the cheese is gone? *same*

74.7

War is like love, it always finds a way.

same

74.8

Don't tell me peace has broken out.

same

75 Bright, John (1811-1889), British radical statesman and orator.

75.1

[*Of the Crimean War*] The Angel of Death has been abroad thoughout the land; you may almost hear the beating of his wings. *Speech, House of Commons, 23 Feb 1855*

75.2

England is the mother of parliaments.

Speech, Birmingham, 18 Jan 1865

75.3

Force is not a remedy.

Speech, Birmingham, 16 Nov 1880

76 Bronowski, Jacob (1908-1974), British scientist and writer.

76.1

The wish to hurt, the momentary intoxication with pain, is the loophole through which the pervert climbs into the minds of ordinary men.

The Face of Violence, Ch.5

76.2
The world is made of people who never quite get into the first team and who just miss the prizes at the flower show. *same, Ch.6*

77 Brontë, Emily (1818-1848), English poet and novelist.

77.1
No coward soul is mine,
No trembler in the world's storm-troubled sphere:
I see Heaven's glories shine,
And faith shines equal, arming me from fear. *Last Lines*

77.2
Vain are the thousand creeds
That move men's hearts: unutterably vain;
Worthless as wither'd weeds. *same*

77.3
O! dreadful is the check—intense the agony—
When the ear begins to hear, and the eye begins to see;
When the pulse begins to throb—the brain to think again—
The soul to feel the flesh, and the flesh to feel the chain. *The Prisoner*

78 Brooke, Rupert (1887-1915), English poet.

78.1
Just now the lilac is in bloom
All before my little room.
The Old Vicarage, Grantchester

78.2
Stands the Church clock at ten to three?
And is there honey still for tea?
same

78.3
If I should die, think only this of me:
That there's some corner of a foreign field
That is forever England.
The Soldier

79 Brown, Thomas (1663-1704), English satirist.

79.1
I do not love thee, Doctor Fell,
The reason why I cannot tell;
But this alone I know full well,
I do not love thee, Doctor Fell.
Translation of Martial's Epigrams, I:32

80 Brown, Thomas Edward (1830-1897), English poet.

80.1
A garden is a lovesome thing, God wot! *My Garden*

81 Browne, Charles Farrar, see **Ward, Artemus**

82 Browne, Sir Thomas (1605-1682), English doctor and writer.

82.1
He who discommendeth others obliquely commendeth himself.
Christian Morals

82.2
All things are artificial, for nature is the art of God. *Religio Medici, I:16*

82.3
It is the common wonder of all men, how among so many million of faces, there should be none alike.
same, II:2

82.4
No man can justly censure or condemn another, because indeed no man truly knows another. *same, II:4*

82.5
Charity begins at home, is the voice of the world. *same, II:4*

82.6
Lord, deliver me from myself. *same, II:10*

82.7
For the world, I count it not an inn, but an hospital, and a place, not to live, but to die in. *same, II:12*

82.8
There is surely a piece of divinity in us, something that was before the elements, and owes no homage unto the sun. *same, II:12*

82.9
Man is a noble animal, splendid in ashes, and pompous in the grave. *Urn Burial, Ch.5*

83 **Browning, Robert** (1812–1889), English poet.

83.1
So free we seem, so fettered fast we are! *Andrea del Sarto*

83.2
Ah, but a man's reach should exceed his grasp,
Or what's a heaven for? *same*

83.3
Just when we are safest, there's a sunset-touch,
A fancy from a flower-bell, some one's death,
A chorus-ending from Euripides, —
And that's enough for fifty hopes and fears
As old and new at once as Nature's self,
To rap and knock and enter in our soul.
Bishop Blougram's Apology

83.4
No, when the fight begins within himself,
A man's worth something. *same*

83.5
Dauntless the slug-horn to my lips I set,
And blew. *Childe Roland to the Dark Tower came.* *Childe Roland, 34*

83.6
Oh, to be in England
Now that April's there.
Home-Thoughts, from Abroad

83.7
That's the wise thrush; he sings each song twice over,
Lest you should think he never could recapture
The first fine careless rapture!
same

83.8
I sprang to the stirrup, and Joris, and he;
I galloped, Dirck galloped, we galloped all three. *How they brought the Good News from Ghent to Aix*

83.9
Just for a handful of silver he left us,
Just for a riband to stick in his coat.
The Lost Leader

83.10
Never the time and the place
And the loved one all together!
Never the Time and the Place

83.11
Rats!
They fought the dogs and killed the cats,
And bit the babies in the cradles.
The Pied Piper of Hamelin, 2

83.12
'You threaten us, fellow? Do your worst,

Blow your pipe there till you burst!'
same, 9

83.13
The year's at the spring,
And day's at the morn;
Morning's at seven;
The hill-side's dew-pearled;
The lark's on the wing;
The snail's on the thorn;
God's in His heaven—
All's right with the world.
Pippa Passes, 1, Morning

83.14
Gr-r-r- there go, my heart's abhorrence!
Water your damned flower-pots, do!
Soliloquy of the Spanish Cloister

83.15
I the Trinity illustrate,
Drinking watered orange-pulp—
In three sips the Arian frustrate;
While he drains his at one gulp.
same

83.16
There's a great text in Galatians,
Once you trip on it, entails
Twenty-nine distinct damnations,
One sure, if another fails. *same*

83.17
My scrofulous French novel
On grey paper with blunt type!
same

83.18
What of soul was left, I wonder, when the kissing had to stop?
A Toccata of Galuppi's

83.19
What's become of Waring
Since he gave us all the slip?
Waring

84 Buchanan, Robert Williams (1841-1901), British poet, novelist and dramatist.

84.1
[*Of Swinburne, William Morris, D.G. Rossetti, etc.*] The Fleshly School of Poetry. *Title of article in the Contemporary Review, Oct 1871*

84.2
She just wore
Enough for modesty—no more.
White Rose and Red, I:5

85 Buckingham, George Villiers, 2nd Duke of (1628-1687), English royalist and writer.

85.1
The world is made up for the most part of fools and knaves.
To Mr. Clifford, on his Humane Reason

85.2
Ay, now the plot thickens very much upon us. *The Rehearsal, III:1*

86 Buffon, Georges-Louis Leclerc, Comte de (1707-1788), French naturalist.

86.1
Style is the man himself.
Discours sur le style

87 Buller, Arthur Henry Reginald (1874-1944), English botanist.

87.1
There was a young lady named Bright,
Whose speed was far faster than light;
She set out one day
In a relative way,
And returned home the previous night.
Limerick

88 Bulwer-Lytton, Edward (1803-1873), English novelist, poet and politician.

88.1
Beneath the rule of men entirely great,
The pen is mightier than the sword.
Richelieu, II:2

89 Buñuel, Luis (b. 1900), Mexican film director.

89.1
I am an atheist still, thank God.
Luis Buñuel: an Introduction (Ado Kyrou)

90 Bunyan, John (1628-1688), English writer and preacher.

90.1
As I walked through the wilderness of this world. *Pilgrim's Progress, Part 1*

90.2
The name of the slough was Despond. *same*

90.3
The gentleman's name that met him was Mr Worldly Wiseman. *same*

90.4
It beareth the name of Vanity Fair, because the town where 'tis kept is lighter than vanity. *same*

90.5
A castle called Doubting Castle, the owner whereof was Giant Despair. *same*

90.6
So I awoke, and behold it was a dream. *same*

90.7
He that is down needs fear no fall;
He that is low, no pride.
same, Shepherd Boy's Song

91 Burke, Edmund (1729-1797), British statesman and philosopher.

91.1
The concessions of the weak are the concessions of fear. *Speech on Conciliation with America, 22 Mar 1775*

91.2
The use of force alone is but *temporary*. It may subdue for a moment; but it does not remove the necessity of subduing again: and a nation is not governed, which is perpetually to be conquered. *same*

91.3
I do not know the method of drawing up an indictment against an whole people. *same*

91.4
All government, indeed every human benefit and enjoyment, every virtue, and every prudent act, is founded on compromise and barter. *same*

91.5
The people are the masters.
Speech on the Economical Reform, 11 Feb 1780

91.6
[*Of Pitt the Younger's first speech*] He was not merely a chip of the old block, but the old block itself.
Remark, 26 Feb 1781

91.7
There is, however, a limit at which forbearance ceases to be a virtue.
Observations on 'The Present State of the Nation', 1769

91.8
But the age of chivalry is gone. That of sophisters, economists, and calculators, has succeeded; and the glory of Europe is extinguished for ever.
Reflections on the Revolution in France

91.9
Man is by his constitution a religious animal. *same*

91.10
Superstition is the religion of feeble minds. *same*

91.11
Example is the school of mankind, and they will learn at no other.
Letters on a Regicide Peace, 1, 1796

91.12
And having looked to government for bread, on the very first scarcity they will turn and bite the hand that fed them. *Thoughts and Details on Scarcity*

91.13
When bad men combine, the good must associate; else they will fall one by one, an unpitied sacrifice in a contemptible struggle. *Thoughts on the Cause of the Present Discontents, 1770*

91.14
Liberty, too, must be limited in order to be possessed. *Letter to the Sherrifs of Bristol, 1777*

91.15
Among a people generally corrupt, liberty cannot long exist. *same*

91.16
The greater the power, the more dangerous the abuse. *Speech, House of Commons, 7 Feb 1771*

91.17
I am convinced that we have a degree of delight, and that no small one, in the real misfortunes and pains of others. *On the Sublime and Beautiful, I:14*

92 Burnet, Gilbert (1643-1715), Bishop of Salisbury.

92.1
There was a sure way to see it lost, and that was to die in the last ditch.
History of his own Times, I

93 Burns, Robert (1759-1796), Scottish poet.

93.1
O Thou! Whatever title suit thee—
Auld Hornie, Satan, Nick, or Clootie.
Address to the Deil

93.2
Should auld acquaintance be forgot,
And never brought to min'?
Auld Lang Syne

93.3
We'll tak a cup o' kindness yet,
For auld lang syne. *same*

93.4
Gin a body meet a body
Coming through the rye;
Gin a body kiss a body,
Need a body cry? *Coming through the Rye*

93.5
I wasna fou, but just had plenty.
Death and Doctor Hornbrook

93.6
On ev'ry hand it will allow'd be,
He's just—nae better than he should be. *A Dedication to Gavin Hamilton*

93.7
A man's a man for a' that.
For a' that and a' that

93.8
Green grow the rashes O,
Green grow the rashes O,
The sweetest hours that e'er I spend,
Are spent amang the lasses O!
Green Grow the Rashes

93.9
John Anderson my jo, John,
When we were first acquent,
Your locks were like the raven,
Your bonnie brow was brent.
John Anderson My Jo

93.10
Man's inhumanity to man
Makes countless thousands mourn!
Man was Made to Mourn

93.11
Wee, sleekit, cow'rin', tim'rous beastie,
O what a panic's in thy breastie!
To a Mouse

93.12
The best laid schemes o' mice an' men
Gang aft a-gley,
An' lea'e us nought but grief an' pain
For promis'd joy. *same*

93.13
My heart's in the Highlands, my heart is not here;
My heart's in the Highlands a-chasing the deer;
Chasing the wild deer, and following the roe,
My heart's in the Highlands, wherever I go. *My Heart's in the Highlands*

93.14
My love is like a red red rose
That's newly sprung in June:
My love is like the melodie
That's sweetly play'd in tune.
A Red, Red Rose

93.15
Scots, wha hae wi' Wallace bled,
Scots, wham Bruce has aften led,
Welcome to your gory bed,
Or to victorie. *Scots, Wha Hae*

93.16
Liberty's in every blow!
Let us do or die! *same*

93.17
Ye banks and braes o' bonnie Doon,
How can ye bloom sae fresh and fair?
How can ye chant, ye little birds,
And I sae weary fu' o' care?
Ye Banks and Braes

94 Burton, Robert (1577-1640), English cleric and writer.

94.1
All my joys to this are folly,
Naught so sweet as Melancholy.
Anatomy of Melancholy, Abstract

94.2
Hinc quam sit calamus saevior ense patet.
From this it is clear how much more cruel the pen is than the sword.
same, 1

94.3
England is a paradise for women, and hell for horses: Italy a paradise for horses, hell for women. *same, 3*

94.4
One religion is as true as another.
same

95 Bussy-Rabutin, Roger, Comte de (1618-1693), French soldier and writer.

95.1
Absence is to love what wind is to fire; it extinguishes the small, it inflames the great. *Histoire Amoureuse des Gaules*

96 Butler, Samuel (1612-1680), English satirist.

96.1
When civil fury first grew high,
And men fell out they knew not why.
Hudibras, I:1:1

96.2
For every why he had a wherefore.
same, I:1:132

96.3
Love is a boy, by poets styl'd,
Then spare the rod, and spoil the child.
same, I:1:844

96.4
Through perils both of wind and limb,
Through thick and thin she follow'd him.
same, II:1:369

96.5
Oaths are but words, and words but wind.
same, II:2:107

96.6
What makes all doctrines plain and clear?
About two hundred pounds a year.
same, III:1:1277

96.7
He that complies against his will,
Is of his own opinion still.
same, III:3:547

96.8
The souls of women are so small,
That some believe they've none at all.
Miscellaneous Thoughts

97 Butler, Samuel (1835-1902), English author, painter and musician.

97.1
It has been said that the love of money is the root of all evil. The want of money is so quite as truly.
Erewhon, Ch.20

97.2
I keep my books at the British Museum and at Mudie's. *The Humour of Homer, Ramblings in Cheapside*

97.3
Life is one long process of getting tired. *Note-books, Life, 7*

97.4
Life is the art of drawing sufficient conclusions from insufficient premises.
same, 9

97.5
All progress is based upon a universal innate desire on the part of every organism to live beyond its income.
same, 16

97.6
The advantage of doing one's praising for oneself is that one can lay it on so thick and exactly in the right places.
The Way of All Flesh, Ch. 34

97.7
'Tis better to have loved and lost than never to have lost at all.
same, Ch.77

97.8
Brigands demand your money or your life; women require both.
Attributed

98 Byron, George Gordon, 6th Baron (1788-1824), English poet.

98.1
In short, he was a perfect cavaliero,
And to his very valet seem'd a hero.
Beppo, 33

98.2
I like the weather, when it is not rainy,
That is, I like two months of every year.
same, 48

98.3
Adieu, adieu! my native shore
Fades o'er the waters blue.
Childe Harold's Pilgrimage, I:13

98.4
My native Land—Good Night!
same, I:13

98.5
War, war is still the cry, 'War even to the knife!' *same, I:85*

98.6
Hereditary bondsmen! know ye not
Who would be free themselves must strike the blow? *same, I:86*

98.7
There was a sound of revelry by night,
And Belgium's capital had gather'd then
Her Beauty and her Chivalry, and bright
The lamps shone o'er fair women and brave men. *same, III:21*

98.8
On with the dance! let joy be unconfined;
No sleep till morn, when Youth and Pleasure meet
To chase the glowing Hours with flying feet. *same, III:22*

98.9
While stands the Coliseum, Rome shall stand;
When falls the Coliseum, Rome shall fall;
And when Rome falls—the World. *same, IV:145*

98.10
There is a pleasure in the pathless woods,
There is a rapture on the lonely shore,
There is society, where none intrudes,
By the deep Sea, and music in its roar:
I love not Man the less, but Nature more. *same, IV:178*

98.11
What men call gallantry, and gods adultery,
Is much more common where the climate's sultry. *Don Juan, I:63*

98.12
Man's love is of man's life a thing apart,
'Tis woman's whole existence. *same, I:194*

98.13
Man, being reasonable, must get drunk;
The best of life is but intoxication. *same, II:179*

98.14
All tragedies are finish'd by a death,
All comedies are ended by a marriage. *same, III:9*

98.15
The isles of Greece, the isles of Greece!
Where burning Sappho loved and sung,
Where grew the arts of war and peace,
Where Delos rose, and Phoebus sprung!
Eternal summer gilds them yet,
But all, except their sun, is set. *same, III:86*

98.16
The mountains look on Marathon—
And Marathon looks on the sea:
And musing there an hour alone,
I dream'd that Greece might still be free. *same*

98.17
There is a tide in the affairs of women,
Which, taken at the flood, leads—God knows where. *same, VI:2*

98.18
A lady of a 'certain age', which means
Certainly aged. *same, VI:69*

98.19
Now hatred is by far the longest pleasure;
Men love in haste, but they detest at leisure. *same, XIII:6*

98.20
Society is now one polish'd horde,
Form'd of two mighty tribes, the *Bores* and *Bored.* *same, XIII:95*

98.21
'Tis strange—but true; for truth is always strange;
Stranger than fiction: if it could be told,
How much would novels gain by the exchange! *same, XIV:101*

98.22
I'll publish, right or wrong:
Fools are my theme, let satire be my song. *English Bards and Scotch Reviewers, 5*

98.23
'Tis pleasant, sure, to see one's name in print;
A book's a book, although there's nothing in't. *same, 51*

98.24
A man must serve his time to every trade
Save censure—critics all are ready made. *same, 63*

98.25
She walks in beauty, like the night
Of cloudless climes and starry skies;
And all that's best of dark and bright
Meet in her aspect and her eyes.
She Walks in Beauty

98.26
So, we'll go no more a roving
So late into the night,
Though the heart be still as loving,
And the moon be still as bright.
So, we'll go no more a roving

98.27
Though the night was made for loving,
And the day returns too soon,
Yet we'll go no more a roving
By the light of the moon. *same*

98.28
If I should meet thee
After long years,
How should I greet thee?—
With silence and tears. *When we two parted*

98.29
[*After the publication of 'Childe Harold'*] I awoke one morning and found myself famous. *Entry in Memoranda*

99 Byron, Henry James (1834-1884), English dramatist.

99.1
Life's too short for chess.
Our Boys, Act I

C

100 Caesar Augustus, (63 B.C.-A.D. 14), Roman emperor.

100.1
[*Of Rome*] He so improved the city that he justly boasted that he found it brick and left it marble.
The Lives of the Caesars (Suetonius), Augustus

101 Julius Caesar, (102 B.C.?-44 B.C.), Roman general, statesman and historian.

101.1
All Gaul is divided into three parts.
De Bello Gallico, I:1

101.2
Veni, vidi, vici.
I came, I saw, I conquered.
The Twelve Caesars (Suetonius)

101.3
The die is cast. *On crossing the Rubicon, 49 B.C.*

101.4
Et tu, Brute.
You too, Brutus? *Last words, attributed*

102 Camden, William (1551-1623), English scholar, antiquary and historian.

102.1
Betwixt the stirrup and the ground
Mercy I asked, mercy I found.
Epitaph for a Man killed by falling from his Horse

103 Campbell, Roy (1902-1957), South African poet and journalist.

103.1
Now Spring, sweet laxative of Georgian strains,
Quickens the ink in literary veins,
The Stately Homes of England ope their doors
To piping Nancy-boys and Crashing Bores. *The Georgiad, I*

104 Campbell, Thomas (1777-1844), Scottish poet.

104.1
O leave this barren spot to me!
Spare, woodman, spare the beechen tree. *The Beech-Tree's Petition*

104.2
'Tis distance lends enchantment to the view,
And robes the mountain in its azure hue. *Pleasures of Hope*

104.3
Now Barabbas was a publisher.
Attributed

105 Campion, Thomas (1567-1620), English poet.

105.1
There is a garden in her face,
Where roses and white lilies grow.
There is a Garden in her Face

105.2
There cherries grow, which none may buy
Till 'Cherry Ripe' themselves do cry.
same

106 Camus, Albert (1913-1960), French writer.

106.1
Style, like sheer silk, too often hides eczema. *The Fall*

106.2
A single sentence will suffice for modern man: he fornicated and read the papers. *same*

106.3
How many crimes committed merely because their authors could not endure being wrong! *same*

106.4
No man is a hypocrite in his pleasures.
same

106.5
Don't wait for the Last Judgement. It takes place every day. *same*

106.6
One cannot be a part-time nihilist.
The Rebel

106.7
What is a rebel? A man who says no.
same

106.8
All modern revolutions have ended in a reinforcement of the power of the State. *same*

106.9
He who despairs over an event is a coward, but he who holds hopes for the human condition is a fool.
same

107 Canning, George (1770–1827), English statesman.
107.1
I called the New World into existence to redress the balance of the Old.
Speech, 12 Dec 1826
107.2
But of all plagues, good Heaven, thy wrath can send,
Save me, oh, save me, from the candid friend. *New Morality*

108 Carey, Henry (1693?–1743), English poet and musician.
108.1
God save our Gracious King,
Long live our noble King,
God save the King.
Send him victorious,
Happy and glorious. *God Save the King*
108.2
Of all the girls that are so smart
There's none like pretty Sally;
She is the darling of my heart
And she lives in our alley. *Sally in our Alley*

109 Carlyle, Thomas (1795–1881), Scottish essayist and historian.
109.1
A witty statesman said, you might prove anything by figures. *Essay on Chartism*
109.2
The three great elements of modern civilization, Gunpowder, Printing, and the Protestant Religion. *Essay on German Literature*
109.3
History is the essence of innumerable biographies. *Essay on History*
109.4
A well-written Life is almost as rare as a well-spent one. *Essay on Richter*
109.5
Genius (which means transcendent capacity of taking trouble, first of all).
Frederick the Great, IV:3
109.6
No great man lives in vain. The history of the world is but the biography of great men. *Heroes and Hero-Worship, 1*
109.7
The true University of these days is a collection of books. *same, 5*
109.8
France was a long despotism tempered by epigrams. *History of the French Revolution, I:1:1*
109.9
A whiff of grapeshot. *same, I:5:3*
109.10
[*Of Robespierre*] The seagreen Incorruptible. *same, II:4:4*
109.11
Respectable Professors of the Dismal Science. (*Political Economy*) *Latter-Day Pamphlets, 1*
109.12
Nature admits no lie. *same, 5*
109.13
Captains of industry. *Past and Present, III:9*
109.14
No man who has once heartily and wholly laughed can be altogether irreclaimably bad. *Sartor Resartus.*

109.15
I don't pretend to understand the Universe—it's a great deal bigger than I am... People ought to be modester.
Remark

109.16
MARGARET FULLER. I accept the universe.
CARLYLE. Gad! she'd better!
Attributed

110 Carnegie, Dale (1888-1955), American writer.

110.1
How to Win Friends and Influence People. *Title of Book*

111 Carroll, Lewis (Charles Lutwidge Dodgson) (1832-1898), English writer and mathematician.

111.1
'What is the use of a book, ' thought Alice, 'without pictures or conversation?' *Alice's Adventures in Wonderland, Ch. 1*

111.2
'Curiouser and curiouser!' cried Alice.
same, Ch. 2

111.3
WHITE RABBIT. The Duchess! The Duchess! Oh my dear paws! Oh my fur and whiskers! *same, Ch. 4*

111.4
'You are old, Father William, ' the young man said,
'And your hair has become very white;
And yet you incessantly stand on your head—
Do you think at your age, it is right?'
same, Ch. 5

111.5
'If everybody minded their own business, ' the Duchess said in a hoarse growl, 'the world would go round a deal faster than it does.' *same, Ch. 6*

111.6
HATTER. Twinkle, twinkle, little bat!
How I wonder what you're at!
same, Ch. 7

111.7
'Take some more tea, ' the March Hare said to Alice, very earnestly.
'I've had nothing yet, ' Alice replied in an offended tone, 'so I can't take more.'
'You mean you can't take *less*, ' said the Hatter: 'it's very easy to take *more* than nothing.' *same, Ch. 7*

111.8
'Off with his head!' *same, Ch. 8*

111.9
DUCHESS. Everything's got a moral, if only you can find it. *same, Ch. 9*

111.10
DUCHESS. Take care of the sense, and the sounds will take care of themselves. *same, Ch. 9*

111.11
MOCK TURTLE. Will you, won't you, will you, won't you, will you join the dance? *same, Ch. 10*

111.12
MOCK TURTLE. Soup of the evening, beautiful Soup! *same, Ch. 10*

111.13
WHITE RABBIT. The Queen of Hearts, she made some tarts,
All on a summer day:
The Knave of Hearts, he stole those tarts,
And took them quite away!
same, Ch. 11

111.14
'Where shall I begin, please your Majesty?' he asked.
'Begin at the beginning' the King said, gravely, 'and go on till you come to the end: then stop.' *same, Ch. 11*

111.15
'No, no!' said the Queen. 'Sentence first—verdict afterwards.'
same, Ch. 12

111.16
For the Snark *was* a Boojum, you see.
The Hunting of the Snark

111.17
'Twas brillig, and the slithy toves
Did gyre and gimble in the wabe;
All mimsy were the borogoves,
And the mome raths outgrabe.
Through the Looking-Glass, Ch. 1

111.18
RED QUEEN. Now, *here*, you see, it takes all the running *you* can do, to keep in the same place. If you want to get somewhere else, you must run at least twice as fast as that!
same, Ch. 2

111.19
Tweedledum and Tweedledee
Agreed to have a battle;
For Tweedledum said Tweedledee
Had spoiled his nice new rattle.
same, Ch. 4

111.20
'Contrariwise,' continued Tweedledee, 'if it was so, it might be; and if it were so, it would be: but as it isn't, it ain't. That's logic.' *same, Ch. 4*

111.21
The Walrus and the Carpenter
Were walking close at hand;
They wept like anything to see
Such quantities of sand:
'If this were only cleared away,'
They said, 'it *would* be grand!'
same, Ch. 4

111.22
'The time has come,' the Walrus said,
'To talk of many things:
Of shoes—and ships—and sealing-wax—
Of cabbages—and kings—
And why the sea is boiling hot—
And whether pigs have wings.'
same, Ch. 4

111.23
RED QUEEN. The rule is, jam tomorrow and jam yesterday—but never jam today. *same, Ch. 5*

111.24
'They gave it me,' Humpty Dumpty continued thoughtfully, ...'for an un-birthday present.' *same, Ch. 6*

111.25
'When *I* use a word,' Humpty Dumpty said in rather a scornful tone, 'it means just what I choose it to mean—neither more nor less.' *same, Ch.6*

111.26
WHITE KING. He's an Anglo-Saxon Messenger—and those are Anglo-Saxon attitudes. *same, Ch. 7*

111.27
HAIGHA. It's as large as life, and twice as natural! *same, Ch. 7*

111.28
The Lion looked at Alice wearily. 'Are you animal—or vegetable—or mineral?' he said, yawning at every other word. *same, Ch. 7*

111.29
WHITE KNIGHT. I'll tell thee everything I can;
There's little to relate.
I saw an aged aged man,
A-sitting on a gate. *same, Ch. 8*

111.30
'Speak when you're spoken to!' the Red Queen sharply interrupted her.
same, Ch. 9

111.31
'You look a little shy; let me introduce you to that leg of mutton,' said the Red Queen. 'Alice—Mutton; Mutton—Alice.' *same, Ch. 9*

111.32
RED QUEEN. It isn't etiquette to cut any one you've been introduced to. Remove the joint. *same, Ch. 9*

112 Cary, Phoebe (1824-1871), American poet.

112.1
And though hard be the task,
'Keep a stiff upper lip.' *Keep a Stiff Upper Lip*

113 Cato, Marcus Porcius (234-149 B.C.), Roman statesman and orator.

113.1
Delenda est Carthago.
Carthage must be destroyed. *Life of Cato (Plutarch)*

114 Catullus, Gaius Valerius (87-54? B.C.), Roman poet.

114.1
Vivamus, mea Lesbia, atque amemus.
Let us live, my Lesbia, and let us love. *Carmina, 5*

114.2
Odi et amo.
I hate and love. *same, 85*

114.3
Atque in perpetuum, frater, ave atque vale.
And for ever, brother, hail and farewell! *same, 101*

115 Cavell, Edith (1865-1915), English nurse.

115.1
I realize that patriotism is not enough. I must have no hatred or bitterness towards anyone. *Last Words*

116 Cervantes, Miguel de (1547-1616), Spanish writer.

116.1
Every man is as Heaven made him, and sometimes a great deal worse. *Don Quixote, II:4*

116.2
The best sauce in the world is hunger. *same, II:5*

116.3
There are only two families in the world, my old grandmother used to say, The *Haves* and the *Have-Nots.* *same, II:20*

116.4
A private sin is not so prejudicial in the world as a public indecency. *same, II:22*

116.5
Tell me what company thou keepest, and I'll tell thee what thou art. *same, II:23*

117 Chamberlain, Joseph (1836-1914), British statesman.

117.1
Provided that the City of London remains as at present, the Clearing-house of the World. *Speech, Guildhall, London, 19 Jan 1904*

117.2
The day of small nations has long passed away. The day of Empires has come. *Speech, Birmingham, 12 May 1904*

118 Chamberlain, Neville (1869-1940), British statesman and prime minister.

118.1
In war, whichever side may call itself the victor, there are no winners, but all are losers. *Speech, Kettering, 3 July 1938*

118.2
I believe it is peace for our time...peace with honour.
Broadcast after Munich Agreement, 1 Oct 1938

118.3
Hitler has missed the bus.
Speech, House of Commons, 4 Apr 1940

119 Chandler, John (1806-1876), English writer.

119.1
Conquering kings their titles take.
Title of poem

120 Chandler, Raymond (1888-1959), American writer.

120.1
It was a blonde. A blonde to make a bishop kick a hole in a stained-glass window.
Farewell, My Lovely, Ch. 13

120.2
She gave me a smile I could feel in my hip pocket. *same, Ch. 18*

120.3
When I split an infinitive, god damn it, I split it so it stays split.
Letter to his publisher

121 Chaplin, Charles (1889-1977), English film actor and director.

121.1
I am for people. I can't help it.
Observer 'Sayings of the week', 28 Sept 1952

121.2
All I need to make a comedy is a park, a policeman and a pretty girl.
My Autobiography

121.3
I remain just one thing, and one thing only—and that is a clown.
It places me on a far higher plane than any politician *Observer 'Sayings of the Week', 17 June 1960*

122 Charles I, (1600-1649), King of England.

122.1
Never make a defence or apology before you be accused. *Letter to Lord Wentworth, 3 Sept 1636*

123 Charles II, (1630-1685), King of England.

123.1
He had been, he said, a most unconscionable time dying; but he hoped that they would excuse it. *History of England (Macaulay), I:4*

123.2
[*Of Presbyterianism*] Not a religion for gentlemen. *History of My Own Time (Burnet), I:2:2*

123.3
[*Of Nell Gwynne*] Let not poor Nelly starve. *Said on his death bed*

123.4
[*Of the House of Lords Debate on the Divorce Bill*] Better than a play.
Remark, 1670

124 Charles V, (1500-1558), Holy Roman Emperor.

124.1
I speak Spanish to God, Italian to women, French to men, and German to my horse. *Attributed*

125 Charles, Prince of Wales (b. 1948), heir to the throne of the United Kingdom.

125.1
All the faces here this evening seem to be bloody Poms. *Remark at Australia Day dinner, 1973*

125.2
British management doesn't seem to understand the importance of the human factor.
Speech, Parliamentary and Scientific Committee lunch, 21 Feb 1979

126 Charles, Hughie, see Parker, Ross

127 Chaucer, Geoffrey (1340?-1400), English poet.

127.1
Whan that Aprille with his shoures sote
The droghte of Marche hath perced to the rote. *The Canterbury Tales, Prologue*

127.2
[*Of the knight*] He was a verray parfit gentil knight. *same*

127.3
[*Of the squire*] He was as fresh as is the month of May. *same*

127.4
[*Of the Prioress*] Ful wel she song the service divyne,
Entuned in hir nose ful semely.
same

127.5
A Clerk ther was of Oxenford also,
That un-to logik hadde longe y-go.
same

127.6
As lene was his hors as is a rake.
same

127.7
[*Of the Clerk*] Souninge in moral vertu was his speche,
And gladly wolde he lerne, and gladly teche. *same*

127.8
[*Of The Man of Law*] No-wher so bisy a man as he ther nas,
And yet he semed bisier than he was.
same

127.9
[*Of The Doctor*] For gold in phisik is a cordial,
Therfore he lovede gold in special.
same

127.10
[*Of the Wife of Bath*] She was a worthy womman al hir lyve,
Housbondes at chirche-dore she hadde fyve,
Withouten other companye in youthe.
same

127.11
The smyler with the knyf under the cloke. *The Knight's Tale*

127.12
This world nis but a thurghfare ful of wo,
And we ben pilgrimes, passinge to and fro;
Deeth is an ende of every worldly sore. *same*

127.13
So was hir joly whistle wel y-wet.
The Reve's Tale

127.14
Tragedie is to seyn a certeyn storie,
As olde bokes maken us memorie,
Of him that stood in greet prosperitee
And is y-fallen out of heigh degree
Into miserie, and endeth wrecchedly.
The Monk's Prologue

127.15
Mordre wol out, that see we day by day. *The Nun's Priest's Tale*

127.16
The lyf so short, the craft so long to lerne,
Th'assay so hard, so sharp the conquering. *The Parlement of Foules*

127.17
For of fortunes sharp adversitee
The worst kinde of infortune is this,
A man to have ben in prosperitee,
And it remembren, what is passed is.
Troilus and Criseyde, 3

127.18
Go, litel book, go litel myn tragedie.
O moral Gower, this book I directe To thee. *same, 5*

128 Chesterfield, Philip Dormer Stanhope, 4th Earl of (1694-1773) English statesman and man of letters.

128.1
Be wiser than other people if you can, but do not tell them so. *Letter to his son, 19 Nov 1745*

128.2
Whatever is worth doing at all is worth doing well. *same, 10 Mar 1746*

128.3
An injury is much sooner forgotten than an insult. *same, 9 Oct 1746*

128.4
Take the tone of the company you are in. *same, 9 Oct 1747*

128.5
Do as you would be done by is the surest method that I know of pleasing. *same, 16 Oct 1747*

128.6
I recommend you to take care of the minutes: for hours will take care of themselves. *same, 6 Nov 1747*

128.7
Advice is seldom welcome; and those who want it the most always like it the least. *same, 29 Jan 1748*

128.8
Idleness is only the refuge of weak minds. *same, 20 July 1749*

128.9
Women are much more like each other than men: they have; in truth, but two passions, vanity and love; these are their universal characteristics.
same, 19 Dec 1749

128.10
Every woman is infallibly to be gained by every sort of flattery, and every man by one sort or other.
same, 16 Mar 1752

128.11
A chapter of accidents.
same, 16 Feb 1753

128.12
Religion is by no means a proper subject of conversation in a mixed company. *Letter to his godson*

129 Chesterton, Gilbert Keith (1874-1936), English writer.

129.1
The strangest whim has seized me... After all
I think I will not hang myself today.
A Ballade of Suicide

129.2
The devil's walking parody
On all four footed things.
The Donkey

129.3
Fools! For I also had my hour;
One far fierce hour and sweet;
There was a shout about my ears,
And palms before my feet. *same*

129.4
A great deal of contemporary criticism reads to me like a man saying: 'Of course I do not like green cheese: I am very fond of brown sherry.'
All I Survey

129.5
The modern world...has no notion except that of simplifying something by destroying nearly everything.
same

129.6
The rich are the scum of the earth in every country. *The Flying Inn*

129.7
The word 'orthodoxy' not only no longer means being right; it practically means being wrong. *Heretics, Ch. 1*

129.8
As enunciated today, 'progress' is simply a comparative of which we have not settled the superlative.
same, Ch. 2

129.9
There is no such thing on earth as an uninteresting subject; the only thing that can exist is an uninterested person.
Heretics, Ch. 1

129.10
We ought to see far enough into a hypocrite to see even his sincerity.
same, Ch. 5

129.11
Happiness is a mystery like religion, and should never be rationalized.
same, Ch. 7

129.12
Charity is the power of defending that which we know to be indefensible. Hope is the power of being cheerful in circumstances which we know to be desperate. *same, Ch. 12*

129.13
Carlyle said that men were mostly fools. Christianity, with a surer and more reverend realism, says that they are all fools. *same*

129.14
A good novel tells us the truth about its hero; but a bad novel tells us the truth about its author. *same, Ch. 15*

129.15
The artistic temperament is a disease that afflicts amateurs. *same, Ch. 17*

129.16
The human race, to which so many of my readers belong.
The Napoleon of Notting Hill, I:1

129.17
The madman is not the man who has lost his reason. The madman is the man who has lost everything except his reason. *Orthodoxy, Ch. 1*

129.18
The cosmos is about the smallest hole that a man can hide his head in.
same

129.19
Reason is itself a matter of faith. It is an act of faith to assert that our thoughts have any relation to reality at all. *same, Ch. 3*

129.20
Mr Shaw is (I suspect) the only man on earth who has never written any poetry. *same*

129.21
All conservatism is based upon the idea that if you leave things alone you leave them as they are. But you do not. If you leave a thing alone you leave it to a torrent of change.
same, Ch. 7

129.22
Angels can fly because they take themselves lightly. *same*

129.23
Compromise used to mean that half a loaf was better than no bread. Among modern statesmen it really seems to mean that half a loaf is better than a whole loaf. *What's Wrong with the World*

129.24
Mankind is not a tribe of animals to which we owe compassion. Mankind is a club to which we owe our subscription. *Daily News, 10 Apr 1906*

129.25
A puritan's a person who pours righteous indignation into the wrong things. *Attributed*

129.26
New roads: new ruts. *Attributed*

130 Chevalier, Maurice (1888–1972), French actor and singer.

130.1
I prefer old age to the alternative.
Remark, 1962

131 Churchill, Charles (1731–1764), English poet.

131.1
Be England what she will,
With all her faults, she is my country still. *The Farewell*

131.2
The danger chiefly lies in acting well,
No crime's so great as daring to excel.
Epistle to William Hogarth

131.3
Keep up appearances; their lies the test
The world will give thee credit for the rest. *Night*

132 Churchill, Lord Randolph Spencer (1849–1895), English statesman.

132.1
[*Of Gladstone*] An old man in a hurry.
Speech, June 1886

132.2
Ulster will fight; Ulster will be right.
Letter, 7 May 1886

132.3
The duty of an opposition is to oppose.
Lord Randolph Churchill (W. S. Churchill)

132.4
[*Of decimal points*] I never could make out what those damned dots meant.
same

133 Churchill, Winston Leonard Spencer (1874–1965), English statesman, writer and prime minister.

133.1
It cannot in the opinion of His Majesty's Government be classified as slavery in the extreme acceptance of the word without some risk of terminological inexactitude. *Speech, House of Commons, 22 Feb 1906*

133.2
Men will forgive a man anything except bad prose. *Election speech, Manchester, 1906*

133.3
[*Over Irish Home Rule*] *The Times* is speechless and takes three columns to express its speechlessness.
Speech, Dundee, 14 May 1908

133.4
[*Of Lord Charles Beresford*] He is one of those orators of whom it was well said, 'Before they get up they do not know what they are going to say; when they are speaking, they do not know what they are saying; and when they sit down, they do not know what they have said'. *Speech, House of Commons, 20 Dec 1912*

133.5
The maxim of the British people is 'Business as usual'.
Speech, Guildhall, 9 Nov 1914

133.6
Labour is not fit to govern.
Election speech, 1920

133.7
[*Of the British*] They are the only people who like to be told how bad things are—who like to be told the worst. *Speech, 1921*

133.8
India is a geographical term. It is no more a united nation than the Equator.
Speech, Royal Albert Hall, 18 Mar 1931

133.9
We have sustained a defeat without a war. *Speech, House of Commons, 5 Oct 1938*

133.10
I have nothing to offer but blood, toil, tears and sweat. *Speech, House of Commons, 13 May 1940*

133.11
Victory at all costs, victory in spite of all terror, victory however long and hard the road may be; for without victory there is no survival. *same*

133.12
We shall not flag or fail. We shall fight in France, we shall fight on the seas and oceans, we shall fight with growing confidence and growing strength in the air, we shall defend our island, whatever the cost may be, we shall fight on the beaches, we shall fight on the landing grounds, we shall fight in the fields and in the streets, we shall fight in the hills; we shall never surrender. *same, 4 June 1940*

133.13
This was their finest hour.
same, 18 June 1940

133.14
The battle of Britain is about to begin.
same, 1 July 1940

133.15
Never in the field of human conflict was so much owed by so many to so few. *same, 20 Aug 1940*

133.16
Give us the tools, and we will finish the job. *Radio Broadcast, 9 Feb 1941*

133.17
You [*Hitler*] do your worst, and we will do our best.
Speech, 14 July 1941

133.18
Do not let us speak of darker days; let us rather speak of sterner days. These are not dark days: these are great days—the greatest days our country has ever lived. *Address, Harrow School, 29 Oct 1941*

133.19
When I warned them [*the French Government*] that Britain would fight on alone whatever they did, their Generals told their Prime Minister

and his divided Cabinet: 'In three weeks England will have her neck wrung like a chicken.'
Some chicken! Some neck!

Speech, Canadian Parliament, 30 Dec 1941

133.20
[*Of the Battle of Egypt*] This is not the end. It is not even the beginning of the end. But it is, perhaps, the end of the beginning. *Speech, Mansion House, 10 Nov 1942*

133.21
I have not become the King's First Minister in order to preside over the liquidation of the British Empire.

same

133.22
There is no finer investment for any community than putting milk into babies. *Radio Broadcast, 21 Mar 1943*

133.23
An iron curtain has descended across the Continent.

Address, Westminster College, Fulton, U.S.A., 5 Mar 1946

133.24
We must build a kind of United States of Europe. *Speech, Zurich, 19 Sept 1946*

133.25
Perhaps it is better to be irresponsible and right than to be responsible and wrong. *Party Political Broadcast, London, 26 Aug 1950*

133.26
By being so long in the lowest form [*at Harrow school*] I gained an immense advantage over the cleverest boys...I got into my bones the essential structure of the normal British sentence—which is a noble thing.

My Early Life, Ch. 2

133.27
Headmasters have powers at their disposal with which Prime Ministers have never yet been invested.

same, Ch. 2

133.28
It is a good thing for an uneducated man to read books of quotations.

same, Ch. 9

133.29
Those who can win a war well can rarely make a good peace and those who could make a good peace would never have won the war.

same, Ch. 26

133.30
The redress of the grievances of the vanquished should precede the disarmament of the victors.

The Gathering Storm, Ch. 3

133.31
I felt as if I were walking with destiny, and that all my past life had been but a preparation for this hour and this trial.

same, Ch. 38

133.32
No one can guarantee success in war, but only deserve it. *Their Finest Hour*

133.33
[*Of Dunkirk*] Wars are not won by evacuations. *same*

133.34
When I look back on all these worries I remember the story of the old man who said on his deathbed that he had had a lot of trouble in his life, most of which had never happened. *same*

133.35
I have only one purpose, the destruction of Hitler, and my life is much simplified thereby. If Hitler invaded Hell I would make at least a favourable reference to the Devil in the House of

Commons. *The Grand Alliance, Ch. 20*

133.36
Before Alamein we never had a victory. After Alamein we never had a defeat. *The Hinge of Fate, Ch. 33*

133.37
Peace with Germany and Japan on our terms will not bring much rest.... As I observed last time, when the war of the giants is over the wars of the pygmies will begin.
Triumph and Tragedy, Ch. 25

133.38
[*When asked whether the Niagara Falls looked the same as when he first saw them*] Well, the principle seems the same. The water still keeps falling over. *Closing the Ring, Ch. 5*

133.39
I said that the world must be made safe for at least fifty years. If it was only for fifteen to twenty years then we should have betrayed our soldiers.
same, Ch. 20

133.40
We must have a better word than 'prefabricated'. Why not 'ready-made'? *same, Appendix C*

133.41
Everybody has a right to pronounce foreign names as he chooses.
Observer 'Sayings of the Week', 5 Aug 1951

133.42
The nation had the lion's heart. I had the luck to give the roar. *Said on his 80th birthday*

133.43
[*Of Viscount Montgomery*] In defeat unbeatable; in victory unbearable.

133.44
[*Of Mr Baldwin*] It is a fine thing to be honest but it is also very important to be right.

134 Cibber, Colley (1671-1757), English actor and dramatist.

134.1
One had as good be out of the world, as out of the fashion. *Love's Last Shift, Act 2*

134.2
Stolen sweets are best.
The Rival Fools, Act 1

135 Cicero, Marcus Tullius (106-43 B.C.), Roman statesman and orator.

135.1
There is nothing so absurd but some philosopher has said it.
De Divinatione, II:58

135.2
The good of the people is the chief law. *De Legibus, III:3*

135.3
Summum bonum.
The greatest good. *De Officiis, I:2*

135.4
O tempora! O mores!
What times! What customs!
In Catilinam, I:1

135.5
Cui bono.
To whose profit. *Pro Milone, IV:9*

136 Clarke, John (*fl.* 1639), English writer.

136.1
Home is home, though it be never so homely. *Paroemiologia Anglo-Latina*

137 Clay, Henry (1777-1852), American statesman.

137.1
I had rather be right than be President. *Speech, 1850*

138 Clemens, Samuel Langhorne, see **Twain, Mark**

139 Clive, Lord Robert (1725-1774), English soldier.

139.1
By God, Mr Chairman, at this moment I stand astonished at my own moderation! *Reply during Parliamentary Inquiry, 1773*

140 Clough, Arthur Hugh (1819-1861), English poet.

140.1
A world where nothing is had for nothing. *The Bothie of Tober-na-Vuolich, VIII:5*

140.2
How pleasant it is to have money. *Dipsychus, I:4*

140.3
Thou shalt have one God only; who
Would be at the expense of two?
The Latest Decalogue, 1

140.4
Thou shalt not kill; but needst not strive
Officiously to keep alive. *same, 11*

140.5
'Tis better to have fought and lost,
Than never to have fought at all.
Peschiera

141 Cobbett, William (1762-1835), English farmer, politician and writer.

141.1
To be poor and independent is very nearly an impossibility. *Advice to Young Men*

141.2
[*Of London*] But what is to be the fate of the great wen of all? *Rural Rides*

142 Coke, Desmond (1879-1931), English writer.

142.1
All rowed fast but none so fast as stroke. *Sandford of Merton*
(Popular quotation derived from the sentence: 'His blade struck the water a full second before any other... until... as the boats began to near the winning-post, his own was dipping into the water twice as often as any other.*')*

143 Coke, Sir Edward (1552-1634), English jurist.

143.1
A man's house is his castle.
Third Institute

144 Coleridge, Samuel Taylor (1772-1834), English poet, philosopher and critic.

144.1
It is an ancient Mariner,
And he stoppeth one of three.
'By thy long grey beard and glittering eye,
Now wherefore stopp'st thou me?'
The Rime of the Ancient Mariner, I:1

144.2
The Sun came up upon the left,
Out of the sea came he!
And he shone bright, and on the right
Went down into the sea. *same, I:25*

144.3
The ice was here, the ice was there,
The ice was all around:

It cracked and growled, and roared and howled,
Like noises in a swound! *same, I:59*

144.4
With my cross-bow
I shot the albatross. *same, I:81*

144.5
We were the first that ever burst
Into that silent sea. *same, II:103*

144.6
Water, water, every where,
And all the boards did shrink;
Water, water, every where,
Nor any drop to drink. *same, II:119*

144.7
Alone, alone, all, all alone,
Alone on a wide wide sea!
And never a saint took pity on
My soul in agony. *same, IV:232*

144.8
The many men, so beautiful!
And they all dead did lie:
And a thousand thousand slimy things
Lived on; and so did I. *same, IV:236*

144.9
The moving Moon went up the sky,
And no where did abide:
Softly she was going up,
And a star or two beside.
same, IV:263

144.10
Oh sleep! it is a gentle thing,
Beloved from pole to pole!
same, V:292

144.11
Quoth he, 'The man hath penance done, And penance more will do.'
same, V:408

144.12
Like one, that on a lonesome road
Doth walk in fear and dread,
And having once turned round walks on,
And turns no more his head;
Because he knows, a frightful fiend
Doth close behind him tread.
same, VI:446

144.13
No voice; but oh! the silence sank
Like music on my heart.
same, VI:498

144.14
He prayeth well, who loveth well
Both man and bird and beast.
same, VII:612

144.15
He prayeth best, who loveth best
All things both great and small;
For the dear God who loveth us,
He made and loveth all.
same, VII:614

144.16
A sadder and a wiser man,
He rose the morrow morn.
same, VII:624

144.17
A sight to dream of, not to tell!
Christabel, I:253

144.18
I may not hope from outward forms to win
The passion and the life, whose fountains are within.
Dejection: An Ode

144.19
In Xanadu did Kubla Khan
A stately pleasure-dome decree:
Where Alph, the sacred river, ran
Through caverns measureless to man
Down to a sunless sea. *Kubla Khan*

144.20
A savage place! as holy and enchanted
As e'er beneath a waning moon was haunted
By woman wailing for her demon-lover! *same*

144.21
Weave a circle round him thrice,
And close your eyes with holy dread,
For he on honey-dew hath fed,
And drunk the milk of Paradise.
same

144.22
That willing suspension of disbelief for the moment, which constitutes poetic faith. *Biographia Literaria, Ch. 14*

144.23
Our myriad-minded Shakespeare.
same, Ch. 15

144.24
Summer has set in with its usual severity. *Remark quoted in C. Lamb's letter to V. Novello, 9 May 1826*

144.25
I wish our clever young poets would remember my homely definitions of prose and poetry; that is, prose = words in their best order;—poetry = the best words in the best order.
Table Talk

144.26
No mind is thoroughly well organized that is deficient in a sense of humour.
same

144.27
What comes from the heart, goes to the heart. *same*

145 Colette, Sidonie Gabrielle (1873-1954), French novelist.

145.1
Total absence of humour renders life impossible. *Chance Acquaintances*

145.2
When she raises her eyelids it's as if she were taking off all her clothes.
Claudine and Annie

145.3
My virtue's still far too small, I don't trot it out and about yet.
Claudine at School

145.4
Don't ever wear artistic jewellery; it wrecks a woman's reputation.
Gigi

145.5
Don't eat too many almonds; they add weight to the breasts *same*

146 Collins, Mortimer (1827-1876), English writer.

146.1
A man is as old as he's feeling,
A woman as old as she looks.
The Unknown Quantity

147 Colman, George (1762-1836), English dramatist and theatrical manager.

147.1
Mum's the word. *The Battle of Hexham, II:1*

147.2
Lord help you! Tell'em Queen Anne's dead. *Heir-at-Law, I:1*

147.3
Not to be sneezed at. *same, II:1*

148 Colton, Charles Caleb (1780?-1832), English clergyman and writer.

148.1
Men will wrangle for religion; write for it; fight for it; anything but—live for it. *Lacon, I:25*

148.2
When you have nothing to say, say nothing. *same, I:183*

148.3
Imitation is the sincerest of flattery.
same, I:217

148.4
Examinations are formidable even to the best prepared, for the greatest fool may ask more than the wisest man can answer. *same, II:322*

148.5
The debt which cancels all others.
same, II:66

149 The Book of Common Prayer

149.1
We have erred, and strayed from thy ways like lost sheep.
Morning Prayer, General Confession

149.2
We have left undone those things which we ought to have done; and we have done those things we ought not to have done. *same*

149.3
As it was in the beginning, is now, and ever shall be: world without end.
same, Gloria

149.4
Give peace in our time, O Lord.
same, Versicles

149.5
When two or three are gathered together in thy Name thou wilt grant their requests. *same, Prayer of St Chrysostom*

149.6
Defend us from all perils and dangers of this night. *same*

149.7
All the deceits of the world, the flesh, and the devil. *same*

149.8
In the hour of death, and in the day of judgement. *same*

149.9
Read, mark, learn and inwardly digest.
Collect, 2nd Sunday in Advent

149.10
All our doings without charity are nothing worth.
Collect, Quinquagesima Sunday

149.11
Renounce the devil and all his works.
Publick Baptism of Infants

149.12
Being now come to the years of discretion. *Order of Confirmation*

149.13
If any of you know cause, or just impediment. *Solemnization of Matrimony*

149.14
Let him now speak, or else hereafter for ever hold his peace. *same*

149.15
To have and to hold from this day forward, for better for worse, for richer for poorer, in sickness and in health, to love and to cherish, till death us do part. *same*

150 Confucius, (K'ung Fu-tse)
(551–479 B.C.), Chinese philosopher.

150.1
Men's natures are alike; it is their habits that carry them far apart.
Analects

150.2
Study the past, if you would divine the future. *same*

150.3
Learning without thought is labour lost; thought without learning is perilous. *same*

150.4
Fine words and an insinuating appearance are seldom associated with true virtue. *same*

150.5
Have no friends not equal to yourself. *same*

150.6
When you have faults, do not fear to abandon them. *same*

150.7
To be able to practise five things everywhere under heaven constitutes perfect virtue.... gravity, generosity of soul, sincerity, earnestness, and kindness. *same*

150.8
The superior man is satisfied and composed; the mean man is always full of distress. *same*

150.9
The people may be made to follow a course of action, but they may not be made to understand it. *same*

150.10
Recompense injury with justice, and recompense kindness with kindness. *same*

150.11
The superior man is distressed by his want of ability. *same*

150.12
What you do not want done to yourself, do not do to others. *same*

151 Congreve, William (1670-1729), English dramatist.

151.1
She lays it on with a trowel.
The Double Dealer, III:10

151.2
See how love and murder will out.
same, IV:6

151.3
ALMERIA. Music has charms to soothe a savage breast.
The Mourning Bride, Act 1

151.4
ZARA. Heaven has no rage like love to hatred turned,
Nor hell a fury like a woman scorned.
same, Act 3

151.5
Say what you will, 'tis better to be left than never to have been loved.
The Way of the World, II:1

151.6
MRS MILLAMENT. I nauseate walking; 'tis a country diversion, I loathe the country and everything that relates to it. *same, IV:4*

151.7
LADY WISHFORT. I hope you do not think me prone to any iteration of nuptials. *same, IV:12*

151.8
WAITWELL. O, she is the antidote to desire. *same, IV:14*

151.9
Alack he's gone the way of all flesh.
Squire Bickerstaff Detected, attributed

152 Connell, James (1852-1929), English socialist and poacher.

152.1
Then raise the scarlet standard high!
Beneath its shade we'll live and die!
Though cowards flinch, and traitors jeer,
We'll keep the Red Flag flying here!
The Red Flag

153 Connolly, Cyril (1903-1974), English journalist and writer.

153.1
It is closing time in the gardens of the West. *The Condemned Playground*

153.2
The ape-like virtues without which no one can enjoy a public school.
Enemies of Promise, Ch. 1

153.3
An author arrives at a good style when his language performs what is required of it without shyness. *same, Ch. 3*

153.4
As repressed sadists are supposed to become policemen or butchers so those with irrational fear of life become publishers. *same*

153.5
Literature is the art of writing something that will be read twice; journalism what will be grasped at once. *same*

153.6
Whom the gods wish to destroy they first call promising. *same*

153.7
There is no more sombre enemy of good art than the pram in the hall.
same

153.8
I have always disliked myself at any given moment; the total of such moments is my life. *same, Ch. 18*

153.9
Boys do not grow up gradually. They move forward in spurts like the hands of clocks in railway stations. *same*

153.10
Better to write for yourself and have no public, than write for the public and have no self. *Turnstile One (edited by V. S. Pritchett)*

153.11
The man who is master of his passions is Reason's slave. *same*

154 Conrad, Joseph (1857-1924), English novelist.

154.1
Exterminate all brutes. *Heart of Darkness*

154.2
The horror! The horror! *same*

154.3
Mistah Kurtz—he dead. *same*

154.4
You shall judge of a man by his foes as well as by his friends.
Lord Jim, Ch. 34

154.5
A work that aspires, however humbly, to the condition of art should carry its justification in every line.
The Nigger of the Narcissus, Preface

154.6
The belief in a supernatural source of evil is not necessary; men alone are quite capable of every wickedness.
Under Western Eyes, Part 2

155 Coolidge, Calvin (1872-1933), President of the United States.

155.1
The business of America is business.
Speech, Washington, 17 Jan 1925

155.2
[*Of the Boston police strike*] There is no right to strike against the public safety by anybody, anywhere, any time.
Remark, 14 Sept 1919

155.3
[*When asked what a clergyman had said in a sermon on sin*] He said he was against it.

156 Cooper, James Fenimore (1789-1851), American novelist.

156.1
The Last of the Mohicans. *Title of Novel*

157 Corbusier, Le (Charles Édouard Jeanneret) (1887-1965), Swiss architect.

157.1
A house is a machine for living in. *Towards an architecture*

158 Corneille, Pierre (1606-1684), French dramatist.

158.1
We triumph without glory when we conquer without danger. *Le Cid, II:2*

158.2
Do your duty and leave the rest to the Gods. *Horace, II:8*

158.3
The manner of giving is worth more than the gift. *Le Menteur, I:1*

158.4
A good memory is needed after one has lied. *same, IV:5*

159 Cornuel, Anne-Marie Bigot de (1605-1694), Frenchwoman noted for her salon.

159.1
No man is a hero to his valet. *Lettres de Mlle Aissé, 13 Aug 1728*

160 Coubertin, Baron Pierre de (1863-1937), French founder of the modern Olympic games.

160.1
The most important thing in the Olympic Games is not winning but taking part.... The essential thing in life is not conquering but fighting well. *Speech at Banquet to Officials of Olympic Games, London, 24 July 1908*

161 Coué, Émile (1857-1926), French doctor.

161.1
Tous les jours, à tous points de vue, je vais de mieux en mieux.
Every day, in every way, I am getting better and better. *Formula for a cure by auto-suggestion*

162 Cousin, Victor (1792-1867), French philosopher.

162.1
L'art pour l'art.
Art for art's sake. *Lecture at Sorbonne, 1818*

163 Coward, Sir Noel (1899-1973), English actor and dramatist.

163.1
Everybody was up to something, especially, of course, those who were up to nothing. *Future Indefinite*

163.2
The Stately Homes of England
How beautiful they stand,
To prove the upper classes
Have still the upper hand.
Operette, II:7, 'The Stately Homes of England'

163.3
Strange how potent cheap music is. *Private Lives, Act 1*

163.4
Very flat, Norfolk. *same*

163.5
Certain women should be struck regularly, like gongs. *same, Act 2*

163.6
Never mind, dear, we're all made the same, though some more than others.
The Café de la Paix

163.7
Sunburn is very becoming—but only when it is even—one must be careful not to look like a mixed grill.
The Lido Beach

163.8
I've over-educated myself in all the things I shouldn't have known at all.
Wild Oats

163.9
Mad dogs and Englishmen go out in the mid-day sun. *Title of song*

163.10
Don't put your daughter on the stage, Mrs Worthington. *Title of song*

163.11
Twentieth-Century Blues.
Title of song

163.12
Poor Little Rich Girl. *Title of song*

163.13
Don't let's be beastly to the Germans.
Title of song

163.14
Dance, dance, dance little lady.
Title of song

163.15
Mad about the boy. *Title of song*

163.16
Work is much more fun than fun.
Observer 'Sayings of the Week', 21 June 1963

164 Cowley, Abraham (1618-1667), English poet.

164.1
God the first garden made, and the first city Cain. *The Garden*

164.2
Life is an incurable disease.
To Dr Scarborough

165 Cowper, William (1731-1800), English poet.

165.1
We perish'd, each alone:
But I beneath a rougher sea,
And whelm'd in deeper gulphs than he. *The Castaway*

165.2
He found it inconvenient to be poor.
Charity

165.3
God made the country, and man made the town. *The Task*

165.4
England, with all thy faults, I love thee still,
My country. *same*

165.5
Variety's the very spice of life
That gives it all its flavour. *same*

165.6
While the bubbling and loud-hissing urn
Throws up a steamy column, and the cups,
That cheer but not inebriate, wait on each,
So let us welcome peaceful evening in.
same

165.7
Nature is but a name for an effect
Whose cause is God. *same*

166 Craig, Sir Edward Gordon (1872-1966), English actor and stage designer.

166.1
Farce is the essential theatre. Farce refined becomes high comedy: farce

brutalized becomes tragedy.
The Story of my Days, Index

167 Crane, Stephen (1871-1900), American writer.

167.1
The Red Badge of Courage. *Title of novel*

168 Cranmer, Thomas (1489-1556), English Archbishop.

168.1
This hand hath offended.
Memorials of Cranmer (Strype)

169 Creighton, Mandell (1843-1901), English churchman and historian.

169.1
No people do so much harm as those who go about doing good. *Life*

170 Croce, Benedetto (1866-1952), Italian philosopher and critic.

170.1
Art is ruled uniquely by the imagination. *Esthetic, Ch. 1*

171 Croker, John Wilson (1780-1857), Irish politician.

171.1
A game which a sharper once played with a dupe, entitled 'Heads I win, tails you lose.' *Croker Papers*

172 Cromwell, Oliver (1599-1658), English soldier and statesman.

172.1
I beseech you, in the bowels of Christ, think it possible you may be mistaken.
Letter to the General Assembly of the Church of Scotland, 3 Aug 1650

172.2
What shall we do with this bauble? There, take it away.
Speech dismissing Parliament, 20 Apr 1653

172.3
It is not fit that you should sit here any longer!...you shall now give place to better men. *Speech to the Rump Parliament, 22 Jan 1654*

172.4
Warts and all. *Anecdotes of Painting (Horace Walpole), Ch. 12*
(Popular quotation derived from the sentence: 'Mr Lely, I desire you would use all your skill to paint my picture truly like me, and not flatter me at all; but remark all these roughnesses, pimples, warts, and everything as you see me, otherwise I will never pay a farthing for it.')

173 Curran, John Philpot (1750-1817), Irish orator.

173.1
The condition upon which God hath given liberty to man is eternal vigilance. *Speech on the Right of Election of Lord Mayor of Dublin, 10 July 1790 vigilance*

D

174 The Daily Mail

174.1
Perhaps the real reason why we have always been able to champion free speech in this country is that we know perfectly well that hardly anybody has got anything to say, and that no one will listen to anyone that has.
Editorial (date unknown)

175 Dana, Charles Anderson (1819-1897), American newspaper editor.

175.1
When a dog bites a man that is not news, but when a man bites a dog, that is news. *The New York Sun, 1882*

176 Dante, Alighieri (1265-1321), Italian poet.

176.1
Abandon hope, all ye who enter here. *Divine Comedy, Inferno, III:9*

176.2
There is no greater sorrow than to recall a time of happiness when in misery. *same, V:121*

177 Danton, Georges Jacques (1759-1794), French politician.

177.1
Boldness, and again boldness, and always boldness! *Speech, French Legislative Committee, 2 Sept 1792*

178 Darling, Charles John, 1st Baron (1849-1936), English judge.

178.1
The Law of England is a very strange one; it cannot compel anyone to tell the truth....But what the Law can do is to give you seven years for not telling the truth. *Lord Darling* (*D. Walker-Smith*)

179 Darwin, Charles Galton (1887-1962), English scientist.

179.1
The evolution of the human race will not be accomplished in the ten thousand years of tame animals, but in the million years of wild animals, because man is and will always be a wild animal. *The Next Ten Million Years, Ch. 4*

180 Darwin, Charles Robert (1809-1882), English scientist.

180.1
Man with all his noble qualities...still bears in his bodily frame the indelible stamp of his lowly origin. *The Descent of Man*

180.2
I have called this principle, by which each slight variation, if useful, is preserved, by the term of Natural Selection. *The Origin of Species, Ch. 3*

180.3
The expression often used by Mr Herbert Spencer of the Survival of the Fittest is more accurate, and is sometimes equally convenient. *same*

181 Davies, William Henry (1871-1940), English poet.

181.1
What is this life if, full of care,
We have no time to stand and stare? *Leisure*

182 Day-Lewis, Cecil (1904-1972), English poet.

182.1
It is the logic of our times,
No subject for immortal verse—
That we who lived by honest dreams
Defend the bad against the worse. *Where are the War Poets?*

183 Decatur, Stephen (1779-1820), American naval commander.

183.1
Our country! In her intercourse with foreign nations, may she always be in the right; but our country, right or

wrong. *Speech, Norfolk, Virginia, Apr 1816*

184 Defoe, Daniel (1660?-1731), English writer.

184.1
The good die early, and the bad die late. *Character of the late Dr. Annesley*

184.2
I takes my man Friday with me.
Robinson Crusoe

184.3
And of all plagues with which mankind are curst,
Ecclesiastic tyranny's the worst.
The True-Born Englishman, 2

185 Dekker, Thomas (1570?-1641?), English dramatist.

185.1
Golden slumbers kiss your eyes,
Smiles awake you when you rise.
Patient Grissil, IV:2

186 Denman, Thomas, 1st Baron (1779-1854), English judge.

186.1
Trial by jury itself, instead of being a security to persons who are accused, will be a delusion, a mockery, and a snare. *Judgment in O'Connell v The Queen, 4 Sept 1844*

187 Dennis, John (1657-1734), English critic.

187.1
A man who could make so vile a pun would not scruple to pick a pocket.
The Gentleman's Magazine, 1781

188 De Quincey, Thomas (1785-1859), English writer.

188.1
Murder considered as one of the Fine Arts. *Title of Essay*

189 Descartes, René (1596-1650), French philosopher and mathematician.

189.1
Cogito, ergo sum.
I think, therefore I am.
Le Discours de la Méthode

190 De Vries, Peter (b. 1910), American novelist.

190.1
We know the human brain is a device to keep the ears from grating on one another.
Comfort me with Apples, Ch. 1

190.2
Gluttony is an emotional escape, a sign something is eating us.
same, Ch. 7

190.3
Probably a fear we have of facing up to the real issues. Could you say we were guilty of Noel Cowardice?
same, Ch. 8

190.4
I wanted to be bored to death, as good a way to go as any. *same, Ch. 17*

190.5
It is the final proof of God's omnipotence that he need not exist in order to save us.
The Mackerel Plaza, Ch. 2

190.6
Let us hope...that a kind of Providence will put a speedy end to the acts of God under which we have been labouring. *same, Ch. 3*

191 Dickens, Charles (1812-1870), English novelist.

191 Dickens

191.1
'There are strings', said Mr Tappertit, 'in the human heart that had better not be wibrated.'
Barnaby Rudge, Ch. 22

191.2
This is a London particular...A fog, miss. *Bleak House, Ch. 3*

191.3
MISS FLITE. I expect a judgment. Shortly. *same*

191.4
It is a melancholy truth that even great men have their poor relations.
same, Ch. 28

191.5
'God bless us every one!' said Tiny Tim, the last of all.
A Christmas Carol

191.6
'I am a lone lorn creetur, ' were Mrs Gummidge's words...'and everythink goes contrairy with me.'
David Copperfield, Ch. 3

191.7
BARKIS. Barkis is willin'. *same, Ch. 5*

191.8
MICAWBER. Annual income twenty pounds, annual expenditure nineteen nineteen six, result happiness. Annual income twenty pounds, annual expenditure twenty pounds ought and six, result misery. *same, Ch. 12*

191.9
URIAH HEEP. We are so very 'umble.
same, Ch. 17

191.10
MICAWBER. Accidents will occur in the best-regulated families. *same, Ch. 28*

191.11
MR PEGGOTTY. I'm Gormed—and I can't say no fairer than that.
same, Ch. 63

191.12
CAPTAIN CUTTLE. When found, make a note of. *Dombey and Son, Ch. 15*

191.13
GRADGRIND. Now, what I want is Facts...Facts alone are wanted in life.
Hard Times, I:1

191.14
Whatever was required to be done, the Circumlocution Office was beforehand with all the public departments in the art of perceiving—HOW NOT TO DO IT.
Little Dorrit, I:10

191.15
MR PECKSNIFF. Let us be moral. Let us contemplate existence.
Martin Chuzzlewit, Ch. 10

191.16
JONAS CHUZZLEWIT. Here's the rule for bargains: 'Do other men, for they would do you.' That's the true business precept. *same, Ch. 11*

191.17
MRS GAMP. He'd make a lovely corpse.
same, Ch. 25

191.18
Every baby born into the world is a finer one than the last.
Nicholas Nickleby, Ch. 36

191.19
GENTLEMEN IN THE SMALLCLOTHES. All is gas and gaiters. *same, Ch. 49*

191.20
MR BUMBLE. Oliver Twist has asked for more. *Oliver Twist, Ch. 2*

191.21
Known by the *sobriquet* of 'The artful Dodger.' *same, Ch. 8*

191.22
'If the law supposes that, ' said Mr Bumble..., 'the law is a ass— a idiot.'
same, Ch. 51

191.23
The question [*Mr. Podsnap asked himself*] about everything was, would it bring a blush to the cheek of a young person?
Our Mutual Friend, I:11

191.24
JINGLE. Kent, sir—everybody knows Kent—apples, cherries, hops and women. *Pickwick Papers, Ch. 2*

191.25
JOE, THE FAT BOY. I wants to make your flesh creep. *same, Ch. 8*

191.26
It's always best on these occasions to do what the mob do.'
'But suppose there are two mobs?' suggested Mr Snodgrass.
'Shout with the largest, ' replied Mr Pickwick. *same, Ch. 13*

191.27
MR WELLER. Take example by your father, my boy, and be very careful o' vidders all your life. *same*

191.28
SAM WELLER. Poverty and oysters always seem to go together.
same, Ch. 22

191.29
SAM WELLER. Wery glad to see you indeed, and hope our acquaintance may be a long 'un, as the gen'l'm'n said to the fi' pun' note.
same, Ch. 25

191.30
MR WELLER. Poetry's unnat'ral; no man ever talked poetry 'cept a beadle on boxin' day. *same, Ch. 33*

191.31
STIGGINS. It's my opinion, sir, that this meeting is drunk. *same*

191.32
MR WELLER. Put it down a we, my lord, put it down a we! *same, Ch. 34*

191.33
SAM WELLER. Anythin' for a quiet life, as the man said wen he took the sitivation at the lighthouse.
same, Ch. 43

191.34
SYDNEY CARTON. It is a far, far, better thing that I do, than I have ever done; it is a far, far, better rest that I go to, than I have ever known. *A Tale of Two Cities, Ch. 15*

192 Dickinson, Emily (1830-1886), American poet.

192.1
Success is counted sweetest
By those who ne'er succeed.
Poems, 67

192.2
Parting is all we know of heaven,
And all we need of hell. *same, 1732*

193 Diogenes, (412?-323? B.C.), Cynic philosopher.

193.1
Stand a little less between me and the sun. *Life of Alexander (Plutarch)*

194 Dionysius of Halicarnassus, (40?-8 B.C.), Greek historian and rhetorician.

194.1
History is philosophy teaching by examples. *Ars rhetorica, XI:2*

195 Disraeli, Benjamin, 1st Earl of Beaconsfield (1804-1881), English statesman and novelist.

195.1
I will sit down now, but the time will come when you will hear me.
Maiden Speech, House of Commons, 7 Dec 1837

195.2
[*Of Sir Robert Peel*] The right honourable gentleman caught the Whigs bathing, and walked away with their clothes. *Speech, House of Commons, 28 Feb 1845*

195.3
A Conservative government is an organized hypocrisy.
Speech, 17 Mar 1845

195.4
The question is this: Is man an ape or an angel? I, my lord, am on the side of the angels. *Speech, 25 Nov 1864*

195.5
Lord Salisbury and myself have brought you back peace—but a peace I hope with honour. *Speech, House of Commons, 16 July 1878*

195.6
[*Of Gladstone*] A sophistical rhetorician inebriated with the exuberance of his own verbosity.
Speech, 27 July 1878

195.7
Youth is a blunder; manhood a struggle; old age a regret.
Coningsby, III:1

195.8
His Christianity was muscular.
Endymion, Ch. 14

195.9
Every woman should marry—and no man. *Lothair, Ch. 30*

195.10
'My idea of an agreeable person, ' said Hugo Bohun, 'is a person who agrees with me.' *same, Ch. 35*

195.11
I was told that the Privileged and the People formed Two Nations.
Sybil, IV:8

195.12
[*Of his wife*] She is an excellent creature, but she never can remember which came first, the Greeks or the Romans. *Attributed*

195.13
When I want to read a novel I write one. *Attributed*

196 Dobrée, Bonamy (b. 1891), English scholar and critic.

196.1
It is difficult to be humble. Even if you aim at humility, there is no guarantee that when you have attained the state you will not be proud of the feat.
John Wesley

197 Dodgson, Charles Lutwidge, see Carroll, Lewis

198 Donleavy, James Patrick (b. 1926), American novelist.

198.1
I got disappointed in human nature as well and gave it up because I found it too much like my own. *Fairy Tales of New York*

199 Donne, John (1573-1631), English poet.

199.1
And new Philosophy calls all in doubt,
The Element of fire is quite put out;
The Sun is lost, and th' earth, and no man's wit
Can well direct him where to look for it. *An Anatomy of the World, 205*

199.2
Come live with me, and be my love,
And we will some new pleasures prove
Of golden sands, and crystal brooks,
With silken lines, and silver hooks.
The Bait

199.3
For God's sake hold your tongue and let me love. *The Canonization*

199.4
Love built on beauty, soon as beauty, dies. *Elegies, 2, The Anagram*

199.5
She, and comparisons are odious.
same, 8, The Comparison

199.6
Licence my roving hands, and let them go,
Before, behind, between, above, below.
same, 18, Love's Progress

199.7
O my America! my new-found-land,
My Kingdom, safeliest when with one man man'd. *same, 19, Going To Bed*

199.8
Death be not proud, though some have called thee
Mighty and dreadful, for, thou art not so. *Holy Sonnets, 10*

199.9
Go, and catch a falling star,
Get with child a mandrake root,
Tell me, where all past years are,
Or who cleft the Devil's foot.
Song, Go and Catch a Falling Star

199.10
Busy old fool, unruly Sun,
Why dost thou thus,
Through windows and through curtains call on us? *The Sun Rising*

199.11
But I do nothing upon myself, and yet
I am mine own Executioner.
Devotions, 12

199.12
No man is an Island, entire of itself; every man is a piece of the Continent, a part of the main. *same, 17*

199.13
Any man's death diminishes me, because I am involved in Mankind; And therefore never send to know for whom the bell tolls; it tolls for thee.
same, 17

200 Dowson, Ernest Christopher (1867-1900), English poet.

200.1
I have been faithful to thee, Cynara! in my fashion. *Non Sum Qualis Eram Bonae Sub Regno Cynarae*

200.2
I have forgot much, Cynara! gone with the wind,
Flung roses, roses riotously with the throng. *same*

200.3
They are not long, the days of wine and roses. *Vitae Summa Brevis Spem Nos Vetat Incohare Longam*

201 Doyle, Sir Arthur Conan (1859-1930), English writer.

201.1
It is an old maxim of mine that when you have excluded the impossible, whatever remains, however improbable, must be the truth.
The Beryl Coronet

201.2
You know my method. It is founded upon the observance of trifles.
The Boscombe Valley Mystery

201.3
It has long been an axiom of mine that the little things are infinitely the most important. *A Case of Identity*

201.4
Depend upon it, there is nothing so unnatural as the commonplace.
same

201.5
'Excellent!' I [*Dr Watson*] cried. 'Elementary,' said he [*Holmes*].
same

201.6
[*Of Professor Moriarty*] He is the Napoleon of crime.
The Final Problem

201.7
It is quite a three-pipe problem.
The Red-Headed League

201.8
An experience of women which extends over many nations and three continents. *The Sign of Four*

201.9
'Is there any point to which you would wish to draw my attention?'
'To the curious incident of the dog in the night-time.'
'The dog did nothing in the night-time.'
'That was the curious incident,' remarked Sherlock Holmes.
Silver Blaze

202 Drake, Sir Francis (1540?-1596), English navigator and naval commander.

202.1
[*Of the raid on Cadiz harbour*] I have singed the Spanish king's beard.
Remark, 1587

202.2
[*On the Armada being sighted during a game of bowls*] There is plenty of time to win this game, and to thrash the Spaniards too.
Remark, 20 July 1588

203 Drayton, Michael (1563-1631), English poet.

203.1
Fair stood the wind for France
When we our sails advance.
Agincourt

203.2
Since there's no help, come let us kiss and part—
Nay, I have done, you get no more of me;
And I am glad, yea glad with all my heart
That thus so cleanly I myself can free.
Sonnets, 61

204 Drummond, Thomas (1797-1840), Scottish engineer and statesman.

204.1
Property has its duties as well as its rights. *Letter to the Earl of Donoughmore, 22 May 1838*

205 Dryden, John (1631-1700), English poet and dramatist.

205.1
In pious times, e'r Priest-craft did begin,
Before Polygamy was made a Sin.
Absalom and Achitophel, I:1

205.2
What e'r he did was done with so much ease,
In him alone, 'twas Natural to please.
same, I:27

205.3
Great Wits are sure to Madness near alli'd
And thin Partitions do their Bounds divide. *same, I:163*

205.4
Bankrupt of Life, yet Prodigal of Ease. *same, I:168*

205.5
For Politicians neither love nor hate. *same, I:223*

205.6
But far more numerous was the Herd of such,
Who think too little, and who talk too much. *same, I:533*

205.7
A man so various, that he seem'd to be
Not one, but all Mankind's Epitome.
Stiff in Opinions, always in the wrong;
Was Everything by starts, and Nothing long. *same, I:545*

205.8
Did wisely from Expensive Sins refrain,
And never broke the Sabbath, but for Gain. *same, I:587*

205.9
During his Office, Treason was no Crime.
The Sons of Belial had a Glorious Time. *same, I:597*

205.10
Nor is the Peoples Judgment always true:
The Most may err as grosly as the Few. *same, I:781*

205.11
Beware the Fury of a Patient Man. *same, I:1005*

205.12
None but the Brave deserves the Fair. *Alexander's Feast*

205.13
All humane things are subject to decay,
And, when Fate summons, Monarchs must obey. *Mac Flecknoe*

205.14
Happy the Man, and happy he alone,
He who can call to-day his own:
He who, secure within, can say,
Tomorrow do thy worst, for I have liv'd today. *Translation of Horace, III:65*

205.15
Errors, like Straws, upon the surface flow;
He who would search for Pearls must dive below. *All for Love, Prologue*

205.16
[*Of Shakespeare*] He was the man who of all modern, and perhaps ancient poets had the largest and most comprehensive soul.
Essay of Dramatic Poesy

205.17
[*Of Shakespeare*] He was naturally learned; he needed not the spectacles of books to read nature; he looked inwards, and found her there.
same

206 Dumas, Alexandre (1803-1870), French novelist.

206.1
All for one, and one for all.
The Three Musketeers

207 Dunning, John, Baron Ashburton (1731-1783), English lawyer and politician.

207.1
The influence of the Crown has increased, is increasing, and ought to be diminished. *Motion passed by the House of Commons, 1780*

E

208 Eden, Sir Anthony, 1st Earl of Avon (1897-1977), British statesman and prime minister.

208.1
Everybody is always in favour of general economy and particular expenditure. *Observer 'Sayings of the Week', 17 June 1956*

208.2
We are not at war with Egypt. We are in an armed conflict. *Speech, House of Commons, 4 Nov 1956*

209 Edison, Thomas Alva (1847-1931), American inventor.

209.1
Genius is one per cent inspiration and ninety-nine per cent perspiration. *Newspaper interview*

210 Edward III, (1312-1377), King of England.

210.1
[*Of the Black Prince*] Let the boy win his spurs. *Remark at the battle of Crécy, 1345*

211 Edward VIII, (Duke of Windsor) (1894-1972), King of Great Britain.

211.1
I have found it impossible to carry the heavy burden of responsibility and to discharge my duties as King as I would wish to do without the help and support of the woman I love. *Radio broadcast, 11 Dec 1936*

212 Einstein, Albert (1879-1955), Swiss scientist.

212.1
I never think of the future. It comes soon enough. *Interview, 1930*

213 Eliot, George (Mary Ann Evans) (1819-1880), English novelist.

213.1
It's but little good you'll do a-watering the last year's crop. *Adam Bede, Ch. 18*

213.2
Animals are such agreeable friends—they ask no questions, they pass no criticisms. *Scenes of Clerical Life, 'Mr Gilfil's Love Story', Ch. 7*

214 Eliot, Thomas Stearns (1888-1965), British poet, dramatist and critic.

214.1
Because I do not hope to turn again
Because I do not hope
Because I do not hope to turn.
Ash-Wednesday

214.2
Time present and time past
Are both perhaps present in time future,
And time future contained in time past.
Burnt Norton

214.3
Human kind
Cannot bear very much reality.
same

214.4
Here I am, an old man in a dry month,
Being read to by a boy, waiting for rain.
Gerontion

214.5
We are the hollow men
We are the stuffed men
Leaning together

Headpiece filled with straw.
The Hollow Men

214.6
This is the way the world ends
Not with a bang but a whimper.
same

214.7
Let us go then, you and I,
When the evening is spread out against the sky
Like a patient etherized upon a table.
The Love Song of J. Alfred Prufrock

214.8
In the room the women come and go
Talking of Michelangelo. *same*

214.9
I have measured out my life with coffee spoons. *same*

214.10
I grow old... I grow old...
I shall wear the bottoms of my trousers rolled. *same*

214.11
Shall I part my hair behind? Do I dare to eat a peach?
I shall wear white flannel trousers, and walk upon the beach.
I have heard the mermaids singing, each to each. *same*

214.12
The winter evening settles down
With smell of steaks in passageways.
Preludes, 1

214.13
'Put your shoes at the door, sleep, prepare for life.'
The last twist of the knife.
Rhapsody on a Windy Night

214.14
Birth, and copulation, and death.
That's all the facts when you come to brass tacks. *Sweeney Agonistes, Fragment of an Agon*

214.15
The host with someone indistinct
Converses at the door apart,
The nightingales are singing near
The Convent of the Sacred Heart.
Sweeney among the Nightingales

214.16
April is the cruellest month, breeding
Lilacs out of the dead land, mixing
Memory and desire, stirring
Dull roots with spring rain.
The Waste Land, 'The Burial of the Dead'

214.17
Hell is oneself;
Hell is alone, the other figures in it
Merely projections. There is nothing to escape from
And nothing to escape to. One is always alone.
The Cocktail Party, I:3

214.18
THOMAS. The last temptation is the greatest treason:
To do the right deed for the wrong reason. *Murder in the Cathedral, Act I*

214.19
No poet, no artist of any sort, has his complete meaning alone. His significance, his appreciation is the appreciation of his relation to the dead poets and artists. *Tradition and the Individual Talent*

215 Elizabeth I, (1533-1603), Queen of England.

215.1
I will make you shorter by a head.
Sayings of Queen Elizabeth (Chamberlin)

215.2
I know I have the body of a weak and feeble woman, but I have the heart and stomach of a King, and of a King of England too. *Speech at Tilbury on the Approach of the Spanish Armada*

215.3
Though God hath raised me high, yet this I count the glory of my crown: that I have reigned with your loves. *The Golden Speech, 1601*

215.4
All my possessions for a moment of time. *Last words*

216 Ellis, Henry Havelock (1859–1939), English psychologist.

216.1
What we call progress is the exchange of one nuisance for another nuisance. *Remark*

217 Éluard, Paul (Eugène Grindal) (1895–1952), French poet.

217.1
Adieu tristesse
Bonjour tristesse
Tu es inscrite dans les lignes du plafond.
Farewell sadness
Good day sadness
You are written in the lines of the ceiling. *La Vie immédiate*

218 Emerson, Ralph Waldo (1803–1882), American poet and essayist.

218.1
Art is a jealous mistress. *Conduct of Life, Wealth*

218.2
Nothing great was ever achieved without enthusiasm. *Essays, Circles*

218.3
A Friend may well be reckoned the masterpiece of Nature. *same, Friendship*

218.4
There is properly no history; only biography. *same, History*

218.5
All mankind love a lover. *same, Love*

218.6
The reward of a thing well done is to have done it. *same, New England Reformers*

218.7
Every man is wanted, and no man is wanted much. *same, Nominalist and Realist*

218.8
In skating over thin ice, our safety is in our speed. *same, Prudence*

218.9
Whoso would be a man must be a nonconformist. *same, Self-Reliance*

218.10
To be great is to be misunderstood. *same*

218.11
Every hero becomes a bore at last. *Representative Men, 'Uses of Great Men'*

218.12
Hitch your wagon to a star. *Society and Solitude, 'Civilization'*

218.13
We boil at different degrees. *same, 'Eloquence'*

218.14
America is a country of young men. *same, 'Old Age'*

218.15
If a man write a better book, preach a better sermon, or make a better mouse-trap than his neighbour, though he build his house in the woods, the world will make a beaten path to his door.
Attributed

219 Estienne, Henri (1528-1598), French scholar and editor.
219.1
Si jeunesse savait; si vieillesse pouvait.
If only youth knew, if only age could.
Les Prémices

220 Euclid, (c. 300 B.C.), Greek mathematician.
220.1
Quod erat demonstrandum.
Which was to be proved.
Elements, I:5

221 Euripides, (c. 485-406 B.C.), Greek dramatist.
221.1
Those whom God wishes to destroy, he first makes mad. *Fragment*

222 Everage, Dame Edna (Barry Humphries), 'Australian housewife and super-star'.
222.1
In the world of success and failure
Have you noticed the Genius Spark
Seems brightest in folk from Australia?
We all leave an indelible mark.
You just have to go to the Opera
Or an Art show, or glance at your shelves
To see in a trice that Australians
Have done *terribly* well for themselves.
Terribly Well

222.2
Did you know that Rolf Harris was Australian? *same*

F

223 Farquhar, George (1678-1707), Irish dramatist.
223.1
There's no scandal like rags, nor any crime so shameful as poverty.
The Beaux' Strategem, I:1
223.2
Lady Bountiful. *same*
223.3
Spare all I have, and take my life.
same, V:2

224 Ferdinand I, (1503-1568), Holy Roman Emperor.
224.1
Let justice be done, though the world perish. *Attributed*

225 Fielding, Henry (1707-1754), English novelist.
225.1
These are called the pious frauds of friendship. *Amelia, III:4*
225.2
I am as sober as a Judge.
Don Quixote in England, III:14
225.3
Oh! the roast beef of England,
And old England's roast beef.
The Grub Street Opera, III:3
225.4
Public schools are the nurseries of all vice and immorality.
Joseph Andrews, III:5

226 Fields, William Claude

(1879-1946), American actor and comedian.

226.1
It ain't a fit night out for man or beast.
The Fatal Glass of Beer, film

226.2
Anybody who hates children and dogs can't be all bad. *Attributed*

226.3
I am free of all prejudice. I hate everyone equally. *Attributed*

227 Firbank, Ronald (1886-1926), English novelist.

227.1
It is said, I believe, that to behold the Englishman at his *best* one should watch him play tip-and-run.
The Flower Beneath the Foot, Ch. 14

227.2
To be sympathetic without discrimination is so very debilitating.
Vainglory, Ch.7

228 Fitzgerald, Edward (1809-1883), English scholar, poet and translator.

228.1
Awake! for Morning in the Bowl of Night
Has flung the Stone that puts the Stars to Flight:
And Lo! the Hunter of the East has caught
The Sultan's Turret in a Noose of Light. *Rubáiyát of Omar Khayyám, 1*

228.2
Come, fill the Cup, and in the Fire of Spring
The Winter Garment of Repentance fling:
The Bird of Time has but a little way
To fly — and Lo! the Bird is on the Wing. *same, 7*

228.3
Here with a Loaf of Bread beneath the Bough,
A Flask of Wine, a Book of Verse—and Thou
Beside me singing in the Wilderness—
And Wilderness is Paradise enow.
same, 11

228.4
One thing is certain, that Life flies;
One thing is certain, and the Rest is Lies;
The Flower that once has blown for ever dies. *same, 26*

228.5
I came like Water, and like Wind I go.
same, 28

228.6
Ah, fill the Cup:—what boots it to repeat
How Time is slipping underneath our Feet:
Unborn TOMORROW, and dead YESTERDAY,
Why fret about them if TODAY be sweet! *same, 37*

228.7
'Tis all a Chequer-board of Nights and Days
Where Destiny with Men for Pieces plays:
Hither and thither moves, and mates, and slays,
And one by one back in the Closet lays. *same, 49*

228.8
The Moving Finger writes; and, having writ,
Moves on: nor all thy Piety nor Wit
Shall lure it back to cancel half a Line,
Nor all thy Tears wash out a Word of it. *same, 51*

229 Fitzgerald, Francis Scott (1896-1940), American novelist.

229.1
Beware of the artist who's an intellectual also. The artist who doesn't fit.
This Side of Paradise, II:5

229.2
'I know myself,' he cried, 'but that is all.' *same*

229.3
A big man has no time really to do anything but just sit and be big.
same, III:2

229.4
FITZGERALD. The rich are different from us.
HEMINGWAY. Yes, they have more money. *Notebooks, E*

229.5
All good writing is *swimming under water* and holding your breath.
Letter to Frances Scott Fitzgerald

229.6
[*Of himself and his wife*] Sometimes I don't know whether Zelda and I are real or whether we are characters in one of my novels. *A Second Flowering (Malcolm Cowley)*

230 Fitzsimmons, Robert Prometheus (1862-1917), British boxer.

230.1
The bigger they come the harder they fall. *Saying*

231 Flecker, James Elroy (1884-1915), English poet.

231.1
For lust of knowing what should not be known,
We take the Golden Road to Samarkand. *Hassan, V:2*

232 Fletcher, John see **Beaumont,** Francis

233 Florio, John (1553?-1625), English translator.

233.1
England is the paradise of women, the purgatory of men, and the hell of horses. *Second Fruits*

234 Ford, Henry (1863-1947), American engineer and industrialist.

234.1
History is more or less bunk. It's tradition. We don't want tradition. We want to live in the present and the only history that is worth a tinker's damn is the history we make today.
Chicago Tribune, 25 May 1916

235 Ford, John (c. 1586-c. 1640), English dramatist.

235.1
'Tis Pity She's a whore. *Title of play*

236 Forgy, Howell Maurice (b. 1908), American soldier.

236.1
Praise the Lord and pass the ammunition. *Said at Pearl Harbour, 7 Dec 1941*

237 Forster, Edward Morgan (1879-1970), English novelist.

237.1
Only connect. *Howard's End, Epigraph*

237.2
It is not that the Englishman can't feel—it is that he is afraid to feel. He has been taught at his public school that feeling is bad form. He must not express great joy or sorrow, or even open his mouth too wide when he

talks—his pipe might fall out if he did.
Abinger Harvest, 'Notes on the English character'

237.3
Yes—oh dear, yes—the novel tells a story. *Aspects of the Novel, Ch. 2*

238 Fosdick, Harry Emerson (1878-1969), American Baptist minister.

238.1
An atheist is a man who has no invisible means of support.
Attributed

239 Franklin, Benjamin (1706-1790), American statesman and scientist.

239.1
Remember that time is money.
Advice to a Young Tradesman

239.2
No nation was ever ruined by trade.
Essays, Thoughts on Commercial Subjects

239.3
We must indeed all hang together, or most assuredly, we shall all hang separately. *Remark on signing the Declaration of Independence, 4 July 1776*

239.4
There never was a good war or a bad peace. *Letter to Josiah Quincy, 11 Sept 1783*

239.5
In this world nothing is certain but death and taxes. *Letter to Jean-Baptiste Leroy, 13 Nov 1789*

240 Frayn, Michael (b. 1933), British novelist and dramatist.

240.1
To be absolutely honest, what I feel really bad about is that I don't feel worse. There's the ineffectual liberal's problem in a nutshell.
Observer, 8 Aug 1965

241 Frederick the Great, (1712-1786), King of Prussia.

241.1
My people and I have come to an agreement which satisfies us both. They are to say what they please, and I am to do what I please.
Attributed

242 Freud, Sigmund (1856-1939), Austrian neurologist and psychoanalyst.

242.1
The psychic development of the individual is a short repetition of the course of development of the race.
Leonardo da Vinci

242.2
Religion is an illusion and it derives its strength from the fact that it falls in with our instinctual desires.
New Introductory Lectures on Psychoanalysis, 'A Philosophy of Life'

242.3
Conscience is the internal perception of the rejection of a particular wish operating within us.
Totem and Taboo

242.4
At bottom God is nothing more than an exalted father. *same*

242.5
The great question... which I have not been able to answer, despite my thirty years of research into the feminine

soul, is 'What does a woman want'?
Psychiatry in American Life (Charles Rolo)

243 Frost, Robert (1875-1963), American poet.

243.1
Most of the change we think we see in life
Is due to truths being in and out of favour. *The Black Cottage*

243.2
Home is the place where, when you have to go there,
They have to take you in.
The Death of the Hired Man

244 Fry, Christopher (b. 1907), English dramatist.

244.1
THOMAS. Where in this small-talking world can I find
A longitude with no platitude?
The Lady's Not for Burning, Act 3

244.2
PRIVATE PETER ABLE. Try thinking of love, or something.
Amor vincit insomnia. *A Sleep of Prisoners*

245 Fuller, Thomas (1608-1661), English writer and antiquarian.

245.1
There is a great difference between painting a face and not washing it.
Church History, 7

245.2
It is a silly game where nobody wins.
Gnomologia, 2880

245.3
A proverb is much matter decorated into few words. *The History of the Worthies of England, Ch. 2*

245.4
Learning hath gained most by those books by which the printers have lost.
The Holy and Profane State, 'Of Books'

G

246 Gabor, Zsa Zsa (b. 1923), American actress.

246.1
I never hated a man enough to give him diamonds back.
Observer 'Sayings of the Week', 28 Aug 1957

247 Galbraith, John Kenneth (b. 1908), Canadian economist.

247.1
Wealth is not without its advantages, and the case to the contrary, although it has often been made, has never proved widely persuasive.
The Affluent Society, Ch. 1

247.2
Wealth has never been a sufficient source of honour in itself. It must be advertised, and the normal medium is obtrusively expensive goods.
same, Ch. 7

247.3
Few things are as immutable as the addiction of political groups to the ideas by which they have once won office. *same, Ch. 13*

248 Galilei, Galileo (1564-1642), Italian astronomer.

248.1
[*Of the earth*] But it does move.
Remark made after his recantation of belief in the Copernican system

249 Garbo, Greta (b. 1905), Swedish film actress.

249.1
I want to be alone. *Grand Hotel, film, 1932*

250 Gavarni, Paul (1801-1866), French illustrator and caricaturist.

250.1
Les enfants terribles.
The embarrassing young. *Title of series of prints*

251 Gay, John (1685-1732), English poet and dramatist.

251.1
PEACHUM. Do you think your mother and I should have liv'd comfortably so long together, if ever we had been married? *The Beggar's Opera, I:8*

251.2
ASTARBE. She who has never loved has never lived. *Captives, I:2*

251.3
Life is a jest; and all things show it.
I thought so once; but now I know it. *My Own Epitaph*

252 George, Dan (b. 1910?), Canadian Indian chief and film actor.

252.1
When the white man came we had the land and they had the Bibles; now they have the land and we have the Bibles. *Remark*

253 George, Daniel (b. 1890), English writer and editor.

253.1
O Freedom, what liberties are taken in thy name! *The Perpetual Pessimist*

254 George II, (1683-1760), King of Great Britain.

254.1
[*Of General Wolfe*] Oh! he is mad, is he? Then I wish he would *bite* some other of my generals. *Remark*

255 Gibbon, Edward (1737-1794), English historian.

255.1
[*Of his time at Oxford*] I spent fourteen months at Magdalen College; they proved the fourteen months the most idle and unprofitable of my whole life. *Autobiography*

255.2
[*Of London*] Crowds without company, and dissipation without pleasure. *same*

255.3
Corruption, the most infallible symptom of constitutional liberty. *Decline and Fall of the Roman Empire, Ch. 21*

255.4
All that is human must retrograde if it does not advance. *same, Ch. 71*

256 Gibbons, Stella (b. 1902), English novelist.

256.1
Something nasty in the woodshed. *Cold Comfort Farm*

257 Gilbert, Sir William Schwenk (1836-1911), English parodist and librettist.

257.1
DUKE OF PLAZA-TORO. He led his regiment from behind
He found it less exciting. *The Gondoliers, Act 1*

257.2

CHORUS OF PEERS. Bow, bow, ye lower middle classes!
Bow, bow, ye tradesmen, bow, ye masses! *Iolanthe, Act 1*

257.3

LORD CHANCELLOR. The Law is the true embodiment
Of everything that's excellent.
It has no kind of fault or flaw,
And I, my lords, embody the Law.
same

257.4

PRIVATE WILLIS. I often think it's comical
How Nature always does contrive
That every boy and every gal
That's born into the world alive
Is either a little Liberal
Or else a little Conservative!
same, Act 2

257.5

LORD MOUNTARARAT. The House of Peers, throughout the war,
Did nothing in particular,
And did it very well. *same*

257.6

LORD CHANCELLOR. For you dream you are crossing the Channel, and tossing about in a steamer from Harwich—
Which is something between a large bathing machine and a very small second-class carriage. *same*

257.7

Pooh-Bah (Lord High Everything Else) *The Mikado, Dramatis Personae*

257.8

NANKI-POO. A wandering minstrel I—
A thing of shreds and patches,
Of ballads, songs and snatches,
And dreamy lullaby! *same, Act 1*

257.9

KO-KO. As some day it may happen that a victim must be found,
I've got a little list—I've got a little list
Of society offenders who might well be underground,
And who never would be missed—who never would be missed! *same*

257.10

YUM-YUM, PEEP-BO and PITTI-SING.
Three little maids from school are we,
Pert as a school-girl well can be,
Filled to the brim with girlish glee.
same

257.11

MIKADO. My object all sublime
I shall achieve in time—
To let the punishment fit the crime—
The punishment fit the crime.
same, Act 2

257.12

KO-KO. The flowers that bloom in the spring,
Tra la,
Have nothing to do with the case.
I've got to take under my wing,
Tra la,
A most unattractive old thing,
Tra la,
With a caricature of a face. *same*

257.13

KO-KO. On a tree by a river a little tom-tit
Sang 'Willow, titwillow, titwillow!'
same

257.14

BUNTHORNE If this young man expresses himself in terms too deep for *me*,
Why, what a very singularly deep young man this deep young man must be! *Patience, Act 1*

257.15
CAPTAIN. I'm never, never sick at sea!
ALL. What, never?
CAPTAIN. No, never!
ALL. What, *never*?
CAPTAIN. Hardly ever!
HMS Pinafore, Act 1

257.16
SIR JOSEPH PORTER. When I was a lad I served a term
As office boy to an Attorney's firm.
I cleaned the windows and I swept the floor,
And I polished up the handle of the big front door.
I polished up that handle so carefullee
That now I am the Ruler of the Queen's Navee! *same*

257.17
MAJOR-GENERAL STANLEY. I am the very model of a modern Major-General,
I've information vegetable, animal and mineral,
I know the kings of England, and I quote the fights historical,
From Marathon to Waterloo, in order categorical. *The Pirates of Penzance, Act 1*

257.18
SERGEANT. When the foeman bares his steel,
Tarantara! tarantara!
We uncomfortable feel.
same, Act 2

257.19
SERGEANT. When constabulary duty's to be done—
A policeman's lot is not a happy one.
same

257.20
JUDGE. She may very well pass for forty-three
In the dusk, with a light behind her!
Trial by Jury

257.21
Sir, I view the proposal to hold an international exhibition at San Francisco with an equanimity bordering on indifference. *Gilbert, His Life and Strife (Hesketh Pearson)*

257.22
[*Of Irving's Hamlet*] Funny without being vulgar. *Attributed*

258 Gladstone, William Ewart (1809–1898), British prime minister.

258.1
You cannot fight against the future. Time is on our side. *Speech on Reform Bill, 1866*

258.2
All the world over, I will back the masses against the classes.
Speech, Liverpool, 28 June 1886

258.3
We are part of the community of Europe, and we must do our duty as such. *Speech, Caenarvon, 10 Apr 1888*

259 Glasse, Hannah (18th century), English habitmaker and writer.

259.1
First catch your hare.
Art of Cookery (Popular quotation derived from the recipe instruction: 'Take your hare when it is cased.')

260 Goering, Hermann (1893–1946), German political and military leader.

260.1
Guns will make us powerful; butter will only make us fat.
Radio broadcast, 1936

260.2
I herewith commission you [*Heydrich*] to carry out all preparations with regard to...a *total solution* of the Jewish question, in those territories of Europe which are under German influence. *The Rise and Fall of the Third Reich* (*William Shirer*)

260.3
When I hear anyone talk of Culture, I reach for my revolver. *Attributed*

261 Goethe, Johann Wolfgang von (1749-1832), German poet, scientist and writer.

261.1
Dear friend, theory is all grey,
And the golden tree of life is green.
Faust, Part 1, Apprentice Scene

261.2
Two souls dwell, alas! in my breast.
same, Before the Gate

261.3
I am the spirit that always denies.
same, Study

261.4
A useless life is an early death.
Iphegenie, I:2

261.5
A talent is formed in stillness, a character in the world's torrent.
Torquato Tasso, I:2

261.6
Mehr Licht!
More light! *Last words, attributed*

262 Goldsmith, Oliver (1728?-1774), Irish dramatist, novelist and poet.

262.1
The dog, to gain some private ends,
Went mad and bit the man.
Elegy on the Death of a Mad Dog

262.2
The man recovered of the bite,
The dog it was that died. *same*

262.3
[*Of Garrick*] On the stage he was natural, simple, affecting;
'Twas only that when he was off he was acting. *same*

262.4
HARDCASTLE. I love everything that's old: old friends, old times, old manners, old books, old wine.
She Stoops to Conquer, Act 1

262.5
HARDCASTLE. This is Liberty Hall, gentlemen. *same, Act 2*

262.6
Where wealth and freedom reign, contentment fails,
And honour sinks where commerce long prevails. *The Traveller, 91*

262.7
Laws grind the poor, and rich men rule the law. *same, 386*

262.8
I...chose my wife, as she did her wedding gown, not for a fine glossy surface, but such qualities as would wear well. *The Vicar of Wakefield, Preface*

262.9
Let us draw upon content for the deficiencies of fortune. *same, Ch. 3*

262.10
When lovely woman stoops to folly,
And finds too late that men betray,
What charm can soothe her melancholy,
What art can wash her guilt away?
same, Ch. 9

263 Goldwyn, Samuel (1882-1974), American film producer.

263.1
In two words: im - possible.
Attributed

263.2
Include me out. *Attributed*

263.3
Anybody who goes to see a psychiatrist ought to have his head examined.
Attributed

263.4
Every director bites the hand that lays the golden egg. *Attributed*

263.5
I'll give you a definite maybe.
Attributed

263.6
A verbal contract isn't worth the paper it's written on. *Attributed*

263.7
You ought to take the bull between the teeth. *Attributed*

263.8
We have all passed a lot of water since then. *Attributed*

263.9
I read part of it all the way through.
Attributed

263.10
Let's have some new clichés.
Observer 'Sayings of the Week', 24 Oct 1948

264 Grahame, Kenneth (1859-1932), Scottish writer.

264.1
RAT. There is nothing—absolutely nothing—half so much worth doing as simply messing about in boats.
The Wind in the Willows, Ch. 1

265 Grant, Ulysses Simpson (1822-1885), American soldier and President of the United States.

265.1
I know no method to secure the repeal of bad or obnoxious laws so effective as their stringent execution.
Inaugural Address, 4 Mar 1869

266 Granville-Barker, Harley (1877-1946), English actor, dramatist and producer.

266.1
Rightly thought of there is poetry in peaches...even when they are canned.
The Madras House, Act 1

266.2
But oh, the farmyard world of sex!
The Madras House, Act 4

266.3
What is the prose for God?
Waste, Act 1

267 Graves, Robert (b. 1895), English poet and novelist.

267.1
Goodbye to All That. *Title of Book*

267.2
In love as in sport, the amateur status must be strictly maintained.
Occupation: Writer

267.3
As for the Freudian, it is a very low, Central European sort of humour.
same

267.4
To be a poet is a condition rather than a profession.
Horizon questionnaire, 1946

267.5
The remarkable thing about Shakespeare is that he is really very good—in spite of all the people who say he is very good.
Observer 'Sayings of the Week', 6 Dec 1964

268 Gray, Thomas (1716-1771), English poet.

268.1
What female heart can gold despise?
What Cat's averse to fish?
Ode on the Death of a Favourite Cat

268.2
Not all that tempts your wand'ring eyes
And heedless hearts, is lawful prize;
Nor all, that glisters, gold. *same*

268.3
Alas, regardless of their doom,
The little victims play! *Ode on a Distant Prospect of Eton College*

268.4
Where ignorance is bliss
'Tis folly to be wise. *same*

268.5
The Curfew tolls the knell of parting day,
The lowing herd winds slowly o'er the lea,
The plowman homeward plods his weary way,
And leaves the world to darkness and to me. *Elegy written in a Country Church-Yard*

268.6
Let not Ambition mock their useful toil,
Their homely joys, and destiny obscure;
Nor Grandeur hear with a disdainful smile,
The short and simple annals of the poor. *same*

268.7
The paths of glory lead but to the grave. *same*

268.8
Full many a gem of purest ray serene,
The dark unfathom'd caves of ocean bear:
Full many a flower is born to blush unseen,
And waste its sweetness on the desert air. *same*

268.9
Some village-Hampden, that with dauntless breast
The little Tyrant of his fields withstood;
Some mute inglorious Milton here may rest,
Some Cromwell guiltless of his country's blood. *same*

268.10
Far from the madding crowd's ignoble strife. *same*

269 Greeley, Horace (1811-1872), American editor and politician.

269.1
Go West, young man, and grow up with the country.
Hints toward Reform

270 Gregory I (540-604), Roman Pope and Saint.

270.1
[*On seeing a group of English captives being sold at Rome*] Not Angles, but angels. *Attributed*

271 Greville, Sir Fulke (1554-1628), English poet.

271.1
Oh wearisome condition of humanity! Born under one law, to another bound. *Mustapha, V:6*

272 Grey of Fallodon, Edward, 1st

Viscount (1862-1933), British statesman.

272.1
[*On the eve of the Great War*] The lamps are going out all over Europe; we shall not see them lit again in our lifetime. *Remark, 3 Aug 1914*

273 Grossmith, George (1847-1912), English comedian and singer, and **Grossmith, Walter Weedon** (1854-1919), his brother.

273.1
What's the good of a home, if you are never in it?
The Diary of a Nobody, Ch. 1

H

274 Halifax, George Saville, 1st Marquis of (1633-1695), English statesman.

274.1
Men are not hanged for stealing horses, but that horses may not be stolen.
Political Thoughts and Reflections of Punishment

275 Hammerstein, Oscar (1895-1960), American librettist and songwriter.

275.1
Ol' man river, dat ol' man river,
He must know sumpin', but don't say nothin',
He just keeps rollin', he keeps on rollin' along. *Ol' Man River*

276 Harcourt, Sir William (1827-1904), British statesman.

276.1
We are all Socialists now. *Speech*

277 Hardy, Thomas (1840-1928), English novelist and poet.

277.1
A local cult called Christianity.
The Dynasts, 1

277.2
My argument is that War makes rattling good history; but Peace is poor reading. *same*

277.3
A lover without indiscretion is no lover at all. *The Hand of Ethelberta, Ch. 20*

277.4
Good, but not religious-good.
Under the Greenwood Tree, Ch. 2

278 Harington, Sir John (1561-1612), English courtier and translator.

278.1
Treason doth never prosper: what's the reason?
For if it prosper, none dare call it treason. *Epigrams, Of Treason*

279 Haskell, Arnold (b. 1903), English writer on ballet.

279.1
[*Of Dame Nellie Melba*] Unlike so many who find success, she remained a 'dinkum hard-swearing Aussie' to the end. *Waltzing Matilda*

280 Hay, Ian (John Hay Beith), (1876-1952), Scottish novelist and dramatist.

280.1
Funny peculiar, or funny ha-ha?
Housemaster, Act 3

281 Hazlitt, William (1778–1830), English essayist.

281.1
[*Of Coleridge*] He talked on for ever; and you wished him to talk on for ever.
Lectures on the English Poets, 8

281.2
The English (it must be owned) are rather a foul-mouthed nation.
On Criticism

281.3
No young man believes he shall ever die. *On the Feeling of Immortality in Youth, 1*

281.4
One of the pleasantest things in the world is going a journey; but I like to go by myself. *On Going a Journey*

281.5
There is not a more mean, stupid, dastardly, pitiful, selfish, spiteful, envious, ungrateful animal than the public. It is the greatest of cowards, for it is afraid of itself.
On Living to Oneself

281.6
The art of pleasing consists in being pleased. *On Manner*

281.7
We never do anything well till we cease to think about the manner of doing it. *On Prejudice*

281.8
There is nothing good to be had in the country, or, if there is, they will not let you have it. *Observations on Wordsworth's 'Excursion'*

281.9
Well, I've had a happy life.
Last words

282 Hegel, Georg Wilhelm Friedrich (1770–1831), German philosopher.

282.1
What experience and history teach is this—that people and governments never have learned anything from history, or acted on principles deduced from it. *Philosophy of History, Introduction*

283 Heller, Joseph (b. 1923), American novelist.

283.1
There was only one catch and that was Catch-22, which specified that a concern for one's own safety in the face of dangers that were real and immediate was the process of a rational mind. *Catch-22, Ch. 5*

283.2
Some men are born mediocre, some men achieve mediocrity, and some men have mediocrity thrust upon them. With Major Major it had been all three. *same, Ch. 9*

284 Hemingway, Ernest (1898–1961), American novelist.

284.1
Bullfighting is the only art in which the artist is in danger of death and in which the degree of brilliance in the performance is left to the fighter's honour.
Death in the Afternoon, Ch. 9

285 Henley, William Ernest (1849–1903), English poet and critic.

285.1
Under the bludgeonings of chance
My head is bloody, but unbowed.
Invictus

285.2
I am the master of my fate;
I am the captain of my soul. *same*

286 Henri IV, (1553–1610), King of France.

286.1
Paris is well worth a mass.
Attributed

286.2
[*Of James I*] The wisest fool in Christendom. *Attributed*

287 Henry II, (1133–1189), King of England.

287.1
[*Of Thomas à Becket*] Will no one free me of this turbulent priest?
Attributed

288 Henry, Matthew (1662–1714), English Nonconformist minister.

288.1
They that die by famine die by inches.
Commentaries, Psalms, LIX:15

288.2
All this and heaven too. *Life of Philip Henry*

289 Henry, Patrick (1736–1799), American statesman.

289.1
I know not what course others may take; but as for me, give me liberty or give me death. *Speech in the Virginia Convention, 23 Mar 1775*

290 Herbert, George (1593–1633), English poet.

290.1
I struck the board, and cried, 'No more;
I will abroad.'
What, shall I ever sigh and pine?
My lines and life are free; free as the road,
Loose as the wind, as large as store.
The Collar

290.2
But as I rav'd and grew more fierce and wild
At every word,
Methought I heard one calling, 'Child';
And I replied, 'My Lord.' *same*

290.3
Oh that I were an orange-tree,
That busy plant!
Then I should ever laden be,
And never want
Some fruit for Him that dressed me.
Employment

290.4
And now in age I bud again,
After so many deaths I live and write;
I once more smell the dew and rain,
And relish versing; O, my only Light,
It cannot be
That I am he
On whom Thy tempests fell all night.
The Flower

290.5
Death is still working like a mole,
And digs my grave at each remove.
Grace

290.6
Love bade me welcome; yet my soul drew back,
Guilty of dust and sin. *Love*

290.7
'You must sit down, ' says Love, 'and taste My meat, '
So I did sit and eat. *same*

290.8
Sweet day, so cool, so calm, so bright,
The bridal of the earth and sky.
Virtue

290.9
Only a sweet and virtuous soul,
Like season'd timber, never gives;
But though the whole world turn to coal,
Then chiefly lives. *same*

291 Herrick, Robert (1591-1674), English poet.

291.1
Cherry ripe, ripe, ripe, I cry.
Full and fair ones; come and buy.
Hesperides, Cherry Ripe

291.2
A sweet disorder in the dress
Kindles in clothes a wantonness.
same, Delight in Disorder

291.3
Fair daffodils, we weep to see
You haste away so soon:
As yet the early-rising sun
Has not attain'd his noon.
same, To Daffodils

291.4
Whenas in silks my Julia goes
Then, then (methinks) how sweetly flows
That liquefaction of her clothes.
same, Upon Julia's Clothes

291.5
Gather ye rosebuds while ye may,
Old time is still a-flying:
And this same flower that smiles today
Tomorrow will be dying. *same, To the Virgins, to make much of Time*

292 Hewart, Gordon, Lord Hewart (1870-1943), British lawyer and statesman.

292.1
Justice should not only be done, but should manifestly and undoubtedly be seen to be done.
The Chief (R. Jackson)

293 Heywood, Thomas (1574?-1641), English dramatist and poet.

293.1
A Woman Killed with Kindness.
Title of play

294 Hickson, William Edward (1803-1870), educational writer.

294.1
If at first you don't succeed,
Try, try again. *Try and Try again*

295 Hill, Rowland (1744-1833), English preacher.

295.1
He did not see any good reasons why the devil should have all the good tunes. *Rev Rowland Hill (E. W. Broome)*

296 Hippocrates, (460?-377? B.C.), Greek physician.

296.1
Art is long, but life is short.
Aphorisms, 1

297 Hitler, Adolf (1889-1945), Chancellor and Führer of Germany.

297.1
All those who are not racially pure are mere chaff. *Mein Kampf, Ch. 2*

297.2
Only constant repetition will finally succeed in imprinting an idea on the memory of the crowd. *same, Ch. 6*

297.3
Germany will be either a world power or will not be at all. *same, Ch. 14*

297.4
In starting and waging a war it is not right that matters, but victory.
The Rise and Fall of the Third Reich (W. L. Shirer), Ch. 16

297.5
The essential thing is the formation of the political will of the nation: that is the starting point for political action.
Speech, Düsseldorf, 27 Jan 1932

297.6
[*Of the invasion of Russia*] When Barbarossa commences, the world will hold its breath and make no comment.
Remark to General Franz Halder

298 Hobbes, Thomas (1588–1679), English philosopher.

298.1
The condition of man...is a condition of war of everyone against everyone.
Leviathan, I:4

298.2
No arts; no letters; no society; and which is worst of all, continual fear and danger of violent death; and the life of man, solitary, poor, nasty, brutish, and short. *same, I:13*

298.3
The Papacy is not other than the Ghost of the deceased Roman Empire, sitting crowned upon the grave thereof.
same, IV:37

298.4
I am about to take my last voyage, a great leap in the dark. *Last words*

299 Hoffman, Heinrich (1809–1874), German writer and illustrator.

299.1
But one day, one cold winter's day,
He screamed out, 'Take the soup away!' *Struwwelpeter, Augustus*

299.2
Look at little Johnny there,
Little Johnny Head-in-Air.
same, Johnny Head-in-Air

299.3
The door flew open, in he ran,
The great, long, red-legged scissor-man. *same, The Little Suck-a-Thumb*

299.4
Anything to me is sweeter
Than to see Shock-headed Peter.
same, Shock-headed Peter

300 Holmes, Oliver Wendell (1809–1894), American writer and physician.

300.1
Man has his will, — but woman has her way. *The Autocrat of the Breakfast Table, Prologue*

300.2
A thought is often original, though you have uttered it a hundred times.
same, Ch. 1

300.3
The world's great men have not commonly been great scholars, nor great scholars great men.
same, Ch. 6

301 Hoover, Herbert Clark (1874–1964), President of the United States.

301.1
The American system of rugged individualism. *Speech, New York, 22 Oct 1928*

302 Hopkins, Gerard Manley (1844–1899), English poet.

302.1
Not, I'll not, carrion comfort, Despair, not feast on thee;
Not untwist—slack they may be—these last strands of man
In me or, most weary, cry *I can no more*. I can;

Can something, hope, wish day come, not choose not to be.
Carrion Comfort

302.2
That night, that year
Of now done darkness I wretch lay wrestling with (my God!) my God.
same

302.3
The world is charged with the grandeur of God. *God's Grandeur*

302.4
Glory be to God for dappled things—
For skies of couple-colour as a brinded cow;
For rose-moles all in stipple upon trout that swim. *Pied Beauty*

303 Horace, (Quintus Horatius Flaccus) (65–8 B.C.), Roman poet and satirist.

303.1
Carpe diem
Seize the day. *Ars Poetica, I:11:8*

303.2
Dulce et decorum est pro patria mori.
It is a sweet and seemly thing to die for one's country. *same, III:2:13*

304 Housman, Alfred Edward (1859–1936), English scholar and poet.

304.1
Loveliest of trees, the cherry now
Is hung with bloom along the bough,
And stands about the woodland ride
Wearing white for Eastertide.
A Shropshire Lad, 2

304.2
Here of a Sunday morning
My love and I would lie,
And see the coloured counties,
And hear the larks so high
About us in the sky. *same, 21*

304.3
Is my team ploughing,
That I was used to drive? *same, 27*

304.4
The goal stands up, the keeper
Stands up to keep the goal. *same*

304.5
With rue my heart is laden
For golden friends I had,
For many a rose-lipt maiden
And many a lightfoot lad. *same, 54*

304.6
Malt does more than Milton can
To justify God's ways to man.
same, 62

304.7
We'll to the woods no more,
The laurels all are cut. *Last Poems, Introductory*

304.8
The candles burn their sockets,
The blinds let through the day,
The young man feels his pockets
And wonders what's to pay.
same, 21

305 Hoyle, Edmond (1672–1769), English writer on card games.

305.1
When in doubt, win the trick.
Hoyle's Games, Whist, Twenty-four Short Rules for Learners

306 Hubbard, Elbert (1856–1915), American writer and editor.

306.1
Life is just one damned thing after another. *A Thousand and One Epigrams*

306.2
One machine can do the work of fifty ordinary men. No machine can do the

work of one extraordinary man.
Roycroft Dictionary and Book of Epigrams

306.3
Little minds are interested in the extraordinary; great minds in the commonplace. *same*

307 Hughes, Thomas (1822-1896), English novelist.

307.1
Life isn't all beer and skittles.
Tom Brown's Schooldays, I:2

307.2
[*Of cricket*] It's more than a game. It's an institution. *same, II:7*

308 Humphries, Barry (Dame Edna Everage) (b. 1934), Australian actor and writer.

308.1
[*Of 'Barry McKenzie'*] His favourite word to describe the act of involuntary regurgitation is the verb to chunder. This word is not in popular currency in Australia, but the writer recalls that ten years ago it was common in Victoria's more expensive public schools. It is now used by the Surfies, a repellent breed of sun-bronzed hedonists who actually hold chundering contests on the famed beaches of the Commonwealth. I understand...that the word derives from a nautical expression 'watch under', an ominous courtesy shouted from the upper decks for the protection of those below. *Times Literary Supplement, 'Barry McKenzie', 16 Sept 1965*

309 Hungerford, Margaret (1855?-1897), Irish novelist.

309.1
Beauty is altogether in the eye of the beholder. *Molly Bawn*

310 Huxley, Aldous Leonard (1894-1963), English novelist and essayist.

310.1
Since Mozart's day composers have learned the art of making music throatily and palpitatingly sexual.
Along the Road, 'Popular music'

310.2
Christlike in my behaviour,
Like every good believer,
I imitate the Saviour,
And cultivate a beaver. *Antic Hay, Ch. 4*

310.3
He was only the Mild and Melancholy one foolishly disguised as a complete Man. *same, Ch. 9*

310.4
There are few who would not rather be taken in adultery than in provincialism. *same, Ch. 10*

310.5
The time of our Ford. *Brave New World, Ch. 3*

310.6
The proper study of mankind is books.
Chrome Yellow

310.7
We participate in a tragedy; at a comedy we only look.
The Devils of Loudon, Ch. 11

310.8
Consistency is contrary to nature, contrary to life. The only completely consistent people are the dead.
Do What you Will, 'Wordsworth in the Tropics'

310.9
Death...It's the only thing we haven't succeeded in completely vulgarizing.
Eyeless in Gaza, Ch. 31

310.10
Christianity accepted as given a metaphysical system derived from several already existing and mutually incompatible systems.
Grey Eminence, Ch. 3

310.11
The quality of moral behaviour varies in inverse ratio to the number of human beings involved.
same, Ch. 10

310.12
'Bed,' as the Italian proverb succinctly puts it, 'is the poor man's opera.'
Heaven and Hell

310.13
I can sympathize with people's pains, but not with their pleasures. There is something curiously boring about somebody else's happiness.
Limbo, 'Cynthia'

310.14
She was a machine-gun riddling her hostess with sympathy.
Mortal Coils, 'The Gioconda Smile'

310.15
Most of one's life...is one prolonged effort to prevent oneself thinking.
same, 'Green Tunnels'

310.16
She was one of those indispensables of whom one makes the discovery, when they are gone, that one can get on quite as well without them.
same, 'Nuns at Luncheon'

310.17
Happiness is like coke - something you get as a by-product in the process of making something else.
Point Counter Point

310.18
There is no substitute for talent. Industry and all the virtues are of no avail. *same*

310.19
Silence is as full of potential wisdom and wit as the unhewn marble of great sculpture. *same*

310.20
A bad book is as much a labour to write as a good one; it comes as sincerely from the author's soul.
same

310.21
That all men are equal is a proposition to which, at ordinary times, no sane individual has ever given his assent.
Proper Studies

310.22
Those who believe that they are exclusively in the right are generally those who achieve something.
same

310.23
Facts do not cease to exist because they are ignored. *same*

310.24
I'm afraid of losing my obscurity. Genuineness only thrives in the dark. Like celery.
Those Barren Leaves, I:1

310.25
'It's like the question of the authorship of the *Iliad*,' said Mr Cardan. 'The author of that poem is either Homer or, if not Homer, somebody else of the same name.' *same, V:4*

310.26
Knowledge is proportionate to being. ...You know in virtue of what you are. *Time Must Have a Stop, Ch. 26*

310.27
The aristocratic pleasure of displeasing is not the only delight that bad taste can yield. One can love a certain kind of vulgarity for its own sake.
Vulgarity in Literature, Ch. 4

310.28
Defined in psychological terms, a fanatic is a man who consciously over-compensates a secret doubt. *same*

311 Huxley, Julian Sorell (1887-1975), English biologist.

311.1
We all know how the size of sums of money appears to vary in a remarkable way according as they are being paid in or paid out. *Essays of a Biologist, 5*

311.2
Operationally, God is beginning to resemble not a ruler but the last fading smile of a cosmic Cheshire cat.
Religion without Revelation

312 Huxley, Thomas Henry (1825-1895), English biologist.

312.1
It is the customary fate of new truths to begin as heresies and to end as superstitions. *The Coming of Age of the Origin of Species*

I

313 Ibsen, Henrik (1828-1906), Norwegian dramatist and poet.

313.1
Fools are in a terrible, overwhelming majority, all the wide world over.
An Enemy of the People, Act 4

313.2
The minority is always right. *same*

313.3
A man should never put on his best trousers when he goes out to battle for freedom and truth. *same, Act 5*

313.4
What's a man's first duty? The answer's brief: To be himself.
Peer Gynt, IV:1

314 Inge, William Ralph (1860-1954), English Churchman.

314.1
What we know of the past is mostly not worth knowing. What is worth knowing is mostly uncertain. Events in the past may roughly be divided into those which probably never happened and those which do not matter. *Assessments and Anticipations, 'Prognostications'*

314.2
The enemies of Freedom do not argue; they shout and they shoot.
The End of an Age, Ch. 4

314.3
The effect of boredom on a large scale in history is underestimated. It is a main cause of revolutions, and would soon bring to an end all the static Utopias and the farmyard civilization of the Fabians. *same, Ch. 6*

314.4
Many people believe that they are attracted by God, or by Nature, when they are only repelled by man.
More Lay Thoughts of a Dean, II:1

314.5
The proper time to influence the *character* of a *child* is about a *hundred* years before he is born.
Observer, 21 June 1929

314.6
A nation is a society united by a delusion about its ancestry and by a common hatred of its neighbours.
The Perpetual Pessimist (Sagittarius and George)

315 Irving, Washington (1783-1859), American writer.

315.1
Whenever a man's friends begin to compliment him about looking young, he may be sure that they think he is growing old. *Bracebridge Hall, 'Bachelors'*

315.2
A sharp tongue is the only edged tool that grows keener with constant use.
The Sketch Book, 'Rip Van Winkle'

316 Isherwood, Christopher William (b. 1904), English novelist.

316.1
I am a camera with its shutter open, quite passive, recording, not thinking.
A Berlin Diary

J

317 James, Henry (1843-1916), American novelist.

317.1
It takes a great deal of history to produce a little literature. *Life of Nathaniel Hawthorne, Ch. 1*

317.2
[*Of Thoreau*] He was unperfect, unfinished, inartistic; he was worse than provincial—he was parochial.
same, Ch. 4

317.3
Experience was to be taken as showing that one might get a five-pound note as one got a light for a cigarette; but one had to check the friendly impulse to ask for it in the same way.
The Awkward Age, IV:13

317.4
Summer afternoon — summer afternoon; to me those have always been the two most beautiful words in the English language.
A Backward Glance (Edith Wharton), Ch. 10

318 James I, (1566-1625), King of England.

318.1
[*Of smoking*] A custom loathsome to the eye, hateful to the nose, harmful to the brain, dangerous to the lungs, and in the black, stinking fume thereof, nearest resembling the horrible Stygian smoke of the pit that is bottomless.
A Counterblast to Tobacco

319 Jeans, Sir James Hopwood (1877-1946), English scientist and writer.

319.1
Life exists in the universe only because the carbon atom possesses certain exceptional properties.
The Mysterious Universe, Ch. 1

320 Jefferson, Thomas (1743-1826), President of the United States.

320.1
We hold these truths to be self-evident: that all men are created equal; that they are endowed by their Creator with certain unalienable rights; that among these are life, liberty, and the

pursuit of happiness. *Declaration of American Independence, 4 July 1776*

321 Jerome, Jerome Klapka (1859-1927), English humorous writer.

321.1
Love is like the measles; we all have to go through with it. *Idle Thoughts of an Idle Fellow, 'On Being in Love'*

321.2
I like work; it fascinates me. I can sit and look at it for hours. I love to keep it by me; the idea of getting rid of it nearly breaks my heart. *Three Men in a Boat, Ch. 15*

322 Joad, Cyril Edwin Mitchinson (1891-1953), English philosopher.

322.1
It all depends what you mean by... *BBC Brains Trust, 1942-1948*

323 Johnson, Samuel (1709-1784), English lexicographer, critic and poet.

323.1
When I took the first survey of my undertaking, I found our speech copious without order, and energetic without rules. *Dictionary of the English Language, Preface*

323.2
Cricket.—A sport, at which the contenders drive a ball with sticks in opposition to each other. *same, Definitions*

323.3
Lexicographer.—A harmless drudge. *same*

323.4
Network.—Any thing reticulated or decussated, at equal distances, with interstices between the intersections. *same*

323.5
Oats.—A grain, which in England is generally given to horses, but in Scotland supports the people. *same*

323.6
When two Englishmen meet their first talk is of the weather. *The Idler, 11*

323.7
For we that live to please, must please to live. *Prologue at the Opening of the Theatre in Drury Lane, 1747*

323.8
No place affords a more striking conviction of the vanity of human hopes, than a public library. *The Rambler, 23 Mar 1751*

323.9
Human life is every where a state in which much is to be endured, and little to be enjoyed. *Rasselas, Ch. 11*

323.10
The life of a solitary man will be certainly miserable, but not certainly devout. *same, Ch. 21*

323.11
[*Of Lord Chesterfield*] This man I thought had been a Lord among wits; but, I find, he is only a wit among Lords. *Boswell's Life of Johnson, 1754*

323.12
If a man does not make new acquaintances as he advances through life, he will soon find himself left alone. A man, Sir, should keep his friendship in constant repair. *same, 1755*

323.13
BOSWELL. I do indeed come from Scotland, but I cannot help it...
JOHNSON. That Sir, I find, is what a very great many of your countrymen cannot help. *same, 1763*

323.14
The noblest prospect which a Scotchman ever sees, is the high road that leads him to England. *same*

323.15
A man ought to read just as inclination leads him; for what he reads as a task will do him little good. *same*

323.16
It is a sad reflection but a true one, that I knew almost as much at eighteen as I do now. *same*

323.17
Your levellers wish to level down as far as themselves; but they cannot bear levelling up to themselves. They would all have some people under them; why not then have some people above them? *same*

323.18
So far is it from being true that men are naturally equal, that no two people can be half an hour together, but one shall acquire an evident superiority over the other. *same, 1766*

323.19
It matters not how a man dies, but how he lives. *same, 1769*

323.20
I would not give half a guinea to live under one form of Government rather than another. It is of no moment to the happiness of an individual.
same, 1772

323.21
The mass of every people must be barbarous where there is no printing.
same

323.22
People seldom read a book which is given to them; and few are given. The way to spread a work is to sell it at a low price. No man will send to buy a thing that costs even sixpence, without an intention to read it. *same, 1773*

323.23
There are few ways in which a man can be more innocently employed than in getting money. *same*

323.24
There may be other reasons for a man's not speaking in publick than want of resolution: he may have nothing to say. *same*

323.25
Patriotism is the last refuge of a scoundrel. *same*

323.26
Marriage is the best state for a man in general; and every man is a worse man, in proportion as he is unfit for the married state. *same, 1776*

323.27
It is commonly a weak man, who marries for love. *same*

323.28
Melancholy, indeed, should be diverted by every means but drinking.
same

323.29
No man but a blockhead ever wrote, except for money. *same*

323.30
A man who has not been in Italy, is always conscious of an inferiority.
same

323.31
Depend upon it, Sir, when a man knows he is to be hanged in a fortnight, it concentrates his mind wonderfully.
same, 1777

323.32
You find no man, at all intellectual, who is willing to leave London. No, Sir, when a man is tired of London, he is tired of life; for there is in London all that life can afford. *same*

323.33
BOSWELL. Is not the Giant's-Causeway worth seeing?
JOHNSON. Worth seeing? Yes; but not worth going to see. *same, 1779*

323.34
Clear your mind of cant. You may talk as other people do: you may say to a man, 'Sir, I am your most humble servant.' You are *not* his most humble servant. *same, 1783*

323.35
No man is a hypocrite in his pleasures. *same, 1784*

323.36
I look upon every day to be lost, in which I do not make a new acquaintance. *same*

323.37
[*Of a violinist's performance*] Difficult do you call it, Sir? I wish it were impossible. *Anecdotes by William Seward*

323.38
The great source of pleasure is variety. *Lives of the English Poets, Butler*

323.39
A man is in general better pleased when he has a good dinner upon his table, than when his wife talks Greek. *Johnsonian Miscellanies*

324 Jolson, Al (1886-1950), American actor and singer.

324.1
You ain't heard nothin' yet, folks. *The Jazz Singer (the first talking film), 1927*

325 Jonson, Ben (1573-1637), English poet and dramatist.

325.1
Drink to me only with thine eyes
And I will pledge with mine;
Or leave a kiss but in the cup
And I'll not look for wine.
To Celia

325.2
Thou hadst small Latin, and less Greek. *To the Memory of William Shakespeare*

325.3
He was not of an age, but for all time! *same*

325.4
Sweet Swan of Avon! *same*

325.5
VOLPONE. Good morning to the day: and, next, my gold!—
Open the shrine, that I may see my saint. *Volpone, I:1*

325.6
VOLPONE. Come, my Celia, let us prove,
While we can, the sports of love,
Time will not be ours for ever,
He, at length, our good will sever.
same, III:6

325.7
O rare Ben Jonson. *Epitaph in Westminister Abbey*

326 Joyce, James (1882-1941), Irish novelist.

326.1
Ireland is the old sow that eats her farrow. *Portrait of the Artist as a Young Man*

326.2
The snotgreen sea. The scrotumtightening sea. *Ulysses*

326.3
When I makes tea I makes tea, as old mother Grogan said. And when I makes water I makes water. *same*

326.4
History, Stephen said, is a nightmare from which I am trying to awake. *same*

327 Jung, Carl Gustav (1875-1961), Swiss psychologist and psychiatrist.

327.1
Among all my patients in the second half of life...there has not been one whose problem in the last resort was not that of finding a religious outlook on life. *Modern Man in Search of a Soul*

327.2
A man who has not passed through the inferno of his passions has never overcome them. *Memories, Dreams, Reflections*

327.3
We need more understanding of human nature, because the only real danger that exists is man himself.... We know nothing of man, far too little. His psyche should be studied because we are the origin of all coming evil. *Television Interview*

328 Junius, pseudonym of an anonymous writer (1768-1772) to the **London Public Advertiser.**

328.1
The Liberty of the press is the *Palladium* of all the civil, political and religious rights of an Englishman. *Letters, Dedication*

328.2
There is a holy, mistaken zeal in politics, as well as religion. By persuading others we convince ourselves. *Letter 35, 19 Dec 1769*

329 Juvenal, (Decimus Junius Juvenalis) (60-130? A.D.), Roman lawyer and satirist.

329.1
Quis custodiet ipsos
Custodes?
Who is to guard the guards themselves? *Satires, VI:347*

329.2
The people long eagerly for just two things— bread and circuses. *same, X:80*

329.3
Orandum est ut sit mens sana in corpore sano.
Your prayer must be for a sound mind in a sound body. *same, X:356*

K

330 Kafka, Franz (1883-1924), Austrian novelist.

330.1
It's often safer to be in chains than to be free. *The Trial, Ch. 8*

330.2
Let me remind you of the old maxim: people under suspicion are better moving than at rest, since at rest they may be sitting in the balance without knowing it, being weighed together with their sins. *same*

331 Karr, Alphonse (1808-1890), French writer.

331.1
Plus ça change, plus c'est la même chose.

The more it changes, the more it is the same. *Les Guêpes, Jan 1849*

332 Keats, John (1795-1821), English poet.

332.1
Season of mists and mellow fruitfulness,
Close bosom-friend of the maturing sun;
Conspiring with him how to load and bless
With fruit the vines that round the thatch-eaves run. *To Autumn*

332.2
Where are the songs of Spring? Ay, where are they? *same*

332.3
Bright star, would I were steadfast as thou art. *Bright Star*

332.4
A thing of beauty is a joy for ever;
Its loveliness increases; it will never
Pass into nothingness.
Endymion, I:1

332.5
St. Agnes' Eve—Ah, bitter chill it was!
The owl, for all his feathers, was a-cold;
The hare limp'd trembling through the frozen grass,
And silent was the flock in woolly fold. *The Eve of Saint Agnes, 1*

332.6
And they are gone: aye, ages long ago
These lovers fled away into the storm.
same, 43

332.7
The Beadsman, after thousand aves told,
For aye unsought-for slept among his ashes cold. *same, 43*

332.8
Fanatics have their dreams, wherewith they weave
A paradise for a sect. *The Fall of Hyperion, I:1*

332.9
The poet and the dreamer are distinct,
Diverse, sheer opposite, antipodes.
The one pours out a balm upon the world,
The other vexes it. *same, I:199*

332.10
No stir of air was there,
Not so much life as on a summer's day
Robs not one light seed from the feather'd grass,
But where the dead leaf fell, there did it rest. *Hyperion, I:7*

332.11
Oh what can ail thee, Knight at arms
Alone and palely loitering;
The sedge is wither'd from the lake,
And no birds sing. *La Belle Dame Sans Merci*

332.12
La belle Dame sans Merci
Hath thee in thrall! *same*

332.13
Love in a hut; with water and a crust,
Is—Love, forgive us!—cinders, ashes, dust;
Love in a palace is perhaps at last
More grievous torment than a hermit's fast. *Lamia, II:1*

332.14
Do not all charms fly
At the mere touch of cold philosophy?
same, II:229

332.15
Thou still unravish'd bride of quietness,
Thou foster-child of silence and slow time. *Ode on a Grecian Urn*

332.16
Heard melodies are sweet, but those unheard
Are sweeter; therefore, ye soft pipes, play on. *same*

332.17
Thou, silent form, dost tease us out of thought
As doth eternity: Cold Pastoral! *same*

332.18
'Beauty is truth, truth beauty, '—that is all
Ye know on earth, and all ye need to know. *same*

332.19
No, no, go not to Lethe, neither twist
Wolf's-bane, tight-rooted, for its poisonous wine. *Ode on Melancholy*

332.20
Nor let the beetle, nor the death-moth be
Your mournful Psyche. *same*

332.21
Ay, in the very temple of delight
Veil'd Melancholy has her sovran shrine.
Though seen of none save him whose strenuous tongue
Can burst Joy's grape against his palate fine. *same*

332.22
My heart aches, and a drowsy numbness pains
My sense. *Ode to a Nightingale*

332.23
O, for a draught of vintage! that hath been
Cool'd a long age in the deep-delved earth. *same*

332.24
O for a beaker full of the warm South,
Full of the true, the blushful Hippocrene,
With beaded bubbles winking at the brim,
And purple-stained mouth. *same*

332.25
Fade far away, dissolve, and quite forget
What thou among the leaves hast never known,
The weariness, the fever, and the fret,
Here, where men sit and hear each other groan. *same*

332.26
Now more than ever seems it rich to die,
To cease upon the midnight with no pain. *same*

332.27
Thou wast not born for death, immortal Bird!
No hungry generations tread thee down;
The voice I hear this passing night was heard
In ancient days by emperor and clown:
Perhaps the self-same song that found a path
Through the sad heart of Ruth, when sick for home,
She stood in tears amid the alien corn;
The same that oft-times hath
Charm'd magic casements, opening on the foam
Of perilous seas, in faery lands forlorn. *same*

332.28
Much have I travell'd in the realms of gold,
And many goodly states and kingdoms seen. *On first looking into Chapman's Homer*

332.29
Then felt I like some watcher of the skies
When a new planet swims into his ken;
Or like stout Cortez when with eagle eyes
He star'd at the Pacific—and all his men
Look'd at each other with a wild surmise—
Silent, upon a peak in Darien.
same

332.30
O soft embalmer of the still midnight.
To Sleep

332.31
Turn the key deftly in the oiled wards,
And seal the hushed casket of my soul.
same

332.32
A drainless shower
Of light is poesy; 'tis the supreme of power;
'Tis might half slumb'ring on its own right arm. *Sleep and Poetry*

332.33
I am certain of nothing but the holiness of the heart's affections and the truth of imagination—what the imagination seizes as beauty must be truth—whether it existed before or not. *Letter to Benjamin Bailey, 22 Nov 1817*

332.34
O for a life of sensations rather than of thoughts! *same*

332.35
The excellence of every art is its intensity, capable of making all disagreeables evaporate, from their being in close relationship with beauty and truth. *Letter to G. and T. Keats, 21 Dec 1817*

332.36
Negative Capability, that is, when a man is capable of being in uncertainties, mysteries, doubts, without any irritable reaching after fact and reason.
same

332.37
If poetry comes not as naturally as leaves to a tree it had better not come at all. *Letter to John Taylor, 27 Feb 1818*

332.38
Axioms in philosophy are not axioms until they are proved upon our pulses; we read fine things but never feel them to the full until we have gone the same steps as the author. *Letter to J. H. Reynolds, 3 May 1818*

332.39
Love is my religion—I could die for that. *Letter to Fanny Brawne, 13 Oct 1819*

332.40
Here lies one whose name was writ in water. *Epitaph*

333 **Kempis, Thomas À** (1380-1471), German religious writer.

333.1
Man proposes but God disposes.
The Imitation of Christ, I:19

333.2
Sic transit gloria mundi.
Thus the glory of the world passes away. *same, III:6*

334 **Keneally, Thomas** (b. 1935), Australian novelist.

334.1
Pass a law to give every single wingeing bloody Pommie his fare home to England. Back to the smoke and the sun shining ten days a year and shit in

the streets. Yer can have it.
The Chant of Jimmy Blacksmith

335 Kennedy, John Fitzgerald (1917-1963), President of the United States.

335.1
My fellow Americans: ask not what your country can do for you, ask what you can do for your country.
Inaugural address, 20 Jan 1961

335.2
We must use time as a tool, not as a couch. *Observer 'Sayings of the Week', 10 Dec 1961*

335.3
The United States has to move very fast to even stand still.
same, 21 July 1963

335.4
When power narrows the areas of man's concern, poetry reminds him of the richness and diversity of his existence. *Address at Dedication of the Robert Frost Library, 1963*

335.5
In free society art is not a weapon.... Artists are not engineers of the soul.
same

336 Kerouac, Jack (1922-1969), American novelist.

336.1
The beat generation. *Expression*

336.2
You can't teach the old maestro a new tune. *On the Road, I:1*

336.3
We're really all of us bottomly broke. I haven't had time to work in weeks.
same, I:7

336.4
I had nothing to offer anybody except my own confusion. *same, II:3*

337 Keynes, John Maynard, 1st Baron (1883-1946), English economist.

337.1
It is better that a man should tyrannize over his bank balance than over his fellow citizens. *General Theory of Employment, VI:24*

338 Khayyam, Omar, see Fitzgerald, Edward

339 King, Benjamin Franklin (1857-1894), American humorist.

339.1
Nothing to do but work,
Nothing to eat but food,
Nothing to wear but clothes,
To keep one from going nude.
The Pessimist

340 Kingsley, Charles (1819-1875), English writer.

340.1
More ways of killing a cat than choking her with cream.
Westward Ho!, Ch. 20

341 Kipling, Rudyard (1865-1936), English writer and poet.

341.1
Oh, East is East, and West is West, and never the twain shall meet.
The Ballad of East and West

341.2
And a woman is only a woman, but a good cigar is a smoke.
The Betrothed

341.3
But the Devil whoops, as he whooped of old:
'It's clever, but is it art?'
The Conundrum of the Workshops

341.4
For the female of the species is more deadly than the male.
The Female of the Species

341.5
You're a better man than I am, Gunga Din. *Gunga Din*

341.6
If you can keep your head when all about you
Are losing theirs and blaming it on you. *If*

341.7
If you can fill the unforgiving minute
With sixty seconds' worth of distance run,
Yours is the Earth and everything that's in it,
And—which is more—you'll be a Man, my son! *same*

341.8
On the road to Mandalay
Where the flyin'-fishes play.
Mandalay

341.9
Take up the White Man's Burden.
The White Man's Burden

341.10
The silliest woman can manage a clever man; but it needs a very clever woman to manage a fool.
Plain Tales from the Hills, 'Three and—an Extra'

341.11
The Light that Failed. *Title of novel*

342 Knox, John (1505-1572), Scottish religious reformer.

342.1
The First Blast of the Trumpet Against the Monstrous Regiment of Women.
Title of Pamphlet, 1558

343 Knox, Ronald Arbuthnot (1888-1957), English theologian and essayist.

343.1
A loud noise at one end and no sense of responsibility at the other.
Definition of a Baby

344 Krushchev, Nikita (1894-1971), Russian statesman.

344.1
[*To British businessmen*] When you are skinning your customers, you should leave some skin on to grow so that you can skin them again.
Observer 'Sayings of the Week', 28 May 1961

344.2
If you start throwing hedgehogs under me, I shall throw two porcupines under you. *same, 10 Nov 1963*

345 Kubrick, Stanley (b. 1928), American film director.

345.1
The great nations have always acted like gangsters, and the small nations like prostitutes.
The Guardian, 5 Jan 1963

L

346 Laing, Ronald David (b. 1927), Scottish psychiatrist.

346.1
The statesmen of the world who boast and threaten that they have Doomsday weapons are far more dangerous, and far more estranged from 'reality', than many of the people on whom the label 'psychotic' is affixed.
The Divided Self, Preface (Pelican edition)

346.2
Schizophrenia cannot be understood without understanding despair.
same, Ch. 2

346.3
We are effectively destroying ourselves by violence masquerading as love.
The Politics of Experience, Ch.13

346.4
Madness need not be all breakdown. It may also be break-through. It is potential liberation and renewal as well as enslavement and existential death.
same, Ch.16

347 Lamb, Lady Caroline
(1785-1828), English novelist and lover of Byron.

347.1
[*Of Byron*] Mad, bad, and dangerous to know. *Journal*

348 Lamb, Charles (Elia)
(1775-1834), English essayist.

348.1
The human species, according to the best theory I can form of it, is composed of two distinct races, the men who borrow, and the men who lend. *Essays of Elia, The Two Races of Men*

348.2
Borrowers of books—those mutilators of collections, spoilers of the symmetry of shelves, and creators of odd volumes. *same*

348.3
I love to lose myself in other men's minds. When I am not walking, I am reading; I cannot sit and think. Books think for me. *Last Essays of Elia, Detached Thoughts on Books and Reading*

348.4
Newspapers always excite curiosity. No one ever lays one down without a feeling of disappointment. *same*

348.5
The greatest pleasure I know, is to do a good action by stealth, and to have it found out by accident. *Table Talk by the late Elia, The Athenaeum, 4 Jan 1834*

348.6
I have had playmates, I have had companions
In my days of childhood, in my joyful schooldays—
All, all are gone, the old familiar faces.
The Old Familiar Faces

349 Langland, William
(1330?-1400?), English poet.

349.1
In a somer season, when soft was the sonne. *Piers Plowman, B Text, Prologue, 1*

350 Latimer, Hugh (1485?-1555),
English Bishop.

350.1
[*While being burned at the stake with Ridley for heresy*] Be of good comfort, Master Ridley, and play the man; we shall this day light such a candle by God's grace in England, as I trust shall never be put out. *16 Oct 1555*

351 Lawrence, David Herbert (1885-1930), English novelist and poet.

351.1
You may be the most liberal Liberal Englishman, and yet you cannot fail to see the categorical difference between the responsible and the irresponsible classes. *Kangaroo, Ch.1*

351.2
Pornography is the attempt to insult sex, to do dirt on it.
Phoenix, 'Pornography and Obscenity'

351.3
Away with all ideals. Let each individual act spontaneously from the for ever incalculable prompting of the creative wellhead within him. There is no universal law. *same, Preface to 'All Things are Possible', by Leo Shostov*

351.4
It is no good casting out devils. They belong to us, we must accept them and be at peace with them.
same, 'The Reality of Peace'

351.5
When I read Shakespeare I am struck with wonder
That such trivial people should muse and thunder
In such lovely language.
When I Read Shakespeare, 1

352 Lawson, Henry Hertzberg (1867-1922), Australian writer.

352.1
Every true Australian bushman must try his best to tell a bigger outback lie than the last bush-liar.
Prose I:93, 'Stragglers'

353 Leacock, Stephen Butler (1869-1944), Canadian economist and humorist.

353.1
If every day in the life of a school could be the last day but one, there would be little fault to find with it.
College Days, 'Memories and Miseries of a Schoolmaster'

353.2
Get your room full of good air, then shut up the windows and keep it. It will keep for years. Anyway, don't keep using your lungs all the time. Let them rest. *Literary Lapses, 'How to Live to be 200'*

353.3
I detest life-insurance agents; they always argue that I shall some day die, which is not so. *same, 'Insurance. Up to Date'*

353.4
Lord Ronald said nothing; he flung himself from the room, flung himself upon his horse and rode madly off in all directions. *Nonsense Novels, 'Gertrude the Governess'*

353.5
Golf may be played on Sunday, not being a game within the view of the law, but being a form of moral effort.
Other Fancies, 'Why I refuse to play Golf'

354 Lear, Edward (1812-1888), English artist and writer.

354.1
On the Coast of Coromandel
Where the early pumpkins blow,
In the middle of the woods
Lived the Yonghy-Bonghy-Bò.
The Courtship of the Yonghy-Bonghy-Bò

354.2
The Dong!—the Dong!
The wandering Dong through the forest goes!
The Dong!—the Dong!
The Dong with a luminous Nose!
The Dong with a Luminous Nose

354.3
They went to sea in a sieve, they did
In a sieve they went to sea.
The Jumblies

354.4
Far and few, far and few,
Are the lands where the Jumblies live;
Their heads are green, and their hands are blue,
And they went to sea in a sieve.
same

354.5
The Owl and the Pussy-Cat went to sea
In a beautiful pea-green boat,
They took some honey, and plenty of money,
Wrapped up in a five-pound note.
The Owl and the Pussy-Cat

355 Lenin, Nikolai (1870-1924), Russian revolutionary and political leader.

355.1
Under capitalism we have a state in the proper sense of the word, that is, a special machine for the suppression of one class by another. *The State and Revolution, V:2*

355.2
It is true that liberty is precious—so precious that it must be rationed.
Attributed

356 Lessing, Doris (b. 1919), English novelist.

356.1
When a white man in Africa by accident looks into the eyes of a native and sees the human being (which it is his chief preoccupation to avoid), his sense of guilt, which he denies, fumes up in resentment and he brings down the whip.
The Grass is Singing, Ch.8

357 Lévis, Duc de (1764-1830), French soldier.

357.1
Noblesse oblige.
Nobility has its own obligations.
Maximes et Réflexions

358 Lewis, Clive Staples (1898-1963), English writer and academic.

358.1
Friendship is unnecessary, like philosophy, like art.... It has no survival value; rather it is one of those things that give value to survival.
The Four Loves, Friendship

358.2
There is wishful thinking in Hell as well as on earth.
The Screwtape Letters, Preface

359 Lewis, Sinclair (1885-1951), American novelist.

359.1
In other countries, art and literature are left to a lot of shabby bums living in attics and feeding on booze and spaghetti, but in America the successful writer or picture-painter is indistinguishable from any other decent business man. *Babbitt, Ch.14*

359.2
Our American professors like their literature clear and cold and pure and very dead. *'The American Fear of Literature', Nobel Prize Speech, 1930*

360 Lincoln, Abraham (1809-1865), President of the United States.

360.1
No man is good enough to govern another man without that other's consent. *Speech, 1854*

360.2
The ballot is stronger than the bullet. *Speech, 19 May 1856*

360.3
Those who deny freedom to others, deserve it not for themselves. *same*

360.4
What is conservatism? Is it not adherence to the old and tried, against the new and untried? *Speech, 27 Feb 1860*

360.5
I intend no modification of my oft-expressed personal wish that all men everywhere could be free. *Letter to Horace Greeley, 22 Aug 1862*

360.6
That this nation, under God, shall have a new birth of freedom; and that government of the people, by the people, and for the people, shall not perish from the earth. *Address at Dedication of National Cemetery, Gettysburg, 19 Nov 1863*

360.7
An old Dutch farmer, who remarked to a companion once that it was not best to swap horses in mid-stream. *Speech, 9 June 1864*

360.8
You can fool some of the people all the time and all the people some of the time; but you can't fool all the people all the time. *Attributed*

360.9
People who like this sort of thing will find this is the sort of thing they like. *Criticism of book*

361 Livy, (Titus Livius) (59 B.C.-A.D. 17), Roman historian.

361.1
Vae victis.
Woe to the vanquished. *History, V:48*

362 Lloyd, Marie (1870-1922), English music-hall singer.

362.1
A little of what you fancy does you good. *Title of song*

363 Lloyd, Robert (1733-1764), English poet.

363.1
Slow and steady wins the race. *The Hare and the Tortoise*

364 Lloyd George, David, 1st Earl of Dwyfor, (1863-1945), British statesman and prime minister.

364.1
What is our task? To make Britain a fit country for heroes to live in. *Speech, 24 Nov 1918*

364.2
Every man has a House of Lords in his own head. Fears, prejudices, misconceptions—those are the peers, and they are hereditary. *Speech, Cambridge, 1927*

364.3
The world is becoming like a lunatic asylum run by lunatics.
Observer 'Sayings of Our Times', 31 May 1953

365 Loos, Anita (b. 1893), American novelist and script-writer.

365.1
Gentlemen always seem to remember blondes. *Gentlemen Prefer Blondes, Ch.1*

365.2
So this gentleman said a girl with brains ought to do something else with them besides think. *same*

365.3
Kissing your hand may make you feel very very good but a diamond and safire bracelet lasts forever.
same, Ch.4

366 Louis XIV, (1638-1715), King of France.

366.1
L'État c'est moi.
I am the State. *Attributed*

367 Louis XVIII, (1755-1824), King of France.

367.1
Punctuality is the politeness of kings.
Attributed

368 Lovelace, Richard (1618-1658), English poet.

368.1
Stone walls do not a prison make,
Nor iron bars a cage.
To Althea, from Prison

369 Lover, Samuel (1797-1868), Irish artist, song-writer and novelist.

369.1
When once the itch of literature comes over a man, nothing can cure it but the scratching of a pen.
Handy Andy, Ch.36

370 Lowry, Malcolm (1909-1957), English novelist.

370.1
How alike are the groans of love to those of the dying. *Under the Volcano, Ch.12*

371 Lucretius, (Titus Lucretius Carus) (c. 99-55 B.C.), Roman poet.

371.1
Nothing can be created out of nothing.
On the Nature of the Universe, I:155

372 Luther, Martin (1483-1546), German religious reformer.

372.1
Who loves not wine, woman and song,
Remains a fool his whole life long.
Attributed

373 Lutyens, Sir Edwin Landseer (1869-1944), English architect.

373.1
The answer is in the plural and they bounce.
Attributed

373.2
This piece of cod passes all understanding. *Attributed remark in restaurant*

374 Lytton, 1st Earl of see **Meredith, Owen**

M

375 **Macaulay, Thomas Babington, 1st Baron** (1800-1859), British writer and historian.

375.1
The English Bible, a book which, if everything else in our language should perish, would alone suffice to show the whole extent of its beauty and power.
Essay on Dryden, Edinburgh Review.

375.2
The gallery in which the reporters sit has become a fourth estate of the realm. *Essay on Hallam's Constitutional History, same*

375.3
The Puritan hated bear-baiting, not because it gave pain to the bear, but because it gave pleasure to the spectators. *History of England, Ch.2*

376 **MacCarthy, Sir Desmond** (1878-1952), English writer and critic.

376.1
When I meet those remarkable people whose company is coveted, I often wish they would show off a little more.
Theatre, 'Good Talk'

376.2
The whole of art is an appeal to a reality which is not without us but in our minds. *same, 'Modern Drama'*

377 **McLuhan, Marshall** (b. 1911), Canadian writer on the mass media.

377.1
If the nineteenth century was the age of the editorial chair, ours is the century of the psychiatrist's couch.
Understanding the Media, Introduction

378 **Macmillan, Sir Harold** (b. 1894), English prime minister and publisher.

378.1
Most of our people have never had it so good. *Speech, Bedford Football Ground, 20 July 1957*

378.2
When you're abroad you're a statesman: when you're at home you're just a politician. *Speech, 1958*

378.3
The wind of change is blowing through the continent. Whether we like it or not, this growth of national consciousness is a political fact.
Speech, South African Parliament, 3 Feb 1960

379 **Mao Tse-Tung,** (1893-1976), Chinese communist leader.

379.1
All reactionaries are paper tigers.
Quotations from Chairman Mao Tse-Tung, 6

379.2
Letting a hundred flowers blossom and a hundred schools of thought contend is the policy for promoting the progress of the arts and the sciences. *same, 32*

380 **Marie-Antoinette, Josephe Jeanne** (1755-1793), Queen of France.

380.1
[*When told that the people had no bread*] Let them eat cake.
Attributed

381 Marlowe, Christopher (1564–1593), English dramatist and poet.

381.1

GAVESTON. My men, like satyrs grazing on the lawns,
Shall with their goat-feet dance an antic hay. *Edward the Second, I:1:59*

381.2

FAUSTUS. Was this the face that launch'd a thousand ships
And burnt the topless towers of Ilium?
Sweet Helen, make me immortal with a kiss. *Doctor Faustus, Sc.14*

381.3

FAUSTUS. Now hast thou but one bare hour to live,
And then thou must be damn'd perpetually!
Stand still, you ever-moving spheres of heaven,
That time may cease, and midnight never come. *same, Sc.16*

381.4

CHORUS. Cut is the branch that might have grown full straight,
And burned is Apollo's laurel-bough,
That sometime grew within this learned man. *same*

381.5

BARABAS. And, as their wealth increaseth, so inclose
Infinite riches in a little room.
The Jew of Malta, I:1

381.6

FRIAR BARNARDINE. Thou hast committed—
BARABAS. Fornication: but that was in another country;
And beside the wench is dead.
same, IV:1

381.7

Come live with me, and be my love;
And we will all the pleasures prove
That hills and valleys, dales and fields,
Woods or steepy mountain yields.
The Passionate Shepherd to his Love

382 Marquis, Donald Robert (1878–1937), American writer.

382.1

To stroke a platitude until it purrs like an epigram. *New York Sun, 'Sun Dial'*

382.2

An idea isn't responsible for the people who believe in it. *same*

383 Marryat, Frederick (1792–1848), English naval officer and novelist.

383.1

NURSE. [*Of her illegitimate baby*] If you please, ma'am, it was a very little one. *Mr. Midshipman Easy, Ch.3*

383.2

I never knows the children. It's just six of one and half-a-dozen of the other.
The Pirate, Ch.4

383.3

I think it much better that...every man paddle his own canoe.
Settlers in Canada, Ch.8

384 Marvell, Andrew (1621–1678), English poet.

384.1

Had we but world enough, and time,
This coyness, lady, were no crime.
To his Coy Mistress

384.2

But at my back I always hear
Time's winged chariot hurrying near;
And yonder all before us lie
Deserts of vast eternity. *same*

384.3
The grave's a fine and private place,
But none, I think, do there embrace.
same

384.4
How vainly men themselves amaze
To win the palm, the oak, or bays.
The Garden

384.5
Annihilating all that's made
To a green thought in a green shade.
same

384.6
So restless Cromwell could not cease
In the inglorious arts of peace.
An Horatian Ode upon Cromwell's Return from Ireland

384.7
[*Of Charles I*] He nothing common did or mean
Upon that memorable scene,
But with his keener eye
The axe's edge did try. *same*

385 Marx, Groucho (1895-1977), American film comedian.

385.1
You're the most beautiful woman I've ever seen, which doesn't say much for you. *Animal Crackers, film, 1930*

385.2
One morning I shot an elephant in my pajamas.
How he got into my pajamas I'll never know. *same*

385.3
What's a thousand dollars? Mere chicken feed. A poultry matter.
The Cocoanuts, film, 1929

385.4
Your eyes shine like the pants of my blue serge suit. *same*

385.5
A child of five would understand this. Send somebody to fetch a child of five.
Duck Soup, film, 1933

385.6
My husband is dead.
—I'll bet he's just using that as an excuse.
I was with him to the end.
—No wonder he passed away.
I held him in my arms and kissed him.
—So it was murder! *same*

385.7
Go, and never darken my towels again!
same

385.8
There's a man outside with a big black moustache.
—Tell him I've got one.
Horse Feathers, film, 1932

385.9
You're a disgrace to our family name of Wagstaff, if such a thing is possible.
same

385.10
You've got the brain of a four-year-old boy, and I bet he was glad to get rid of it. *same*

385.11
Look at me: I worked my way up from nothing to a state of extreme poverty.
Monkey Business, film, 1931

385.12
I want to register a complaint. Do you know who sneaked into my room at three o'clock this morning?...
—Who?...
Nobody, and that's my complaint.
same

385.13
Do you suppose I could buy back my introduction to you? *same*

385.14
Sir, you have the advantage of me.
—Not yet I haven't, but wait till I get you outside. *same*

385.15
Do they allow tipping on the boat?
—Yes, sir.
Have you got two fives?
—Oh, yes, sir.
Then you won't need the ten cents I was going to give you.
A Night at the Opera, film, 1935

385.16
The strains of Verdi will come back to you tonight, and Mrs Claypool's cheque will come back to you in the morning. *same*

385.17
Send two dozen roses to Room 424 and put 'Emily, I love you' on the back of the bill. *A Night in Casablanca, film, 1945*

385.18
I never forget a face, but I'll make an exception in your case.
The Guardian, 18 June 1965

385.19
[*On resigning from the Friar's Club, Hollywood*] Please accept my resignation. I don't want to belong to any club that will accept me as a member.
Telegram

385.20
No, Groucho is not my real name. I'm breaking it in for a friend.
Attributed

385.21
Whoever named it necking was a poor judge of anatomy. *Attributed*

385.22
A man is only as old as the woman he feels. *Attributed*

386 Marx, Karl (1818-1883), German philosopher and founder of Communism.

386.1
Capitalist production begets, with the inexorability of a law of nature, its own negation. *Capital, Ch.15*

386.2
From each according to his abilities, to each according to his needs.
Criticism of the Gotha Programme

386.3
Religion ... is the opium of the people.
Criticism of the Hegelian Philosophy of Right, Introduction

386.4
The history of all hitherto existing society is the history of class struggles.
Manifesto of the Communist Party, 1

386.5
The workers have nothing to lose but their chains. They have a world to gain. Workers of the world, unite.
same, 4

387 Mary Tudor, (1516-1558), Queen of England.

387.1
When I am dead and opened, you shall find 'Calais' lying in my heart.
Holinshed's Chronicles, III:1160

388 Maugham, William Somerset (1874-1965), English writer and dramatist.

388.1
Like all weak men he laid an exaggerated stress on not changing one's mind. *Of Human Bondage, Ch.37*

388.2
People ask you for criticism, but they only want praise. *same, Ch.50*

388.3
Money is like a sixth sense without which you cannot make a complete use of the other five. *same, Ch.51*

388.4
The mystic sees the ineffable, and the psychopathologist the unspeakable.
The Moon and Sixpence, Ch.1

388.5
Impropriety is the soul of wit.
same, Ch.4

388.6
You can't learn too soon that the most useful thing about a principle is that it can always be sacrificed to expediency.
The Circle, Act 3

388.7
It was such a lovely day I thought it was a pity to get up.
Our Betters, Act 2

388.8
I would sooner read a time-table or a catalogue than nothing at all. They are much more entertaining than half the novels that are written.
The Summing Up

388.9
Life is too short to do anything for oneself that one can pay others to do for one. *same*

388.10
I've always been interested in people, but I've never liked them.
Observer 'Sayings of the Week', 28 Aug 1949

389 Melba, Dame Nellie
(1861-1931), Australian soprano.

389.1
[*To Clara Butt*] So you're going to Australia! Well, I made twenty thousand pounds on my tour there, but of course *that* will never be done again. Still, it's a wonderful country, and you'll have a good time. What are you going to sing? All I can say is—sing 'em muck! It's all they can understand! *Clara Butt: Her Life Story (W. H. Ponder)*

390 Melbourne, William Lamb, 2nd Viscount
(1779-1848), English statesman and prime minister.

390.1
Things have come to a pretty pass when religion is allowed to invade the sphere of private life. *Attributed*

391 Mellon, Andrew William
(1855-1937), American financier.

391.1
A nation is not in danger of financial disaster merely because it owes itself money. *Remark, 1933*

392 Mencken, Henry Louis
(1880-1956), American philologist, editor and satirist.

392.1
Conscience is the inner voice that warns us somebody may be looking.
A Mencken Chrestomathy

392.2
It is now quite lawful for a Catholic woman to avoid pregnancy by a resort to mathematics, though she is still forbidden to resort to physics and chemistry. *Notebooks, 'Minority Report'*

392.3
The chief contribution of Protestantism to human thought is its massive proof that God is a bore. *same*

392.4
The worst government is the most moral. One composed of cynics is often very tolerant and human. But

when fanatics are on top there is no limit to oppression. *same*

392.5
Poetry is a comforting piece of fiction set to more or less lascivious music. *Prejudices, Third Series, 'The Poet and his Art'*

392.6
I've made it a rule never to drink by daylight and never to refuse a drink after dark. *New York Post, 18 Sept 1945*

393 Meredith, George (1828–1909), English novelist and poet.

393.1
I expect that Woman will be the last thing civilized by Man. *The Ordeal of Richard Feverel, Ch.1*

394 Meredith, Owen, Earl of Lytton (1831–1891), English poet and statesman.

394.1
Genius does what it must, and Talent does what it can. *Last Words of a Sensitive Second-rate Poet*

395 Mikes, George (b. 1912), Hungarian-English writer.

395.1
On the Continent people have good food; in England people have good table manners. *How to be an Alien*

395.2
An Englishman, even if he is alone, forms an orderly queue of one. *same*

396 Mill, John Stuart (1806–1873), English philosopher.

396.1
All good things which exist are the fruits of originality. *On Liberty, Ch.3*

396.2
The liberty of the individual must be thus far limited; he must not make himself a nuisance to other people. *same*

396.3
The worth of a State in the long run is the worth of the individuals composing it. *same*

397 Miller, Arthur (b. 1915), American dramatist.

397.1
A good newspaper, I suppose, is a nation talking to itself. *Observer 'Sayings of the Week', 26 Nov 1961*

398 Miller, Jonathan (b. 1934), English academic, broadcaster, stage director and humorist.

398.1
I'm not really a Jew; just Jew-ish, not the whole hog. *Beyond the Fringe, television review*

399 Milligan, Spike (b. 1918), English comic and writer.

399.1
—'Do you come here often?'
'Only in the mating season.'
The Goon Show, television programme

399.2
BLUEBOTTLE. I don't like this game. *same, passim*

399.3
I'm walking backwards till Christmas *same*

400 Milne, Alan Alexander (1882–1956), English writer and dramatist.

400.1
POOH. Time for a little something.
Winnie-the-Pooh, Ch.6

401 Milton, John (1608–1674), English poet.

401.1
Blest pair of Sirens, pledges of Heaven's joy,
Sphere-born harmonious sisters, Voice and Verse. *At a Solemn Music*

401.2
Hence, vain deluding Joys,
The brood of Folly without father bred! *Il Penseroso, 1*

401.3
[*Of the nightingale*] Sweet bird, that shunn'st the noise of folly,
Most musical, most melancholy!
same, 61

401.4
Where glowing embers through the room
Teach light to counterfeit a gloom,
Far from all resort of mirth,
Save the cricket on the hearth.
same, 79

401.5
Where more is meant than meets the ear. *same, 120*

401.6
Come, and trip it as you go
On the light fantastic toe.
L'Allegro, 31

401.7
Then to the spicy nut-brown ale.
same, 100

401.8
Or sweetest Shakespeare, Fancy's child,
Warble his native wood-notes wild.
same, 133

401.9
Yet once more, O ye laurels, and once more,
Ye myrtles brown, with ivy never sere,
I come to pluck your berries harsh and crude,
And with forced fingers rude
Shatter your leaves before the mellowing year. *Lycidas, 1*

401.10
To sport with Amaryllis in the shade,
Or with the tangles of Neaera's hair?
same, 68

401.11
Fame is the spur that the clear spirit doth raise
(That last infirmity of noble mind)
To scorn delights, and live laborious days. *same, 70*

401.12
The hungry sheep look up, and are not fed,
But, swoln with wind and the rank mist they draw,
Rot inwardly, and foul contagion spread. *same, 123*

401.13
At last he rose, and twitched his mantle blue:
To-morrow to fresh woods, and pastures new. *same, 192*

401.14
Of Man's first disobedience, and the fruit
Of that forbidden tree, whose mortal taste
Brought death into the World, and all our woe… *Paradise Lost, I:1*

401.15
What in me is dark
Illumine, what is low raise and support;

That, to the height of this great argument,
I may assert Eternal Providence,
And justify the ways of God to men.
same, I:22

401.16
What though the field be lost?
All is not lost—the unconquerable will,
And study of revenge, immortal hate,
And courage never to submit or yield:
And what is else not to be overcome?
same, I:105

401.17
A mind not to be changed by place or time.
The mind is its own place, and in itself
Can make a Heaven of Hell, a Hell of Heaven. *same, I:253*

401.18
To reign is worth ambition, though in Hell:
Better to reign in Hell than serve in Heaven. *same, I:262*

401.19
From morn
To noon he fell, from noon to dewy eve,
A summer's day, and with the setting sun
Dropped from the zenith, like a falling star. *same, I:742*

401.20
High on a throne of royal state, which far
Outshone the wealth of Ormus and of Ind,
Or where the gorgeous East with richest hand
Showers on her kings barbaric pearl and gold,
Satan exalted sat, by merit raised
To that bad eminence. *same, II:1*

401.21
Which way I fly is Hell; myself am Hell;
And, in the lowest deep, a lower deep
Still threat'ning to devour me opens wide,
To which the Hell I suffer seems a Heaven. *same, IV:73*

401.22
Farewell remorse! All good to me is lost;
Evil, be thou my Good.
same, IV:180

401.23
Now came still Evening on, and Twilight grey
Had in her sober livery all things clad.
same, IV:598

401.24
Midnight brought on the dusky hour
Friendliest to sleep and silence.
same, V:667

401.25
In solitude
What happiness? who can enjoy alone,
Or, all enjoying, what contentment find? *same, VIII:364*

401.26
Revenge, at first though sweet,
Bitter ere long back on itself recoils.
same, IX:171

401.27
The world was all before them, where to choose
Their place of rest, and Providence their guide:
They, hand in hand, with wandering steps and slow,
Through Eden took their solitary way.
same, XII:646

401.28
SAMSON. A little onward lend thy guiding hand

To these dark steps, a little further on.
Samson Agonistes, 1

401.29

SAMSON. Ask for this great deliverer now, and find him
Eyeless in Gaza at the mill with slaves.
same, 40

401.30

SAMSON. O dark, dark, dark, amid the blaze of noon,
Irrecoverably dark, total eclipse,
Without all hope of day! *same, 80*

401.31

How soon hath Time, the subtle thief of youth,
Stolen on his wing my three-and-twentieth year! *Sonnet, On being arrived at the age of twenty-three*

401.32

When I consider how my light is spent
Ere half my days in this dark world and wide,
And that one talent which is death to hide
Lodged with me useless. *Sonnet, On his Blindness*

401.33

God doth not need
Either man's work or his own gifts. Who best
Bear his mild yoke, they serve him best: his state
Is kingly; thousands at his bidding speed,
And post o'er land and ocean without rest;
They also serve who only stand and wait. *same*

401.34

New Presbyter is but old Priest writ large. *Sonnet, On the new Forcers of Conscience under the Long Parliament*

401.35

Who kills a man kills a reasonable creature, God's image; but he who destroys a good book, kills reason itself, kills the image of God, as it were in the eye. *Areopagitica*

401.36

A good book is the precious life-blood of a master spirit, embalmed and treasured up on purpose to a life beyond life. *same*

401.37

Let her and Falsehood grapple; who ever knew Truth put to the worse, in a free and open encounter? *same*

401.38

None can love freedom heartily, but good men; the rest love not freedom, but licence. *Tenure of Kings and Magistrates*

402 Molière, (Jean Baptiste Poquelin) (1622–1673), French dramatist and actor.

402.1

One should eat to live, not live to eat.
L'Avare, III:5

402.2

Good heavens! I have been talking prose for over forty years without realizing it.
Le Bourgeois Gentilhomme, II:4

402.3

It is a public scandal that gives offence, and it is no sin to sin in secret.
Tartuffe, IV:5

403 Montaigne, Michel de (1533–1592), French essayist.

403.1

The greatest thing in the world is to know how to be self-sufficient.
Essays, I:39

403.2
A man must keep a little back shop where he can be himself without reserve. In solitude alone can he know true freedom. *same*

403.3
When I play with my cat, who knows whether she is not amusing herself with me more than I with her? *same, II:12*

403.4
Marriage is like a cage; one sees the birds outside desperate to get in, and those inside equally desperate to get out. *same, III:5*

404 More, Sir Thomas (1478–1535), English statesman and divine.

404.1
[*On mounting the scaffold*] I pray you, Master Lieutenant, see me safe up, and for coming down let me shift for myself. *Life of Sir Thomas More (William Roper)*

405 Morgan, Augustus de (1806–1871), English mathematician.

405.1
Great fleas have little fleas upon their backs to bite 'em,
And little fleas have lesser fleas, and so *ad infinitum.* *A Budget of Paradoxes*

406 Morris, Desmond (b. 1928), English biologist and writer.

406.1
There are one hundred and ninety-three living species of monkeys and apes. One hundred and ninety-two of them are covered with hair. The exception is a naked ape self-named *Homo sapiens.*
The Naked Ape, Introduction

407 Mosley, Sir Oswald (b. 1896), English politician and fascist leader.

407.1
I am not and never have been, a man of the right. My position was on the left and is now in the centre of politics. *The Times, 26 Apr 1968*

408 Motley, John Lothrop (1814–1877), American historian and diplomat.

408.1
Give us the luxuries of life, and we will dispense with its necessities. *The Autocrat of the Breakfast Table (O. W. Holmes), Ch.6*

409 Munro, Hector Hugh see Saki

410 Münster, Ernst Friedrich Herbert (1766–1839), Hanoverian statesman.

410.1
[*Of the Russian Constitution*] Absolutism tempered by assassination. *Letter*

411 Mussolini, Benito (1883–1945), Italian dictator.

411.1
[*Of Hitler's seizure of power*] Fascism is a religion; the twentieth century will be known in history as the century of Fascism. *Sawdust Caesar (George Seldes), Ch.24*

N

412 Nabokov, Vladimir (1899–1977), Russian novelist and lepidopterist.

412 Napoleon

412.1
Lolita, light of my life, fire of my loins. My sin, my Soul. *Lolita, I:1*

412.2
Spring and summer did happen in Cambridge almost every year.
The Real Life of Sebastian Knight, Ch.5

412.3
Literature and butterflies are the two sweetest passions known to man.
Radio Times, Oct 1962

413 Napoleon Bonaparte,
(1769–1821), French emperor and general.

413.1
It is only a step from the sublime to the ridiculous. *After the retreat from Moscow, 1812*

413.2
England is a nation of shopkeepers.
Attributed

413.3
An army marches on its stomach.
Attributed

414 Nash, Ogden (1902–1971),
American writer of humorous verse.

414.1
A door is what a dog is perpetually on the wrong side of. *A Dog's Best Friend Is His Illiteracy*

414.2
Home is heaven and orgies are vile
But you need an orgy, once in a while.
Home, 99.44/100% Sweet Home

414.3
Beneath this slab
John Brown is stowed.
He watched the ads
And not the road. *Lather as You Go*

414.4
Children aren't happy with nothing to ignore,
And that's what parents were created for. *The Parents*

414.5
I think that I shall never see
A billboard lovely as a tree.
Perhaps unless the billboards fall,
I'll never see a tree at all.
Song of the Open Road

415 Nelson, Horatio, 1st Viscount
(1758–1805), English admiral.

415.1
England expects every man will do his duty. *Battle of Trafalgar*

415.2
Kiss me, Hardy. *Remark, Battle of Trafalgar, 1805*

416 Newbolt, Sir Henry John
(1862–1938), English poet.

416.1
There's a breathless hush in the Close tonight—
Ten to make and the match to win—
A bumping pitch and a blinding light,
An hour to play and the last man in.
Vitaï Lampada

416.2
But his captain's hand on his shoulder smote—
'Play up! play up! and play the game!'
same

417 Newman, John Henry
(1801–1890), English Catholic theologian.

417.1
It is almost a definition of a gentleman to say that he is one who never inflicts pain. *The Idea of a University, 'Knowledge and Religious Duty'*

418 Nicholas I, (1796-1855), Tsar of Russia.

418.1
Russia has two generals in whom she can confide—Generals Janvier and Février. *Punch, 10 Mar 1853*

419 Nietzsche, Friedrich Wilhelm (1844-1900), German philosopher and critic.

419.1
When a man is in love he endures more than at other times; he submits to everything.
The Antichrist, aphorism 23

419.2
God created woman. And boredom did indeed cease from that moment—but many other things ceased as well! Woman was God's *second* mistake. *same, 48*

419.3
I call Christianity the one great curse, the one enormous and innermost perversion, the one great instinct of revenge, for which no means are too venomous, too underhand, too underground and too petty—I call it the one immortal blemish of mankind.
same, 62

419.4
My doctrine is: Live that thou mayest desire to live again—that is thy duty—for in any case thou wilt live again! *Eternal Recurrence, 27*

419.5
I teach you the Superman. Man is something that is to be surpassed.
Thus Spake Zarathustra, Ch. 3

420 Nixon, Richard Milhous (b. 1913), American politician and President of the United States.

420.1
[*Of the first manned moon landing*] This is the greatest week in the history of the world since the creation.
Remark, 24 July 1969

420.2
I am not a crook.
Remark, 17 Nov 1973

420.3
There can be no whitewash at the White House. *Observer 'Sayings of the Week', 30 Dec 1973*

421 North, Christopher (John Wilson) (1785-1854), Scottish poet, essayist and critic.

421.1
His Majesty's dominions, on which the sun never sets.
Noctes Ambrosianae, 20 Apr 1829

421.2
Laws were made to be broken.
same, 24 May 1830

O

422 Oates, Lawrence Edward Grace (1880-1912), English explorer.

422.1
I am just going outside, and may be some time. *Last words: Recorded in Captain R. F. Scott's Antarctic Diary, 16 Mar 1912*

423 O'Casey, Sean (1884-1964), Irish dramatist.

423.1
There's no reason to bring religion into it. I think we ought to have as great a regard for religion as we can, so as to keep it out of as many things

as possible. *The Plough and the Stars, Act 1*

423.2
[*Of P. G. Wodehouse*] English literature's performing flea. *Remark*

424 Ochs, Adolph Simon (1858–1935), American newspaper publisher.

424.1
All the news that's fit to print. *Motto of New York Times*

425 O'Keefe, Patrick (1872–1934), American advertising agent.

425.1
Say it with flowers. *Slogan for Society of American Florists*

426 Orton, Joe (1933–1967), English dramatist.

426.1
I'd the upbringing a nun would envy and that's the truth. Until I was fifteen I was more familiar with Africa than my own body. *Entertaining Mr Sloane, Act 1*

426.2
It's all any reasonable child can expect if the dad is present at the conception. *same, Act 3*

426.3
The humble and meek are thirsting for blood. *Funeral Games, Act 1*

426.4
Every luxury was lavished on you—atheism, breast-feeding, circumcision. I had to make my own way. *Loot, Act 1*

426.5
Reading isn't an occupation we encourage among police officers. We try to keep the paper work down to a minimum. *same, Act 2*

427 Orwell, George (Eric Blair) (1903–1950), English novelist and essayist.

427.1
All animals are equal but some animals are more equal than others. *Animal Farm, Ch. 10*

427.2
Big Brother is watching you *Nineteen Eighty-Four*

427.3
War is Peace, Freedom is Slavery, Ignorance is Strength. *same*

427.4
Doublethink means the power of holding two contradictory beliefs in one's mind simultaneously, and accepting both of them. *same, II:9*

427.5
[*Of the middle classes*] We have nothing to lose but our aitches. *The Road to Wigan Pier, Ch. 13*

428 Ovid, (Publius Ovidius Naso) (43 B.C.–17 A.D.), Latin poet.

428.1
Whether they give or refuse, women are glad to have been asked. *Ars Amatoria, I*

428.2
Tu quoque.
You also. *Tristia*

429 Owen, Robert (1771–1858), Welsh social reformer.

429.1
[*Of his business partner, William Allen*] All the world is queer save thee and me, and even thou art a little queer. *Remark, 1828*

430 Owen, Wilfred (1893–1918), English poet.

430.1
Above all I am not concerned with Poetry. My subject is War, and the pity of War. The Poetry is in the pity.
Preface to Poems

430.2
The old Lie: *Dulce et decorum est*
Pro patria mori.
Dulce et decorum est

P

431 Paine, Thomas (1737-1809), English philosopher and writer.

431.1
The sublime and the ridiculous are often so nearly related that it is difficult to class them separately. One step above the sublime makes the ridiculous; and one step above the ridiculous makes the sublime again.
The Age of Reason, Part 2

431.2
Government, even in its best state, is but a necessary evil; in its worst state, an intolerable one.
Common Sense, Ch.1

432 Palmerston, Henry John Temple, 3rd Viscount (1784-1865), English prime minister.

432.1
Die, my dear Doctor, that's the last thing I shall do! *Last words, attributed*

433 Parker, Dorothy (1893-1967), American writer.

433.1
How do people go to sleep? I'm afraid I've lost the knack. I might try busting myself smartly over the temple with the nightlight. I might repeat to myself, slowly and soothingly, a list of quotations beautiful from minds profound; if I can remember any of the damn things. *The Little Hours*

433.2
Men seldom make passes
At girls who wear glasses.
News Item

433.3
Why is it no one ever sent me yet
One perfect limousine, do you suppose?
Ah no, it's always just my luck to get
One perfect rose. *One Perfect Rose*

433.4
Guns aren't lawful;
Nooses give;
Gas smells awful;
You might as well live. *Résumé*

433.5
Sorrow is tranquillity remembered in emotion. *Sentiment*

433.6
By the time you swear you're his,
Shivering and sighing,
And he vows his passion is
Infinite, undying—
Lady, make a note of this:
One of you is lying.
Unfortunate Coincidence

433.7
If all the young ladies who attended the Yale promenade dance were laid end to end, no one would be the least surprised. *While Rome Burns (Alexander Woollcott)*

434 Parkinson, Cyril Northcote (b. 1909), English political scientist and writer.

434.1
Work expands so as to fill the time available for its completion.
Parkinson's Law

435 Pascal, Blaise (1623-1662), French mathematician and theologian.

435.1
The heart has its reasons which reason does not know. *Pensées, IV:277*

436 Pater, Walter Horatio (1839-1894), English critic.

436.1
[*Of the Mona Lisa*] She is older than the rocks among which she sits.
The Renaissance, 'Leonardo da Vinci'

436.2
All art constantly aspires towards the condition of music. *same, 'The School of Giorgione'*

437 Peacock, Thomas Love (1785-1866), English novelist.

437.1
LADY CLARINDA. Respectable means rich, and decent means poor. I should die if I heard my family called decent.
Crotchet Castle, Ch.3

437.2
MR PORTPIPE. There are two reasons for drinking; one is, when you are thirsty, to cure it; the other, when you are not thirsty, to prevent it... Prevention is better than cure.
Melincourt, Ch.16

438 Pepys, Samuel (1633-1703), English diarist.

438.1
And so to bed. *Diary, 6 May 1660 and passim*

438.2
Music and women I cannot but give way to, whatever my business is.
same, 9 Mar 1666

438.3
To church; and with my mourning, very handsome, and new periwig, make a great show. *same, 31 Mar 1667*

439 Perón, Juan Domingo (1895-1974), Argentine soldier and president.

439.1
If I had not been born Perón, I would have liked to be Perón.
Observer 'Sayings of the Week', 21 Feb 1960

440 Pétain, Henri Phillipe (1856-1951), French marshal.

440.1
[*Of the German army*] They shall not pass. *Verdun, Feb 1916*

441 Peter, Laurence (b. 1919), Canadian writer and educationalist.

441.1
The Peter Principle: In a Hierarchy Every Employee Tends to Rise to his Level of Incompetence.
The Peter Principle, Ch.1

441.2
Work is accomplished by those employees who have not yet reached their level of incompetence. *same*

442 Petronius, (*fl.* 1st century A.D), Latin writer.

442.1
Cave canem.
Beware of the dog.
Satyricon, XXIX:1

443 Phelps, Edward John (1822-1900), American lawyer and diplomat.

443.1
The man who makes no mistakes does not usually make anything.
Speech, Mansion House, London, 24 Jan 1899

444 Phillips, Wendell (1811-1884), American reformer.

444.1
One on God's side is a majority.
Speech, Brooklyn, 1 Nov 1859

444.2
Every man meets his Waterloo at last.
same

445 Picasso, Pablo (1881-1973), Spanish painter.

445.1
I hate that aesthetic game of the eye and the mind, played by these connoisseurs, these mandarins who 'appreciate' beauty. What *is* beauty, anyway? There's no such thing. I never 'appreciate', any more than I 'like'. I love or I hate. *Life with Picasso (Gilot and Lake), Ch.2*

445.2
Painting is a blind man's profession. He paints not what he sees, but what he feels, what he tells himself about what he has seen. *Journals (Jean Cocteau), 'Childhood'*

446 Pinter, Harold (b. 1930), English dramatist.

446.1
DAVIES. If only I could get down to Sidcup! I've been waiting for the weather to break. He's got my papers, this man I left them with, it's got it all down there, I could prove everything.
The Caretaker, Act 1

447 Pitt, William (1759-1806), English prime minister.

447.1
Necessity is the plea for every infringement of human freedom. It is the argument of tyrants; it is the creed of slaves. *Speech, House of Commons, 18 Nov 1783*

447.2
[*On hearing of Napoleon's victory at the Battle of Austerlitz*] Roll up that map: it will not be wanted these ten years. *Remark, 1805*

447.3
I think I could eat one of Bellamy's veal pies. *Last words, attributed*

447.4
Oh, my country! How I leave my country! *Last words, attributed*

448 Plato, (429?-347? B.C.), Greek philosopher.

448.1
The good is the beautiful. *Lysis*

448.2
Our object in the construction of the state is the greatest happiness of the whole, and not that of any one class.
Republic, 4

449 Pliny the Elder, (Gaius Plinius Secundus) (23-79), Roman soldier and writer.

449.1
In vino veritas.
Truth comes out in wine.
Historia Naturalis, XIV:141

450 Poe, Edgar Allan (1809-1849), American poet and writer.

450.1
Take thy beak from out my heart, and take thy form from off my door!
Quoth the Raven, 'Nevermore.'
The Raven

451 Pompadour, Madame de (1721-1764), mistress of Louis XV of France.

451.1
Après nous le déluge.
After us the deluge. *After the Battle of Rossbach, 1757*

452 Pope, Alexander (1688-1744), English poet.

452.1
The right divine of kings to govern wrong. *The Dunciad, IV:188*

452.2
The Muse but serv'd to ease some friend, not Wife,
To help me through this long disease, my life.
Epistle to Dr. Arbuthnot, 131

452.3
Damn with faint praise, assent with civil leer,
And, without sneering, teach the rest to sneer. *same, 201*

452.4
Curst be the verse, how well so'er it flow,
That tends to make one worthy man my foe. *same, 283*

452.5
Wit that can creep, and pride that licks the dust. *same, 333*

452.6
In wit a man; simplicity a child.
Epitaph on Mr Gay

452.7
'Tis hard to say, if greater want of skill
Appear in writing or in judging ill.
An Essay on Criticism, 1

452.8
'Tis with our judgments as our watches, none
Go just alike, yet each believes his own. *same, 9*

452.9
Of all the causes which conspire to blind
Man's erring judgment, and misguide the mind,
What the weak head with strongest bias rules,
Is Pride, the never-failing vice of fools.
same, 201

452.10
A little learning is a dangerous thing;
Drink deep, or taste not the Pierian spring:
There shallow draughts intoxicate the brain,
And drinking largely sobers us again.
same, 215

452.11
Whoever thinks a faultless piece to see,
Thinks what ne'er was, nor is, nor e'er shall be. *same, 253*

452.12
True wit is nature to advantage dress'd;
What oft was thought, but ne'er so well express'd. *same, 297*

452.13
True ease in writing comes from art, not chance,
As those move easiest who have learn'd to dance.
'Tis not enough no harshness gives offence,
The sound must seem an echo to the sense. *same, 362*

452.14
Fondly we think we honour merit then,
When we but praise ourselves in other men. *same, 454*

452.15
To err is human, to forgive, divine. *same, 525*

452.16
For fools rush in where angels fear to tread. *same, 625*

452.17
Hope springs eternal in the human breast;
Man never is, but always to be blest. *An Essay on Man, I:95*

452.18
Know then thyself, presume not God to scan,
The proper study of Mankind is Man. *same, II:1*

452.19
That true self-love and social are the same;
That virtue only makes our bliss below;
And all our knowledge is, ourselves to know. *same, IV:396*

452.20
'Tis education forms the common mind,
Just as the twig is bent, the tree's inclined. *Moral Essays, I:149*

452.21
Men, some to business, some to pleasure take;
But every woman is at heart a rake. *same, II:215*

452.22
Woman's at best a contradiction still. *same, II:270*

452.23
The ruling passion, be it what it will
The ruling passion conquers reason still. *same, III:153*

452.24
I am His Highness' dog at Kew;
Pray tell me sir, whose dog are you? *On the collar of a dog given to Frederick, Prince of Wales*

452.25
What dire offence from am'rous causes springs,
What mighty contests rise from trivial things. *The Rape of the Lock, I:1*

452.26
Here thou great Anna! whom three realms obey,
Dost sometimes counsel take—and sometimes Tea. *The Rape of the Lock, III:7*

452.27
Not louder shrieks to pitying heav'n are cast,
When husbands, or when lap-dogs breathe their last. *same, III:157*

452.28
The hungry judges soon the sentence sign,
And wretches hang that jury-men may dine. *same, III:21*

452.29
Coffee which makes the politician wise,
And see through all things with his half-shut eyes. *same, III:117*

453 Potter, Stephen (1900-1969), English writer and radio producer.

453.1
Gamesmanship or The Art of Winning Games Without Actually Cheating.
Title of book

453.2
How to be one up—how to make the other man feel that something has gone wrong, however slightly.
Lifemanship, Introduction

454 Pound, Ezra Loomis (1885-1972), American poet and critic.

454.1
Winter is icummen in,
Lhude sing Goddamm,
Raineth drop and staineth slop
And how the wind doth ramm!
Sing: Goddamm. *Ancient Music*

454.2
Great Literature is simply language charged with meaning to the utmost possible degree. *How to Read*

455 Powell, Anthony (b. 1905), English novelist.

455.1
'He fell in love with himself at first sight and it is a passion to which he has always remained faithful. Self-love seems so often unrequited.'
The Acceptance World, Ch.1

455.2
Dinner at the Huntercombes' possessed 'only two dramatic features —the wine was a farce and the food a tragedy'. *same, Ch.4*

456 Prescott, William (1726-1795), American revolutionary soldier.

456.1
Don't fire until you see the whites of their eyes. *Bunker Hill,*

457 Proudhon, Pierre Joseph (1809-1865), French socialist.

457.1
Property is theft. *Qu'est-ce que la proprieté?, Ch.1*

458 Proust, Marcel (1871-1922), French novelist.

458.1
There can be no peace of mind in love, since the advantage one has secured is never anything but a fresh starting-point for further desires.
À l'Ombre des Jeunes Filles en Fleur

458.2
As soon as one is unhappy one becomes moral. *same*

458.3
As soon as he ceased to be mad he became merely stupid. There are maladies we must not seek to cure because they alone protect us from others that are more serious.
Le Côté de Guermantes, 1

458.4
There is nothing like desire for preventing the thing one says from bearing any resemblance to what one has in mind. *same, 2*

458.5
It has been said that the highest praise of God consists in the denial of Him by the atheist, who finds creation so perfect that he can dispense with a creator. *same*

458.6
I have a horror of sunsets, they're so romantic, so operatic. *Sodome et Gomorrhe, 2*

458.7
Everything great in the world is done by neurotics; they alone founded our religions and created our masterpieces.
The Perpetual Pessimist (Sagittarius and George)

Q

459 Quesnay, François (1694–1774), French physician and economist.
459.1
Laissez faire, laissez passer.
Let it be, let it pass. *Attributed*

R

460 Rabelais, Francois (1494?–1553?), French satirist.
460.1
Appetite comes with eating.
Gargantua, I:5
460.2
Ring down the curtain, the farce is over. *Last words, attributed*
460.3
I am going in search of a great perhaps.
Last words, attributed

461 Rae, John (b. 1931), English teacher and novelist.
461.1
War is, after all, the universal perversion. We are all tainted: if we cannot experience our perversion at first hand we spend our time reading war stories, the pornography of war; or seeing war films, the blue films of war; or titillating our senses with the imagination of great deeds, the masturbation of war. *The Custard Boys, Ch. 6*

462 Raleigh, Sir Walter (1552?–1618), English courtier, navigator and writer.
462.1
Even such is Time, that takes in trust
Our youth, our joys, our all we have,
And pays us but with age and dust;
Who in the dark and silent grave,
When we have wandered all our ways,
Shuts up the story of our days;
But from this earth, this grave, this dust,
My God shall raise me up, I trust.
Written the night before his death
462.2
[*On feeling the edge of the axe*] Tis a sharp remedy, but a sure one for all ills. *Remark made before his execution*
462.3
[*On laying his head on the block*] So the heart be right, it is no matter which way the head lies. *same*

463 Raleigh, Sir Walter Alexander (1861–1922), English scholar and critic.
463.1
An anthology is like all the plums and orange peel picked out of a cake.
Letter to Mrs. Robert Bridges, 15 Jan 1915

464 Reade, Charles (1814–1884), English novelist.
464.1
Make 'em laugh; make 'em cry; make 'em wait. *Advice to young writer*

465 Reed, Henry (b. 1914), English poet and dramatist.

465.1
Today we have naming of parts. Yesterday,
We had daily cleaning. And tomorrow morning
We shall have what to do after firing. But today,
Today we have naming of parts.
Naming of Parts

465.2
They call it easing the Spring: it is perfectly easy
If you have any strength in your thumb: like the bolt,
And the breech, and the cocking-piece, and the point of balance,
Which in our case we have not got.
same

466 Reynolds, Sir Joshua (1723-1792), English portrait painter.

466.1
If you have great talents, industry will improve them: if you have but moderate abilities, industry will supply their deficiency. *Discourses, 2*

467 Rhodes, Cecil John (1853-1902), South African statesman.

467.1
So little done, so much to do.
Last words

468 Rimsky-Korsakov, Nikolai (1844-1908), Russian composer.

468.1
[*Of Debussy's music*] I have already heard it. I had better not go: I will start to get accustomed to it and finally like it. *Conversations with Stravinsky (Robert Craft and Igor Stravinsky)*

469 Robinson, James Harvey (1863-1936), American historian and educator.

469.1
Partisanship is our great curse. We too readily assume that everything has two sides and that it is our duty to be on one or the other.
The Mind in the Making

470 Roche, Sir Boyle (1743-1807), English politician.

470.1
Mr Speaker, I smell a rat; I see him forming in the air and darkening the sky; but I'll nip him in the bud.
Attributed

471 Rochefoucauld, Duc de la (1613-1680), French writer.

471.1
Everyone complains of his memory, but no one complains of his judgement.
Les Maximes, 89

471.2
The intellect is always fooled by the heart. *same, 102*

471.3
Hypocrisy is the homage paid by vice to virtue. *same, 218*

471.4
The height of cleverness is to conceal one's cleverness. *same, 245*

471.5
In the misfortunes of our best friends, we find something that is not displeasing. *Maximes supprimées, 583*

471.6
Self-love is the greatest of all flatterers.
Reflections, 2

471.7
We all have strength enough to endure the misfortunes of others. *same, 19*

471.8
We need greater virtues to sustain good fortune than bad. *same, 25*

471.9
If we had no faults of our own, we would not take so much pleasure in noticing those of others. *same, 31*

471.10
Self-interest speaks all sorts of tongues, and plays all sorts of roles, even that of disinterestedness. *same, 39*

471.11
We are never so happy nor so unhappy as we imagine. *same, 49*

471.12
To succeed in the world, we do everything we can to appear successful. *same, 50*

471.13
There are very few people who are not ashamed of having been in love when they no longer love each other. *same, 71*

471.14
The love of justice in most men is simply the fear of suffering injustice. *same, 78*

471.15
Silence is the best tactic for him who distrusts himself. *same, 79*

472 Rogers, Will (1879-1935), American actor and humorist.

472.1
You can't say civilization don't advance, however, for in every war they kill you a new way.
Autobiography, Ch. 12

472.2
Everything is funny, as long as it's happening to somebody else.
The Illiterate Digest

473 Rochester, John Wilmot, 2nd Earl of (1647-1680), English courtier and poet.

473.1
Here lies our sovereign lord the King,
Whose word no man relies on;
He never said a foolish thing,
Nor ever did a wise one.
Epitaph on Charles II

474 Roland, Madame Marie Jeanne Philipon (1754-1793), French revolutionist.

474.1
[*On viewing the statue of Liberty*] Oh liberty, liberty, what crimes are committed in your name!
Remark from the scaffold

475 Roosevelt, Franklin Delano (1882-1945), President of the United States.

475.1
I pledge you, I pledge myself, to a new deal for the American people.
Speech accepting nomination for Presidency, Chicago, 2 July 1932

475.2
A radical is a man with both feet firmly planted in the air.
Broadcast, 26 Oct 1939

475.3
We look forward to a world founded upon four essential human freedoms. The first is freedom of speech and expression—everywhere in the world. The second is freedom of every person to worship God in his own way—everywhere in the world. The

third is freedom from want...everywhere in the world. The fourth is freedom from fear...anywhere in the world. *Speech to Congress, 6 Jan 1941*

475.4
We all know that books burn—yet we have the greater knowledge that books cannot be killed by fire. People die, but books never die. No man and no force can abolish memory...In this war, we know, books are weapons.
Message to American Booksellers Association, 23 Apr 1942

475.5
More than an end to war, we want an end to the beginnings of all wars.
Speech written for broadcast, 13 Apr 1945 (the day after his death)

476 Roosevelt, Theodore (1858-1919), President of the United States.

476.1
I wish to preach, not the doctrine of ignoble ease, but the doctrine of the strenuous life.. *Speech, Chicago, 10 Apr 1899*

476.2
There is no room in this country for hyphenated Americanism.
Speech, New York, 12 Oct 1915

476.3
No man is justified in doing evil on the ground of expediency.
The Strenuous Life

477 Rosebery, Archibald Philip Primrose, 5th Earl of (1847-1929), British statesman.

477.1
The Empire is a Commonwealth of Nations. *Speech, Adelaide, 18 Jan 1884*

477.2
It is beginning to be hinted that we are a nation of amateurs.
Rectorial Address, Glasgow, 16 Nov 1900

478 Ross, Alan Strode Campbell (b.1907), English academic.

478.1
U and Non-U, An Essay in Sociological Linguistics. *Title of Essay in 'Noblesse Oblige', 1956*

479 Rossetti, Dante Gabriel (1828-1882), English poet and painter.

479.1
I have been here before.
But when or how I cannot tell:
I know the grass beyond the door,
The sweet keen smell,
The sighing sound, the lights around the shore. *Sudden Light*

480 Rouget de Lisle, Claude Joseph (1760-1836), French army officer.

480.1
Allons, enfants, de la patrie,
Le jour de gloire est arrivé.
Come, children of our native land,
The day of glory has arrived.
La Marseillaise

481 Rousseau, Jean Jacques (1712-1778), Swiss political philosopher.

481.1
Man was born free and everywhere he is in chains.
Du Contrat Social, Ch. 1

482 Routh, Martin Joseph (1755-1854), English scholar.

482.1
Always verify your references.
Attributed

483 Runyon, Damon (1884-1946), American writer and journalist.

483.1
More than somewhat. *Title of a collection of stories*

483.2
My boy...always try to rub up against money, for if you rub up against money long enough, some of it may rub off on you. *Furthermore, 'A Very Honourable Guy'*

484 Ruskin, John (1819-1900), English writer and art critic.

484.1
If a book is worth reading, it is worth buying. *Sesame and Lilies*

484.2
Remember that the most beautiful things in the world are the most useless; peacocks and lilies for instance. *The Stones of Venice*

484.3
Fine art is that in which the hand, the head, and the heart of man go together.
The Two Paths

485 Russell, Bertrand Arthur William, 3rd Earl (1872-1970), English philosopher and mathematician.

485.1
Three passions, simple but overwhelmingly strong, have governed my life: the longing for love, the search for knowledge, and unbearable pity for the suffering of mankind.
Autobiography, 1, Prologue

485.2
The megalomaniac differs from the narcissist by the fact that he wishes to be powerful rather than charming, and seeks to be feared rather than loved. To this type belong many lunatics and most of the great men of history.
The Conquest of Happiness, Ch. 1

485.3
Of all forms of caution, caution in love is perhaps the most fatal to true happiness. *Marriage and Morals*

485.4
Mathematics possesses not only truth, but supreme beauty—a beauty cold and austere, like that of sculpture.
The Study of Mathematics

485.5
Few people can be happy unless they hate some other person, nation or creed. *Attributed*

485.6
Patriots always talk of dying for their country, and never of killing for their country. *Attributed*

S

486 Saki, (Hector Hugh Munro) (1870-1916), English novelist and short-story writer.

486.1
The people of Crete unfortunately make more history than they can consume locally. *The Jesting of Arlington Stringham*

486.2
All decent people live beyond their incomes nowadays, and those who aren't respectable live beyond other people's. A few gifted individuals

manage to do both.

The Match Maker

486.3
I always say beauty is only sin deep.

Reginald's Choir Treat

486.4
The cook was a good cook, as cooks go; and as cooks go she went.

Reginald on Besetting Sins

486.5
People may say what they like about the decay of Christianity; the religious system that produced green Chartreuse can never really die. *Reginald on Christmas Presents*

486.6
I think she must have been very strictly brought up, she's so desperately anxious to do the wrong thing correctly. *Reginald on Worries*

487 Samuel, Herbert Louis, 1st Viscount (1870-1963), English statesman and writer.

487.1
It takes two to make a marriage a success and only one a failure.

A Book of Quotations

487.2
A truism is on that account none the less true. *same*

487.3
A library is thought in cold storage.

same

487.4
Without doubt the greatest injury... was done by basing morals on myth, for sooner or later myth is recognized for what it is, and disappears. Then morality loses the foundation on which it has been built.

Romanes Lecture, 1947

488 Santayana, George (1863-1952), American philosopher and poet.

488.1
The working of great institutions is mainly the result of a vast mass of routine, petty malice, self interest, carelessness, and sheer mistake. Only a residual fraction is thought.

The Crime of Galileo

488.2
The young man who has not wept is a savage, and the old man who will not laugh is a fool.

Dialogues in Limbo, Ch. 3

488.3
Those who cannot remember the past are condemned to repeat it.

The Life of Reason, I:12

488.4
Happiness is the only sanction of life; where happiness fails, existence remains a mad and lamentable experiment. *same*

488.5
Life is not a spectacle or a feast; it is a predicament.

The Perpetual Pessimist (Sagittarius and George)

489 Sartre, Jean-Paul (b. 1905), French philosopher, dramatist and novelist.

489.1
I hate victims who respect their executioners. *Altona, 1*

489.2
Things are entirely what they appear to be and *behind them*...there is nothing. *Nausea*

489.3
My thought is *me*: that is why I can't stop. I exist by what I think...and I can't prevent myself from thinking.

same

489.4
I know perfectly well that I don't want to do anything; to do something is to create existence — and there's quite enough existence as it is. *same*

490 Schelling, Friedrich William (1775-1854), German philosopher.
490.1
Architecture in general is frozen music. *Philosophie der Kunst*

491 Schweitzer, Albert (1875-1965), French clergyman, musician and missionary.
491.1
[*To an African who refused to carry out a humdrum task on the grounds that he was an intellectual*] I too had thoughts once of being an intellectual, but I found it too difficult.
Attributed

492 Scott, Robert Falcon (1868-1912), English Antarctic explorer.
492.1
[*Of the South Pole*] Great God! this is an awful place. *Journal, 17 Jan 1912*
492.2
Had we lived, I should have had a tale to tell of the hardihood, endurance, and courage of my companions which would have stirred the heart of every Englishman. These rough notes and our dead bodies must tell the tale.
Message to the Public

493 Scott, William, 1st Baron Stowell (1745-1836), English judge.
493.1
A dinner lubricates business.
Boswell's Life of Johnson, 1781

494 Selden, John (1584-1654), English historian and antiquary.
494.1
Preachers say, Do as I say, not as I do.
Table Talk
494.2
A king is a thing men have made for their own sakes, for quietness' sake. Just as if in a family one man is appointed to buy the meat.
Table Talk
494.3
Every law is a contract between the king and the people and therefore to be kept. *same*
494.4
Ignorance of the law excuses no man; not that all men know the law, but because 'tis an excuse every man will plead, and no man can tell how to confute him. *same*
494.5
Pleasure is nothing else but the intermission of pain. *same*

495 Sellar, Walter Carruthers (1898-1951) and **Yeatman, Robert Julian** (1897-1968), English humorous writers.
495.1
1066 And All That. *Title of Book*
495.2
The Roman Conquest was, however, a *Good Thing*, since the Britons were only natives at the time.
1066 And All That, Ch. 1
495.3
Napoleon's armies used to march on their stomachs, shouting: 'Vive l'intérieur!' *same, Ch. 48*
495.4
Do not on any account attempt to write on both sides of the paper at once. *same, Test Paper 5*

496 Service, Robert William (1874–1958), Canadian poet.

496.1
A promise made is a debt unpaid.
The Cremation of Sam McGee

496.2
This is the Law of the Yukon, that only the strong shall thrive;
That surely the weak shall perish, and only the Fit survive. *The Law of the Yukon*

496.3
When we, the Workers, all demand: 'What are we fighting for?'...
Then, then we'll end that stupid crime, that devil's madness—War.
Michael

497 Shadwell, Thomas (1642?–1692), English dramatist.

497.1
Words may be false and full of art,
Sighs are the natural langauge of the heart. *Psyche, Act 3*

497.2
'Tis the way of all flesh.
The Sullen Lovers, V:2

497.3
Every man loves what he is good at.
A True Widow, V:1

498 Shakespeare, William (1564–1616), English dramatist and poet.

498.1
HELENA. Our remedies oft in ourselves do lie,
Which we ascribe to heaven.
All's Well that End's Well, I:1:202

498.2
2ND LORD. The web of our life is of a mingled yarn, good and ill together.
same, IV:3:67

498.3
KING. Th' inaudible and noiseless foot of Time. *same, V:3:41*

498.4
PHILO. The triple pillar of the world transform'd
Into a strumpet's fool. *Antony and Cleopatra, I:1:12*

498.5
ANTONY. There's beggary in the love that can be reckon'd. *same, I:1:15*

498.6
ANTONY. Where's my serpent of old Nile? *same, I:5:25*

498.7
CLEOPATRA. My salad days,
When I was green in judgment, cold in blood,
To say as I said then! *same, I:5:73*

498.8
ENOBARBUS. The barge she sat in, like a burnish'd throne,
Burn'd on the water. The poop was beaten gold;
Purple the sails, and so perfumed that
The winds were love-sick with them; the oars were silver,
Which to the tune of flutes kept stroke and made
The water which they beat to follow faster,
As amorous of their strokes. For her own person,
It beggar'd all description.
same, II:2:195

498.9
ENOBARBUS. Age cannot wither her, nor custom stale
Her infinite variety. Other women cloy
The appetites they feed, but she makes hungry
Where most she satisfies.
same, II:2:239

498.10

ENOBARBUS. I will praise any man that will praise me. *same, II:6:88*

498.11

CLEOPATRA. Celerity is never more admir'd
Than by the negligent.
same, III:7:24

498.12

ANTONY. To business that we love we rise betime,
And go to't with delight.
same, IV:4:20

498.13

ANTONY. Unarm Eros; the long day's task is done,
And we must sleep. *same, IV:14:35*

498.14

ANTONY. I am dying, Egypt, dying; only
I here importune death awhile, until
Of many thousand kisses the poor last
I lay upon thy lips. *same, IV:15:18*

498.15

CLEOPATRA. O, wither'd is the garland of the war,
The soldier's pole is fall'n! Young boys and girls
Are level now with men. The odds is gone,
And there is nothing left remarkable
Beneath the visiting moon.
same, IV:15:64

498.16

IRAS. The bright day is done,
And we are for the dark.
same, V:2:192

498.17

CLEOPATRA. Dost thou not see my baby at my breast
That sucks the nurse asleep?
same, V:2:307

498.18

CELIA. Well said; that was laid on with a trowel. *As You Like It, I:2:94*

498.19

TOUCHSTONE. I had rather bear with you than bear you. *same, II:4:9*

498.20

SILVIUS. If thou rememb'rest not the slightest folly
That ever love did make thee run into,
Thou hast not lov'd. *same, II:4:31*

498.21

AMIENS. Under the greenwood tree
Who loves to lie with me,
And turn his merry note
Unto the sweet bird's throat,
Come hither, come hither, come hither.
Here shall he see
No enemy
But winter and rough weather.
same, II:5:1

498.22

JACQUES. And so, from hour to hour, we ripe and ripe,
And then, from hour to hour, we rot and rot;
And thereby hangs a tale.
same, II:7:26

498.23

JACQUES. All the world's a stage,
And all the men and women merely players;
They have their exits and their entrances;
And one man in his time plays many parts,
His acts being seven ages.
same, II:7:139

498.24

JACQUES. Last scene of all,
That ends this strange eventful history,
Is second childishness and mere oblivion;

Sans teeth, sans eyes, sans taste, sans every thing. *same, II:7:159*

498.25

AMIENS. Blow, blow, thou winter wind,
Thou art not so unkind
As man's ingratitude. *same, II:7:174*

498.26

AMIENS. Most friendship is feigning, most loving mere folly.
same, II:7:181

498.27

CORIN. He that wants money, means, and content, is without three good friends. *same, III:2:23*

498.28

ROSALIND. Do you not know I am a woman? When I think, I must speak.
same, III:2:234

498.29

ORLANDO. I do desire we may be better strangers. *same, III:2:243*

498.30

TOUCHSTONE. The truest poetry is the most feigning. *same, III:3:16*

498.31

ROSALIND. Men have died from time to time, and worms have eaten them, but not for love. *same, IV:1:94*

498.32

TOUCHSTONE. Your If is the only peace-maker; much virtue in If.
same, V:4:97

498.33

ROSALIND. If it be true that good wine needs no bush, 'tis true that a good play needs no epilogue.
same, Epilogue

498.34

CORIOLANUS. Custom calls me to't.
What custom wills, in all things should we do't,
The dust on antique time would lie unswept,
And mountainous error be too highly heap'd
For truth to o'erpeer.
Coriolanus, II:3:114

498.35

CORIOLANUS. Like a dull actor now
I have forgot my part and I am out,
Even to a full disgrace. *same, V:3:40*

498.36

BELARIUS. O, this life
Is nobler than attending for a check,
Richer than doing nothing for a bribe,
Prouder than rustling in unpaid-for silk. *Cymbeline, II:3:21*

498.37

IMOGEN. Society is no comfort
To one not sociable. *same, IV:2:12*

498.38

GUIDERIUS. Fear no more the heat o' th' sun
Nor the furious winter's rages;
Thou thy worldly task hast done,
Home art gone, and ta'en thy wages.
Golden lads and girls all must,
As chimney-sweepers, come to dust.
same, IV:2:259

498.39

FRANCISCO. For this relief much thanks. 'Tis bitter cold,
And I am sick at heart.
Hamlet, I:1:8

498.40

HAMLET. A little more than kin, and less than kind. *same, I:2:65*

498.41

HAMLET. But I have that within which passes show—
these but the trappings and the suits of woe. *same, I:2:85*

498.42

HAMLET. How weary, stale, flat, and unprofitable,
Seem to me all the uses of this world!
same, I:2:129

498.43
HAMLET. Frailty, thy name is woman!
same, I:2:146

498.44
HAMLET. It is not, nor it cannot come to good. *same, I:2:156*

498.45
HAMLET. 'A was a man, take him for all in all,
I shall not look upon his like again.
same, I:2:187

498.46
OPHELIA. Do not, as some ungracious pastors do,
Show me the steep and thorny way to heaven,
Whiles, like a puff'd and reckless libertine,
Himself the primrose path of dalliance treads
And recks not his own rede.
same, I:3:47

498.47
POLONIUS. Costly thy habit as thy purse can buy,
But not express'd in fancy; rich, not gaudy;
For the apparel oft proclaims the man.
same, I:3:70

498.48
POLONIUS. Neither a borrower nor a lender be;
For loan oft loses both itself and friend,
And borrowing dulls the edge of husbandry.
This above all - to thine own self be true,
And it must follow, as the night the day,
Thou canst not then be false to any man. *same, I:3:75*

498.49
HAMLET. But to my mind, though I am native here
And to the manner born, it is a custom
More honour'd in the breach than the observance. *same, I:4:14*

498.50
MARCELLUS. Something is rotten in the state of Denmark. *same, I:4:90*

498.51
GHOST. Murder most foul, as in the best it is;
But this most foul, strange, and unnatural. *same, I:5:27*

498.52
HAMLET. There are more things in heaven and earth, Horatio,
Than are dreamt of in your philosophy.
same, I:5:166

498.53
POLONIUS. Brevity is the soul of wit.
same, II:2:90

498.54
HAMLET. To be honest, as this world goes, is to be one man pick'd out of ten thousand. *same, II:2:177*

498.55
POLONIUS. Though this be madness, yet there is method in't. *same, II:2:204*

498.56
HAMLET. There is nothing either good or bad, but thinking makes it so.
same, II:2:248

498.57
HAMLET. What a piece of work is a man! How noble in reason! how infinite in faculties! in form and moving, how express and admirable! in action, how like an angel! in apprehension, how like a god! the beauty of the world! the paragon of animals! And yet, to me, what is this quintessence of dust? Man delights

not me—no, nor woman neither.
same, II:2:303

498.58

HAMLET. The play, I remember, pleas'd not the million; 'twas caviare to the general. *same, II:2:429*

498.59

HAMLET. Use every man after his desert, and who shall scape whipping?
same, II:2:523

498.60

HAMLET. The play's the thing
Wherein I'll catch the conscience of the King. *same, II:2:600*

498.61

HAMLET. To be, or not to be — that is the question;
Whether 'tis nobler in the mind to suffer
The slings and arrows of outrageous fortune,
Or to take arms against a sea of troubles,
And by opposing end them? To die, to sleep—
No more; and by a sleep to say we end
The heart-ache and the thousand natural shocks
That flesh is heir to, 'tis a consummation
Devoutly to be wish'd. To die, to sleep;
To sleep, perchance to dream. Ay, there's the rub;
For in that sleep of death what dreams may come,
When we have shuffled off this mortal coil,
Must give us pause. *same, III:1:56*

498.62

HAMLET. The dread of something after death—
The undiscover'd country, from whose bourn
No traveller returns. *same, III:1:78*

498.63

HAMLET. Thus conscience does make cowards of us all;
And thus the native hue of resolution
Is sicklied o'er with the pale cast of thought. *same, III:1:83*

498.64

CLAUDIUS. Madness in great ones must not unwatch'd go. *same, III:1:188*

498.65

HAMLET. It out-herods Herod.
same, III:2:14

498.66

HAMLET. Suit the action to the word, the word to the action; with this special observance, that you o'erstep not the modesty of nature. *same, III:2:17*

498.67

GERTRUDE. The lady doth protest too much, methinks. *same, III:2:225*

498.68

POLONIUS. Very like a whale.
same, III:2:372

498.69

HAMLET. A king of shreds and patches.
same, III:4:102

498.70

HAMLET. Some craven scruple
Of thinking too precisely on th' event.
same, IV:4:40

498.71

CLAUDIUS. When sorrows come, they come not single spies,
But in battalions! *same, IV:5:75*

498.72

CLAUDIUS. There's such divinity doth hedge a king
That treason can but peep to what it would. *same, IV:5:120*

498.73

HAMLET. Alas, poor Yorick! I knew him, Horatio: a fellow of infinite jest, of most excellent fancy.

same, V:1:179

498.74

HAMLET. There's a divinity that shapes our ends,
Rough-hew them how we will.

same, V:2:10

498.75

HAMLET. If thou didst ever hold me in thy heart,
Absent thee from felicity awhile,
And in this harsh world draw thy breath in pain,
To tell my story. *same, V:2:338*

498.76

HAMLET. The rest is silence.

same, V:2:350

498.77

PRINCE. If all the year were playing holidays, To sport would be as tedious as to work. *Henry the Fourth, Part One, I:2:197*

498.78

PRINCE. Falstaff sweats to death
And lards the lean earth as he walks along. *same, II:2:104*

498.79

FALSTAFF. I have more flesh than another man, and therefore more frailty. *same, III:3:167*

498.80

FALSTAFF. Honour pricks me on. Yea, but how if honour prick me off when I come on? How then? Can honour set to a leg? No. Or an arm? No. Or take away the grief of a wound? No. Honour hath no skill in surgery, then? No. What is honour? A word. What is in that word? Honour. What is that honour? Air. *same, V:1:129*

498.81

HOTSPUR. But thoughts, the slaves of life, and life, time's fool,
And time, that takes survey of all the world,
Must have a stop. *same, V:4:81*

498.82

FALSTAFF. The better part of valour is discretion; in the which better part I have saved my life. *same, V:4:120*

498.83

FALSTAFF. I am not only witty in myself, but the cause that wit is in other men. I do here walk before thee like a sow that hath overwhelm'd all her litter but one. *King Henry the Fourth, Part Two, I:2:7*

498.84

FALSTAFF. Well, I cannot last ever; but it was always yet the trick of our English nation, if they have a good thing, to make it too common.

same, I:2:200

498.85

FALSTAFF. I can get no remedy against this consumption of the purse; borrowing only lingers and lingers it out, but the disease is incurable.

same, I:2:223

498.86

HOSTESS. He hath eaten me out of house and home. *same, II:1:71*

498.87

POINS. Is it not strange that desire should so many years outlive performance? *same, II:4:250*

498.88

HENRY IV. Uneasy lies the head that wears a crown. *same, III:1:26*

498.89

FALSTAFF. We have heard the chimes at midnight. *same, III:2:210*

498.90
FEEBLE. I care not; a man can die but once; we owe God a death.
same, III:2:228

498.91
Care I for the limb, the thews, the stature, bulk, and big assemblance of a man! Give me the spirit.
same, III:2:251

498.92
NYM. I dare not fight; but I will wink and hold out mine iron. *King Henry the Fifth, II:1:6*

498.93
NYM. Though patience be a tired mare, yet she will plod. *same, II:1:24*

498.94
HOSTESS. His nose was as sharp as a pen, and 'a babbl'd of green fields.
same, II:3:17

498.95
HENRY V. Once more unto the breach, dear friends, once more;
Or close the wall up with our English dead. *same, III:1:1*

498.96
BOY. Men of few words are the best men. *same, III:2:36*

498.97
HENRY V. I think the King is but a man as I am: the violet smells to him as it doth to me. *same, IV:1:101*

498.98
HENRY V. Every subject's duty is the King's; but every subject's soul is his own. *same, IV:1:175*

498.99
HENRY V. Old men forget; yet all shall be forgot,
But he'll remember, with advantages,
What feats he did that day.
same, IV:3:49

498.100
FLUELLEN. There is occasions and causes why and wherefore in all things.
same, V:1:3

498.101
NORFOLK. Heat not a furnace for your foe so hot
That it do singe yourself. We may outrun
By violent swiftness that which we run at,
And lose by over-running.
King Henry the Eighth, I:1:140

498.102
ANNE. I would not be a queen
For all the world. *same, II:3:45*

498.103
WOLSEY. Farewell, a long farewell, to all my greatness!
This is the state of man: to-day he puts forth
The tender leaves of hopes: to-morrow blossoms
And bears his blushing honours thick upon him;
The third day comes a frost, a killing frost,
And when he thinks, good easy man, full surely
His greatness is a-ripening, nips his root,
And then he falls, as I do.
same, III:2:351

498.104
WOLSEY. Had I but serv'd my God with half the zeal
I serv'd my King, he would not in mine age
Have left me naked to mine enemies.
same, III:2:455

498.105
GRIFFITH. Men's evil manners live in brass: their virtues
We write in water. *same, IV:2:45*

498.106
SOOTHSAYER. Beware the ides of March.
Julius Caesar, I:2:18

498.107
CAESAR. Let me have men about me that are fat;
Sleek-headed men, and such as sleep o' nights.
Yond Cassius has a lean and hungry look;
He thinks too much. Such men are dangerous. *same, I:2:192*

498.108
CASCA. For mine own part, it was Greek to me. *same, I:2:283*

498.109
CAESAR. Cowards die many times before their deaths:
The valiant never taste of death but once. *same, II:2:32*

498.110
CAESAR. *Et tu, Brute?* *same, III:1:77*

498.111
CASSIUS. Why, he that cuts off twenty years of life
Cuts off so many years of fearing death. *same, III:1:102*

498.112
ANTONY. O mighty Caesar! dost thou lie so low?
Are all thy conquests, glories, triumphs, spoils,
Shrunk to this little measure?
same, III:1:149

498.113
ANTONY. O, pardon me, thou bleeding piece of earth,
That I am meek and gentle with these butchers!
Thou art the ruins of the noblest man
That ever lived in the tide of times.
same, III:1:255

498.114
ANTONY. Cry 'Havoc!' and let slip the dogs of war. *same, III:1:274*

498.115
BRUTUS. Not that I lov'd Caesar less, but that I lov'd Rome more.
same, III:2:20

498.116
ANTONY. Friends, Romans, countrymen, lend me your ears;
I come to bury Caesar, not to praise him.
The evil that men do lives after them;
The good is oft interred with their bones. *same, III:2:73*

498.117
ANTONY. For Brutus is an honourable man;
So are they all, all honourable men.
same, III:2:82

498.118
ANTONY. Ambition should be made of sterner stuff. *same, III:2:92*

498.119
ANTONY. If you have tears, prepare to shed them now. *same, III:2:169*

498.120
ANTONY. For I have neither wit, nor words, nor worth,
Action, nor utterance, nor the power of speech,
To stir men's blood; I only speak right on. *same, III:2:221*

498.121
CASSIUS. A friend should bear his friend's infirmities,
But Brutus makes mine greater than they are. *same, IV:3:85*

498.122
BRUTUS. There is a tide in the affairs of men
Which, taken at the flood, leads on to fortune;
Omitted, all the voyage of their life

Is bound in shallows and in miseries.
On such a full sea are we now afloat,
And we must take the current when it serves,
Or lose our ventures.

same, IV:3:216

498.123

ANTONY. This was the noblest Roman of them all.
All the conspirators save only he
Did that they did in envy of great Caesar. *same, V:5:68*

498.124

ANTONY. His life was gentle; and the elements
So mix'd in him that Nature might stand up
And say to all the world 'This was a man!' *same, V:5:73*

498.125

BASTARD. Well, whiles I am a beggar, I will rail
And say there is no sin but to be rich;
And being rich, my virtue then shall be
To say there is no vice but beggary.

King John, II:1:593

498.126

BASTARD. Bell, book, and candle, shall not drive me back,
When gold and silver becks me to come on. *same, III:3:12*

498.127

LEWIS. Life is as tedious as a twice-told tale
Vexing the dull ear of a drowsy man.

same, III:4:108

498.128

SALISBURY. To gild refined gold, to paint the lily,
To throw a perfume on the violet,
To smooth the ice, or add another hue
Unto the rainbow, or with taper-light
To seek the beauteous eye of heaven to garnish,
Is wasteful and ridiculous excess.

same, IV:2:11

498.129

KING JOHN. I beg cold comfort.

same, V:7:42

498.130

LEAR. Nothing will come of nothing.
Speak again. *King Lear, I:1:89*

498.131

EDMUND. This is the excellent foppery of the world, that, when we are sick in fortune, often the surfeits of our own behaviour, we make guilty of our disasters the sun, the moon, and stars.

same, I:2:112

498.132

LEAR. Ingratitude, thou marble-hearted fiend,
More hideous when thou show'st thee in a child
Than the sea-monster! *same, I:4:259*

498.133

LEAR. O, let me not be mad, not mad, sweet heaven!
Keep me in temper; I would not be mad! *same, I:5:43*

498.134

KENT. Thou whoreson zed! thou unnecessary letter! *same, II:2:58*

498.135

LEAR. *Hysterica passio*—down, thou climbing sorrow,
Thy element's below. *same, II:4:56*

498.136

LEAR. O, reason not the need! Our basest beggars
Are in the poorest thing superfluous.
Allow not nature more than nature needs,
Man's life is cheap as beast's.

same, II:4:263

498.137
LEAR. Blow, winds, and crack your cheeks; rage, blow.
You cataracts and hurricanoes, spout
Till you have drench'd our steeples, drown'd the cocks. *same, III:2:1*

498.138
LEAR. Rumble thy bellyful. Spit, fire; spout rain.
Nor rain, wind, thunder, fire, are my daughters
I tax not you, you elements, with unkindness. *same, III:2:14*

498.139
LEAR. I am a man
More sinn'd against than sinning.
same, III:2:59

498.140
LEAR. Poor naked wretches, wheresoe'er you are,
That bide the pelting of this pitiless storm,
How shall your houseless heads and unfed sides,
Your loop'd and window'd raggedness, defend you
From seasons such as these?
same, III:4:28

498.141
LEAR. Take physic, pomp;
Expose thyself to feel what wretches feel. *same, III:4:33*

498.142
CORNWALL. Out vile jelly!
Where is thy lustre now?
same, III:7:82

498.143
EDGAR. The worst is not
So long as we can say 'This is the worst'. *same, IV:1:28*

498.144
GLOUCESTER. As flies to wanton boys are we to th' gods—
They kill us for their sport.
same, IV:1:37

498.145
LEAR. Ay, every inch a king.
same, IV:6:107

498.146
LEAR. The wren goes to't, and the small gilded fly
Does lecher in my sight.
same, IV:6:112

498.147
LEAR. Through tatter'd clothes small vices do appear;
Robes and furr'd gowns hide all.
same, IV:6:164

498.148
LEAR. Get thee glass eyes,
And, like a scurvy politician, seem
To see the things thou dost not.
same, IV:6:170

498.149
LEAR. When we are born, we cry that we are come
To this great stage of fools.
same, IV:6:183

498.150
LEAR. Thou art a soul in bliss; but I am bound
Upon a wheel of fire, that mine own tears
Do scald like molten lead.
same, IV:7:46

498.151
EDGAR. Men must endure
Their going hence, even as their coming hither:
Ripeness is all. *same, V:2:9*

498.152
LEAR. And my poor fool is hang'd! No, no, no life!
Why should a dog, a horse, a rat have life,
And thou no breath at all? Thou'lt come no more,

Never, never, never, never.
same, V:3:305

498.153
BEROWNE. At Christmas I no more desire a rose
Than wish a snow in May's new-fangled shows. *Love's Labour's Lost, I:1:105*

498.154
SIR NATHANIEL. He hath never fed of the dainties that are bred in a book; he hath not eat paper, as it were; he hath not drunk ink; his intellect is not replenished. *same, IV:2:22*

498.155
BEROWNE. For where is any author in the world
Teaches such beauty as a woman's eye?
Learning is but an adjunct to oneself.
same, IV:3:308

498.156
BEROWNE. A jest's prosperity lies in the ear
Of him that hears it, never in the tongue
Of him that makes it. *same, V:2:849*

498.157
WINTER. When icicles hang by the wall,
And Dick the shepherd blows his nail,
And Tom bears logs into the hall,
And milk comes frozen home in pail,
When blood is nipp'd, and ways be foul,
Then nightly sings the staring owl:
'Tu-who;
Tu-whit, Tu-who'—A merry note,
While greasy Joan doth keel the pot.
same, V:2:899

498.158
MACBETH. So foul and fair a day I have not seen. *Macbeth, I:3:38*

498.159
MACBETH. This supernatural soliciting
Cannot be ill; cannot be good.
same, I:3:130

498.160
MACBETH. Come what come may,
Time and the hour runs through the roughest day. *same, I:3:146*

498.161
MALCOLM. Nothing in his life
Became him like the leaving it: he died
As one that had been studied in his death
To throw away the dearest thing he ow'd
As 'twere a careless trifle.
same, I:4:7

498.162
LADY MACBETH. Yet do I fear thy nature;
It is too full o' th' milk of human kindness
To catch the nearest way.
same, I:5:13

498.163
MACBETH. If it were done when 'tis done, then 'twere well
It were done quickly. *same, I:7:1*

498.164
MACBETH. That but this blow
Might be the be-all and the end-all here—
But here upon this bank and shoal of time—
We'd jump the life to come.
same, I:7:4

498.165
MACBETH. I have no spur
To prick the sides of my intent, but only
Vaulting ambition, which o'er-leaps itself,
And falls on th' other. *same, I:7:25*

498.166
MACBETH. False face must hide what the false heart doth know.
same, I:7:82

498.167
MACBETH. Sleep that knits up the ravell'd sleave of care,
The death of each day's life, sore labour's bath,
Balm of hurt minds, great nature's second course,
Chief nourisher in life's feast.
same, II:2:35

498.168
PORTER. It provokes the desire, but it takes away the performance. Therefore much drink may be said to be an equivocator with lechery.
same, II:3:28

498.169
LADY MACBETH. Nought's had, all's spent,
Where our desire is got without content.
'Tis safer to be that which we destroy,
Than by destruction dwell in doubtful joy. *same, III:2:4*

498.170
MACBETH. I had else been perfect,
Whole as the marble, founded as the rock,
As broad and general as the casing air,
But now I am cabin'd, cribb'd, confin'd, bound in
To saucy doubts and fears.
same, II:4:21

498.171
LADY MACBETH. Stand not upon the order of your going,
But go at once. *same, III:4:119*

498.172
MACBETH. I am in blood
Stepp'd in so far that, should I wade no more,
Returning were as tedious as go o'er.
same, III:4:136

498.173
LADY MACBETH. Out, damned spot! out, I say! *same, V:1:33*

498.174
LADY MACBETH. Here's the smell of the blood still. All the perfumes of Arabia will not sweeten this little hand.
same, V:1:48

498.175
MACBETH. I have liv'd long enough. My way of life
Is fall'n into the sear, the yellow leaf;
And that which should accompany old age,
As honour, love, obedience, troops of friends,
I must not look to have.
same, V:3:22

498.176
MACBETH. I have supp'd full with horrors. *same, V:5:13*

498.177
MACBETH. Tomorrow, and tomorrow, and tomorrow,
Creeps in this petty pace from day to day
To the last syllable of recorded time,
And all our yesterdays have lighted fools
The way to dusty death. Out, out, brief candle!
Life's but a walking shadow, a poor player,
That struts and frets his hour upon the stage,
And then is heard no more; it is a tale
Told by an idiot, full of sound and fury,
Signifying nothing. *same, V:5:17*

498.178
MACBETH. I gin to be aweary of the sun,
And wish th' estate o' th' world were now undone. *same, V:5:49*

498.179
MACBETH. I bear a charmed life, which must not yield
To one of woman born.
MACDUFF. Despair thy charm;
And let the angel whom thou still hast serv'd
Tell thee Macduff was from his mother's womb
Untimely ripp'd. *same, V:8:12*

498.180
ISABELLA. But man, proud man
Dress'd in a little brief authority,
Most ignorant of what he's most assur'd,
His glassy essence, like an angry ape,
Plays such fantastic tricks before high heaven
As makes the angels weep.
Measure for Measure, II:2:117

498.181
ISABELLA. That in the captain's but a choleric word
Which in the soldier is flat blasphemy.
same, II:2:130

498.182
CLAUDIO. The miserable have no other medicine
But only hope. *same, III:1:12*

498.183
DUKE. Thou has nor youth nor age;
But, as it were, an after-dinner's sleep,
Dreaming on both. *same, III:1:32*

498.184
CLAUDIO. Ay, but to die, and go we know not where;
To lie in cold obstruction, and to rot;
This sensible warm motion to become
A kneaded clod; and the delighted spirit
To bathe in fiery floods or to reside
In thrilling region of thick-ribbed ice.
same, III:1:119

498.185
LUCIO. I am a kind of burr; I shall stick. *same, IV:3:173*

498.186
DUKE. Haste still pays haste, and leisure answers leisure;
Like doth quit like, and Measure still for Measure. *same, V:1:408*

498.187
GRATIANO. As who should say 'I am Sir Oracle,
And when I ope my lips let no dog bark'. *The Merchant of Venice, I:1:93*

498.188
PORTIA. If to do were as easy as to know what were good to do, chapels had been churches, and poor men's cottages princes' palaces.
same, I:2:11

498.189
ANTONIO. The devil can cite Scripture for his purpose. *same, I:3:93*

498.190
LAUNCELOT GOBBO. It is a wise father that knows his own child.
same, II:2:69

498.191
JESSICA. But love is blind, and lovers cannot see
The pretty follies that themselves commit. *same, II:6:36*

498.192
NERISSA. The ancient saying is no heresy:
Hanging and wiving goes by destiny.
same, II:9:82

498.193

SHYLOCK. Hath not a Jew eyes? Hath not a Jew hands, organs, dimensions, senses, affections, passions, fed with the same food, hurt with the same weapons, subject to the same diseases, healed by the same means, warmed and cooled by the same winter and summer, as a Christian is? If you prick us, do we not bleed? If you tickle us, do we not laugh? If you poison us, do we not die? And if you wrong us, shall we not revenge? *same, III:1:49*

498.194

PORTIA. The quality of mercy is not strain'd;
It droppeth as the gentle rain from heaven
Upon the place beneath. It is twice blest;
It blesseth him that gives and him that takes. *same, IV:1:179*

498.195

JESSICA. I am never merry when I hear sweet music. *same, V:1:69*

498.196

LORENZO. The man that hath no music in himself,
Nor is not mov'd with concord of sweet sounds,
Is fit for treasons, stratagems, and spoils. *same, V:1:83*

498.197

PORTIA. How far that little candle throws his beams!
So shines a good deed in a naughty world. *same, V:1:90*

498.198

PORTIA. For a light wife doth make a heavy husband. *same, V:1:130*

498.199

PISTOL. Why, then the world's mine oyster,
Which I with sword will open.
The Merry Wives of Windsor, II:2:4

498.200

FALSTAFF. They say there is divinity in odd numbers, either in nativity, chance, or death. *same, V:1:3*

498.201

LYSANDER. For aught that I could ever read,
Could ever hear by tale or history,
The course of true love never did run smooth. *A Midsummer Night's Dream, I:1:132*

498.202

HELENA. Love looks not with the eyes, but with the mind;
And therefore is wing'd Cupid painted blind. *same, I:1:234*

498.203

SNUG. I am slow of study.
same, I:2:59

498.204

BOTTOM. A lion among ladies is a most dreadful thing; for there is not a more fearful wild-fowl than your lion living. *same, III:1:27*

498.205

PUCK. Lord, what fools these mortals be! *same, III:2:115*

498.206

THESEUS. The lunatic, the lover, and the poet,
Are of imagination all compact.
same, V:1:7

498.207

THESEUS. The poet's eye, in a fine frenzy rolling,
Doth glance from heaven to earth, from earth to heaven;
And as imagination bodies forth
The forms of things unknown, the poet's pen

Turns them to shapes, and gives to airy nothing
A local habitation and a name.
same, V:1:12

498.208
BENEDICK. Would you have me speak after my custom, as being a professed tyrant to their sex? *Much Ado About Nothing, I:1:144*

498.209
CLAUDIO. Friendship is constant in all other things
Save in the office and affairs of love.
same, II:1:154

498.210
CLAUDIO. Silence is the perfectest herald of joy: I were but little happy if I could say how much.
same, II:1:275

498.211
BENEDICK. Doth not the appetite alter? A man loves the meat in his youth that he cannot endure in his age.
same, II:3:215

498.212
DOGBERRY. To be a well-favoured man is the gift of fortune; but to write and read comes by nature.
same, III:3:13

498.213
VERGES. I thank God I am as honest as any man living that is an old man and no honester than I. *same, III:5:13*

498.214
DOGBERRY. Comparisons are odorous.
same, III:5:16

498.215
DOGBERRY. Our watch, sir, have indeed comprehended two aspicious persons.
same, III:5:42

498.216
DOGBERRY. Write down that they hope they serve God; and write God first; for God defend but God should go before such villains! *same, IV:2:17*

498.217
LEONATO. For there was never yet philosopher
That could endure the toothache patiently. *same, V:1:35*

498.218
DUKE. To mourn a mischief that is past and gone
Is the next way to draw new mischief on. *Othello, I:3:204*

498.219
IAGO. Put money in thy purse.
same, I:3:338

498.220
IAGO. For I am nothing if not critical.
same, II:1:119

498.221
IAGO. To suckle fools and chronicle small beer. *same, II:1:159*

498.222
CASSIO. Reputation, reputation, reputation! O, I have lost my reputation! I have lost the immortal part of myself, and what remains is bestial.
same, II:3:254

498.223
IAGO. Good name in man and woman, dear my lord,
Is the immediate jewel of their souls:
Who steals my purse steals trash; 'tis something, nothing;
'Twas mine, 'tis his, and has been slave to thousands;
But he that filches from me my good name
Robs me of that which not enriches him
And makes me poor indeed.
same, III:3:159

498.224

IAGO. O, beware, my lord, of jealousy;
It is the green-ey'd monster which doth mock
The meat it feeds on.

same, III:3:169

498.225

OTHELLO. O curse of marriage,
That we can call these delicate creatures ours,
And not their appetites! I had rather be a toad,
And live upon the vapour of a dungeon,
Than keep a corner in the thing I love
For others' uses. *same, III:3:272*

498.226

OTHELLO. He that is robb'd, not wanting what is stol'n,
Let him not know't, and he's not robb'd at all. *same, III:3:346*

498.227

OTHELLO. Farewell the neighing steed and the shrill trump,
The spirit-stirring drum, th' ear-piercing fife,
The royal banner, and all quality.
Pride, pomp, and circumstance, of glorious war! *same, III:3:351*

498.228

OTHELLO. Put out the light, and then put out the light.
If I quench thee, thou flaming minister,
I can again thy former light restore,
Should I repent me; but once put out thy light,
Thou cunning'st pattern of excelling nature,
I know not where is that Promethean heat
That can thy light relume.

same, V:2:7

498.229

OTHELLO. Then must you speak
Of one that lov'd not wisely, but too well;
Of one not easily jealous, but, being wrought,
Perplexed in the extreme; of one whose hand,
Like the base Indian, threw a pearl away
Richer than all his tribe.

same, V:2:7

498.230

PERICLES. Kings are earth's gods; in vice their law's their will.

Pericles, I:1:103

498.231

3RD FISHERMAN. Master, I marvel how the fishes live in the sea.
1ST FISHERMAN. Why, as men do a-land—the great ones eat up the little ones. *same, II:1:27*

498.232

MOWBRAY. The purest treasure mortal times afford
Is spotless reputation; that away,
Men are but gilded loam or painted clay. *King Richard the Second, I:1:177*

498.233

GAUNT. Things sweet to taste prove in digestion sour. *same, I:3:236*

498.234

GAUNT. Teach thy necessity to reason thus:
There is no virtue like necessity.

same, I:3:275

498.235

GAUNT. This royal throne of kings, this sceptred isle,
This earth of majesty, this seat of Mars,
This other Eden, demi-paradise

This precious stone set in the silver sea,
Which serves it in the office of a wall,
Or as a moat defensive to a house,
Against the envy of less happier lands;
This blessed plot, this earth, this realm, this England,
This nurse, this teeming womb of royal kings,
Fear'd by their breed, and famous by their birth. *same, II:1:40*

498.236

RICHARD. Not all the water in the rough rude sea
Can wash the balm from an anointed king;
The breath of worldly men cannot depose
The deputy elected by the Lord.
same, III:2:54

498.237

RICHARD. For God's sake let us sit upon the ground
And tell sad stories of the death of kings:
How some have been depos'd, some slain in war,
Some haunted by the ghosts they have depos'd,
Some poison'd by their wives, some sleeping kill'd,
All murder'd—for within the hollow crown
That rounds the mortal temples of a king
Keeps Death his court.
same, III:2:155

498.238

RICHARD. How sour sweet music is
When time is broke and no proportion kept!
So is it in the music of men's lives.
same, V:5:42

498.239

GLOUCESTER. Now is the winter of our discontent
Made glorious summer by this sun of York. *King Richard III, I:1:1*

498.240

CLARENCE. O Lord, methought what pain it was to drown,
What dreadful noise of waters in my ears,
What sights of ugly death within my eyes! *same, I:4:21*

498.241

RICHARD III. A horse! a horse ! my kingdom for a horse. *same, V:4:7*

498.242

JULIET. O Romeo, Romeo! wherefore art thou Romeo? *Romeo and Juliet, II:2:33*

498.243

JULIET. What's in a name? That which we call a rose
By any other name would smell as sweet. *same, II:2:43*

498.244

JULIET. O, swear not by the moon, th' inconstant moon,
That monthly changes in her circled orb,
Lest that thy love prove likewise variable. *same, II:2:109*

498.245

JULIET. Good night, good night! Parting is such sweet sorrow
That I shall say good night till it be morrow. *same, II:2:185*

498.246

FRIAR LAWRENCE. Wisely and slow; they stumble that run fast.
same, II:3:94

498.247

FRIAR LAWRENCE. Therefore love moderately: long love doth so;
Too swift arrives as tardy as too slow.
same, II:6:14

498.248

MERCUTIO. A plague o' both your houses!
They have made worms' meat of me.
same, III:1:103

498.249

CAPULET. Thank me no thankings, nor proud me no prouds.
same, III:5:152

498.250

SERVINGMAN. 'Tis an ill cook that cannot lick his own fingers.
same, IV:2:6

498.251

TRANIO. No profit grows where is no pleasure ta'en;
In brief, sir, study what you most affect. *The Taming of the Shrew, I:1:39*

498.252

PETRUCHIO. This is a way to kill a wife with kindness. *same, IV:1:192*

498.253

PETRUCHIO. Our purses shall be proud, our garments poor;
For 'tis the mind that makes the body rich;
And as the sun breaks through the darkest clouds,
So honour peereth in the meanest habit. *same, IV:3:167*

498.254

ARIEL. Full fathom five thy father lies;
Of his bones are coral made;
Those are pearls that were his eyes;
Nothing of him that doth fade
But doth suffer a sea-change
Into something rich and strange.
The Tempest, I:2:396

498.255

TRINCULO. When they will not give a doit to relieve a lame beggar, they will lay out ten to see a dead Indian.
same, II:2:29

498.256

TRINCULO. Misery acquaints a man with strange bedfellows.
same, II:2:38

498.257

STEPHANO. He that dies pays all debts.
same, III:2:126

498.258

PROSPERO. Our revels now are ended. These our actors,
As I foretold you, were all spirits, and
Are melted into air, into thin air;
And, like the baseless fabric of this vision,
The cloud-capp'd towers, the gorgeous palaces,
The solemn temples, the great globe itself,
Yea, all which it inherit, shall dissolve,
And, like this insubstantial pageant faded,
Leave not a rack behind. We are such stuff
As dreams are made on; and our little life
Is rounded with a sleep.
same, IV:1:148

498.259

PROSPERO. I'll break my staff,
Bury it certain fathoms in the earth,
And deeper than did ever plummet sound
I'll drown my book. *same, V:1:54*

498.260

MIRANDA. How beauteous mankind is! O brave new world
That has such people in't!
same, V:1:183

498.261

CRESSIDA. That she belov'd knows nought that knows not this:
Men prize the thing ungain'd more than it is. *Troilus and Cressida, I:2:278*

498.262

ULYSSES. O, when degree is shak'd,
Which is the ladder of all high designs,
The enterprise is sick! *same, I:3:101*

498.263

CRESSIDA. To be wise and love
Exceeds man's might.
same, III:2:152

498.264

ULYSSES. Time hath, my lord, a wallet at his back,
Wherein he puts alms for oblivion,
A great-siz'd monster of ingratitudes.
same, III:3:145

498.265

THERSITES. Lechery, lechery! Still wars and lechery! Nothing else holds fashion. *same, V:2:193*

498.266

ORSINO. If music be the food of love, play on,
Give me excess of it, that, surfeiting,
The appetite may sicken and so die.
Twelfth Night, I:1:1

498.267

SIR TOBY. Is it a world to hide virtues in? *same, I:3:123*

498.268

FESTE. Many a good hanging prevents a bad marriage. *same, I:5:18*

498.269

SIR TOBY. Not to be abed after midnight is to be up betimes. *same, II:3:1*

498.270

FESTE. What is love? 'Tis not hereafter;
Present mirth hath present laughter;
What's to come is still unsure.
In delay there lies no plenty,
Then come kiss me, sweet and twenty;
Youth's a stuff will not endure.
same, II:3:46

498.271

SIR TOBY. Dost thou think, because thou art virtuous, there shall be no more cakes and ale? *same, II:3:109*

498.272

VIOLA. She never told her love,
But let concealment, like a worm i' th' bud,
Feed on her damask cheek. She pin'd in thought;
And with a green and yellow melancholy
She sat like Patience on a monument,
Smiling at grief. *same, II:4:109*

498.273

MALVOLIO. Some are born great, some achieve greatness, and some have greatness thrust upon 'em.
same, II:5:129

498.274

OLIVIA. Love sought is good, but given unsought is better.
same, III:1:153

498.275

FABIAN. If this were play'd upon a stage now, I could condemn it as an improbable fiction. *same, III:4:121*

498.276

FABIAN. Still you keep o' th' windy side of the law. *same, III:4:156*

498.277

VIOLA. I hate ingratitude more in a man
Than lying, vainness, babbling drunkenness,
Or any taint of vice whose strong corruption
Inhabits our frail blood.
same, III:4:338

498.278
VALENTINE. Home-keeping youth have ever homely wits.
The Two Gentlemen of Verona, I:1:2

498.279
LUCETTA. I have no other but a woman's reason:
I think him so, because I think him so.
same, I:2:23

498.280
Who is Silvia? What is she,
That all our swains commend her?
Holy, fair, and wise is she.
same, IV:2:38

498.281
PAULINA. What's gone and what's past help
Should be past grief.
The Winter's Tale, III:2:219

498.282
Exit, pursued by a bear. *same, Stage Direction, II:3:58*

498.283
SHEPHERD. I would there were no age between ten and three and twenty, or that youth would sleep out the rest; for there is nothing in the between but getting wenches with child, wronging the ancientry, stealing, fighting.
same, III:3:59

498.284
AUTOLYCUS. A snapper-up of unconsidered trifles. *same, IV:3:26*

498.285
AUTOLYCUS. Though I am not naturally honest, I am so sometimes by chance.
same, IV:3:734

498.286
CLOWN. Though authority be a stubborn bear, yet he is oft led by the nose with gold. *same, IV:3:835*

498.287
From fairest creatures we desire increase,
That thereby beauty's rose might never die. *Sonnet 1*

498.288
Shall I compare thee to a summer's day?
Thou art more lovely and more temperate.
Rough winds do shake the darling buds of May,
And summer's lease hath all too short a date. *Sonnet 18*

498.289
A woman's face, with Nature's own hand painted,
Hast thou, the Master Mistress of my passion. *Sonnet 20*

498.290
When in disgrace with fortune and men's eyes
I all alone beweep my outcast state,
And trouble deaf heaven with my bootless cries,
And look upon myself, and curse my fate,
Wishing me like to one more rich in hope
Featur'd like him, like him with friends possess'd,
Desiring this man's art, and that man's scope,
With what I most enjoy contented least. *Sonnet 29*

498.291
When to the sessions of sweet silent thought
I summon up remembrance of things past,
I sigh the lack of many a thing I sought,
And with old woes new wail my dear time's waste. *Sonnet 30*

498.292
Not marble, nor the gilded monuments
Of princes, shall outlive this powerful rhyme. *Sonnet 55*

498.293
Like as the waves make towards the pebbled shore,
So do our minutes hasten to their end. *Sonnet 60*

498.294
That time of year thou mayst in me behold
When yellow leaves, or none, or few, do hang
Upon those boughs which shake against the cold,
Bare ruin'd choirs, where late the sweet birds sang. *Sonnet 73*

498.295
Farewell! thou art too dear for my possessing,
And like enough thou know'st thy estimate:
The charter of thy worth gives thee releasing;
My bonds in thee are all determinate. *Sonnet 87*

498.296
For sweetest things turn sourest by their deeds:
Lilies that fester smell far worse than weeds. *Sonnet 94*

498.297
When in the chronicle of wasted time
I see descriptions of the fairest wights. *Sonnet 106*

498.298
Let me not to the marriage of true minds
Admit impediments. Love is not love
Which alters when it alteration finds,
Or bends with the remover to remove.
O, no! it is an ever-fixed mark,
That looks on tempests and is never shaken. *Sonnet 116*
Love alters not with his brief hours and weeks,
But bears it out even to the edge of doom.
If this be error, and upon me prov'd,
I never writ, nor no man ever lov'd. *Sonnet 116*

498.299
Th' expense of spirit in a waste of shame
Is lust in action; and till action, lust
Is perjur'd, murd'rous, bloody, full of blame,
Savage, extreme, rude, cruel, not to trust;
Enjoy'd no sooner but despised straight. *Sonnet 129*

498.300
My mistress' eyes are nothing like the sun;
Coral is far more red than her lips' red. *Sonnet 130*

498.301
And yet, by heaven, I think my love as rare
As any she belied with false compare. *Sonnet 130*

498.302
Two loves I have, of comfort and despair,
Which like two spirits do suggest me still;
The better angel is a man right fair,
The worser spirit a woman colour'd ill. *Sonnet 144*

498.303
Crabbed age and youth cannot live together:
Youth is full of pleasure, age is full of care;
Youth like summer morn, age like winter weather;

Youth like summer brave, age like winter bare.
The Passionate Pilgrim, 12

498.304
Beauty itself doth of itself persuade
The eyes of men without an orator.
The Rape of Lucrece, I:29

499 Shaw, George Bernard
(1856-1950), Irish dramatist and critic.

499.1
All great truths begin as blasphemies.
Annajanska

499.2
One man that has a mind and knows it, can always beat ten men who havnt and dont. *The Apple Cart, Act 1*

499.3
I never resist temptation, because I have found that things that are bad for me do not tempt me. *same, Act 2*

499.4
You can always tell an old soldier by the inside of his holsters and cartridge boxes. The young ones carry pistols and cartridges: the old ones, grub.
Arms and the Man, Act 1

499.5
My father is a very hospitable man: he keeps six hotels. *same, Act 1*

499.6
I never apologize. *same, Act 3*

499.7
You're not a man, you're a machine.
same, Act 3

499.8
Every genuine scientist must be ...a metaphysician. *Back to Methuselah, Preface*

499.9
Well, as the serpent used to say, why not? *same, Act 2*

499.10
When a stupid man is doing something he is ashamed of, he always declares that it is his duty. *Caesar and Cleopatra, Act 3*

499.11
We have no more right to consume happiness without producing it than to consume wealth without producing it.
Candida, Act 1

499.12
Do you think that the things people make fools of themselves about are any less real and true than the things they behave sensibly about?
same, Act 1

499.13
I'm only a beer teetotaller, not a champagne teetotaller. *same, Act 3*

499.14
Man can climb to the highest summits, but he cannot dwell there long.
same, Act 3

499.15
The worst sin towards our fellow creatures is not to hate them, but to be indifferent to them.
The Devil's Disciple, Act 2

499.16
I never expect a soldier to think.
same, Act 3

499.17
All professions are conspiracies against the laity. *The Doctor's Dilemma, Act 1*

499.18
It's easier to replace a dead man than a good picture. *same, Act 2*

499.19
Morality consists in suspecting other people of not being legally married.
same, Act 3

499.20
I don't believe in morality. I'm a disciple of Bernard Shaw.
same, Act 4

499.21
You don't expect me to know what to say about a play when I don't know who the author is, do you?
Fanny's First Play, Epilogue

499.22
What God hath joined together no man shall ever put asunder: God will take care of that. *Getting Married*

499.23
I cannot bear men and women.
Heartbreak House, Act 2

499.24
Go anywhere in England, where there are natural, wholesome, contented, and really nice English people; and what do you always find? That the stables are the real centre of the household.
same, Act 3

499.25
Do you think the laws of God will be suspended in favour of England because you were born in it?
same, Act 3

499.26
An Irishman's heart is nothing but his imagination. *John Bull's Other Island, Act 1*

499.27
What really flatters a man is that you think him worth flattering.
same, Act 4

499.28
There are only two qualities in the world: efficiency and inefficiency; and only two sorts of people: the efficient and the inefficient. *same, Act 4*

499.29
We must be thoroughly democratic and patronize everybody without distinction of class. *same, Act 4*

499.30
The greatest of evils and the worst of crimes is poverty.
Major Barbara, Preface

499.31
He is always breaking the law. He broke the law when he was born: his parents were not married.
same, Act 1

499.32
I am a Millionaire. That is my religion.
same, Act 1

499.33
I cant talk religion to a man with bodily hunger in his eyes.
same, Act 1

499.34
Nothing is ever done in this world until men are prepared to kill one another if it is not done. *same, Act 3*

499.35
Our political experiment of democracy, the last refuge of cheap misgovernment.
Man and Superman, Epistle Dedicatory

499.36
The more things a man is ashamed of, the more respectable he is.
same, Act 1

499.37
A lifetime of happiness: no man alive could bear it: it would be hell on earth. *same, Act 1*

499.38
The true artist will let his wife starve, his children go barefoot, his mother drudge for his living at seventy, sooner than work at anything but his art.
same, Act 1

499.39
Is the devil to have all the passions as well as all the good tunes?
same, Act 1

499.40
An Englishman thinks he is moral when he is only uncomfortable.
same, Act 3

499.41
What is virtue but the Trade Unionism of the married? *same, Act 3*

499.42
I am a gentleman: I live by robbing the poor. *same, Act 3*

499.43
If you go to Heaven without being naturally qualified for it, you will not enjoy yourself there. *same, Act 3*

499.44
In the arts of peace Man is a bungler.
same, Act 3

499.45
There are two tragedies in life. One is not to get your heart's desire. The other is to get it. *same, Act 4*

499.46
Do not do unto others as you would they should do unto you. Their tastes may not be the same.
same, Maxims for Revolutionists

499.47
Beware of the man whose god is in the skies. *same*

499.48
The golden rule is that there are no golden rules. *same*

499.49
Democracy substitutes election by the incompetent many for appointment by the corrupt few. *same*

499.50
Liberty means responsibility. That is why most men dread it. *same*

499.51
He who can, does. He who cannot, teaches. *same*

499.52
Marriage is popular because it combines the maximum of temptation with the maximum of opportunity.
same

499.53
The reasonable man adapts himself to the world: the unreasonable one persists in trying to adapt the world to himself. Therefore all progress depends on the unreasonable man *same*

499.54
The man who listens to Reason is lost: Reason enslaves all whose minds are not strong enough to master her.
same

499.55
Home is the girl's prison and the woman's workhouse. *same*

499.56
Every man over forty is a scoundrel.
same

499.57
In heaven an angel is nobody in particular. *same*

499.58
Decency is Indecency's Conspiracy of Silence. *same*

499.59
There is nothing so bad or so good that you will not find Englishmen doing it; but you will never find an Englishman in the wrong.
The Man of Destiny

499.60
There is no satisfaction in hanging a man who does not object to it.
same

499.61
There is only one universal passion: fear. *same*

499.62
An English army led by an Irish general: that might be a match for a French army led by an Italian general. *same*

499.63
The fickleness of the women I love is only equalled by the infernal constancy of the women who love me. *The Philanderer, Act 2*

499.64
It is clear that a novel cannot be too bad to be worth publishing.... It certainly is possible for a novel to be too good to be worth publishing. *Plays Pleasant and Unpleasant, 1, Preface*

499.65
There is only one religion, though there are a hundred versions of it. *same, 2, Preface*

499.66
It is impossible for an Englishman to open his mouth, without making some other Englishman despise him. *Pygmalion, Preface*

499.67
ELIZA DOOLITTLE. I dont want to talk grammar. I want to talk like a lady. *same, Act 2*

499.68
Not bloody likely. *same, Act 2*

499.69
Assassination is the extreme form of censorship. *The Rejected Statement, Act 1*

499.70
We were not fairly beaten, my lord. No Englishman is ever fairly beaten. *St. Joan, Sc. 4*

499.71
Must then a Christ perish in torment in every age to save those that have no imagination? *same, Epilogue*

499.72
No woman can shake off her mother. There should be no mothers, only women. *Too True to be Good*

499.73
We dont bother much about dress and manners in England, because as a nation we don't dress well and we've no manners. *You Never Can Tell, Act 1*

499.74
My speciality is being right when other people are wrong. *same, Act 2*

499.75
Money is indeed the most important thing in the world; and all sound and successful personal and national morality should have this fact for its basis. *The Irrational Knot, Preface*

499.76
A man who has no office to go to—I don't care who he is—is a trial of which you can have no conception. *same, Ch. 18*

499.77
Martyrdom is the only way in which a man can become famous without ability. *Fabian Essays*

499.78
People must not be forced to adopt me as their favourite author, even for their own good. *Letter to Alma Murray, 20 Oct 1886*

499.79
We are a nation of governesses. *New Statesman, 12 Apr 1913*

499.80
Very few books of any nationality are worth reading. *Table-Talk of George Bernard Shaw*

499.81
A coquette is a woman who rouses passions she has no intentions of gratifying. *Attributed*

499.82
If all economists were laid end to end, they would not reach a conclusion.
Attributed

500 Shelley, Percy Bysshe (1792-1822), English poet.

500.1
He has outsoared the shadow of our night;
Envy and calumny and hate and pain,
And that unrest which men miscall delight,
Can touch him not and torture not again;
From the contagion of the world's slow stain
He is secure, and now can never mourn
A heart grown cold, a head grown gray in vain. *Adonais, 352*

500.2
The One remains, the many change and pass;
Heaven's light forever shines, Earth's shadows fly;
Life, like a dome of many-coloured glass,
Stains the white radiance of Eternity.
same, 460

500.3
I never was attached to that great sect,
Whose doctrine is, that each one should select
Out of the crowd a mistress or a friend,
And all the rest, though fair and wise, commend
To cold oblivion.
Epipsychidion, 149

500.4
Good-night? ah! no; the hour is ill
Which severs those it should unite;
Let us remain together still,
Then it will be good night.
Good-Night

500.5
Most wretched men
Are cradled into poetry by wrong:
They learn in suffering what they teach in song. *Julian and Maddalo, 543*

500.6
I met Murder on the way—
He had a mask like Castlereagh.
The Mask of Anarchy, 5

500.7
O Wild West Wind, thou breath of Autumn's being,
Thou, from whose unseen presence the leaves dead
Are driven, like ghosts from an enchanter fleeing,
Yellow, and black, and pale, and hectic red,
Pestilence-stricken multitudes.
Ode to the West Wind, 1

500.8
Oh, lift me as a wave, a leaf, a cloud!
I fall upon the thorns of life! I bleed!
A heavy weight of hours has chained and bowed
One too like thee: tameless, and swift, and proud. *same, 53*

500.9
If Winter comes, can Spring be far behind? *same, 66*

500.10
'My name is Ozymandias, king of kings:
Look on my works, ye Mighty, and despair!'
Nothing beside remains. Round the decay

Of that colossal wreck, boundless and bare
The lone and level sands stretch far away. *Ozymandias*

500.11
Hell is a city much like London—
A populous and a smoky city.
Peter Bell the Third, Part 3, Hell, 1

500.12
Familiar acts are beautiful through love. *Prometheus Unbound, IV:403*

500.13
Hail to thee, blithe Spirit!
Bird thou never wert,
That from Heaven, or near it,
Pourest thy full heart
In profuse strains of unpremeditated art. *To a Skylark*

500.14
Rarely, rarely, comest thou,
Spirit of Delight! *Song, Rarely, Rarely, Comest Thou*

500.15
Poetry lifts the veil from the hidden beauty of the world, and makes familiar objects be as if they were not familiar. *A Defence of Poetry*

500.16
Poets are the unacknowledged legislators of the world. *same*

501 Sheridan, Philip Henry
(1831-1888), American soldier.

501.1
The only good Indian is a dead Indian. *Attributed*

502 Sheridan, Richard Brinsley
(1751-1816), English dramatist.

502.1
TILBURINA. An oyster may be crossed in love. *The Critic, III:1*

502.2
MRS MALAPROP. Thought does not become a young woman. *The Rivals, I:2*

502.3
MRS MALAPROP. Illiterate him, I say, quite from your memory. *same, I:2*

502.4
MRS MALAPROP. 'Tis safest in matrimony to begin with a little aversion. *same, I:2*

502.5
MRS MALAPROP. A supercilious knowledge in accounts. *same, I:2*

502.6
MRS MALAPROP. If I reprehend any thing in this world it is the use of my oracular tongue and a nice derangement of epitaphs. *same, III:3*

502.7
MRS MALAPROP. As headstrong as an allegory on the banks of the Nile. *same*

502.8
ACRES. Too civil by half. *same, III:4*

502.9
SIR PETER TEAZLE. What is principle against the flattery of a handsome, lively young fellow? *same, IV:2*

502.10
[*Of Mr. Dundas*] The Right Honourable gentleman is indebted to his memory for his jests, and to his imagination for his facts. *Reply in the House of Commons*

503 Sherman, William Tecumseh
(1820-1891), American general.

503.1
There is many a boy here today who looks on war as all glory, but, boys, it is all hell. *Speech, 1880*

504 Sibelius, Jean (1865-1957), Finnish composer.

504.1
Pay no attention to what the critics say; no statue has ever been put up to a critic. *Attributed*

505 Sidney, Algernon (1622-1683), English politician.

505.1
Liars ought to have good memories.
Discourses Concerning Government, Ch. 2, 15

506 Sidney, Sir Philip (1554-1586), English poet.

506.1
Biting my truant pen, beating myself for spite:
'Fool!' said my Muse to me, 'look in thy heart and write.'
Astrophel and Stella, Sonnet 1

506.2
With a tale forsooth he cometh unto you, with a tale which holdeth children from play, and old men from the chimney corner. *The Defence of Poesy*

506.3
[*On giving water to a dying soldier*]
Thy necessity is greater than mine.
After the battle of Zutphen, 1586

507 Simpson, Norman Frederick (b. 1919), English dramatist.

507.1
I eat merely to put food out of my mind. *The Hole*

507.2
It'll do him good to lie there unconscious for a bit. Give his brain a rest.
One Way Pendulum, 1

507.3
You should have thought of all this before you were born. *same*

507.4
We've got nothing against apes, Sylvia. As such. *same*

508 Sitwell, Sir Osbert (1892-1969), English writer and poet.

508.1
The British Bourgeoisie
Is not born,
And does not die,
But, if it is ill,
It has a frightened look in its eyes.
At the House of Mrs Kinfoot

509 Smedley, Francis Edward (1818-1864), English novelist.

509.1
You are looking as fresh as paint.
Frank Fairleigh, Ch. 41

510 Smith, Adam (1723-1790), Scottish economist.

510.1
No society can surely be flourishing and happy, of which the far greater part of the members are poor and miserable.
The Wealth of Nations, I:8

510.2
To found a great empire for the sole purpose of raising up a people of customers may at first sight appear a project fit only for a nation of shopkeepers. It is, however, a project altogether unfit for a nation of shopkeepers; but extremely fit for a nation that is governed by shopkeepers. *same, II:4*

511 Smith, Logan Pearsall (1865-1946), American writer.

511.1
The indefatigable pursuit of an unobtainable perfection, even though it consist in nothing more than in the pounding of an old piano, is what alone gives a meaning to our life on this unavailing star. *Afterthoughts*

511.2
Happiness is a wine of the rarest vintage, and seems insipid to a vulgar taste. *same*

511.3
There are few sorrows, however poignant, in which a good income is of no avail. *same*

511.4
The wretchedness of being rich is that you live with rich people. *same*

511.5
People say that Life is the thing, but I prefer Reading. *same*

511.6
How awful to reflect that what people say of us is true! *All Trivia*

511.7
Solvency is entirely a matter of temperament and not of income. *same*

511.8
There is more felicity on the far side of baldness than young men can possibly imagine. *same*

511.9
We need two kinds of acquaintances, one to complain to, while we boast to the others. *same*

511.10
Thank heavens the sun has gone in, and I don't have to go out and enjoy it. *same, last words*

511.11
A friend who loved perfection would be the perfect friend, did not that love shut his door on me. *Great Turnstile (edited by V. S. Pritchett)*

512 Smith, Sydney (1771-1845), English journalist, clergyman and wit.

512.1
Poverty is no disgrace to a man, but it is confoundedly inconvenient. *His Wit and Wisdom*

512.2
It requires a surgical operation to get a joke well into a Scotch understanding. Their only idea of wit...is laughing immoderately at stated intervals. *Lady Holland, Memoir, I:2*

512.3
[*When it was proposed to put a wooden pavement around St. Paul's*] Let the Dean and Canons lay their heads together and the thing will be done. *same*

512.4
Death must be distinguished from dying, with which it is often confused. *same*

512.5
No furniture so charming as books. *same*

512.6
Praise is the best diet for us, after all. *same*

512.7
I never read a book before reviewing it; it prejudices a man so. *The Smith of Smiths (H. Pearson), Ch. 3*

512.8
I am convinced digestion is the great secret of life. *Letter to Arthur Kinglake, 30 Sept 1837*

512.9
I have no relish for the country; it is a kind of healthy grave. *Letter to Miss G. Harcourt, 1838*

513 Smollett, Tobias George (1721-1771), English novelist.

513.1
Some folk are wise, and some are otherwise. *Roderick Random, Ch. 6*

513.2
I consider the world as made for me, not me for the world. It is my maxim therefore to enjoy it while I can, and let futurity shift for itself. *same, Ch. 45*

513.3
True patriotism is of no party. *Sir Launcelote Greavers*

514 Snagge, John (b. 1904), English broadcaster.

514.1
I can't see who's ahead—it's either Oxford or Cambridge. *BBC Commentary on Boat Race, 1949*

515 Socrates, (469-399 B.C.), Athenian philosopher.

515.1
Having the fewest wants, I am nearest to the gods. *Diogenes Laertius, II:27*

515.2
There is only one good, knowledge, and one evil, ignorance. *same, II:31*

515.3
I know nothing except the fact of my ignorance. *same, II:32*

515.4
Bad men live that they may eat and drink, whereas good men eat and drink that they may live. *How a Young Man Ought to Hear Poems (Plutarch), 4*

515.5
I am not an Athenian or a Greek, but a citizen of the world. *Of Banishment (Plutarch)*

516 Solon, (640?-558? B.C.), Athenian lawgiver.

516.1
Call no man happy until he dies; he is at best fortunate. *Histories (Herodotus), I:32*

517 Soule, John Babsone Lane (1815-1891), American editor and writer.

517.1
Go west, young man. *Article in the Terre Haute Express, Indiana, 1851*

518 Spencer, Herbert (1820-1903), English philosopher.

518.1
Time: that which man is always trying to kill, but which ends in killing him. *Definitions*

518.2
Science is organized knowledge. *Education, Ch. 2*

518.3
The ultimate result of shielding men from the effects of folly is to fill the world with fools. *Essays, 'State Tamperings with Money Banks'*

518.4
Survival of the fittest. *Principles of Biology*

518.5
We all decry prejudice, yet are all prejudiced. *Social Statics, 2*

518.6
Education has for its object the formation of character. *same, 2*

518.7
Hero-worship is strongest where there is least regard for human freedom. *same, 3*

518.8
Opinion is ultimately determined by the feelings, and not by the intellect. *same, 4*

519 Spenser, Edmund (1552?-1599), English poet.

519.1
Sleep after toil, port after stormy seas,
Ease after war, death after life does greatly please. *The Fairie Queen, I:9:40*

519.2
And as she looked about, she did behold,
How over that same door was likewise writ,
Be bold, be bold, and everywhere Be bold. *same, III:11:54*

519.3
The gentle mind by gentle deeds is known,
For a man by nothing is so well bewrayed
As by his manners. *same, VI:3:1*

519.4
Sweet Thames! run softly, till I end my Song. *Prothalamion, 18*

519.5
So now they have made our English tongue a gallimaufry or hodgepodge of all other speeches. *The Shepherd's Calendar, Letter to Gabriel Harvey*

520 Spooner, William Archibald (1844-1930), English clergyman and academic.

520.1
Sir, you have tasted two whole worms; you have hissed all my mystery lectures and have been caught fighting a liar in the quad; you will leave by the next town drain. *Attributed*

520.2
Let us drink to the queer old Dean. *Attributed*

520.3
I remember your name perfectly, but I just can't think of your face. *Attributed*

521 Squire, Sir John Collings (1884-1958), English writer.

521.1
But I'm not so think as you drunk I am. *Ballade of Soporific Absorption*

522 Stanley, Sir Henry Morton (1841-1904), British explorer and journalist.

522.1
[*On meeting Livingstone*] Dr Livingstone, I presume? *Ujiji, Central Africa, 10 Nov 1871*

523 Staël, Madame de (1766-1817), French writer.

523.1
To know all makes one tolerant. *Corinne*

523.2
Love is the whole history of a woman's life, it is but an episode in a man's. *De l'Influence des Passions*

524 Steele, Sir Richard (1672-1729), English essayist, dramatist and politician.

524.1
Among all the diseases of the mind there is not one more epidemical or more pernicious than the love of flattery. *The Spectator, No. 238*

524.2
There are so few who can grow old with a good grace. *same, No. 263*

524.3
Reading is to the mind what exercise is to the body. *The Tatler, No. 147*

525 Stein, Gertrude (1874-1946), American writer.

525.1
In the United States there is more space where nobody is than where anybody is. That is what makes America what it is.
The Geographical History of America

525.2
Rose is a rose is a rose is a rose.
Sacred Emily

525.3
Just before she died she asked, 'What *is* the answer?' No answer came. She laughed and said, 'In that case what is the question?' Then she died.
G.S., a Biography of her Work (Duncan Sutherland), final words

526 Stephen, James Kenneth (1859-1892), English writer of light verse.

526.1
Two voices are there: one is of the deep…
And one is of an old half-witted sheep
Which bleats articulate monotony
And indicates that two and one are three. *Lapsus Calami, Sonnet (Parody of Wordsworth)*

526.2
When the Rudyards cease from kipling
And the Haggards ride no more.
same, To R.K.

527 Sterne, Laurence (1713-1768), English novelist.

527.1
As an Englishman does not travel to see Englishmen, I retired to my room.
A Sentimental Journey, Preface

527.2
There are worse occupations in the world than feeling a woman's pulse.
same, The Pulse

527.3
So that when I stretched out my hand, I caught hold of the fille de chambre's—. *same, Last words*

527.4
'L—d!' said my mother, 'what is all this story about?'
'A Cock and a Bull,' said Yorick.
Tristram Shandy, III:11

528 Stevens, Wallace (1879-1955), American poet.

528.1
The only emperor is the emperor of ice-cream.
The Emperor of Ice-Cream

528.2
Poetry is the supreme fiction, madame.
A High-toned Old Christian Woman

529 Stevenson, Robert Louis (1850-1894), Scottish writer.

529.1
Even if we take matrimony at its lowest, even if we regard it as no more than a sort of friendship recognised by the police. *Virginibus Puerisque, Part 1*

529.2
Extreme busyness, whether at school or college, kirk or market, is a symptom of deficient vitality.
same, An Apology for Idlers

529.3
There is no duty we so much underrate as the duty of being happy. *same*

529.4
To travel hopefully is a better thing than to arrive, and the true success is to labour. *same, El Dorado*

530 Stravinsky, Igor (1882-1971), Russian composer.

530.1
Nothing is likely about masterpieces, least of all whether there will be any.
Conversations with Igor Stravinsky (Robert Craft)

530.2
My music is best understood by children and animals.
Observer, 'Sayings of the Week', 8 Oct 1961

531 Suckling, Sir John (1609-1642), English poet.

531.1
Out upon it, I have loved
Three whole days together;
And am like to love three more,
If it prove fair weather.
A Poem with the Answer

532 Suetonius, (Gaius Suetonius Tranquillus) (75?-150? A.D.), Roman biographer and antiquarian.

532.1
Festina lente.
Hasten slowly. *The Twelve Caesars, Augustus*

532.2
Hail, Emperor, those about to die salute you. *same, Claudius*

533 Surtees, Robert Smith (1803-1864), English sporting writer.

533.1
The only infallible rule we know is, that the man who is always talking about being a gentleman never is one.
Ask Mamma, Ch. 1

533.2
He was a gentleman who was generally spoken of as having nothing a-year, paid quarterly.
Mr. Sponge's Sporting Tour, Ch. 24

534 Svevo, Italo (Ettore Schmitz) (1861-1928), Italian novelist.

534.1
There are three things I always forget. Names, faces, and—the third I can't remember. *Attributed*

535 Swift, Jonathan (1667-1745), English satirist.

535.1
The two noblest of things, which are sweetness and light. *The Battle of the Books, Preface*

535.2
'Tis an old maxim in the schools,
That flattery's the food of fools;
Yet now and then your men of wit
Will condescend to take a bit.
Cadenus and Vanessa

535.3
Yet malice never was his aim;
He lash'd the vice, but spared the name;
No individual could resent,

Where thousands equally were meant.
On the Death of Dr Swift, 512

535.4
Big-endians and small -endians.
Gulliver's Travels, Voyage to Lilliput, Ch. 4

535.5
Whoever could make two ears of corn or two blades of grass to grow upon a spot of ground where only one grew before would deserve better of mankind and do more essential service to his country than the whole race of politicians put together.
same, Voyage to Brobdingnag, Ch. 7

535.6
Proper words in proper places make the true definition of a style.
Letter to a young clergyman, 9 Jan 1720

535.7
So, naturalists observe, a flea
Hath smaller fleas that on him prey,
And these have smaller fleas to bite 'em,
And so proceed *ad infinitum.*
On Poetry, 337

535.8
The sight of you is good for sore eyes.
Polite Conversation, 1

535.9
She's no chicken: she's on the wrong side of thirty, if she be a day.
same, 1

535.10
She wears her clothes, as if they were thrown on her with a pitchfork.
same, 1

535.11
He was a bold man that first eat an oyster. *same, 2*

535.12
That's as well said, as if I had said it myself. *same, 2*

535.13
She has more goodness in her little finger, than he has in his whole body.
same, 2

535.14
Lord, I wonder what fool it was that first invented kissing! *same, 2*

535.15
I'll give you leave to call me anything, if you don't call me spade.
same, 2

535.16
We have just enough religion to make us hate, but not enough to make us love one another. *Thoughts on Various Subjects*

535.17
Few are qualified to shine in company; but it is in most men's power to be agreeable. *same*

535.18
A nice man is a man of nasty ideas.
same

535.19
[*Of 'A Tale of a Tub'*] Good God! What a genius I had when I wrote that book. *Attributed*

T

536 Talleyrand, Charles Maurice de (1754-1838), French statesman.

536.1
[*Of Napoleon's defeat at Borodino*] It is the beginning of the end.
Remark to Napoleon, 1813

536.2
They have learnt nothing, and forgotten nothing. *Attributed*
536.3
Speech was given to man to disguise his thoughts. *Attributed*
536.4
Not too much zeal. *Attributed*
536.5
War is much too serious a thing to be left to military men. *Attributed*

537 Tarkington, Booth (1869-1946), American writer.
537.1
There are two things that will be believed of any man whatsoever, and one of them is that he has taken to drink. *Penrod, Ch. 10*

538 Taylor, Alan John Percivale (b. 1906), English historian.
538.1
A racing tipster who only reached Hitler's level of accuracy would not do well for his clients.
The Origins of the Second World War, Ch. 7
538.2
They say that men become attached even to Widnes.
Observer, 15 Sept 1963

539 Tennyson, Alfred, 1st Baron (1809-1892), English poet.
539.1
For men may come and men may go
But I go on for ever. *The Brook, 33*
539.2
Half a league, half a league,
Half a league onward,
All in the valley of Death
Rode the six hundred.
The Charge of the Light Brigade
539.3
Their's not to make reply,
Their's not to reason why,
Their's but to do and die. *same*
539.4
Sunset and evening star,
And one clear call for me!
And may there be no moaning of the bar
When I put out to sea.
Crossing the Bar
539.5
God made the woman for the man,
And for the good and increase of the world. *Edwin Morris, 43*
539.6
His honour rooted in dishonour stood,
And faith unfaithful kept him falsely true. *Idylls of the King, Lancelot and Elaine, 871*
539.7
He makes no friend who never made a foe. *same, 1082*
539.8
And slowly answer'd Arthur from the barge:
'The old order changeth, yielding place to new,
And God fulfils himself in many ways.'
same, The Passing of Arthur, 407
539.9
Our little systems have their day;
They have their day and cease to be.
In Memoriam A.H.H., Prologue
539.10
For words, like Nature, half reveal
And half conceal the Soul within.
same, 5
539.11
I hold it true, whate'er befall;
I feel it, when I sorrow most;
'Tis better to have loved and lost
Than never to have loved at all.
same, 27

539.12
Are God and Nature then at strife
That Nature lends such evil dreams?
So careful of the type she seems,
So careless of the single life.
same, 55

539.13
So many worlds, so much to do,
So little done, such things to be.
same, 73

539.14
One God, one law, one element,
And one far-off divine event,
To which the whole creation moves.
same, 131

539.15
Kind hearts are more than coronets,
And simple faith than Norman blood.
Lady Clara Vere de Vere

539.16
'The curse is come upon me,' cried
The Lady of Shalott.
The Lady of Shalott, 3

539.17
In the Spring a young man's fancy lightly turns to thoughts of love.
Locksley Hall, 20

539.18
Music that gentlier on the spirit lies,
Than tir'd eyelids upon tir'd eyes.
The Lotos Eaters

539.19
Come into the garden, Maud,
For the black bat, night, has flown,
Come into the garden, Maud,
I am here at the gate alone.
Maud, I:22

539.20
But the churchmen fain would kill their church,
As the churches have kill'd their Christ.
same, V:2

539.21
The splendour falls on castle walls
And snowy summits old in story.
The Princess, IV, Song

539.22
Tears, idle tears, I know not what they mean,
Tears from the depth of some divine despair.
same, 2nd Song

539.23
Man is the hunter; woman is his game:
The sleek and shining creatures of the chase,
We hunt them for the beauty of their skins.
same, V:147

539.24
The moan of doves in immemorial elms,
And murmuring of innumerable bees.
same, VII:203

539.25
My strength is as the strength of ten,
Because my heart is pure.
Sir Galahad

539.26
The woods decay, the woods decay and fall,
The vapours weep their burthen to the ground,
Man comes and tills the field and lies beneath,
And after many a summer dies the swan.
Tithonus, 1

539.27
We are not now that strength which in old days
Moved earth and heaven; that which we are, we are;
One equal temper of heroic hearts,
Made weak by time and fate, but strong in will
To strive, to seek, to find, and not to yield.
Ulysses, 44

540 Terence, (Publius Terentius Afer) (c. 190–159 B.C.), Roman poet.

540.1
Fortune favours the brave.
Phormio, 203

540.2
So many men, so many opinions.
same, 454

541 Thackeray, William Makepeace (1811–1863), English novelist.

541.1
He who meanly admires mean things is a Snob. *The Book of Snobs, Ch. 2*

541.2
It is impossible, in our condition of society, not to be sometimes a Snob.
same, Ch. 3

541.3
RICHARD STEELE. 'Tis not the dying for a faith that's so hard, Master Harry—every man of every nation has done that—'tis the living up to it that is difficult. *Henry Esmond, I:6*

541.4
'Tis strange what a man may do, and a woman yet think him an angel.
same, Ch. 7

541.5
A woman with fair opportunities and without a positive hump, may marry whom she likes. *Vanity Fair, Ch. 4*

541.6
BECKY SHARP. I think I could be a good woman if I had five thousand a year.
same, Ch. 36

542 Thomas, Brandon (1857–1914), English actor and dramatist.

542.1
LORD FANCOURT BABERLEY. I'm Charley's aunt from Brazil, where the nuts come from. *Charley's Aunt, Act 1*

543 Thomas, Dylan (1914–1953), Welsh poet.

543.1
Do not go gentle into that good night,
Old age should burn and rave at close of day;
Rage, rage, against the dying of the light. *Do not go gentle into that good night*

543.2
The force that through the green fuse drives the flower
Drives my green age.
The Force that through the green Fuse drives the Flower

543.3
After the first death, there is no other.
A Refusal to Mourn the Death, by Fire, of a Child in London

543.4
These poems, with all their crudities, doubts, and confusions, are written for the love of Man and in praise of God, and I'd be a damn' fool if they weren't.
Collected Poems, Note

543.5
[*Wales*] The land of my fathers. My fathers can have it. *Dylan Thomas (John Ackerman)*

543.6
Too many of the artists of Wales spend too much time about the position of the artist of Wales. There is only one position for an artist anywhere: and that is, upright.
New Statesman, 18 Dec 1964

544 Thomson, James (1700–1748), Scottish poet.

544.1
When Britain first, at Heaven's command,
Arose from out the azure main,
This was the charter of the land,

And guardian angels sung this strain:
'Rule, Britannia, rule the waves:
Britons never will be slaves.'
Alfred: A Masque, II:5

544.2
Oh! Sophonisba! Sophonisba! oh!
Sophonisba, III:2

545 Thoreau, Henry David (1817-1862), American essayist and poet.

545.1
The mass of men lead lives of quiet desperation. *Walden, 'Economy'*

545.2
As for doing good, that is one of the professions which are full. *same*

545.3
Things do not change; we change. *same*

545.4
It is not all books that are as dull as their readers. *same, 'Reading'*

545.5
Our life is frittered away by detail...Simplify, simplify. *same, 'Where I Lived and What I Lived For'*

545.6
It takes two to speak the truth—one to speak, and another to hear. *A Week on the Concord and Merrimack Rivers, Wednesday*

545.7
Not that the story need be long, but it will take a long while to make it short. *Letter*

546 Thurber, James (1894-1961), American humorist and cartoonist.

546.1
Early to rise and early to bed makes a male healthy and wealthy and dead. *Fables for Our Time, 'The Shrike and the Chipmunks'*

546.2
No man...who has wrestled with a self-adjusting card table can ever quite be the man he once was. *Let Your Mind Alone, 'Sex ex Machina'*

546.3
You wait here and I'll bring the etchings down. *Cartoon caption, 'Men, Woman, and Dogs'*

546.4
I said the hounds of spring are on winter's traces—but let it pass, let it pass! *Cartoon caption*

546.5
Well, if I called the wrong number, why did you answer the phone? *Cartoon Caption*

546.6
[*Of a play*] It had only one fault. It was kind of lousy. *Remark*

546.7
The difference between our decadence and the Russians' is that while theirs is brutal, ours is apathetic. *Observer 'Sayings of the Week', 5 Feb 1961*

547 Tolstoy, Leo (1828-1910), Russian writer.

547.1
All happy families resemble one another, each unhappy family is unhappy in its own way. *Anna Karenina, I:1*

547.2
If you want to be happy, be. *Kosma Prutkov*

547.3
Pure and complete sorrow is as impossible as pure and complete joy. *War and Peace, XV:1*

548 Tree, Sir Herbert Beerbohm (1853–1917), English actor and manager.

548.1
I was born old and get younger every day. At present I am sixty years young
Beerbohm Tree (Hesketh Pearson), Ch. 1

548.2
[*To a man carrying a grandfather clock*] My poor fellow, why not carry a watch? *same*

548.3
[*Of Israel Zangwill*] He is an old bore; even the grave yawns for him.
same

549 Trotsky, Leon (Lev Davidovich Bronstein) (1879–1940), Russian revolutionary.

549.1
The fundamental premise of a revolution is that the existing social structure has become incapable of solving the urgent problems of development of the nation.
History of the Russian Revolution, III:6

550 Trollope, Anthony (1815–1882), English novelist.

550.1
It's dogged as does it. It ain't thinking about it. *Last Chronicle of Barset, Ch. 61*

550.2
Three hours a day will produce as much as a man ought to write.
Autobiography, Ch. 15

551 Truman, Harry S. (1884–1972), President of the United States.

551.1
The buck stops here. *Notice on the Presidential desk*

551.2
The President spends most of his time kissing people on the cheek in order to get them to do what they ought to do without getting kissed.
Observer 'Sayings of the Week', 6 Feb 1949

552 Tuer, Andrew White (1838–1900), English publisher and writer.

552.1
English as she is Spoke, *Title of Portuguese-English Conversation Guide*

553 Twain, Mark (Samuel Langhorne Clemens) (1835–1910), American writer.

553.1
There are three kinds of lies: lies, damned lies, and statistics.
Autobiography

553.2
Soap and education are not as sudden as a massacre, but they are more deadly in the long run. *The Facts concerning the Recent Resignation*

553.3
I must have a prodigious quantity of mind; it takes me as much as a week, sometimes, to make it up.
The Innocents Abroad, Ch. 7

553.4
Familiarity breeds contempt—and children. *Notebooks*

553.5
Adam was but human—this explains it all. He did not want the apple for the apple's sake, he wanted it only because

it was forbidden.
Pudd'nhead Wilson's Calendar, Ch. 2

553.6
A classic is something that everybody wants to have read and nobody wants to read. *Speech, The Disapperance of Literature*

553.7
Reports of my death are greatly exaggerated. *Cable to the Associated Press*

554 Tynan, Kenneth (b. 1927), English theatre critic and producer.

554.1
William Congreve is the only sophisticated playwright England has produced; and like Shaw, Sheridan, and Wilde, his nearest rivals, he was brought up in Ireland.
Curtains, 'The Way of the World'

554.2
A novel is a static thing that one moves through; a play is a dynamic thing that moves past one. *same*

554.3
What, when drunk, one sees in other women, one sees in Garbo sober.
Sunday Times, 25 Aug 1963

U

555 Ustinov, Peter (b. 1921), English actor, dramatist and humorist.

555.1
GENERAL. As for being a General, well, at the age of four with paper hats and wooden swords we're all Generals. Only some of us never grow out of it.
Romanoff and Juliet, Act 1

555.2
GENERAL. A diplomat these days is nothing but a head-waiter who's allowed to sit down occasionally.
same

V

556 Vanburgh, Sir John (1664-1726), English dramatist and architect.

556.1
Once a woman has given you her heart you can never get rid of the rest of her. *The Relapse, II:1*

556.2
No man worth having is true to his wife, or can be true to his wife, or ever was, or ever will be so. *same, III:2*

557 Vegetius, (Flavius Vegetius Renatus) (fl. 375 A.D.), Latin writer.

557.1
Let him who desires peace, prepare for war. *Epitoma Rei Militaris, 3, Prologue*

558 Victoria, (1819-1901), Queen of England.

558.1
We are not amused. *Notebooks of a Spinster Lady, 2 Jan 1900*

558.2
[*Of Gladstone*] He speaks to Me as If I was a public meeting.
Collections and Recollections (Russell), Ch. 14

559 Villon, François (1431-1485), French poet.

559.1
Mais où sont les neiges d'antan?
But where are the snows of yesteryear?
Ballade des Dames du Temps Jadis

560 **Virgil, (Publius Vergilius Maro)** (70–19 B.C.), Latin poet.

560.1
Arms and the man I sing. *Aeneid, I:1*

560.2
Woman is always fickle and changing. *same, IV:569*

560.3
The way down to Hell is easy. *same, VI:126*

560.4
Love conquers all, and we too succumb to love. *same, X:69*

560.5
Meanwhile, time is flying — flying, never to return. *same, III:284*

561 **Voltaire, François Marie Arouet** (1694–1778), French writer.

561.1
All is for the best in the best of possible worlds. *Candide, Ch. 1*

561.2
[*Of England*] In this country it is good to kill an admiral from time to time, to encourage the others. *same, Ch. 23*

561.3
'That is well said,' replied Candide, 'but we must cultivate our garden.' *same, Ch. 30*

561.4
The best is the enemy of the good. *Dictionnaire Philosophique, 'Art Dramatique'*

561.5
If God did not exist, it would be necessary to invent Him. *Épîtres, 96, À L'Auteur du livre des Trois Imposteurs*

W

562 **Wallace, Lew** (1827–1905), American soldier and writer.

562.1
Beauty is altogether in the eye of the beholder. *The Prince of India, III:6:78*

563 **Walpole, Sir Robert, 1st Earl of Orford** (1676–1745), English statesman.

563.1
The balance of power. *Speech, House of Commons, 1741*

563.2
All those men have their price. *Memoirs of Walpole (W. Coxe)*

563.3
Anything but history, for history must be false. *Walpoliana*

564 **Walpole, Horace, 4th Earl of Orford** (1717–1797), English writer.

564.1
It is charming to totter into vogue. *Letter to G. A. Selwyn, 1765*

564.2
The world is a comedy to those who think, a tragedy to those who feel. *Letter to Sir Horace Mann, 1769*

565 **Walton, Izaak** (1593–1683), English writer.

565.1
Angling may be said to be so like the mathematics, that it can never be fully

learnt. *The Compleat Angler, Epistle to the Reader*

565.2
We may say of angling as Dr Boteler said of strawberries, 'Doubtless God could have made a better berry, but doubtless God never did.'
same, Ch. 5

566 Ward, Artemus (Charles Farrar Browne) (1834-1867), American humorist.

566.1
I prefer temperance hotels—although they sell worse kinds of liquor than any other kind of hotels.
Artemus Ward's Lecture

566.2
Why is this thus? What is the reason of this thusness? *same*

566.3
I am happiest when I am idle. I could live for months without performing any kind of labour, and at the expiration of that time I should feel fresh and vigorous enough to go right on in the same way for numerous more months. *Pyrotechny*

567 Washington, George (1732-1799), first President of the United States.

567.1
Associate yourself with men of good quality if you esteem your own reputation; for 'tis better to be alone than in bad company. *Rules of Civility*

567.2
Father, I cannot tell a lie. I did it with my little hatchet. *Attributed*

568 Watts, Isaac (1674-1748), English hymn-writer.

568.1
For Satan finds some mischief still
For idle hands to do.
Against Idleness

568.2
'Tis the voice of the sluggard, I heard him complain:
'You have waked me too soon, I must slumber again.' *The Sluggard*

569 Waugh, Evelyn (1903-1966), English novelist.

569.1
I expect you'll be becoming a schoolmaster sir. That's what most of the gentlemen does sir, that gets sent down for indecent behaviour.
Decline and Fall, Prelude

569.2
We class schools, you see, into four grades: Leading School, First-rate School, Good School, and School.
same, I:1

569.3
Meanwhile you will write an essay on 'self-indulgence'. There will be a prize of half a crown for the longest essay, irrespective of any possible merit.
same, I:5

569.4
I can't quite explain it, but I don't believe one can ever be unhappy for long provided one does just exactly what one wants to and when one wants to. *same,- I:5*

569.5
Nonconformity and lust stalking hand in hand through the country, wasting and ravaging. *same, I:5*

569.6
'The Welsh, ' said the Doctor, 'are the only nation in the world that has produced no graphic or plastic art, no architecture, no drama. They just sing,'

he said with disgust, 'sing and blow down wind instruments of plated silver.' *same, I:8*

569.7
I have noticed again and again since I have been in the Church that lay interest in ecclesiastical matters is often a prelude to insanity. *same, I:8*

569.8
I have often observed in women of her type a tendency to regard all athletics as inferior forms of fox-hunting. *same, I:10*

569.9
I haven't been to sleep for over a year. That's why I go to bed early. One needs more rest if one doesn't sleep. *same, II:3*

569.10
There is a species of person called a 'Modern Churchman' who draws the full salary of a beneficed clergyman and need not commit himself to any religious belief. *same, II:4*

569.11
I came to the conclusion many years ago that almost all crime is due to the repressed desire for aesthetic expression. *same, III:1*

569.12
Anyone who has been to an English public school will always feel comparatively at home in prison. *same, III:4*

569.13
He was greatly pained at how little he was pained by the events of the afternoon. *same, III:4*

569.14
Instead of this absurd division into sexes they ought to class people as static and dynamic. *same, III:7*

569.15
She had heard someone say something about an Independent Labour Party, and was furious that she had not been asked. *Vile Bodies, Ch. 4*

569.16
All this fuss about sleeping together. For physical pleasure I'd sooner go to my dentist any day. *same, Ch. 6*

569.17
Assistant masters came and went.... Some liked little boys too little and some too much. *A Little Learning*

569.18
You never find an Englishman among the underdogs—except in England of course. *The Loved One*

569.19
In the dying world I come from quotation is a national vice. It used to be the classics, now it's lyric verse. *same*

569.20
News is what a chap who doesn't care much about anything wants to read. And it's only news until he's read it. After that it's dead. *Scoop, I:5*

569.21
Pappenhacker says that every time you are polite to a proletarian you are helping to bolster up the capitalist system. *same, I:5*

569.22
'I will not stand for being called a woman in my own house,' she said. *same*

569.23
Other nations use 'force'; we Britons alone use 'Might'. *same, II:5*

569.24
Enclosing every thin man, there's a fat man demanding elbow-room. *Officers and Gentlemen, Interlude*

569.25
Manners are especially the need of the plain. The pretty can get away with anything. *Observer 'Sayings of the Year,' 1962*

570 Webb, Sidney, 1st Baron Passfield (1859-1947), English social reformer.

570.1
The inevitability of gradualness.
Presidential Address to Labour Party Conference, 1923

571 Webster, Daniel (1782-1852), American statesman.

571.1
[*When advised not to become a lawyer*] There is always room at the top.
Remark

571.2
The people's government, made for the people, made by the people, and answerable to the people.
Second Speech on Foote's Resolution, Jan 26 1830

572 Webster, John (1580?-1625?), English dramatist.

572.1
BOSOLA. Other sins only speak; murder shrieks out.
The Duchess of Malfi, IV:2

572.2
BIRD LIME. I saw him even now going the way of all flesh, that is to say towards the kitchen.
Westward Hoe, II:2

573 Wellington, Arthur Wellesley, 1st Duke of (1769-1852), English general and statesman.

573.1
[*Of the British army*] Ours is composed of the scum of the earth.
Remark, 4 Nov 1831

573.2
Up, Guards, and at 'em. *Order at the battle of Waterloo, 18 June 1815, attributed*

573.3
The battle of Waterloo was won on the playing fields of Eton.
Attributed

573.4
Publish and be damned.
Attributed

574 Wells, Herbert George (1866-1946), English writer.

574.1
The cat is the offspring of a cat and the dog of a dog, but butlers and lady's maids do not reproduce their kind. They have other duties. *Bealby, I:1*

574.2
The Shape of Things to Come.
Title of Book

575 Wesley, John (1703-1791), English founder of Methodism.

575.1
I look upon all the world as my parish.
Journal, 11 June 1739

576 West, Mae (b. 1893), American film actress.

576.1
Come up and see me sometime.
Diamond Lil, film, 1932

576.2
—My goodness those diamonds are lovely!

576.3
Goodness had nothing whatever to do with it. *same*

576.4
Beulah, peel me a grape.
I'm No Angel, film, 1933

576.5
[*When asked what she wanted to be remembered for*] Everything.
Remark

576.6
When I'm good I'm very good, but when I'm bad I'm better. *Remark*

576.7
Whenever I'm caught between two evils, I take the one I've never tried.
Remark

577 Whistler, James Abbott McNeill (1834–1903). American painter.

577.1
I am not arguing with you—I am telling you. *Gentle Art of Making Enemies*

577.2
Nature is usually wrong. *same*

577.3
—I only know of two painters in the world: yourself and Velasquez.
Why drag in Velasquez?
Whistler Stories (D. C. Seitz)

577.4
You shouldn't say it is not good. You should say you do not like it; and then, you know, you're perfectly safe.
same

577.5
—For two days' labour, you ask two hundred guineas?
No, I ask it for the knowledge of a lifetime. *same*

577.6
—This landscape reminds me of your work.
Yes madam, Nature is creeping up.
same

577.7
OSCAR WILDE. I wish I had said that.

WHISTLER. You will, Oscar, you will.
Oscar Wilde (L. C. Ingleby)

578 White, Elwyn Brooks (b. 1899), American journalist and humorist.

578.1
As in the sexual experience, there are never more than two persons present in the act of reading—the writer who is the impregnator, and the reader who is the respondent. *The Second Tree from the Corner*

578.2
To perceive Christmas through its wrapping becomes more difficult with every year. *same*

579 White, Patrick (b. 1912), Australian novelist.

579.1
But bombs *are* unbelievable until they actually fall. *Riders in the Chariot, I:4*

579.2
'I dunno, ' Arthur said. 'I forget what I was taught. I only remember what I've learnt.' *The Solid Mandala, Ch. 2*

579.3
All my novels are an accumulation of detail. I'm a bit of a bower-bird.
Southerly, 139

579.4
Well, good luck to you, kid! I'm going to write the Great Australian Novel.
The Vivisector, 112

580 Whitehead, Alfred North (1861-1947), English mathematician and philosopher.

580.1
There are no whole truths; all truths are half-truths. It is trying to treat them as whole truths that plays the devil. *Dialogues, 16*

580.2
Intelligence is quickness to apprehend as distinct from ability, which is capacity to act wisely on the thing apprehended. *same, 135*

580.3
Art is the imposing of a pattern on experience, and our aesthetic enjoyment is recognition of the pattern. *same, 228*

581 Whitlam, Gough (b. 1916), Australian prime minister.

581.1
I do not mind the Liberals, still less do I mind the Country Party, calling me a bastard. In some circumstances I am only doing my job if they do. But I hope you will not publicly call me a bastard, as some bastards in the Caucus have. *Speech to the Australian Labour Party, 9 June 1974*

582 Whitman, Walt (1819-1892), American poet.

582.1
If anything is sacred the human body is sacred. *I Sing the Body Electric, 8*

582.2
I celebrate myself, and sing myself,
And what I assume you shall assume.
Song of Myself, 1

582.3
I think I could turn and live with animals, they're so placid and self-contain'd,
I stand and look at them long and long. *same, 32*

582.4
I have said that the soul is not more than the body,
And I have said that the body is not more than the soul,
And nothing, not God, is greater to one than one's self is. *same, 48*

582.5
Do I contradict myself?
Very well then I contradict myself,
(I am large, I contain multitudes).
same, 51

582.6
No one will ever get at my verses who insists upon viewing them as a literary performance. *A Backward Glance O'er Travel'd Roads*

582.7
After you have exhausted what there is in business, politics, conviviality, and so on—have found that none of these finally satisfy, or permanently wear—what remains? Nature remains. *Specimen Days, 'New Themes Entered Upon'*

583 Wilcox, Ella Wheeler (1850-1919), American poet.

583.1
Laugh, and the world laughs with you;
Weep, and you weep alone,
For the sad old earth must borrow its mirth,
But has trouble enough of its own.
Solitude

584 Wilde, Oscar Fingall O'Flahertie Wills (1856–1900), Irish poet, dramatist and wit.

584.1
Yet each man kills the thing he loves,
By each let this be heard,
Some do it with a bitter look,
Some with a flattering word.
The coward does it with a kiss,
The brave man with a sword!
The Ballad of Reading Gaol, I:7

584.2
Something was dead in each of us,
And what was dead was Hope.
same, III:31

584.4
For he who lives more lives than one
More deaths than one must die.
same, III:37

584.5
LORD GORING. To love oneself is the beginning of a lifelong romance.
An Ideal Husband, Act 3

584.6
ALGERNON. In married life three is company and two is none.
The Importance of Being Earnest, Act 1

584.7
LADY BRACKNELL. Ignorance is like a delicate exotic fruit; touch it, and the bloom is gone. *same*

584.8
LADY BRACKNELL. To lose one parent, Mr Worthing, may be regarded as a misfortune; to lose both looks like carelessness. *same*

584.9
JACK. In a hand-bag.
LADY BRACKNELL. A hand-bag?
same

584.10
GWENDOLEN. I never travel without my diary. One should always have something sensational to read in the train. *same, Act 2*

584.11
LADY BRACKNELL. No woman should ever be quite accurate about her age. It looks so calculating. *same, Act 3*

584.12
LORD DARLINGTON. It is absurd to divide people into good and bad. People are either charming or tedious.
Lady Windermere's Fan, Act 1

584.13
LORD DARLINGTON. I can resist everything except temptation. *same*

584.14
LORD ILLINGWORTH. One knows so well the popular idea of health. The English country gentleman galloping after a fox—the unspeakable in full pursuit of the uneatable. *A Woman of No Importance, Act 1*

584.15
LORD ILLINGWORTH. One should never trust a woman who tells one her real age. A woman who would tell one that, would tell one anything.
same

584.16
LORD ILLINGWORTH. Moderation is a fatal thing, Lady Hunstanton. Nothing succeeds like excess. *same, Act 3*

584.17
All Art is quite useless.
The Picture of Dorian Gray, Preface

584.18
There is only one thing in the world worse than being talked about, and that is not being talked about.
same, 1

584.19
The only way to get rid of a temptation is to yield to it. *same, 2*

584.20
The man who sees both sides of a question is a man who sees absolutely nothing at all. *The Critic as Artist, Part 2*

584.21
A little sincerity is a dangerous thing, and a great deal of it is absolutely fatal. *same*

584.22
Ah! don't say you agree with me. When people agree with me I always feel that I must be wrong. *same*

584.23
There is no sin except stupidity. *same*

584.24
Art is the most intense mode of individualism that the world has known. *The Soul of Man Under Socialism*

584.25
Over the piano was printed a notice: Please do not shoot the pianist. He is doing his best. *Impressions of America, Leadville*

584.26
I have nothing to declare except my genius. *At New York Customs House*

584.27
[*When told that an operation would be expensive*] I suppose that I shall have to die beyond my means. *Life of Wilde (Sherard)*

584.28
Work is the curse of the drinking classes. *Attributed*

585 Wilhelm II, (1859-1941), King of Prussia and German Emperor.

585.1
[*Of the British Expeditionary Force*] A contemptible little army. *Remark, 1914*

586 William III, (1650-1702), King of Great Britain.

586.1
I will die in the last ditch. *History of England (Hume)*

586.2
Every bullet has its billet. *Journal (John Wesley), 6 June 1765*

587 William of Wykeham, (1324-1404), English churchman and statesman.

587.1
Manners maketh man. *Motto of Winchester College and New College, Oxford, his foundations*

588 Wilson, Charles Erwin (1890-1961), American engineer and industrialist.

588.1
I thought what was good for the country was good for General Motors and vice versa. *Statement to U.S. Congressional Committee, 23 Jan 1953*

589 Wilson, Sir Harold (b. 1916), British prime minister.

589.1
If I had the choice between smoked salmon and tinned salmon, I'd have it tinned. With vinegar. *Observer 'Sayings of the Week', 11 Nov 1962*

589.2
From now, the pound is worth 14 per cent or so less in terms of other currencies. It does not mean, of course, that the pound here in Britain, in your pocket or purse or in your bank, has been devalued. *Speech after devaluation of the pound, 20 Nov 1967*

589.3
One man's wage rise is another man's price increase. *Observer 'Sayings of the Week', 11 Jan 1970*

590 Wilson, John, see North, Christopher

591 Wilson, Thomas Woodrow (1856-1924), President of the United States.

591.1
No nation is fit to sit in judgement upon any other nation.
Address, Apr 1915

591.2
There is such a thing as a man being too proud to fight. *Address to foreign-born citizens, 10 May 1915*

591.3
[*To Congress, asking for a declaration of war*] The world must be made safe for democracy. *Address, 2 Apr 1917*

592 Wodehouse, Pelham Grenville (1881-1975), English humorous novelist.

592.1
All the unhappy marriages come from the husbands having brains. What good are brains to a man? They only unsettle him. *The Adventures of Sally*

592.2
It is no use telling me that there are bad aunts and good aunts. At the core they are all alike. Sooner or later, out pops the cloven hoof. *The Code of the Woosters, Ch. 2*

592.3
I spent the afternoon musing on Life. If you come to think of it, what a queer thing Life is! So unlike anything else, don't you know, if you see what I mean. *My Man Jeeves, 'Rallying Round Old George'*

592.4
The Right Hon. was a tubby little chap who looked as if he had been poured into his clothes and had forgotten to say 'When!'
Very Good Jeeves!, 'Jeeves and the Impending Doom'

592.5
The stationmaster's whiskers are of a Victorian bushiness and give the impression of having been grown under glass. *Wodehouse at Work (R. Usborne), Ch. 2*

593 Wolsey, Thomas (1475?-1530), English cardinal and statesman.

593.1
Had I but served God as diligently as I have served the king, he would not have given me over in my gray hairs.
To Sir William Kingston

594 Wood, Mrs Henry (1814-1887), English novelist.

594.1
Dead! and...never called me mother.
East Lynne (dramatized version; the words do not occur in the novel)

595 Wordsworth, William (1770-1850), English poet.

595.1
The good die first,
And they whose hearts are dry as summer dust
Burn to the socket.
The Excursion, I:500

595.2
I wandered lonely as a cloud
That floats on high o'er vales and hills,
When all at once I saw a crowd,
A host, of golden daffodils.
I Wandered Lonely as a Cloud

595.3
For oft, when on my couch I lie
In vacant or in pensive mood,
They flash upon that inward eye
Which is the bliss of solitude.
same

595.4
There was a time when meadow, grove, and stream,
The earth, and every common sight,
To me did seem
Apparelled in celestial light,
The glory and the freshness of a dream.
Ode, Intimations of Immortality from Recollections of Early Childhood

595.5
Our birth is but a sleep and a forgetting:
The Soul that rises with us, our life's Star,
Hath had elsewhere its setting,
And cometh from afar:
Not in entire forgetfulness,
And not in utter nakedness,
But trailing clouds of glory do we come
From God, who is our home:
Heaven lies about us in our infancy!
Shades of the prison-house begin to close
Upon the growing Boy. *same*

595.6
To me the meanest flower that blows can give
Thoughts that do often lie too deep for tears. *same*

595.7
Have I not reason to lament
What man has made of man?
Lines Written in Early Spring

595.8
There is a comfort in the strength of love;
'Twill make a thing endurable, which else
Would overset the brain, or break the heart. *Michael, 448*

595.9
The world is too much with us; late and soon
Getting and spending, we lay waste our powers:
Little we see in Nature that is ours.
Miscellaneous Sonnets, I:33

595.10
I'd rather be
A Pagan suckled in a creed outworn;
So might I, standing on this pleasant lea,
Have glimpses that would make me less forlorn;
Have sight of Proteus rising from the sea;
Or hear old Triton blow his wreathèd horn. *same*

595.11
Earth has not anything to show more fair:
Dull would he be of soul who could pass by
A sight so touching in its majesty:

This City now doth, like a garment, wear
The beauty of the morning; silent, bare,
Ships, towers, domes, theatres, and temples lie
Open unto the fields, and to the sky;
All bright and glittering in the smokeless air. *same, II:36*

595.12
Dear God! the very houses seem asleep;
And all that mighty heart is lying still! *same*

595.13
The Child is father of the Man;
And I could wish my days to be
Bound each to each by natural piety. *My Heart leaps up*

595.14
Bliss was it in that dawn to be alive,
But to be young was very Heaven! *The Prelude, II:108*

595.15
Still glides the Stream, and shall for ever glide;
The Form remains, the Function never dies. *The River Duddon, 34, After-Thought*

595.16
A slumber did my spirit seal;
I had no human fears:
She seemed a thing that could not feel
The touch of earthly years.

No motion has she now, no force;
She neither hears nor sees;
Rolled round in earth's diurnal course,
With rocks, and stones, and trees. *A Slumber did my Spirit seal*

595.18
Come forth into the light of things,
Let Nature be your Teacher. *The Tables Turned*

595.19
One impulse from a vernal wood
May teach you more of man,
Of moral evil and of good,
Than all the sages can. *same*

595.20
That best portion of a good man's life,
His little, nameless, unremembered acts
Of kindness and of love. *Lines composed a few miles above Tintern Abbey, 33*

595.21
That blessed mood,
In which the burthen of the mystery,
In which the heavy and the weary weight
Of all this unintelligible world,
Is lightened. *same, 37*

595.22
We are laid asleep
In body, and become a living soul:
While with an eye made quiet by the power
Of harmony, and the deep power of joy,
We see into the life of things. *same, 45*

595.23
I have learned
To look on nature, not as in the hour
Of thoughtless youth; but hearing often-times
The still, sad music of humanity. *same, 88*

595.24
Nature never did betray
The heart that loved her. *same, 122*

595.25
Poetry is the spontaneous overflow of powerful feelings: it takes its origin from emotion recollected in tranquillity. *Lyrical Ballads, Preface*

596 Wotton, Sir Henry (1568–1639), English traveller, diplomatist and poet.

596.1
An Ambassador is an honest man sent to lie abroad for his country.
Written in Mr Christopher Fleckamore's Album

597 Wren, Sir Christopher (1632–1723), English architect.

597.1
If you seek my monument, look around you. *Inscription in St Paul's Cathedral, London*

598 Wykeham, William of, see William of Wykeham

X

599 Xenophon, (435?–354? B.C.), Greek historian and soldier.

599.1
The sea! the sea! *Anabasis, IV:7*

600 Yeatman, Robert Julian, see Sellar, Walter Carruthers

601 Yeats, William Butler (1865–1939), Irish poet and dramatist.

601.1
O chestnut tree, great rooted blossomer,
Are you the leaf, the blossom or the bole?
O body swayed to music, O brightening glance,
How can we know the dancer from the dance? *Among School Children*

601.2
Now that my ladder's gone,
I must lie down where all the ladders start,
In the foul rag-and-bone shop of the heart. *The Circus Animals' Desertion*

601.3
Though leaves are many, the root is one;
Through all the lying days of my youth
I swayed my leaves and flowers in the sun;
Now I may wither into the truth.
The Coming of Wisdom with Time

601.4
But Love has pitched his mansion in
The place of excrement. *Crazy Jane Talks with the Bishop*

601.5
Wine comes in at the mouth
And love comes in at the eye;
That's all we shall know for truth
Before we grow old and die.
A Drinking Song

601.6
All changed, changed utterly:
A terrible beauty is born.
Easter 1916

601.7
When I play on my fiddle in Dooney,
Folk dance like a wave of the sea.
The Fiddler of Dooney

601.8
For the good are always the merry,
Save by an evil chance,
And the merry love the fiddle,
And the merry love to dance *same*

601.9
But I, being poor, have only my dreams;
I have spread my dreams under your feet;

Tread softly because you tread on my dreams. *He Wishes for the Cloths of Heaven*

601.10
I will arise and go now, and go to Innisfree,
And a small cabin build there, of clay and wattles made;
Nine bean rows will I have there, a hive for the honey bee,
And live alone in the bee-loud glade.
The Lake Isle of Innisfree

601.11
Never to have lived is best, ancient writers say;
Never to have drawn the breath of life, never to have looked into the eye of day
The second best's a gay goodnight and quickly turn away. *Oedipus at Colonus*

601.12
In dreams begins responsibility.
Old Play, Epigraph, Responsibilities

601.13
A pity beyond all telling
Is hid in the heart of love.
The Pity of Love

601.14
Things fall apart; the centre cannot hold;
Mere anarchy is loosed upon the world,
The blood-dimmed tide is loosed, and everywhere
The ceremony of innocence is drowned;
The best lack all conviction, while the worst
Are full of passionate intensity.
The Second Coming

602 Young, Edward (1683-1765), English poet.

602.1
Some for renown, on scraps of learning dote,
And think they grow immortal as they quote. *Love of Fame, I:89*

602.2
Be wise with speed,
A fool at forty is a fool indeed,
same, II:281

602.3
Procrastination is the thief of time.
Night Thoughts, I:393

Index

A

Abandon A. hope, all ye who enter 176.1
Abed Not to be a. after midnight 498.269
Abhorrence my heart's a. 83.14
Abilities From each according to his a. 386.2
Ability a.... capacity to act wisely 580.2
distressed by his want of a. 150.11
man can become famous without a. 499.77
Abroad a. you're a statesman 378.2
Absence A. is to love 95.1
A. makes the heart grow fonder 43.1
total a. of humour 145.1
Absent A. thee from felicity awhile 498.75
Absolutism A. tempered by assassination 410.1
Absurd something rather a. about the past 51.2
There is nothing so a. 135.1
Abuse more dangerous the a. 91.16
Accident good action... found out by a. 348.5
Accidents A. will occur 191.10
chapter of a. 128.11
Accounts supercilious knowledge in a. 502.5
Accused Never make a defence... before you be a. 122.1
Accustomed I will start to get a. to it 468.1
Aches My heart a. 332.22
Achieve those who a. something 310.22
Achieved Nothing great was ever a. 218.2
Acquaintance auld a. be forgot 93.2
day... in which I do not make a new a. 323.36
Acquaintances If a man does not make new a. 323.12
We need two kinds of a. 511.9
Act ability, which is capacity to a. wisely 580.2
Acting danger chiefly lies in a. well 131.2
Action lust in a. 498.299
Suit the a. to the word 498.66
Actor Like a dull a. now 498.35
Acts Familiar a. are beautiful 500.12
He who desires but a. not 67.21
Providence... end to the a. of God 190.6
unremembered a. 595.20
Adam A. was but human 553.5
When A. delved 37.1
Adapts reasonable man a. himself 499.53
Addiction a. of political groups to ideas 247.3
Adieu A.! my native shore 98.3
Ad infinitum And so proceed a. 535.7
fleas have lesser fleas... a. 405.1
Admiral good to kill an a. 561.2
Admires He who meanly a. 541.1
Adolescence man suffering from petrified a. 61.2
Adopt a. me as their favourite author 499.78
Ads He watched the a. 414.3
Adultery and gods a. 98.11
taken in a. than in provincialism 310.4
Thou shalt not commit a. 62.19
Advantage a. of doing one's praising 97.6
you have the a. of me 385.14
Advantages Wealth is not without its a. 247.1
Adversity a. doth best discover virtue 30.7
Advertised Wealth... must be a. 247.2
Advice A. is seldom welcome 128.7
woman seldom asks a. 4.7
Aesthetic crime is due to... a. expression 569.11
degree of my a. emotion 54.2
Affairs tide in the a. of men 498.122

Affect study what you most a. 498.251
Affliction Remembering mine a. 62.103
Afford purest treasure mortal times a. 498.232
Afraid A. of Virginia Woolf? 9.1
Englishman ... is a. to feel 237.2
Africa more familiar with A. than my own body 426.1
After-dinner a.'s sleep 498.183
Afternoon Summer a.... most beautiful words 317.4
Against every man's hand a. him 62.6
He said he was a. it 155.3
He that is not with me is a. me 62.134
Age A. cannot wither her 498.9
a. is full of care 498.303
a. of chivalry is gone 91.8
A. shall not weary them 64.1
A. will not be defied 30.29
Cool'd a long a. in the deep-delved earth 332.23
Crabbed a. and youth cannot live together 498.303
Do you think at your a., it is right?' 111.4
Drives my green a. 543.2
lady of a certain a. 98.18
meat ... cannot endure in his a. 498.211
no a. between ten and three and twenty 498.283
not of an a., but for all time 325.3
now in a. I bud again 290.4
No woman should ... be ... accurate about her a. 584.11
tells one her real a. 584.15
that which should accompany old a. 498.175
Thou has nor youth nor a. 498.183
Aged I saw an a. a. man 111.29
Agents I detest life-insurance a. 353.3
Ages His acts being seven a. 498.23
Agnes St. A.' Eve—Ah, bitter chill it was 332.5
Agree When people a. with me ... I must be wrong 584.22
Agreeable it is in most men's power to be a. 535.17
My idea of an a. person 195.10
Agreement My people and I have come to an a. 241.1
Agrees person who a. with me 195.10
Ahead I can't see who's a. 514.1
Ail what can a. thee, knight at arms 332.11
Air both feet firmly planted in the a. 475.2
Get your room full of good a. 353.2
I see him forming in the a. 470.1
No stir of a. was there 332.10
waste its sweetness on the desert a. 268.8
Aitches nothing to lose but our a. 427.5
Alamein Before A. we never had a victory 133.36
Alarms confused a. of struggle and flight 20.2
Albatross I shot the a. 144.4
Aldershot burnish'd by A. sun 60.3
Ale no more cakes and a. 498.271
spicy nut-brown a. 401.7
Alice A. mutton; mutton A. 111.31
Alien amid the a. corn 332.27
Alike among so many million of faces ... none a. 82.3
Alive Bliss was it in that dawn to be a. 595.14
he is no longer a. 59.4
needst not strive ... to keep a. 140.4
All A. art is quite useless 584.17
A. for one, and one for a. 206.1
a. our yesterdays 498.177
A. things to a. men 62.185
are you sure they are a. horrid 27.5
man, take him for a. in a. 498.45
Ripeness is a. 498.151
To know a. makes one tolerant 523.1
Allegory a. on the banks of the Nile 502.7
Alley she lives in our a. 108.2
Almonds Don't eat too many a. 145.5
Alms a. for oblivion 498.264
Alone A., a., all, all a. 144.7
A. and palely loitering 332.11
better to be a. than in bad company 567.1
I am here at the gate a. 539.19

I want to be a. 249.1
Man shall not live by bread a. 62.117
No poet...has...meaning a. 214.19
One is always a. 214.17
Weep, and you weep a. 583.1
We perish'd, each a. 165.1
who can enjoy a. 401.25
Alph Where A., the sacred river, ran 144.19
Alpha I am A. and Omega 62.212
Also You a. 428.2
Alternative I prefer old age to the a. 130.1
Alters Love is not love which a. 498.298
Am I a. that I am 62.11
I think therefore I a. 189.1
Amaryllis sport with A. in the shade 401.10
Amateur In love...the a. status 267.2
Amateurs disease that afflicts a. 129.15
nation of a. 477.2
Amaze vainly men themselves a. 384.4
Ambassador A. is an honest man sent to lie abroad 596.1
Ambition A. should be made of sterner stuff 498.118
Vaulting a., which o'er-leaps itself 498.165
America A. is a country of young men 218.14
business of A. is business 155.1
my A.! my new-found-land 199.7
what makes A. what it is 525.1
American A. system of rugged individualism 301.1
Americanism hyphenated A. 476.2
Ammunition pass the a. 236.1
Amo *Odi et a.* 114.2
Amor *A. vincit insomnia* 244.2
Amused We are not a. 558.1
Amusing whether she is not a. herself 403.3
Anarchy a. is loosed upon the world 601.14
Anatomy poor judge of a. 385.21
Ancient a. Mariner 144.1
A. of days 62.107
Anderson John A. my jo 93.9
Angel a. is nobody in particular 499.57
A. of Death has been abroad 75.1
in action, how like an a. 498.57
Is man an ape or an a. 195.4
woman yet think him an a. 541.4
Angels A. can fly 129.22
Not Angles, but a. 270.1
where a. fear to tread 452.16
Angles Not A., but angels 270.1
Angling A. may be said to be so like the mathematics 565.1
Anglo-Saxon those are A. attitudes 111.26
Animal Are you a.—or vegetable—or mineral? 111.28
information vegetable, a. and mineral 257.17
man is and will always be a wild a. 179.1
Man is a noble a. 82.9
man is...a religious a. 91.9
Man is by nature a political a. 17.2
Animals All a. are equal 4
A. are such agreeable friends 213.2
I think I could...live with a. 582.3
paragon of a. 498.57
Anna great A.! whom three realms obey 452.26
Annals simple a. of the poor 268.6
Annihilating A. all that's made 384.5
Annual A. income twenty pounds 191.8
Anomaly Poverty is an a. to rich people 32.3
Another He who would do good to a. 67.4
Life is just one damned thing after a. 306.1
No man can...condemn a. 82.4
Answer more than the wisest man can a. 148.4
What *is* the a.? 525.3
why did you a. the phone? 546.5
would not stay for an a. 30.2
Ant Go to the a., thou sluggard 62.64
Antan *les neiges d'a.* 559.1
Anthology a. is like all the plums...out of a cake 463.1
Antic Hay dance an a. 381.1

Anti-clerical it makes me understand a. things 55.7
Antidote a. to desire 151.8
Anything call me a. if you don't call me spade 535.15
pretty can get away with a. 569.25
Apart Man's love is...a thing a. 98.12
Things fall a. 601.14
Ape exception is a naked a. 406.1
Is man an a. or an angel 195.4
Ape-like a. virtues without which 153.2
Apes We've got nothing against a. 507.4
Apologize I never a. 499.6
Apparel a. oft proclaims the man 498.47
Appear Things are...what they a. to be 489.2
Appearances Keep up a. 131.3
Appetite A. comes with eating 460.1
a. may sicken and so die 498.266
Apple a. of his eye 62.29
want the a. for the a.'s sake 553.5
Appointment a. by the corrupt few 499.49
Appreciate I never a. 445.1
Apprehend Intelligence is quickness to a. 580.2
Après *A. nous le déluge* 451.1
April A. is the cruellest month 214.16
Now that A.'s there 83.6
Aprille Whan that A. with his shoures sote 127.1
Arabia All the perfumes of A. 498.174
Architecture A. in general is frozen music 490.1
Arguing I am not a. with you 577.1
Arian In three sips the A. frustrate 83.15
Arise I will a. and go now 601.10
Arm Human on my faithless a. 25.6
Armies ignorant a. clash by night 20.2
Napoleon's a. used to march on their stomachs 495.3
Arms A. and the man I sing 560.1
Army a. marches on its stomach 413.3
contemptible little a. 585.1
English a. led by an Irish general 499.62
Arrive travel...better thing than to a. 529.4
Art a....aspires towards the condition of music 436.2
A. for a.'s sake 162.1
A. is a jealous mistress 218.1
A. is long 296.1
a. is not a weapon 335.5
A. is ruled uniquely by the imagination 170.1
A. is the imposing of a pattern 580.3
A. is the most intense mode of individualism 584.24
a....left to a lot of shabby bums 359.1
a. of pleasing consists 281.6
Bullfighting is the only a. in which the artist is in danger of death 284.1
Desiring this man's a. 498.290
excellence of every a. is its intensity 332.35
Fine a. is that in which the hand 484.3
It's clever but is it a. 341.3
more sensitive one is to great a. 51.4
nature is the a. of God 82.2
object of a. 14.1
sombre enemy of good a. 153.7
strains of unpremeditated a. 500.13
True ease in writing comes from a. 452.13
Welsh...produced no...a. 569.6
whole of a. is an appeal to a reality 376.2
Words...full of a. 497.1
work that aspires...to the condition of a. 154.5
Artful a. Dodger 191.21
Artificial All things are a. 82.2
Artist Beware of the a. who's an intellectual 229.1
only one position for an a. anywhere 543.6
true a. will let his wife starve 499.38
Artistic a. temperament is a disease that afflicts amateurs 129.15
Artists A. are not engineers of the soul 335.5
Arts inglorious a. of peace 384.6
Murder...one of the Fine A. 188.1
Ashamed few people who are not a. of having been in love 471.13

man is doing something he is a. of 499.10
more things a man is a. of 499.36
Asked furious that she had not been a. 569.15
women are glad to have been a. 428.1
Asleep laid a. in body 595.22
Aspect Meet in her a. 98.25
Aspicious two a. persons 498.215
Ass law is a a. 191.22
Assassination Absolutism tempered by a. 410.1
A. is the extreme form of censorship 499.69
Assemblance Care I for the ...a. of a man? 498.91
Associate good must a. 91.13
I...like to a. with...priests 55.7
Assume what I a. you shall a. 582.2
Astonished a. at my own moderation 139.1
Astray like sheep have gone a. 62.100
Asunder let no man put a. 62.149
no man shall ever put a. 499.22
Asylum world is...like a lunatic a. 364.3
Atheist a. is a man who has no invisible means of support 238.1
denial of Him by the a. 458.5
I am an a. still, thank God 89.1
Athletics a. as inferior forms of fox-hunting 569.8
Attached men become a. even to Widnes 538.2
Attic glory of the A. stage 20.6
Attitudes Anglo-Saxon a. 111.26
Auld a. acquaintance be forgot 93.2
Aunt Charley's a. from Brazil 542.1
Aunts bad a. and good a. 592.2
Aussie dinkum hard-swearing A. 279.1
Australia Genius Spark Seems brightest in folk from A. 222.1
Australian Did you know that Rolf Harris was A.? 222.2
Every true A. bushman 352.1
Great A. Novel 579.4
Australians A. Have done *terribly* well for themselves 222.1
Author adopt me as their favourite a. 499.78
bad novel tells us...about its a. 129.14
when I don't know who the a. is 499.21
Authority a. be a stubborn bear 498.286
man Dress'd in a little brief a. 498.180
No morality can be founded on a. 29.1
Nothing destroyeth a. so much 30.22
Authors a. could not endure being wrong 106.3
Autumn breath of A.'s being 500.7
Ave A. atque vale 114.3
Aversion in matrimony to begin with a little a. 502.4
Aves Beadsman, after thousand a. told 332.7
Avon Sweet Swan of A. 325.4
Awake 'A. for Morning in the Bowl of Night 228.1
Away Take the soup a. 299.1
Aweary I gin to be a. of the sun 498.178
Awoke I a. one morning 98.29
Axe a.'s edge did try 384.7
Axioms A. in philosophy are not a. 332.38

B

Babbl'd 'a b. of green fields 498.94
Babes Out of the mouth of b. 62.42
Babies bit the b. in the cradles 83.11
putting milk into b. 133.22
Baby b.... loud noise at one end 343.1
Every b. born into the world 191.8
my b. at my breast 498.17
When the first b. laughed 40.1
Babylon By the rivers of B. 62.62
Back But at my b. I always hear 384.2
Bacon When their lordships asked B. 59.1
Bad b. die late 184.1
b. novel tells us the truth about its author 129.14
Defend the b. against the worse 182.1
never was a b. peace 239.4
novel cannot be too b. 499.64

too b. to be worth publishing 499.64
what I feel really b. about 240.1
When b. men combine 91.13
when... I'm b. I'm better 576.6
Badge Red B. of Courage 167.1
Balance b. of power 563.1
Balances weighed in the b. 62.105
Baldness felicity on the far side of b. 511.8
Baldwin fine thing to be honest 133.44
Ballot b. is stronger than the bullet 360.2
Balm wash the b. from an anointed king 498.236
Bang Not with a b. but a whimper 214.6
Bank b. and shoal of time 498.164
Bank balance better that a man should tyrannize over his b. 337.1
Bankrupt B. of Life 205.4
Banks Ye b. and braes 93.17
Bar no moaning of the b. 539.4
Barabbas B. was a publisher 104.3
Barbarians B., Philistines, Populace 20.15
Bargains rule for b. 191.16
Barge b. she sat in, like a burnish'd throne 498.8
Bark let no dog b. 498.187
Barkis B. is willin' 191.7
Bars Nor iron b. a cage 368.1
Based All progress is b. 97.5
Bastard I hope you will not... call me a b. 581.1
Bat black b., night, has flown 539.19
Twinkle, twinkle, little b. 111.6
Bathing right honourable gentleman caught the Whigs b. 195.2
Bathing machine something between a large b. 257.6
Battalions not single spies but in b. 498.71
Battle b. of Britain 133.14
Bauble What shall we do with this b. 172.2
Bays To win the palm, the oak, or b. 384.4
Be If you want to b. happy, b. 547.2
To b., or not to b. 498.61
Beaches we shall fight on the b. 133.12
Beadle b. on boxin' day 191.30
Beadsman B., after thousand aves told 332.7
Beaker b. full of the warm South 332.24
Be-all b. and the end-all here 498.164
Bean rows Nine b. will I have there 601.10
Bear authority be a stubborn b. 498.286
B. ye one another's burdens 62.195
Exit, pursued by a b. 498.282
Human kind cannot b. 214.3
I cannot b. men and women 499.23
I had rather b. with you than b. you 498.19
no man alive could b. it 499.37
Thou shalt not b. false witness 62.21
Bear-baiting Puritan hated b. 375.3
Beard singed the Spanish king's b. 202.1
Beast for man or b. 226.1
Man's life is cheap as b.'s 498.136
Beastie Wee, sleekit, cow'rin', tim'rous b. 93.11
Beastly Don't let's be b. to the Germans 163.13
Beaten We were not fairly b. 499.70
Beautiful good is the b. 448.1
many men, so b. 144.8
most b. things... are the most useless 484.2
Beauty B. and the lust for learning 51.7
B. is... in the eye of the beholder 309.1
B. is... in the eye of the beholder 562.1
b. is only sin deep 486.3
B. itself doth of itself persuade The eyes of men 498.304
Exuberance is B. 67.24
Love built on b. 199.4
Mathematics possesses... b. 485.4
She walks in b. 98.25
Teaches such b. as a woman's eye 498.155
terrible b. is born 601.6
There is no excellent b. 30.34
thing of b. is a joy for ever 332.4
What *is* b., anyway? There's no such thing 445.1
Beaver And cultivate a b. 310.2
Becket this turbulent priest 287.1

Become What's b. of Waring? 83.19
Becoming Sunburn is very b. 163.7
Bed And so to b. 438.1
b. be blest 5.1
B.... is the poor man's opera 310.12
Bedfellows Misery acquaints... strange b. 498.256
Beechen spare the b. tree 104.1
Beef roast b. of England 225.3
Beer chronicle small b. 498.221
Life isn't all b. and skittles 307.1
only a b. teetotaller 499.13
Bees murmuring of innumerable b. 539.24
Before I have been here b. 479.1
Begat and our fathers that b. us 62.113
Beggary b. in the love that can be reckon'd 498.5
no vice but b. 498.125
Begin B. at the beginning 111.14
If a man will b. with certainties 30.1
Beginning As it was in the b. 149.3
Begin at the b. 111.14
b. and the ending 62.212
b. of fairies 40.1
b. of the end 536.1
end of the b. 133.20
In the b. God 62.1
In the b. was the Word 62.161
Beginnings end to the b. of all wars 475.5
Behaviour quality of moral b. varies 310.11
sent down for indecent b. 569.1
Behind Get thee b. me, Satan 62.138
In the dusk, with a light b. her 257.20
led his regiment from b. 257.1
part my hair b. 214.11
Behold b. it was a dream 90.6
time of year thou mayst in me b. 498.294
Beholder Beauty is... in the eye of the b. 309.1
Beauty is... in the eye of the b. 562.1
Being Knowledge is proportionate to b. 310.26
live, and move, and have our b. 62.176
Belial Sons of B. 205.9
Beliefs holding two contradictory b. 427.4
Believe b. in the life to come 47.1
I don't b. in fairies 40.2
what we b. is not necessarily true 54.3
Believed two things that will be b. of any man 537.1
Bell B., book, and candle 498.126
for whom the b. tolls 199.13
Bellamy B.'s veal pies 447.3
Bellies their b. were full 74.2
Bellyful Rumble thy b. 498.138
Belong I don't want to b. to any club 385.19
Below Down and away b. 20.4
Ben Jonson O rare B. 325.7
Berries I come to pluck your b. 401.9
Berry Doubtless God could have made a better b. 565.2
Beside star or two b. 144.9
Best all that's b. of dark and bright 98.25
as in the b. it is 498.51
b. is the enemy of the good 561.4
b. lack all conviction 601.14
b. of life is but intoxication 98.13
b. of possible worlds 561.1
b. that is known and thought in the world 20.17
Culture, the acquainting ourselves with the b. 20.18
He is doing his b. 584.25
Men of few words are the b. 498.96
Never to have lived is b. 601.11
Stolen sweets are b. 134.2
we will do our b. 133.17
Bestial what remains is b. 498.222
Betimes to be up b. 498.269
Betray Nature never did b. the heart 595.24
Better b. strangers 498.29
b. than a play 123.4
b. to be alone 567.1
b. to have loved and lost 539.11
b. to have no opinion of God 30.19
far, far, b. thing 191.34
for b. for worse 149.15
He is no b. 28.1
I am getting b. and b. 161.1

if you knows of a b. 'ole 33.1
nae b. than he should be 93.6
no b. than you should be 45.1
when I'm bad I'm b. 576.6
Beulah B., peel me a grape 576.4
Beware B. of the artist who's an intellectual 229.1
B. of the dog 442.1
Beyond live b. their incomes 486.2
Bible English B. 375.1
Bibles they have the land and we have the B. 252.1
Big b. man has no time 229.3
Big Brother B. is watching you 427.2
Big-endians B. and small-endians 535.4
Bigger b. they come 230.1
it's a great deal b. than I am 109.15
Bill put 'Emily, I love you' on the back of the b. 385.17
Billboard b. lovely as a tree 414.5
Billet Every bullet has its b. 586.2
Biographies History...essence of...b. 109.3
Biography B. is about chaps 59.2
no history; only b. 218.4
Bird B. is on the Wing 228.2
B. thou never wert 500.13
Birds no b. sing 332.11
that make fine b. 6.3
where late the sweet b. sang 498.294
Birth B., and copulation, and death 214.14
Our b. is but a sleep and a forgetting 595.5
Bishop blonde to make a b. kick a hole 120.1
Bisier he semed b. than he was 127.8
Bite b. some other of my generals 254.1
b. the hand that fed them 91.12
Bites Every director b. the hand 263.4
When a man b. a dog 175.1
Black future is...b. 34.3
Black Prince Let the boy win his spurs. 210.1
Blasphemies truths begin as b. 499.1
Blasphemy in the soldier is flat b. 498.181
Bled Scots wha hae wi' Wallace b. 93.15
Bleed If you prick us, do we not b. 498.193
Bless B. relaxes 67.23
God b. us, every one 191.5
Blessed B. are the meek 62.118
B. are the pure in heart 62.119
B. are they that have not seen 62.173
b. be the name of the Lord 62.38
Blest bed be b. 5.1
It is twice b. 498.194
Man never is, but always to be b. 452.17
Blind If the b. lead the b. 62.137
love is b. 498.191
wing'd Cupid painted b. 498.202
Bliss b. of solitude 595.3
B. was it in that dawn to be alive 595.14
Where ignorance is b. 268.4
Blithe Hail to thee, b. Spirit 500.13
Block chip of the old b. 91.6
Blockhead No man but a b. ever wrote 323.29
Blonde b. to make a bishop kick a hole 120.1
Blondes Gentlemen always seem to remember b. 365.1
Blood b., toil, tears and sweat 133.10
humble and meek are thirsting for b. 426.3
I am in b. Stepp'd in so far 498.172
Bloody All the faces...b. Poms 125.1
My head is b., but unbowed 285.1
Bloom lilac is in b. 78.1
touch it, and the b. is gone 584.7
Blossom letting a hundred flowers b. 379.2
Blossomer great rooted b. 601.1
Blow B., b., thou winter wind 498.25
B....till you burst 83.12
B., winds, and crack your cheeks 498.137
themselves must strike the b. 98.6
this b. Might be the be-all and the end-all 498.164
Bloweth wind b. where it listeth 62.165
Blowing b. through the continent 378.3
Blown Flower that once has b. 228.4
Blows meanest flower that b. 595.6
Blues Twentieth-Century B. 163.11

Blunder Youth is a b. 195.7
Blush b. to the cheek of a young person 191.23
flower is born to b. unseen 268.8
Board I struck the b. 290.1
Boat beautiful pea-green b. 354.5
Boats messing about in b. 264.1
Bodies our dead b. must tell the tale 492.2
Body Absent in b. 62.183
b. of a weak and feeble woman 215.2
human b. is sacred 582.1
laid asleep In b. 595.22
mind that makes the b. rich 498.253
more familiar with Africa than my own b. 426.1
O b. swayed to music 601.1
soul is not more than the b. 582.4
than he has in his whole b. 535.13
what exercise is to the b. 524.3
Boil b. at different degrees 218.13
Bold Be b., be b., and everywhere Be b. 519.2
Boldness B., and again b., and always b. 177.1
Bolster helping to b. up the capitalist system 569.21
Bombs b. *are* unbelievable 579.1
Bones Of his b. are coral made 498.254
Bonjour *B. tristesse* 217.1
Bono *Cui b.* 135.5
Bonum *Summum b.* 135.3
Boojum Snark was a B. 111.16
Book bad b. is as much a labour to write 310.20
Bell, b., and candle 498.126
b.'s a b., although there's nothing in't 98.23
dainties that are bred in a b. 498.154
do not throw this b. about 55.1
Go, litel b. 127.18
good b. is the precious life-blood 401.36
he who destroys a good b., kills reason 401.35
If a b. is worth reading 484.1
I'll drown my b. 498.259
People seldom read a b. which is given 323.22
What a genius I had when I wrote that b. 535.19
What is the use of a b. 111.1
Books b. by which the printers have lost 245.4
b. cannot be killed by fire 475.4
B. think for me 348.3
Borrowers of b. 348.2
but b. never die 475.4
few b.... are worth reading 499.80
His b. were read 55.4
I keep my b. at the British Museum 97.2
No furniture so charming as b. 512.5
not all b. that are as dull as their readers 545.4
Of making many b. there is no end 62.85
proper study of mankind is b. 310.6
Some b. are to be tasted 30.38
true University is a collection of b. 109.7
We all know that b. burn 475.4
Bore B., a person who talks 63.1
Every hero becomes a b. 218.11
He is an old b. 548.3
proof that God is a b. 392.3
Bored Bores and B. 98.20
I wanted to be b. to death 190.4
Boredom effect of b. on a large scale 314.3
Bores B. and Bored 98.20
Boring something... b. about... happiness 310.13
Born B. under one law 271.1
British Bourgeoisie Is not b. 508.1
He broke the law when he was b. 499.31
He was b. an Englishman 52.1
I was b. old 548.1
Man that is b. of a woman 62.39
Man was b. free 481.1
natural to die as to be b. 30.4
One is not b. a woman 46.1
one of woman b. 498.179
powerless to be b. 20.7
Some are b. great 498.273
Some men are b. mediocre 283.2
sucker b. every minute 39.1
terrible beauty is b. 601.6

thought of all this before you were b. 507.3
to the manner b. 498.49
unto us a child is b. 62.95
We are all b. mad 47.5
Ye must be b. again 62.164
Borrow men who b. 348.1
Borrower Neither a b. nor a lender be 498.48
Borrowers B. of books 348.2
Borrowing b. dulls the edge of husbandry 498.48
Both Dreaming on b. 498.183
man who sees b. sides 584.20
said on b. sides 4.6
women require b. 97.8
Bottles new wine into old b. 62.154
Bottomless b. pit 62.217
Bough Loaf of Bread beneath the B. 228.3
Bounce in the plural and they b. 373.1
Bountiful Lady B. 223.2
Bourgeoisie British B. is not born 508.1
Bourn from whose b. No traveller returns 498.62
Bow B., b., ye lower middle classes 257.2
Bowels in the b. of Christ 172.1
Bower-bird I'm a bit of a b. 579.3
Bowl love in a golden b. 67.3
Morning in the B. of Night 228.1
Boxing day beadle on b. 191.30
Boy brain of a four-year-old b. 385.10
every b. and every gal That's born into the world alive 257.4
Love is a b. 96.3
Mad about the b. 163.15
Upon the growing B. 595.5
Boys As flies to wanton b. 498.144
B. do not grow up gradually 153.9
Some liked little b. too little 569.17
Bracelet diamond and safire b. lasts forever 365.3
Braces Damn b. 67.23
Braes Ye banks and b. 93.17
Brain B., an apparatus with which we think 63.2
Give his b. a rest 507.2
human b. is a device to keep the ears from grating 190.1
You've got the b. of a four-year-old boy 385.10
Brains girl with b. ought to do something else 365.2
What good are b. to a man 592.1
Branch Cut is the b. that might have grown 381.4
Brass Men's evil manners live in b. 498.105
Brave B. deserves the Fair 205.12
b. new world...such people in't 498.260
Fortune favours the b. 540.1
Brazil B., where the nuts come from 542.1
Breach custom more honour'd in the b. 498.49
Once more unto the b. 498.95
Bread b. and circuses 329.2
b. eaten in secret is pleasant 62.66
Cast thy b. upon the waters 62.84
give him b. 62.75
Loaf of B. beneath the Bough 228.3
Man does not live by b. only 62.27
Man shall not live by b. alone 62.117
Breakdown Madness need not be all b. 346.4
Breaking b. it in for a friend 385.20
Break-through Madness...may also be b. 346.4
Breast charms to soothe a savage b. 151.3
my baby at my b. 498.17
Two souls dwell...in my b. 261.2
Breasts they add weight to the b. 145.5
Breath b. of Autumn's being 500.7
world will hold its b. 297.6
Breathe when lap-dogs b. their last 452.27
Breed happy b. of men 498.235
Breeds Familiarity b.... children 553.4
Brevity B. is the soul of wit 498.53
Bribe doing nothing for a b. 498.36
Bribes How many b. he had taken 59.1
Brick he found it b. 100.1
Bride prepared as a b. adorned for her husband 62.219

unravish'd b. of quietness 332.15
Brief Out, out, b. candle 498.177
Brigands B. demand your money 97.8
Bright Tiger! burning b. 67.12
young lady named B. 87.1
Brilliant far less b. pen than mine 51.3
Brillig 'Twas b., and the slithy toves 111.17
Britain battle of B. is about to begin 133.14
B. fit country for heroes to live in 364.1
B. Land of Hope and Glory 57.1
B. nation of amateurs 477.2
B. nation of governesses 499.79
When B. first, at Heaven's command 544.1
Britannia Rule, B., rule the waves 544.1
British B. like to be told the worst 133.7
B. management doesn't... understand 125.2
maxim of the B. 133.5
British Empire liquidation of the B. 133.21
British Museum I keep my books at the B. 97.2
Britons B. alone use 'Might' 569.23
B. never will be slaves 544.1
B. were only natives 495.2
Broke We're really all of us bottomly b. 336.3
Broken Laws were made to be b. 421.2
peace has b. out 74.8
Brother my b.'s keeper 62.5
Brought never b. to min' 93.2
Brute Et tu, B. 498.110
Brutes Exterminate all b. 154.1
Brutus B. is an honourable man 498.117
B. noblest Roman of them all 498.123
You too, B. 101.4
Bubbles beaded b. winking at the brim 332.24
Buck b. stops here 551.1
Bud I'll nip him in the b. 470.1
like a worm i' th' b. 498.272
now in age I b. again 290.4
Buds darling b. of May 498.288
Builders stone which the b. refused 62.59
Built till we have b. Jerusalem 67.7
Bull Cock and a B. 527.4
take the b. between the teeth 263.7
Bullet ballot is stronger than the b. 360.2
Every b. has its billet 586.2
Bullfighting B. is the only art 284.1
Bums art... left to a lot of shabby b. 359.1
Bungler Man is a b. 499.44
Bunk History is more or less b. 234.1
Burden White Man's B. 341.9
Burdens Bear ye one another's b. 62.195
Burr kind of b.; I shall stick 498.185
Burst Blow your pipe there till you b. 83.12
first that ever b. 144.5
Burthen b. of the mystery 595.21
Bury I come to b. Caesar 498.116
Bus Hitler has missed the b. 118.3
Bush good wine needs no b. 498.33
Bush-liar bigger outback lie than the last b. 352.1
Bushman Every true Australian b. 352.1
Business B. as usual 133.5
B.... may bring money 27.3
b. of America is b. 155.1
dinner lubricates b. 493.1
do b. in great waters 62.57
If everybody minded their own b. 111.5
That's the true b. precept 191.16
To b. that we love we rise betime 498.12
Busyness b.... symptom of deficient vitality 529.2
Butlers b. and lady's maids do not reproduce 574.1
Butter b. will only make us fat 260.1
Buy I could b. back my introduction 385.13
Buying book... is worth b. 484.1
Byron Mad, bad, and dangerous 347.1

C

Cabbages c. and kings 111.22
Cabin small c. build there 601.10
Cabin'd c., cribb'd, confin'd, bound in 498.170

Caesar C.! dost thou lie so low 498.112
I come to bury C. 498.116
Not that I lov'd C. less 498.115
Render therefore unto C. 62.141
Cage Marriage is like a c. 403.4
Nor iron bars a c. 368.1
robin redbreast in a c. 67.2
Cain first city C. 164.1
Cake anthology...plums...picked out of a c. 463.1
Let them eat c. 380.1
Cakes no more c. and ale 498.271
Calais C. lying in my heart 387.1
Call leave to c. me anything 535.15
one clear c. for me 539.4
Called c. a cold a cold 56.1
many are c. 62.140
never c. me mother 594.1
Calm sea is c. to-night 20.1
Cambridge ahead...either Oxford or C. 514.1
Spring and summer did happen in C. 412.2
Came I c., I saw, I conquered 101.2
I c. like Water 228.5
Camera I am a c. 316.1
Can cry c. no more. I c. 302.1
He who c., does 499.51
Talent does what it c. 394.1
Cancel c. half a Line 228.8
Cancels debt which c. all others 148.5
Candid save me, from the c. friend 107.2
Candle Bell, book, and c. 498.126
little c. throws his beams 498.197
Out, out, brief c. 498.177
we shall this day light such a c. 350.1
Canem Cave c. 442.1
Canoe every man paddle his own c. 383.3
Cant Clear your mind of c. 323.34
Capability Negative C. 332.36
Capitalism c....machine for the suppression 355.1
Capitalist C. production begets...its own negation 386.1
helping to bolster up the c. system 569.21
Captain I am the c. of my soul 285.2
Captains C. of industry 109.13
Carbon c. atom possesses certain exceptional properties 319.1
Card table wrestled with a self-adjusting c. 546.2
Care age is full of c. 498.303
Sleep that knits up the ravell'd sleave of c. 498.167
Career nothing which might damage his c. 40.4
Careful be very c. of vidders 191.27
Careless first fine c. rapture 83.7
Carelessness to lose both looks like c. 584.8
Carpe C. diem 303.1
Carpenter Walrus and the C. 111.21
Carriage very small second-class c. 257.6
Carry why not c. a watch? 548.2
Carthage C. must be destroyed 113.1
Carthago delenda est C. 113.1
Case in our c. we have not got 465.2
Casements Charm'd magic c. 332.27
Casket seal the hushed c. of my soul 332.31
Cassius C. has a lean and hungry look 498.107
Cast die is c. 101.3
pale c. of thought 498.63
Casting It is no good c. out devils 351.4
Castle c. called Doubting C. 90.5
man's house is his c. 143.1
Castlereagh He had a mask like C. 500.6
Cat c. is the offspring of a c. 574.1
God...a cosmic Cheshire c. 311.2
More ways of killing a c. 340.1
What C.'s averse to fish 268.1
When I play with my c. 403.3
Catch First c. your hare 259.1
Go, and c. a falling star 199.9
only one c. and that was C.-22 283.1
Catholic lawful for a C. woman to avoid pregnancy 392.2
Caught I c. hold of the fille de chambre's...527.3
Causes dire offence from amorous c. 452.25
Home of lost c. 20.16
Caution c. in love is...fatal 485.3

Cavaliero perfect c. 98.1
Cave *C. canem* 442.1
Caverns c. measureless to man 144.19
Caviare c. to the general 498.58
Cease c. upon the midnight 332.26
have their day and c. to be 539.9
I will not c. from mental fight 67.7
poor shall never c. 62.28
Ceases forbearance c. to be a virtue 91.7
Celebrate I c. myself 582.2
Celerity C. is never more admir'd 498.11
Celia Come, my C., let us prove 325.6
Censorship Assassination is...form of c. 499.69
Centre c. cannot hold. 601.14
stables are the real c. 499.24
Cents you won't need the ten c. 385.15
Century twentieth c....c. of Fascism 411.1
Ceremony c. of innocence is drowned 601.14
Certain nothing is c. but death and taxes 239.5
One thing is c. 228.4
Certainties begin with c. 30.1
Chain flesh to feel the c. 77.3
Chains It's often safer to be in c. 330.1
Man...everywhere he is in c. 481.1
nothing to lose but their c. 386.5
Champagne not a c. teetotaller 499.13
Chance bludgeonings of c. 285.1
honest...sometimes by c. 498.285
Change If you leave a thing alone you leave it to a torrent of c. 129.21
Most of the c. we think we see 243.1
Plus ça c., plus c'est la même chose 331.1
Things do not c.; we c. 545.3
wind of c. is blowing through the continent 378.3
Changed All c., c. utterly 601.6
Changeth old order c. 539.8
Changing stress on not c. one's mind 388.1
Channel dream you are crossing the C. 257.6
Chapels c. had been churches 498.188
Chaps Biography is about C. 59.2
Chapter c. of accidents 128.11
Character c. in the world's torrent 261.5
Education...formation of c. 518.6
time to influence the c. of a child 314.5
Characteristic typically English c. 3.1
Characters c. in one of my novels 229.6
Chariot Time's winged c. hurrying near 384.2
Charity C. begins at home 82.5
C. is the power of defending...indefensible 129.12
C. shall cover the multitude of sins 62.209
faith, hope, c. 62.188
greatest of these is c. 62.188
In c. there is no excess 30.15
living need c. 19.1
without c. are nothing worth 149.10
Charles I He nothing common did or mean 384.7
Charley I'm C.'s aunt from Brazil 542.1
Charming People are either c. or tedious 584.12
Chastity Give me c. and continence 26.1
Cheating Winning Games Without...C. 453.1
Check dreadful is the c. 77.3
Cheek c., turn to him the other also 62.122
Cheeks Blow, winds, and crack your c. 498.137
Cheer cups, That c. but not inebriate 165.6
Cheese I do not like green c. 129.4
when the c. is gone 74.6
Cheque Mrs Claypool's c. will come back to you 385.16
Chequer-board C. of Nights and Days 228.7
Cherry C. ripe, ripe, ripe 291.1
C. Ripe themselves do cry 105.2
Loveliest of trees, the c. 304.1
Chess Life's too short for c. 99.1
Chewing c. little bits of String 55.2
Chicken mere c. feed 385.3
She's no c. 535.9
Some c. 133.19

Chickens Don't count your c. 6.4
Child all any reasonable c. can expect 426.2
C.! do not throw this book about 55.1
C. is father of the Man 595.13
c. is known by his doings 62.73
c. of five would understand this 385.5
getting wenches with c. 498.283
I heard one called C. 290.2
In...simplicity a c. 452.6
little c. shall lead them 62.96
proper time to influence the *character* of a c. is 314.5
spoil the c. 96.3
unto us a c. is born 62.95
wise father that knows his own c. 498.190
Childe C. Roland to the Dark Tower 83.5
Childish I put away c. things 62.186
Childishness second c. 498.24
Children Anybody who hates c. and dogs 226.2
C. aren't happy with nothing to ignore 414.4
c. fear to go in the dark 30.3
C. sweeten labours 30.9
Come dear c. 20.4
Familiarity breeds...c. 553.4
My music is best understood by c. 530.2
Rachel weeping for her c. 62.114
Suffer the little c. to come unto me 62.150
tale which holdeth c. from play 506.2
Chill bitter c. it was 332.5
Chimes c. at midnight 498.89
Chimney corner holdeth...old men from the c. 506.2
Chimney-sweepers As c., come to dust 498.38
Chip c. of the old block 91.6
Chirche-dore housbondes at c. 127.10
Chivalry age of c. is gone 91.8
Choirs Bare ruin'd c. 498.294
Chosen few are c. 62.140
Christ churches have kill'd their C. 539.20
I beseech you, in the bowels of C. 172.1
Must then a C. perish in torment 499.71
Christendom wisest fool in C. 286.2
Christian in what peace a C. can die 4.9
object...to form C. men 21.2
Christianity C. accepted...a metaphysical system 310.10
C. one great curse 419.3
C....says that they are all fools 129.13
decay of C. 486.5
His C. was muscular 195.8
local cult called C. 277.1
Christmas At C. I no more desire a rose 498.153
I'm walking backwards till C. 399.3
To perceive C. through its wrapping 578.2
Chronicle c. of wasted time 498.297
c. small beer 498.221
Chunder His favourite word...c. 308.1
Churches chapels had been c. 498.188
c. have kill'd their Christ 539.20
Churchill a man suffering from petrified adolescence 61.2
Churchman species of person called a 'Modern C.' 569.10
Cigar good c. is a smoke 341.2
Circle Weave a c. round him thrice 144.21
Circumcision Every luxury...atheism, breast-feeding, c. 426.4
Circumlocution Office C. 191.14
Circumstance Pride, pomp, and c. 498.227
Circuses bread and c. 329.2
Citizen c. of the world 30.16
I am...a c. of the world 515.5
City C. now doth, like a garment 595.11
first c. Cain 164.1
Civil Too c. by half 502.8
Civilization You can't say c. don't advance 472.1
Civilized Woman will be the last thing c. 393.1
Class history of c. struggles 386.4
machine for the suppression of one c. 355.1

patronize...without distinction of c. 499.29
Classes back the masses against the c. 258.2
curse of the drinking c. 584.28
responsible and the irresponsible c. 351.1
Classic c. is something that everybody wants to have read 553.6
Clearing-house C. of the World 117.1
Clerk C. ther was of Oxenford also 127.5
Clever It's c., but is it art? 341.3
Cleverness height of c. is to conceal 471.4
Clichés Let's have some new c. 263.10
Climate common where the c.'s sultry 98.11
whole c. of opinion 25.3
Clive What I like about C. 59.4
Clock Stands the Church c. at ten to three? 78.2
Clocks hands of c. in railway stations 153.9
Cloke knyf under the c. 127.11
Clootie Satan, Nick, or C. 93.1
Close breathless hush in the C. tonight 416.1
Closing time c. in the gardens of the West 153.1
Clothes as if she were taking off all her c. 145.2
bought her wedding c. 4.7
c.... thrown on her with a pitchfork 535.10
Nothing to wear but c. 339.1
walked away with their c. 195.2
Clothing in sheep's c. 62.132
Cloud fiend hid in a c. 67.11
I wandered lonely as a c. 595.2
Clouds trailing c. of glory 595.5
Clown I remain...a c. 121.3
Club I don't want to belong to any c. 385.19
Mankind is a c. 129.24
Coals heap c. of fire upon his head 62.75
Cock Before the c. crow twice 62.151
C. and a Bull 527.4
Cod piece of c. passes all understanding 373.2
Coffee C. which makes the politician wise 452.29
measured out my life with c. spoons 214.9
Cogito *C., ergo sum* 189.1
Coil shuffled off this mortal c. 498.61
Coke Happiness is like c. 310.17
Cold c. in blood 498.7
C. Pastoral 332.17
c. war 42.1
I beg c. comfort 498.129
We called a c. a c. 56.1
Coleridge He talked on for ever 281.1
Coliseum While stands the C., Rome shall stand 98.9
Collections those mutilators of c. 348.2
Colour'd woman c. ill 498.302
Colours All c. will agree in the dark 30.5
Combine When bad men c. 91.13
Come bigger they c. 230.1
Do you c. here often? 399.1
men may c. and men may go 539.1
Shape of Things to C. 574.2
Thou'lt c. no more 498.152
Whistle and she'll c. to you 45.9
Comedies c. are ended by a marriage 98.14
Comedy All I need to make a c. 121.2
at a c. we only look 310.7
Farce refined becomes high c. 166.1
world is a c. 564.2
Comfort c. in the strength of love 595.8
I beg cold c. 498.129
I'll not, carrion c., Despair 302.1
rod and thy staff c. me 62.48
Society is no c. 498.37
Two loves I have, of c. and despair 498.302
Coming C. through the rye 93.4
Command mortals to c. success 4.1
When Britain first, at Heaven's c. 544.1
Commanded Nature, to be c. 30.41
Commandment new c. I give unto you 62.170
Commandments keep his c. 62.86
Commendeth obliquely c. himself 82.1

Commerce honour sinks where c. long prevails 262.6
Common good thing, to make it too c. 498.84
He nothing c. did or mean 384.7
Commonplace great minds in the c. 306.3
nothing so unnatural as the c. 201.4
Commonwealth C. of Nations 477.1
Community We are part of the c. of Europe 258.3
Company better to be alone than in bad c. 567.1
Crowds without c. 255.2
few are qualified to shine in c. 535.17
In married life three is c. 584.6
people whose c. is coveted 376.1
Take the tone of the c. 128.4
Tell me what c. thou keepest 116.5
Companye other c. in youthe 127.10
Comparative progress is simply a c. 129.8
Compare any she belied with false c. 498.301
c. thee to a summer's day 498.288
Comparisons c. are odious 199.5
C. are odorous 498.214
Complains No one c. of his judgement 471.1
Complaint I want to register a c. 385.12
Complete disguised as a C. Man 310.3
Comprehended c. two aspicious persons 498.215
Compromise C. used to mean that half a loaf 129.23
government... is founded on c. 91.4
Conceal words... half c. 539.10
Concealment c., like a worm i' th' bud 498.272
Concept If the c. of God has 34.1
Conception dad is present at the c. 426.2
Concern power narrows the areas of man's c. 335.4
Concessions c. of the weak are the c. of fear 91.1
Conclusion they would not reach a c. 499.82
Conclusions Life is the art of drawing...c. 97.4
Condemn No man can justly censure or c. another 82.4
Condition c. of man... is a c. of war 298.1
hopes for the human c. 106.9
To be a poet is a c. 267.4
wearisome c. of humanity 271.1
Confin'd cabin'd, cribb'd, c. 498.170
Conflict We are in an armed c. 208.2
Confusion nothing to offer anybody except my own c. 336.4
Congreve C. is the only sophisticated playwright 554.1
Connect Only c. 237.1
Conquer when we c. without danger 158.1
Conquered I came, I saw, I c. 101.2
Conquering C. kings 119.1
not c. but fighting well 160.1
Conquers Love c. all 560.4
Conquest Roman C. was, however, a *Good Thing* 495.2
Conscience c. does make cowards of us all 498.63
C. is the inner voice 392.1
C. is the... rejection of a particular wish 242.3
I'll catch the c. of the King 498.60
Conservatism c.... adherence to the old and tried 360.4
c. is based upon the idea 129.21
Conservative C. government is an organized hypocrisy 195.3
Or else a little C. 257.4
Consistency C. is contrary to nature 310.8
Conspiracies All professions are c. 499.17
Conspiracy Indecency's C. of Silence 499.58
Conspirators All the c. 498.123
Constabulary When c. duty's to be done 257.19
Constancy infernal c. of the women who love me 499.63

Constant Friendship is c. in all other things 498.209
Consume more history than they can c. locally 486.1
no more right to c. happiness 499.11
Consummation c. Devoutly to be wish'd 498.61
Consumption this c. of the purse 498.85
Contagion c. of the world's slow stain 500.1
Contain I c. multitudes 582.5
Contemptible c. little army 585.1
Contend hundred schools of thought c. 379.2
Content desire is got without c. 498.169
draw upon c. for the deficiencies of fortune 262.9
Contented With what I most enjoy c. least 498.290
Contests mighty c. rise from trivial things 452.25
Continence Give me chastity and c. 26.1
Continent On the C. people have good food 395.1
Continents which extends over many nations and three c. 201.8
Continual c. state of inelegance 27.12
Contract Every law is a c. 494.3
verbal c. isn't worth the paper 263.6
Contradict Do I c. myself 582.5
Contradiction Woman's at best a c. 452.22
Contrairy everythink goes c. with me 191.6
Contraries Without C. is no progression 67.18
Contrariwise 'C.,' continued Tweedledee 111.20
Convent C. of the Sacred Heart 214.15
Conversation proper subject of c. 128.12
Conviction best lack all c. 601.14
Cook C. is a little unnerved 60.1
c. was a good c., as cooks go 486.4
ill c. that cannot lick his own fingers 498.250
c. was a good c., as cooks go 486.4
Copulation Birth, and c., and death 214.14
Coquette c. is a woman who rouses passions 499.81
Coral C. is far more red 498.300
Of his bones are c. made 498.254
Cordial gold in phisik is a c. 127.9
Corn amid the alien c. 332.27
Whoever could make two ears of c. 535.5
Corner c. in the thing I love 498.225
head stone of the c. 62.59
some c. of a foreign field 78.3
Coromandel On the Coast of C. 354.1
Coronets Kind hearts are more than c. 539.15
Corpse He'd make a lovely c. 191.17
Correctly anxious to do the wrong thing c. 486.6
Corrupt Among a people generally c. 91.15
Power tends to c. 1.1
Corruption C.... symptom of constitutional liberty 255.3
Cosmos c. is about the smallest hole 129.18
Couch century of the psychiatrist's c. 377.1
time as a tool not as a c. 335.2
Counsel sometimes c. take—and sometimes Tea 452.26
Count Don't c. your chickens 6.4
Counties see the coloured c. 304.2
Country ask not what your c. can do for you 335.1
c. diversion 151.6
c. from whose bourn no traveller returns 498.62
c.; it is a kind of healthy grave 512.9
c. of young men 218.14
Fornication... in another c. 381.6
God made the c. 165.3
How I leave my c. 447.4
I love thee still, my c. 165.4
loathe the c. 151.6
nothing good... in the c. 281.8
our c., right or wrong 183.1
save in his own c. 62.136
she is my c. still 131.1
undiscover'd c. 498.62

what was good for the c. 588.1
Countrymen Friends, Romans, c. 498.116
Courage c. never to submit or yield 401.16
Red Badge of C. 167.1
tale...of...c. of my companions 492.2
Course c. of true love never did run smooth 498.201
earth's diurnal c. 595.16
Courteous If a man be...c. to strangers 30.16
Covet Thou shalt not c. thy neighbour's house 62.22
Cow till the c. comes home 45.8
Coward c. does it with a kiss 584.1
No c. soul is mine 77.1
Cowardice we were guilty of Noel C. 190.3
Cowards C. die many times 498.109
public...is the greatest of c. 281.5
Thus conscience does make c. of us all 498.63
Coyness This c., lady, were no crime 384.1
Cradled c. into poetry by song 500.5
Cradles bit the babies in the c. 83.11
Craft c. so long to lerne 127.16
Cream choking her with c. 340.1
Created c. man in his own image 62.3
Creation greatest week...since the c. 420.1
Creatures call these delicate c. ours 498.225
From fairest c. we desire increase 498.287
Creed suckled in a c. outworn 595.10
Creeds Vain are the thousand c. 77.2
Creep I wants to make your flesh c. 191.25
Wit that can c. 452.5
Creeping Nature is c. up 577.6
Creetur lone lorn c. 191.6
Crete people of C.... make more history 486.1
Cricket C. A sport, at which the contenders drive a ball with sticks 323.2
c. on the hearth 401.4
c. It's more than a game 307.2
Crime coyness, lady, were no c. 384.1
c. is...desire for aesthetic expression 569.11
Napoleon of c. 201.6
no...c. so shameful as poverty 223.1
punishment fit the c. 257.11
Treason was no C. 205.9
Crimes how many c. committed 106.3
liberty, what c. are committed in thy name 474.1
worst of c. is poverty 499.30
Critic function of the c. 54.2
no statue has ever been put up to a c. 504.1
Critical nothing if not c. 498.220
Criticism great deal of contemporary c. 129.4
my own definition of c. 20.17
People ask you for c. 388.2
Critics c. all are ready made 98.24
Cromwell restless C. could not cease 384.6
Some C. guiltless 268.9
Crook I am not a c. 420.2
Crop watering last year's c. 213.1
Cross-bow With my c. I shot 144.4
Crowd Far from the madding c. 268.10
select Out of the c. a mistress or a friend 500.3
Crowds C. without company 255.2
Crown influence of the C. has increased 207.1
I will give thee a c. of life 62.213
Uneasy lies the head that wears a c. 498.88
within the hollow c. 498.237
Crucify C. him 62.152
Cruellest April is the c. month 214.16
Crumbs c. which fell from the rich man's table 62.158
Cry make 'em c. 464.1
Crying one c. in the wilderness 62.115
Cui C. bono 135.5
Cult local c. called Christianity 277.1
Cultivate c. our garden 561.3
Culture C., the acquainting ourselves with the best 20.18

When I hear anyone talk of C. 260.3
Cup Ah, fill the C. 228.6
Come, fill the C. 228.2
tak a c. o' kindness yet 93.3
Cupid wing'd C. painted blind 498.202
Cups c., that cheer but not inebriate 165.6
Cure C. the disease 30.27
maladies we must not seek to c. 458.3
Prevention is better than c. 437.2
Curfew C. tolls the knell of parting day 268.5
Curiosity Newspapers always excite c. 348.4
Curious That was the c. incident 201.9
Curiouser C. and c. 111.2
Curse Christianity the one great c. 419.3
c. is come upon me 539.16
Partisanship is our great c. 469.1
Curst C. be the verse 452.4
Curtain iron c. has descended across the Continent 133.23
Ring down the c. 460.2
Custodes *Quis custodiet ipsos c.?* 329.1
Custom C. calls me to't 498.34
c. loathsome to the eye 318.1
c. More honour'd in the breach than the observance 498.49
c. stale Her infinite variety 498.9
Customers raising up a people of c. 510.2
When you are skinning your c. 344.1
Cut It isn't etiquette to c. any one 111.32
laurels all are c. 304.7
Cuts he that c. off twenty years of life 498.111
Cynara faithful to thee, C. 200.1

D

Dad if the d. is present at the conception 426.2
Daffodils Fair d., we weep to see 291.3
host, of golden d. 595.2
Dainties d. that are bred in a book 498.154
Dalliance primrose path of d. 498.46
Damage nothing which might d. his career 40.4
Dame La belle D. sans Merci 332.12
Damn D. braces 67.24
D. with faint praise 452.3
Damnations Twenty-nine distinct d. 83.16
Damn'd thou must be d. perpetually 381.3
Damned Publish and be d. 573.4
Dance D., d., d. little lady 163.14
Folk d. like a wave of the sea 601.7
know the dancer from the d. 601.1
merry love to d. 601.8
On with the d. 98.8
those move easiest who have learn'd to d. 452.13
will you join the d.? 111.11
Dancer know the d. from the dance 601.1
Danger d.... lies in acting well 131.2
only real d. that exists is man 327.3
when we conquer without d. 158.1
Dangerous little learning is a d. thing 452.10
little sincerity is... d. 584.21
Mad, bad, and d. to know 347.1
more d. the abuse 91.16
Dappled Glory be to God for d. things 302.4
Dare d. to eat a peach 214.11
Darien Silent, upon a peak in D. 332.29
Daring d. to excel 131.2
Dark children fear... the d. 30.3
colours will agree in the d. 30.5
Genuineness only thrives in the d. 310.24
great leap in the d. 298.4
never to refuse a drink after d. 392.6
nightmare of the d. 25.4
O d., d., d., amid the blaze of noon 401.30
we are for the d. 498.16
What in me is d. Illumine 401.15
Darken never d. my towels again 385.7
Darkling as on a d. plain 20.2
Darkly through a glass, d. 62.187

Darkness people that walked in d. 62.94
Daughter Don't put your d. on the stage 163.10
David D. his ten thousands 62.34
Dawn Bliss was it in that d. to be alive 595.14
Day bright d. is done 498.16
compare thee to a summer's d. 498.288
d. returns too soon 98.27
every d.... lost, in which I do not make a new acquaintance 323.36
every dog has his d. 70.1
from this d. forward 149.15
Good morning to the d.: and, next, my gold 325.5
If every d. in the life of a school 353.1
in the d. of judgement 149.8
It takes place every d. 106.5
It was such a lovely d. 388.7
live murmur of a summer's d. 20.9
long d.'s task is done 498.13
Our little systems have their d. 539.9
runs through the roughest d. 498.160
Seize the d. 303.1
So foul and fair a d. 498.158
Sufficient unto the d. 62.129
Sweet d., so cool, so calm 290.8
Without all hope of d. 401.30
Daylight rule never to drink by d. 392.6
Days Ancient of d. 62.107
d. of wine and roses 200.3
Do not let us speak of darker d. 133.18
his d. are as grass 62.56
live laborious d. 401.11
loved three whole d. together 531.1
Shuts up the story of our d. 462.1
Six d. shalt thou labour 62.16
Dead American professors like their literature... d. 359.2
D.... never called me mother 594.1
fairy somewhere... falls down d. 40.2
great deal to be said for being d. 59.4
healthy and wealthy and d. 546.1
It's easier to replace a d. man 499.18
Mistah Kurtz—he d. 154.3
Queen Anne's d. 147.2
Something was d. in each of us 584.2
Deadener Habit is a great d. 47.6
Deadly female... is more d. 341.4
Soap and education... are more d. 553.2
Deal new d. for the American people 475.1
Dean drink to the queer old D. 520.2
Let the D. and Canons lay their heads together 512.3
Dear too d. for my possessing 498.295
Dearer d. still is truth 17.4
Death After the first d., there is no other 543.3
Angel of D. has been abroad 75.1
Any man's d. diminishes me 199.13
artist is in danger of d. 284.1
Be thou faithful unto d. 62.213
Birth, and copulation, and d. 214.14
cuts off... fearing d. 498.111
d. after life does greatly please 519.1
D. be not proud 199.8
D. hath no more dominion 62.179
D. is still working like a mole 290.5
D. must be distinguished from dying 512.4
D.... we haven't succeeded in vulgarizing 310.9
dread of something after d. 498.62
give me liberty or give me d. 289.1
I here importune d. awhile 498.14
I wanted to be bored to d. 190.4
Love is strong as d. 62.89
Men fear d. 30.3
nothing is certain but d. and taxes 239.5
O d., where is thy sting 62.189
one that had been studied in his d. 498.161
Reports of my d. are greatly exaggerated 553.7
sad stories of the d. of kings 498.237
Thou wast not born for d. 332.27
till d. us do part 149.15
tragedies are finished by a d. 98.14
useless life is an early d. 261.4
valiant never taste of d. but once 498.109
valley of the shadow of d. 62.48
wages of sin is d. 62.180
way to dusty d. 498.177
we owe God a d. 498.90

Deaths More d. than one must die 584.4
Debauchee D., one who has... pursued pleasure 63.3
Debt d. which cancels all others 148.5
promise made is a d. unpaid 496.1
Debts He that dies pays all d. 498.257
Decadence difference between our d. and the Russians' 546.7
Decay All humane things are subject to d. 205.13
woods d. and fall 539.26
Deceived Be not d. 62.196
Decency D. is Indecency's Conspiracy of Silence 499.58
Decent d. means poor 437.1
Declare nothing to d. except my genius 584.26
Decorated proverb... much matter d. 245.3
Decorum *Dulce et d. est* 303.2
Dulce et d. est 430.2
Deed good d. in a naughty world 498.197
good d. to forget a poor joke 72.1
right d. for the wrong reason 214.18
Deeds better d. shall be in water writ 45.6
Deep beauty is only sin d. 486.3
one is of the d. 526.1
Thoughts... too d. for tears 595.6
what a very singularly d. young man 257.14
Deeper d. than did ever plummet sound 498.259
whelm'd in d. gulphs 165.1
Deeth D. is an ende of every worldly sore 127.12
Defeat d. without a war 133.9
In d. unbeatable 133.43
Defect Chief D. of Henry King 55.2
Defence Never make a d. or apology 122.1
Deferred Hope d. maketh the heart sick 62.69
Defied Age will not be d. 30.29
Definite d. maybe 263.5
Definition true d. of a style 535.6
Degree d. of delight 91.17
when d. is shak'd 498.262
Degrees we boil at different d. 218.13
Delenda *D. est Carthago* 113.1
Deliberates woman that d. is lost 4.2
Delight degree of d. 91.17
Energy is Eternal D. 67.20
go to't with d. 498.12
Spirit of D. 500.14
Studies serve for d. 30.37
unrest... men miscall d. 500.1
very temple of d. 332.21
Delighted Whosoever is d. in solitude 30.26
Delights Man d. not me 498.57
To scorn d. 401.11
Deliver d. me from myself 82.6
Déluge *Après nous le d.* 451.1
Delved When Adam d. 37.1
Democracy D. substitutes election by the incompetent 499.49
d., the last refuge of cheap misgovernment 499.35
world must be made safe for d. 591.3
Democratic We must be... d. and patronize 499.29
Demon woman wailing for her d.-lover 144.20
Demonstrandum *Quod erat d.* 220.1
Denies spirit that always d. 261.3
Denmark rotten in the state of D. 498.50
Dentist For physical pleasure I'd sooner go to my d. 569.16
Deny Those who d. freedom 360.3
thou shalt d. me thrice 62.151
Derangement nice d. of epitaphs 502.6
Descriptions d. of the fairest wights 498.297
Desert Use every man after his d. 498.59
Deserts D. of vast eternity 384.2
Deserves None but the Brave d. 205.12
Designing I am d. St. Paul's 59.3
Desire antidote to d. 151.8
d. is got without content 498.169
d. should so many years outlive performance 498.87
It provokes the d. 498.168
like d. for preventing the thing one says 458.4

not to get your heart's d. 499.45
to have few things to d. 30.21
universal innate d. 97.5
Desired war which... left nothing to be d. 74.5
Desires He who d. but acts not 67.22
starting-point for further d. 458.1
Despair Giant D. 90.5
I'll not... D., not feast on thee 302.1
Patience, a minor form of d. 63.7
some divine d. 539.22
without understanding d. 346.2
Despairs He who d. over an event is a coward 106.9
Desperation lives of quiet d. 545.1
Despise making some other Englishman d. him 499.66
Despond name of the slough was D. 90.2
Despotism France was a long d. 109.8
Destiny I were walking with d. 133.31
Destroy whom God wishes to d. 221.1
Whom the gods wish to d. 153.6
Destruction one purpose... d. of Hitler 133.35
Pride goeth before d. 62.71
Detail life is frittered away by d. 545.5
novels are an accumulation of d. 579.3
Detest they d. at leisure 98.19
Devil cleft the D.'s foot 199.9
d. can cite Scripture 498.189
d. should have all the good tunes 295.1
d.'s madness—War 496.3
Is the d. to have all the passions 499.39
Renounce the d. 149.11
world, the flesh, and the d. 149.7
Devils It is no good casting out d. 351.4
Diamond d.... bracelet lasts forever 365.3
Diamonds goodness, those d. are lovely! 576.3
to give him d. back 246.1
Diary I never travel without my d. 584.10
Die appointed unto men once to d. 62.203
Before we grow old and d. 601.5
books never d. 475.4
Cowards d. many times 498.109
d. in the last ditch 92.1
d. in the last ditch 586.1
d. is cast 101.3
D.... last thing I shall do 432.1
either do, or d. 45.3
good d. first 595.1
If I should d. 78.3
in what peace a Christian can d. 4.9
I shall have to d. beyond my means 584.27
It is natural to d. 30.4
Let us do or d. 93.16
man can d. but once 498.90
More deaths than one must d. 584.4
No young man believes he shall ever d. 281.3
place... to d. in 82.7
save your world you asked this man to d. 25.2
seems it rich to d. 332.26
Their's but to do and d. 539.3
they... argue that I shall some day d. 353.3
They that d. by famine 288.1
those about to d. salute you 532.2
to d., and go we know not where 498.184
tomorrow we shall d. 62.97
Died dog it was that d. 262.2
Men have d. from time to time 498.31
Diem Carpe d. 303.1
Dies Call no man happy until he d. 516.1
Function never d. 595.15
He that d. pays all debts 498.257
It matters not how a man d. 323.19
king never d. 65.1
Diet Praise is the best d. 512.6
Different rich are d. 229.4
Difficult D. do you call it, Sir? I wish it were impossible 323.37
intellectual... found it too d. 491.1
It is d. to be humble 196.1
Digest mark, learn, and inwardly d. 149.9
Digestion d. is the great secret of life 512.8
Things sweet to taste prove in d. sour 498.233

Diggeth Whoso d. a pit 62.76
Diminished ought to be d. 207.1
Dine wretches hang that jury-men may d. 452.28
Dinkum d. hard-swearing Aussie 279.1
Dinner Breakfast, D., Lunch and Tea 55.3
d. lubricates business 493.1
D.... possessed only two dramatic features 455.2
man is... better pleased when he has a good d. 323.39
Diplomat d. these days is nothing but a head-waiter 555.2
Directions rode madly off in all d. 353.4
Director Every d. bites the hand 263.4
Disarmament precede the d. of the victors 133.30
Disaster nation is not in danger of financial d. 391.1
Disbelief willing suspension of d. 144.22
Disc round d. of fire 67.17
Disciple d. of Bernard Shaw 499.20
Discommendeth He who d. others 82.1
Discontent winter of our d. 498.239
Discretion better part of valour is d. 498.82
years of d. 149.12
Discrimination sympathetic without d. 227.2
Disease Cure the d. 30.27
Life is an incurable d. 164.2
remedy is worse than the d. 30.18
strange d. of modern life 20.10
this long d., my life 452.2
Diseases d. of the mind 524.1
Disgrace d. to our family name of Wagstaff 385.9
Intellectual d. 25.5
Poverty is no d. to a man 512.1
Disguise Speech... to d. his thoughts 536.3
Dishonour honour rooted in d. 539.6
Disliked I have always d. myself 153.8
Dismal D. Science 109.11
Disobedience Of Man's first d. 401.14
Disorder sweet d. in the dress 291.2
Displeasing misfortunes... not d. 471.5
Disposes God d. 333.1
Dissipation d. without pleasure 255.2
Dissolve Fade far away, d. 332.25
Distance d. lends enchantment 104.2
Distress All pray in their d. 67.16
mean man is always full of d. 150.8
Distrusts him who d. himself 471.15
Ditch die in the last d. 92.1
die in the last d. 586.1
Dive search for Pearls must d. below 205.15
Diversion 'tis a country d. 151.6
Divide absurd to d. people into good and bad 584.12
Divided If a house be d. 62.147
Divine to forgive d. 452.15
Divinity d. in odd numbers 498.200
d. that shapes our ends 498.74
piece of d. in us 82.8
There's such d. doth hedge a king 498.72
Division absurd d. into sexes 569.14
Do D. as I say, not as I d. 494.1
D. as you would be done by 128.5
D. not d. unto others 499.46
d. other men 191.16
either d., or die 45.3
far, far, better thing that I d. 191.34
I am to d. what I please 241.1
If to d. were as easy as to know what were good to d. 498.188
Let us d. or die 93.16
so much to d. 467.1
so much to d., So little done 539.13
they would d. you 191.16
to d. something is to create existence 489.4
what you can d. for your country 335.1
Doctor I do not love thee, D. Fell 79.1
Doctrine d. of the strenuous life 476.1
Doctrines What makes all d. plain 96.6
Dodger artful D. 191.21
Does He who can, d. 499.51
It's dogged as d. it 550.1
Dog Beware of the d. 442.1
curious incident of the d. in the night-time 201.9
d. it was that died 262.2

d., to gain some private ends, Went mad and bit the man 262.1
door is what a d. is...on the wrong side of 414.1
every d. has his day 70.1
His Highness' d. at Kew 452.24
I ope my lips let no d. bark 498.187
When a d. bites a man 175.1
whose d. are you 452.24
Dogged It's d. as does it 550.1
Dogs All the d. of Europe bark 25.4
Anybody who hates children and d. 226.2
let slip the d. of war 498.114
Mad d. and Englishmen 163.9
Rats...fought the d. 83.11
woman who is...kind to d. 51.6
Doing we learn by d. 17.1
Whatever is worth d. 128.2
Doings All our d. without charity 149.10
child is known by his d. 62.73
Dollars What's a thousand d.? 385.3
Dominion Death hath no more d. 62.179
Done bright day is d. 498.16
do as you would be d. by 128.5
d. those things...we ought not 149.2
If it were d. when 'tis d. 498.163
Justice...should...be seen to be d. 292.1
Let justice be d. 224.1
let us have d. with you 13.1
long day's task is d. 498.13
Nothing is ever d. 499.34
so little d. 539.13
thy worldly task hast d. 498.38
What you do not want d. to yourself 150.12
Dong D. with a luminous Nose 354.2
Doom even to the edge of d. 498.298
regardless of their d. 268.3
Doon banks and braes o' bonnie D. 93.17
Dooney my fiddle in D. 601.7
Door d. is what a dog is perpetually on the wrong side of 414.1
world will make a beaten path to his d. 218.15
Doors d. of perception were cleansed 67.26
Dots I never could make out what those damned d. 132.4
Doublethink D. means the power of holding two contradictory beliefs 427.4
Doubt fanatic...over-compensates a secret d. 310.28
new Philosophy calls all in d. 199.1
When in d., win the trick 305.1
Doubting castle called D. Castle 90.5
Doubtless D. God could have made a better berry 565.2
Doubts end in d. 30.1
Dove wings like a d. 62.53
Doves moan of d. in immemorial elms 539.24
Down He that is d. 90.7
I'll bring the etchings d. 546.3
put it d. a we 191.32
Drag Why d. in Velasquez? 577.3
Drain you will leave by the next town d. 520.1
Dramatic Dinner...two d. features 455.2
Draught O, for a d. of vintage 332.23
Drawers d. of water 62.30
Dread close your eyes with holy d. 144.21
most men d. it 499.50
Dreadful d. is the check 77.3
some have called thee Mighty and d. 199.8
Dream behold it was a d. 90.6
glory and the freshness of a d. 595.4
old men shall d. dreams 62.109
sight to d. of 144.17
To sleep, perchance to d. 498.61
you d. you are crossing the Channel 257.6
Dreamer poet and the d. are distinct 332.9
Dreaming after-dinner's sleep, d. on both 498.183
d. spires 20.13
Dreams Fanatics have their d. 332.8
In d. begins responsibility 601.12

We are such stuff As d. are made on 498.258
what d. may come 498.61
you tread on my d. 601.9
Dreamt d. of in your philosophy 498.52
Dress as a nation we don't d. well 499.73
sweet disorder in the d. 291.2
Dress'd D. in a little brief authority 498.180
Drink D. deep, or taste not 452.10
d. may be said to be an equivocator with lechery 498.168
D. to me only with thine eyes 325.1
d. to the queer old Dean 520.2
never to d. by daylight 392.6
never to refuse a d. after dark 392.6
Nor any drop to d. 144.6
Drinking curse of the d. classes 584.28
two reasons for d. 437.2
Droghte d. of Marche 127.1
Drop Nor any d. to drink 144.6
Drown I'll d. my book 498.259
what pain it was to d. 498.240
Drowned ceremony of innocence is d. 601.14
Drudge harmless d. 323.3
Drunk man...must get d. 98.13
not so think as you d. I am 521.1
this meeting is d. 191.31
Dry old man in a d. month 214.4
Duchess D.! The D. 111.3
Dulce *D. et decorum est* 303.2
D. et decorum est 430.2
Dull D. would he be of soul 595.11
not all books...are as d. as their readers 545.4
Dunn Miss J. Hunter D. 60.3
Dusk In the d., with a light behind her 257.20
Dust As chimney-sweepers, come to d. 498.38
d. thou art 62.4
pride that licks the d. 452.5
this quintessence of d. 498.57
Duties Property has its d. 204.1
Duty declares that it is his d. 499.10
Do your d. and leave the rest to the Gods 158.2
d. of an Opposition 132.3
d. of being happy 529.3
England expects every man will do his d. 415.1
no d. we so much underrate 529.3
when constablulary d.'s to be done 257.19
whole d. of man 62.86
Dwell he cannot d. there long 499.14
Dying alike are the groans of love to...d. 370.1
Death must be distinguished from d. 512.4
He had been, he said, a most unconscionable time d. 123.1
I am d., Egypt, d. 498.14
Patriots always talk of d. 485.6
'Tis not the d. for a faith 541.3
Dynamic class people as static and d. 569.14
play is a d. thing 554.2

E

Each e. according to his needs 386.2
Ear e. begins to hear 77.3
jest's prosperity lies in the e. 498.156
more is meant than meets the e. 401.5
Early E. to rise and e. to bed 546.1
good die e. 184.1
Ears device to keep the e. from grating 190.1
Romans, countrymen, lend me your e. 498.116
Earth Cool'd...in the deep-delved e. 332.23
E. has not anything to show more fair 595.11
e. was without form 62.1
flowers appear on the e. 62.88
it would be hell on e. 499.37
I will move the e. 16.1
lards the lean e. as he walks 498.78
meek shall inherit the e. 62.51
more things in heaven and e. 498.52

Rolled round in e.'s diurnal course 595.16
salt of the e. 62.120
scum of the e. 573.1
they shall inherit the e. 62.118
This e. of majesty 498.235
thou bleeding piece of e. 498.113
Ease done with so much e. 205.2
Joys in another's loss of e. 67.10
Prodigal of e. 205.4
East E. is E., and West is West 341.1
Easy way down to Hell is e. 560.3
Eat Don't e. too many almonds 145.5
e. to live 402.1
good men e. and drink that they may live 515.4
great ones e. up the little ones 498.231
I e. merely to put food out of my mind 507.1
Let them e. cake 380.1
Let us e. and drink 62.97
Nothing to e. but food 339.1
So I did sit and e. 290.7
Eaten e. me out of house and home 498.86
Eater Out of the e. came forth meat 62.32
Eating Appetite comes with e. 460.1
sign something is e. us 190.2
Ecclesiastic E. tyranny's the worst 184.3
Eclipse Irrecoverably dark, total e. 401.30
Economists If all e. were laid end to end 499.82
Eczema style...often hides e. 106.1
Eden This other E., demi-paradise 498.235
Through E. took their solitary way 401.27
Editorial nineteenth century...age of the e. chair 377.1
Education E. has for its object the formation of character 518.6
Soap and e. are not as sudden as a massacre, but they are more deadly 553.2
'Tis e. forms the common mind 452.20
Travel...is a part of e. 30.20
Efficiency e. and inefficiency 499.28
Effort Golf...a form of moral e. 353.5
Egg hand that lays the golden e. 263.4
Egotist E., a person...more interested in himself 63.4
Egypt I am dying, E., dying 498.14
We are not at war with E. 208.2
Eighteen I knew almost as much at e. as I do now 323.16
Element One God, one law, one e. 539.14
Elementary 'E.,' said he 201.5
Elements I tax not you, you e., with unkindness 498.138
something that was before the e. 82.8
Elephant I shot an e. in my pajamas 385.2
Elms moan of doves in immemorial e. 539.24
Else Lord High Everything E. 257.7
Embalmer soft e. of the still midnight 332.30
Embarras e. des richesses 11.1
Embody I, my lords, e. the Law 257.3
Embrace none, I think, do there e. 384.3
Emily E., I love you 385.17
Emotion degree of my aesthetic e. 54.2
e. recollected in tranquillity 595.25
Sorrow is tranquillity...in e. 433.5
Emperor e. of ice-cream 528.1
Emperors e. can't do it all by themselves 74.4
Empire E. is a Commonwealth 477.1
Empires day of E. has come. 117.2
Employee E.... Rise to his Level of Incompetence 441.1
Enchantment lends e. to the view 104.2
Encourage to e. the others 561.2
End all economists were laid e. to e. 499.82
beginning of the e. 536.1
Big-e.ians and small-e.ians 535.4
e. of the beginning 133.20
e. to the beginnings of all wars 475.5
he shall e. in doubts 30.1
I was with him to the e. 385.6
our minutes hasten to their e. 498.293
world without e. 149.3

young ladies...were laid e. to e. 433.7
Ending beginning and the e. 62.212
Ends divinity that shapes our e. 498.74
Endurable 'Twill make a thing e. 595.8
Endure Men must e. their going 498.151
Youth's a stuff will not e. 498.270
Endured Human life...is to be e. 323.9
Endures man is in love he e. more 419.1
Enemies e. of Freedom 314.2
Love your e. 62.123
Enemy best is the e. of the good 561.4
If thine e. be hungry 62.75
No e. but winter 498.21
no more sombre e. of good art 153.7
Energy E. is Eternal Delight 67.20
Enfants *Allons, e., de la patrie* 480.1
Les e. terribles 250.1
Engineers Artists are not e. of the soul 335.5
England Be E. what she will 131.1
E. expects every man will do his duty 415.1
E. is a nation of shopkeepers 413.2
E. is a paradise for women 94.3
E. is the mother of parliaments 75.2
E. is the paradise of women 233.1
E.'s green and pleasant land 67.7
E.'s pleasant pastures 67.6
E., with all thy faults 165.4
in E. people have good table manners 395.1
Law of E. is a very strange 178.1
Oh, to be in E. 83.6
roast beef of E. 225.3
Stately Homes of E. 163.2
suspended in favour of E. 499.25
that is forever E. 78.3
this realm, this E. 498.235
We dont bother much about dress and manners in E. 499.73
English E. as she is Spoke 552.1
E. (it must be owned) are rather a foul-mouthed nation 281.2
our E. nation, if they have a good thing...make it too common 498.84
our E. tongue a gallimaufry or hodgepodge 519.5
typically E. characteristic 3.1
Englishman E. does not travel to see Englishmen 527.1
E....is afraid to feel 237.2
E....queue of one 395.2
E. thinks he is moral 499.40
He was born an E. 52.1
impossible for an E. to open his mouth 499.66
never find an E. among the underdogs 569.18
No E. is ever fairly beaten 499.70
tale...which would have stirred...E. 492.2
to behold the E. at his best 227.1
You may be the most liberal Liberal E. 351.1
you will never find an E. in the wrong 499.59
Englishmen Englishman does not travel to see E. 527.1
Mad dogs and E. 163.9
nothing so bad...you will not find E. doing it 499.59
When two E. meet 323.6
Enjoy I don't have to go out and e. it 511.10
Enjoyed much is to be endured and little to be e. 323.9
Enough It comes soon e. 212.1
patriotism is not e. 115.1
Enslaves Reason e. all 499.54
Enthusiasm Nothing great was ever achieved without e. 218.2
Enthusiasts so few e. can be trusted 36.1
Entrances their exits and their e. 498.23
Entuned E. in hir nose 127.4
Epigram it purrs like an e. 382.1
Epigrams long despotism tempered by e. 109.8
Epilogue good play needs no e. 498.33
Episode Love...but an e. in a man's 523.2
Epitaphs nice derangement of e. 502.6
Epitome all Mankind's E. 205.7
Equal All animals are e. 427.1
all men are created e. 320.1
Inferiors revolt...that they may be e. 17.3

So far is it from being true that men are naturally e. 323.18
some...are more e. than others 427.1
That all men are e. is a proposition 310.21
Equally I hate everyone e. 226.3
Equanimity e. bordering on indifference 257.21
Equivocator drink...e. with lechery 498.168
Eros Unarm E. 498.13
Err To e. is human 452.15
Erred We have e., and strayed from thy ways 149.1
Errors E., like Straws upon the surface 205.15
Escape Gluttony is an emotional e. 190.2
There is nothing to e. from 214.17
Esprit de corps English characteristic... 3.1
Essay e. on 'self-indulgence' 569.3
Estate e. o' th' world were now undone 498.178
fourth e. of the realm 375.2
État L'é. c'est moi 366.1
Etchings I'll bring the e. down 546.3
Eternal Hope springs e. in the human breast 452.17
Eternity Deserts of vast e. 384.2
E. in an hour 67.1
white radiance of E. 500.2
Ethiopian E. change his skin 62.102
Etiquette It isn't e. to cut any one 111.32
Eton won on the playing fields of E. 573.3
Eureka 16.2
Europe All the dogs of E. bark 25.4
glory of E. is extinguished 91.8
lamps are going out all over E. 272.1
part of the community of E. 258.3
United States of E. 133.24
Evacuations Wars are not won by e. 133.33
Eve St. Agnes' E.—Ah, bitter chill it was 332.5
Evening e. is spread out against the sky 214.7
Now came still E. on 401.23
Soup of the e. 111.12
Event one far-off divine e. 539.14
thinking too precisely on th' e. 498.70
Events E. which...never happened 314.1
Ever for e. hold his peace 149.14
I go on for e. 539.1
thing of beauty is a joy for e. 332.4
What, *never*? Hardly e. 257.15
Every E. day in e. way 161.1
God bless us, e. one 191.5
Everybody E. is always in favour of general economy 208.1
E. was up to something 163.1
Everyone e. against e. 298.1
I hate e. equally 226.3
Everything destroying nearly e. 129.5
E. 576.5
E. by starts 205.7
E. is funny 472.2
E.'s got a moral 111.9
sans e. 498.24
Evil belief in a supernatural source of e. 154.6
E., be thou my Good 401.22
e. that men do lives after them 498.116
Government...is...a necessary e. 431.2
I will fear no e. 62.48
love of money is the root of all e. 62.202
Men's e. manners live in brass 498.105
No man is justified in doing e. 476.3
one e., ignorance 515.2
overcome e. with good 62.182
Sufficient unto the day is the e. 62.129
we are the origin of all coming e. 327.3
Evils greatest of e.... is poverty 499.30
He...must expect new e. 30.24
Whenever I'm caught between two e. 576.7
Evolution e. in...ten thousand years 179.1
Exaggerated Reports of my death are greatly e. 553.7
Example E. is the school of mankind 91.11
Excel daring to e. 131.2
thou shalt not e. 62.8

Excellent everything that's e. 257.3
Exception I'll make an e. in your case 385.18
Excess e. is most exhilarating 14.2
Give me e. of it 498.266
In charity there is no e. 30.15
Nothing succeeds like e. 584.16
road of e. 67.21
Exciting He found it less e. 257.1
Excluded when you have e. the impossible 201.1
Excrement place of e. 601.4
Excuse bet he's just using that as an e. 385.6
Executioner I am mine own E. 199.11
Executioners victims who respect their e. 489.1
Exercise e. is to the body 524.3
Exhausted e. what there is in business, politics, conviviality, and so on 582.7
Exist Facts do not cease to e. 310.23
I e. by what I think 489.3
If God did not e. 561.5
liberty cannot long e. 91.15
Existence Let us contemplate e. 191.15
to do something is to create e. 489.4
woman's whole e. 98.12
Exit E., pursued by a bear 498.282
Exits They have their e. and their entrances 498.23
Expands Work e. to fill the time 434.1
Expect I e. a judgment 191.3
Expediency evil on the ground of e. 476.3
principle...sacrificed to e. 388.6
Expenditure annual e. nineteen nineteen 191.8
in favour of particular e. 208.1
Expense who Would be at the e. of two 140.3
Experience e. of women which extends 201.8
my e. of life has been drawn from life itself 51.8
Experiment existence remains...e. 488.4
Express'd but ne'er so well e. 452.12
Expression crime is due to...desire for...e. 569.11
Exterminate E. all brutes 154.1
Extinguished glory of Europe is e. 91.8
Nature is...seldom e. 30.31
Extraordinary Little minds are interested in the e. 306.3
Exuberance E. is Beauty 67.25
Eye apple of his e. 62.29
Beauty is...in the e. of the beholder 562.1
e. for an e. 62.121
E. for e. 62.23
flash upon that inward e. 595.3
his keener e. The axe's edge did try 384.7
less in this than meets the e. 38.1
love comes in at the e. 601.5
such beauty as a woman's e. 498.155
thine e. offend thee, pluck it 62.139
Eyeless E. in Gaza 401.29
Eyelids tir'd e. upon tir'd eyes 539.18
When she raises her e. 145.2
Eyes Drink to me only with thine e. 325.1
fortune and men's e. 498.290
lift up mine e. unto the hills 62.60
Love looks not with the e. 498.202
pearls that were his e. 498.254
sight of you is good for sore e. 535.8
whites of their e. 456.1
Your e. shine like the pants 385.4

F

Fabric baseless f. of this vision 498.258
Face f. that launch'd a thousand ships 381.2
False f. must hide 498.166
garden in her f. 105.1
I just can't think of your f. 520.3
painting a f. and not washing 245.1
then f. to f. 62.187
To get very red in the f. 59.1
Faces All, all are gone, the old familiar f. 348.6
among so many million of f. 82.3
grind the f. of the poor 62.93

Factor importance of the human f. 125.2
Facts F. alone are wanted in life 191.13
F. do not cease to exist 310.23
his imagination for his f. 502.10
Failed Light that F. 341.11
Fair Brave deserves the F. 205.12
Earth has not anything...more f. 595.11
F. stood the wind for France 203.1
man right f. 498.302
name of Vanity F. 90.4
So foul and f. a day 498.158
Faire Laissez f. 459.1
Fairer I can't say no f. than that 191.11
Fairies beginning of f. 40.1
I don't believe in f. 40.2
Faith f., hope, charity 62.188
F. is the substance of things hoped for 62.204
f. unfaithful kept him falsely true 539.6
F. without works is dead 62.206
Reason itself is a matter of f. 129.19
'Tis not the dying for a f. 541.3
Faithful Be thou f. unto death 62.213
I have been f. to thee 200.1
Fall harder they f. 230.1
Pride goeth...before a f. 62.71
Fallen How are the mighty f. 62.35
Ye are f. from grace 62.194
y-f. out of heigh degree 127.14
False be not f. to others 30.23
F. face must hide what the f. heart 498.166
history must be f. 563.3
Thou canst not then be f. 498.48
Words may be f. 497.1
Falsehood Let her and F. grapple 401.37
Falstaff F. sweats to death 498.78
Fame F. is like a river 30.40
F. is the spur 401.11
Familiar f. objects be as if they were not f. 500.15
old f. faces 348.6
Familiarity F. breeds contempt—and children 553.4
Families All happy f. resemble one another 547.1
best-regulated f. 191.10
There are only two f. in the world 116.3
Famine They that die by f. 288.1
Famous I awoke...found myself f. 98.29
Martyrdom...way...a man can become f. 499.77
Fanatic f....over-compensates a...doubt 310.28
Fanatics F. have their dreams 332.8
when f. are on top there is no limit to oppression 392.4
Fancy In the Spring a young man's f. 539.17
little of what you f. does you good 362.1
Fantastic light f. toe 401.6
Far F. from the madding crowd 268.10
Farce f. is over 460.2
F. is the essential theatre 166.1
wine was a f. 455.2
Farewell F., a long f., to all my greatness 498.103
F.! thou art too dear for my possessing 498.295
hail and f. 114.3
Farmyard f. world of sex 266.2
Fascism F. is a religion 411.1
Fashion as good be out of f. 134.1
faithful to thee, Cynara! in my f. 200.1
Nothing else holds f. 498.265
Fast none so f. as stroke 142.1
they stumble that run f. 498.246
U.S. has to move very f. 335.3
Faster world would go round a deal f. 111.5
Fat butter will only make us f. 260.1
f. of the land 62.7
Let me have men about me that are f. 498.107
Fatal caution in love is...f. 485.3
Moderation is a f. thing 584.16
sincerity is...f. 584.21
Fate I am the master of my f. 285.2
when F. summons 205.13
Father brood of Folly without f. 401.2
Child is f. of the Man 595.13
F., I cannot tell a lie 567.2
f. is a very hospitable man 499.5
Full fathom five thy f. lies 498.254
God is...an exalted f. 242.4
Honour thy f. and mother 62.17

wise f. that knows his own child 498.190
wise son maketh a glad f. 62.67
Fatherhood Mirrors and f. are abominable 69.2
Fathers land of my f. 543.5
our f. that begat us 62.113
Fathom Full f. five thy father lies 498.254
Fault only one f.. It was…lousy 546.6
Faultless Whoever thinks a f. piece to see 452.11
Faults England, with all thy f. 165.4
f., do not fear to abandon them 150.6
If we had no f. of our own 471.9
When you have f. 150.6
Favour truths being in and out of f. 243.1
Fear concessions of f. 91.1
F. God 62.86
F. no more the heat o' th' sun 498.38
f. of suffering injustice 471.14
f. of the Lord is the beginning 62.58
freedom from f. 475.3
have…many things to f. 30.21
I do f. thy nature 498.162
I will f. no evil 62.48
love casteth out f. 62.211
no f. in love 62.211
one universal passion: f. 499.61
those with f. of life become publishers 153.4
Fearful thy f. symmetry 67.12
Fears enough for fifty hopes and f. 83.3
Feast Chief nourisher in life's f. 498.167
life is not…af. 488.5
Feathers not only fine f. 6.3
Fed bite the hand that f. them 91.12
he on honey-dew hath f. 144.21
hungry sheep look up and are not f. 401.12
Feel Englishman…is afraid to f. 237.2
f. what wretches f. 498.141
tragedy to those who f. 564.2
what I f. really bad about 240.1
Feeling man is as old as he's f. 146.1
Feelings Opinion is…determined by the f. 518.8
spontaneous overflow of powerful f. 595.25
Feels as old as the woman he f. 385.22
Feet both f. firmly planted in the air 475.2
spread my dreams under your f. 601.9
those f. in ancient time 67.6
Feigning Most friendship is f. 498.26
truest poetry is the most f. 498.30
Felicity Absent thee from f. awhile 498.75
more f. on the far side of baldness 511.8
Fell Doctor F. 79.1
From morn to noon he f. 401.19
men f. out 96.1
where the dead leaf f. 332.10
Fellow f. of infinite jest 498.73
Fellowship right hands of f. 62.193
Female f. of the species is more deadly 341.4
What f. heart can gold despise 268.1
Festina *F. lente* 532.1
Fettered so f. fast we are 83.1
Few appointment by the corrupt f. 499.49
err as grossly as the F. 205.10
f. are chosen 62.140
f. are qualified to shine 535.17
f. who can grow old with a good grace 524.2
owed by so many to so f. 133.15
Fickle Woman is always f. 560.2
Fickleness f. of the women I love 499.63
Fiction an improbable f. 498.275
one form of continuous f. 61.4
Poetry is a comforting piece of f. 392.5
Poetry is the supreme f. 528.2
Stranger than f. 98.21
Fiddle When I play on my f. in Dooney 601.7
Field flower of the f. 62.56
some corner of a foreign f. 78.3
Fields 'a babbl'd of green f. 498.94
Fiend f. hid in a cloud 67.11
frightful f. Doth close behind him tread 144.12
Ingratitude, thou marble-hearted f. 498.132
Fight I dare not f. 498.92
I will not cease from mental f. 67.7

too proud to f. 591.2
Ulster will f. 132.2
we shall f. on the beaches 133.12
when the f. begins within 83.4
You cannot f. against the future 258.1
Fighting f. a liar in the quad 520.1
not conquering but f. 160.1
What are we f. for 496.3
Figures prove anything by f. 109.1
Fille de chambre I caught hold of the f.'s— 527.3
Filthy f. lucre 62.199
Financial in danger of f. disaster 391.1
Find to f., and not to yield 539.27
Fine f. feathers that make f. birds 6.3
Finer every baby...is a f. one 191.18
Finest their f. hour 133.13
Finger more goodness in her little f. 535.13
Moving F. writes 228.8
Fingers ill cook that cannot lick his own f. 498.250
Fire bound Upon a wheel of f. 498.150
two irons in the f. 45.2
what wind is to f. 95.1
Firmament f. sheweth his handywork 62.45
First good die f. 595.1
If at f. you don't succeed 294.1
which came f., the Greeks or the Romans 195.12
Fish What Cat's averse to f. 268.1
Fishes f. live in the sea 498.231
Fish knives Phone for the f. Norman 60.1
Fit It is not f. that you should sit here 172.3
let the punishment f. the crime 257.11
only the F. survive 496.2
Fittest Survival of the F. 180.3
Survival of the f. 518.4
Five child of f. would understand this 385.5
practise f. things 150.7
Five pound note gentlemen said to the f. 191.29
get a f. as...a light for a cigarette 317.3
Flag keep the Red F. flying here 152.1
Flash f. upon that inward eye 595.3
Flat Very f., Norfolk 163.4
Flatterers Self-love...greatest of all f. 471.6
Flattering think him worth f. 499.27
Flatters What really f. a man 499.27
Flattery f.'s the food of fools 535.2
Imitation is the sincerest of f. 148.3
more pernicious than the love of f. 524.1
What is principle against the f. 502.9
woman...to be gained by...f. 128.10
Flea f. Hath smaller fleas that on him prey 535.7
performing f. 423.2
Fleas flea hath smaller f. that on him prey 535.7
Great f. have little f. upon their backs 405.1
Flee f. from the wrath to come 62.116
Flesh All f. is as grass 62.207
All f. is grass 62.98
f. is weak 62.145
f. to feel the chain 77.3
going the way of all f. 572.2
I have more f. than another man 498.79
I wants to make your f. creep 191.25
thorn in the f. 62.192
way of all f. 151.9
way of all f. 497.2
Word was made f. 62.163
world, the f., and the devil 149.7
Fleshly F. School of Poetry 84.1
Flies As f. to wanton boys 498.144
certain, that Life f. 228.4
Fling I'll have a f. 45.7
Float rather be an opportunist and f. 35.1
Flood Which, taken at the f. 498.122
Flower f. of the field 62.56
F. that once has blown 228.4
many a f. is born to blush unseen 268.8
meanest f. that blows 595.6
Flowers f. appear on the earth 62.88
f. that bloom in the spring 257.12
Letting a hundred f. blossom 379.2
Say it with f. 425.1
Flowing f. with milk and honey 62.10
Flung he f. himself from the room 353.4

Fly small gilded f. Does lecher 498.146
Flying time is f. 560.5
Foam f. Of perilous seas 332.27
Foe Heat not a furnace for your f. 498.101
He...who never made a f. 539.7
make one worthy man my f. 452.4
Foeman When the f. bares his steel 257.18
Foes You shall judge of a man by his f. 154.4
Fog London particular...a f. 191.2
Follies lovers cannot see the pretty f. 498.191
Folly brood of F. without father 401.2
shielding men from the effects of f. 518.3
slightest f. That ever love did make thee run into 498.20
'Tis f. to be wise 268.4
When lovely woman stoops to f. 262.10
Fond f. of resisting temptation 48.1
Fonder Absence makes the heart grow f. 43.1
Food eat...to put f. out of my mind 507.1
f. a tragedy 455.2
Nothing to eat but f. 339.1
On the Continent...good f. 395.1
Fool Busy old f., unruly Sun 199.10
f. at forty is a f. indeed 602.2
f. hath said in his heart 62.44
f. his whole life long 372.1
f. sees not the same tree 67.23
f.... the people 360.8
greatest f. may ask more 148.4
He who holds hopes...is a f. 106.9
more of the f. than of the wise 30.13
needs a very clever woman to manage a f. 341.10
old man who will not laugh is a f. 488.2
strumpet's f. 498.4
what f. it was that first invented kissing 535.14
Wise Man or a F. 67.5
wisest f. in Christendom 286.2
Foolish He never said a f. thing 473.1
Fools Christianity...says they are all f. 129.13
fill the word with f. 518.3
flattery's the food of f. 535.2
F. are in a terrible, overwhelming majority 313.1
For f. rush in 452.16
Pride the...vice of f. 452.9
things people make f. of themselves about 499.12
this great stage of f. 498.149
To suckle f. and chronicle 498.221
what f. these mortals be 498.205
ye suffer f. gladly 62.191
Foot noiseless f. of Time 498.3
Foppery excellent f. of the world 498.131
Forbearance f. ceases to be a virtue 91.7
Forbidden he wanted it only because it was f. 553.5
Force f. alone is but temporary 91.2
F. is not a remedy 75.3
F. that through the green fuse 543.2
Other nations use 'f.' 569.23
Ford time of our F. 310.5
Forefathers Think of your f. 2.1
Foreign pronounce f. names as he chooses 133.41
Forests f. of the night 67.12
Forever diamond...bracelet lasts f. 365.3
That is f. England 78.3
Forget Fade far away, dissolve, and...f. 332.25
I f. what I was taught 579.2
I never f. a face, but I'll make an exception 385.18
Old men f. 498.99
three things I always f. 534.1
Forgetting birth is but a sleep and a f. 595.5
Forgive Father, f. them 62.160
Men will f. a man 133.2
to f., divine 452.15
Forgot I have f. my part 498.35
old acquaintance be f. 93.2
Forgotten They have...f. nothing 536.2
Forlorn faery lands f. 332.27

Form F. remains 595.15
significant f. 54.1
Formation Education...f. of character 518.6
Formidable Examinations are f. 148.4
Forms from outward f. to win 144.18
Fornicated f. and read the papers 106.2
Fornication F.: but that was in another country 381.6
Forsake F. not an old friend 62.111
Fortress f. built by Nature 498.235
Fortunate he is at best f. 516.1
Fortune deficiences of f. 262.9
f. and men's eyes 498.290
F. favours the brave 540.1
F.'s sharp adversitee 127.17
greater virtues to sustain good f. 471.8
hostages to f. 30.10
slings and arrows of outrageous f. 498.61
Forty Every man over f. is a scoundrel 499.56
fool at f. is a fool 602.2
Forty-three She may very well pass for f. 257.20
Foster-child f. of silence and slow time 332.15
Fou I wasna f. 93.5
Fought better to have f. and lost 140.5
Foul Murder most f. 498.51
So f. and fair a day 498.158
Foul-mouthed English...are rather a f. nation 281.2
Found he f. it brick 100.1
I have f. it 16.2
When f., make a note of 191.12
Four at the age of f.... we're all Generals 555.1
f. essential human freedoms 475.3
Four-year-old brain of a f. boy 385.10
Fox-hunting athletics...inferior forms of f. 569.8
Frailty F., thy name is woman 498.43
more flesh...more f. 498.79
Frame all the Human F. requires 55.3
France Fair stood the wind for F. 203.1
F. was a long despotism 109.8
Frauds pious f. of friendship 225.1
Free all men everywhere could be f. 360.5
Greece might still be f. 98.16
Man was born f. 481.1
Mother of the F. 57.1
safer to be in chains than to be f. 330.1
So f. we seem 83.1
Thou art f. 20.12
truth that makes men f. 7.1
Who would be f. 98.6
Freedom enemies of F. 314.2
F. is Slavery 427.3
F., what liberties are taken in thy name 253.1
In solitude alone can he know f. 403.2
least regard for human f. 518.7
Necessity is the plea for every infringement of human f. 447.1
new birth of f. 360.6
None can love f. heartily, but good men 401.38
Those who deny f. to others 360.3
Freedoms four essential human f. 475.3
Freemasonry kind of bitter f. 51.5
French I speak F. to men 124.1
Frenzy poet's eye, in a fine f. rolling 498.207
Fresh as f. as paint 509.1
f. as is the month of May 127.3
Fret weariness, the fever, and the f. 332.25
Freudian F., it is a very low, Central European sort of humour 267.3
Friend Forsake not an old f. 62.111
F.... masterpiece of Nature 218.3
f. should bear his f.'s infirmities 498.121
f. who loved perfection 511.11
He makes no f. 539.7
save me, from the candid f. 107.2
would be the perfect f. 511.11
Friends Animals are such agreeable f. 213.2
F., Romans, countrymen 498.116
Have no f. not equal 150.5
honour, love, obedience, troops of f. 498.175
How to Win F. 110.1
I don't trust him. We're f. 74.3

In the misfortunes of our best f. 471.5
man lay down his life for his f. 62.171
Once more unto the breach, dear f. 498.95
Wealth maketh many f. 62.72
without three good f. 498.27
Friendship f. hardly ever does 27.3
F. is constant in all other things 498.209
F. is unnecessary 358.1
man, Sir, should keep his f. in constant repair 323.12
matrimony…f. recognised by the police 529.1
Most f. is feigning 498.26
pious frauds of f. 225.1
Frittered life is f. away by detail 545.5
Front door polished up the handle of the big f. 257.16
Fruit f. Of that forbidden tree 401.14
Ignorance is like a…f. 584.7
Fruitfulness Season of…mellow f. 332.1
Frustrate In three sips…Arian f. 83.15
Full one of the professions which are f. 545.2
Reading maketh a f. man 30.39
Fun Work is much more f. than f. 163.16
Function F. never dies 595.15
f. of the critic 54.2
Funny Everything is f. 472.2
F. peculiar, or f. ha-ha 280.1
F. without being vulgar 257.22
Fur Oh my f. and whiskers 111.3
Furious f. that she had not been asked 569.15
Furnace Heat not a f. for your foe 498.101
Furniture No f. so charming as books 512.5
Fury full of sound and f. 498.177
F. of a Patient Man 205.11
Fuse force that through the green f. 543.2
Fuss f. about sleeping together 569.16
Future f. is…black 34.3
F., that period of time in which 63.5
if you would divine the f. 150.2
I never think of the f. 212.1
You cannot fight against the f. 258.1
Futurity let f. shift for itself 513.2

G

Gain g. the whole world 62.148
never broke the Sabbath, but for g. 205.8
Gained learning hath g. most 245.4
Gaiters gas and g. 191.19
Galatians great text in G. 83.16
Gall wormwood and the g. 62.103
Gallantry What men call g. 98.11
Gallery g. in which the reporters sit 375.2
Gallimaufry English…g.…of all other speeches 519.5
Galloped I g., Dirck g. 83.8
Game I don't like this g. 399.2
It is a silly g. 245.2
It's more than a g.. It's an institution 307.2
play up! and play the g.! 416.2
win this g. and thrash the Spaniards 202.2
woman is his g. 539.23
Gamesmanship G. or The Art of Winning Games 453.1
Gangsters great nations have always acted like g. 345.1
Garbo one sees in G. sober 554.3
Garden Come into the g., Maud 539.19
cultivate our g. 561.3
g. is a lovesome thing 80.1
God Almighty first planted a g. 30.36
God the first g. made 164.1
There is a g. in her face 105.1
Gardens closing time in the g. of the West 153.1
Garland wither'd is the g. of the war 498.15
Garment City now doth, like a g., wear 595.11
Garrick *G.* On the stage he was natural 262.3
Gas g. and gaiters 191.19

G. smells awful 433.4
Gate aged... man a-sitting on a g. 111.29
I am here at the g. alone 539.19
Gathered two or three are g. together 149.5
Gaul G. is divided into three 101.1
Gave Lord g. 62.38
Gaza Eyeless in G. 401.29
General caviare to the g. 498.58
French army led by an Italian g. 499.62
General Motors what was... good for G. 588.1
Generals at the age of four... we're we're all G. 555.1
Russia has two g. 418.1
wish he would bite... my g. 254.1
Generation O g. of vipers 62.116
Generations No hungry g. tread thee down 332.27
Genius G.... capacity of taking trouble 109.5
G. does what it must 394.1
G. is one per cent inspiration 209.1
nothing to declare except my g. 584.26
What a g. I had when I wrote that book 535.19
Gent what a man is to a g. 35.2
Gentil verray parfit g. knight 127.2
Gentle Do not go g. into that good night 543.1
g. mind by g. deeds is known 519.3
Gentleman g.... I live by robbing the poor 499.42
g.... is one who never inflicts pain 417.1
g. said to the five pound note 191.29
man who is always talking about being a g. 533.1
Who was then the g. 37.1
Gentlemanly secondly, g. conduct 21.1
Gentlemen G.... remember blondes 365.1
religion for g. 123.2
Genuineness G. only thrives in the dark 310.24
Geographical India is a g. term 133.8
Geography G. is about Maps 59.2
Georgian sweet laxative of G. strains 103.1
German I speak G. to my horse 124.1
Germans Don't let's be beastly to the G. 163.13
Get up I thought it was a pity to g. 388.7
Ghosts g. from an enchanter fleeing 500.7
Giant owner whereof was G. Despair 90.5
Giants war of the g. is over 133.37
Giant's-Causeway Is not the G. worth seeing? 323.33
Gift giving is worth more than the g. 158.3
Gild To g. refined gold 498.128
Girl g. with brains 365.2
Home is the g.'s prison 499.55
park, a policeman and a pretty g. 121.2
Poor Little Rich G. 163.12
Girls g. who wear glasses 433.2
Give g. me liberty or g. me death 289.1
more blessed to g. than to receive 62.177
Giving g. is worth more than the gift 158.3
Glade live alone in the bee-loud g. 601.10
Gladstone inebriated with... own verbosity 195.6
Glass impression of having been grown under g. 592.5
Life, like a dome of many-coloured g. 500.2
through a g., darkly 62.187
Glasses girls who wear g. 433.2
Glimpses g. that would make me less forlorn 595.10
Glisters Nor all that g. gold 268.2
Globe great g. itself 498.258
Gloire *Le jour de g. est arrivé* 480.1
gloria *Sic transit g. mundi* 333.2
Glorious Happy and g. 108.1
Glory G. be to God for dappled things 302.4
g. of Europe is extinguished for ever 91.8
Land of Hope and G. 57.1
paths of g. lead but to the grave 268.7
trailing clouds of g. 595.5

Gluttony G. is an emotional escape 190.2
Go as cooks g. she went 486.4
In the name of God, g. 13.1
Let my people g. 62.12
Let's g. 47.4
Let us g. then, you and I 214.7
like Wind I g. 228.5
to die and g. we know not where 498.184
Goal g. stands up 304.4
Goats divideth his sheep from the g. 62.143
God an atheist still, thank G. 89.1
Are G. and Nature then at strife 539.12
better to have no opinion of G. 30.19
but for the grace of G. goes 73.1
charged with the grandeur of G. 302.3
concept of G. has any validity 34.1
dear G. who loveth us 144.15
Doubtless G. could have made a better berry 565.2
effect whose cause is G. 165.7
either a wild beast or a g. 30.26
Fear G. 62.86
Fear G. 62.208
'G. bless us every one!' 191.5
G. disposes 333.1
G.... first planted a garden 30.36
G. is beginning to resemble... a cosmic Cheshire cat 311.2
G. is love 62.210
G. is nothing more than an exalted father 242.4
G. is not mocked 62.196
G. is our refuge and strength 62.52
G. made the country 165.3
G.... need not exist... to save us 190.5
G. save our gracious King 108.1
G. should go before such villains 498.216
G.'s in His heaven 83.13
G. so loved the world 62.166
G. the first garden made 164.1
G. will take care of that 499.22
Had I but serv'd my G. with half the zeal I serv'd my King 498.104
Had I but served G. as diligently 593.1
heavens declare the glory of G. 62.45
highest praise of G. consists in the denial of Him 458.5
If G. did not exist 561.5
In the beginning G. created 62.1
In the name of G., go! 13.1
justify the ways of G. to men 401.15
laws of G. will be suspended in favour of England 499.25
lay wrestling with my G.! my G. 302.2
lovesome thing, God wot 80.1
man whose g. is in the skies 499.47
Many people believe that they are attracted by G. 314.4
mighty G. 62.95
nature is the art of G. 82.2
One G., one law, one element 539.14
One on G.'s side is a majority 444.1
poems... for the love of Man and in praise of G. 543.4
presume not G. to scan 452.18
proof that G. is a bore 392.3
prose for G. 266.3
Providence will... end... acts of G. 190.6
serve G. and mammon 62.127
There is no G. 62.44
they shall see G. 62.119
Thou shalt have one G. only 140.3
unto G. the things that are G.'s 62.141
we owe G. a death 498.90
What... G. hath joined 62.149
What G. hath joined together 499.22
whom G. wishes to destroy 221.1
Woman was G.'s second mistake 419.2
Goddamm Lhude sing G. 454.1
Godot waiting for G. 47.4
Gods g. adultery 98.11
g. help them 6.2
I am nearest to the g. 515.1
Kings are earth's g. 498.230
leave the rest to the G. 158.2
Thou shalt have no other g. 62.13
Whom the g. wish to destroy 153.6
Going Men must endure Their g. hence 498.151
not worth g. to see 323.33

Stand not upon the order of your g. 498.171
Gold For g. in phisik is a cordial 127.9
gild refined g. 498.128
Good morning to the day: and next my g. 325.5
led by the nose with g. 498.286
Nor all that glisters g. 268.2
travell'd in the realms of g. 332.28
What female heart can g. despise 268.1
Golden G. Road to Samarkand 231.1
G. slumbers kiss your eyes 185.1
there are no g. rules 499.48
Golf G.... a form of moral effort 353.5
Gone g. with the wind 200.2
here today and g. tomorrow 53.2
sun has g. in 511.10
Gongs women should be struck... like g. 163.5
Good All g. writing 229.5
As for doing g. 545.2
best is the enemy of the g. 561.4
Every man loves what he is g. at 497.3
Evil, be thou my G. 401.22
General G. is the plea of the scoundrel 67.4
g. are always the merry 601.8
G., but not religious-g. 277.4
g. die early 184.1
g. die first 595.1
g. for sore eyes 535.8
g. is oft interred with their bones 498.116
g. is the beautiful 448.1
g. must associate 91.13
g. novel tells us the truth 129.14
g. of the people 135.2
greatest g. 135.3
He who would do g. to another 67.4
If to do were as easy as to know what were g. 498.188
it cannot come to g. 498.44
little of what you fancy does you g. 362.1
Men have never been g. 41.1
never was a g. war 239.4
nothing g. to be had in the country 281.8
only g. Indian is... dead 501.1
only one g., knowledge 515.2
our people have never had it so g. 378.1
overcome evil with g. 62.182
Roman Conquest... a G. Thing 495.2
those who go about doing g. 169.1
What's the g. of a home? 273.1
what was g. for the country was g. for General Motors 588.1
You shouldn't say it is not g. 577.4
Goodbye G. to All That 267.1
Goodness G. had nothing whatever to do with it 576.3
more g. in her little finger 535.13
Goodnight second best's a gay g. 601.11
Then it will be g. 500.4
Gormed I'm G. 191.11
Got Tell him I've g. one 385.8
Which in our case we have not g. 465.2
Govern Labour is not fit to g. 133.6
No man is good enough to g. another man 360.1
Governesses nation of g. 499.79
Government G.... is but a necessary evil 431.2
g.... is founded on compromise 91.4
g. of the people, by the people 360.6
one form of G. rather than another 323.20
people's g. 571.2
worst g. is the most moral 392.4
Gower moral G. 127.18
Grace but for the g. of God, goes 73.1
fallen from g. 62.194
few who can grow old with a good g. 524.2
Grades We class schools... into four g. 569.2
Gradually Boys do not grow up g. 153.9
Gradualness inevitability of g. 570.1
Grammar I dont want to talk g. 499.67
Grandeur g. of God 302.3
Grape Beulah, peel me a g. 576.4
Grapeshot whiff of g. 109.9
Grasp man's reach should exceed his g. 83.2
Grass All flesh is as g. 62.207
All flesh is g. 62.98

his days are as g. 62.56
Gratifying passions she has no intention of g. 499.81
Grave country... a kind of healthy g. 512.9
g.'s a fine and private place 384.3
g. yawns for him 548.3
jealousy is cruel as the g. 62.89
O g., where is thy victory 62.189
paths of glory lead but to the g. 268.7
Graven any g. image 62.14
Great All things both g. and small 144.15
Everything g.... is done by neurotics 458.7
fate of the g. wen 141.2
g. men have not... been g. scholars 300.3
g. ones eat up the little ones 498.231
Some are born g. 498.273
To be g. is to be misunderstood 218.10
Great Australian Novel write the G. 579.4
Greater g. the power 91.16
Thy necessity is g. than mine 506.3
Greatest g. good 135.3
g. happiness of the g. number 58.1
Greatness long farewell to all my g. 498.103
some achieve g. 498.273
some have g. thrust upon 'em 498.273
Greece G. might still be free 98.16
isles of G. 98.15
Greek it was G. to me 498.108
Greeks G. Had a Word 8.1
uncertainty: a state unknown to the G. 69.1
which came first, the G. or the Romans 195.12
Green g. thought in a g. shade 384.5
G. grow the rashes O 93.8
I was g. in judgment 498.7
tree of life is g. 261.1
Green Chartreuse religious system that produced G. 486.5
Green-ey'd jealousy... g. monster 498.224
Greenwood Under the g. tree 498.21
Grey theory is all g. 261.1
Grief in much wisdom is much g. 62.81
Should be past g. 498.281
Grievances redress of the g. of the vanquished 133.30
Grill be careful not to look like a mixed g. 163.7
Grind g. the faces of the poor 62.93
Groan men sit and hear each other g. 332.25
Groans How alike... g. of love to... dying 370.1
Groucho No, G. is not my real name 385.20
Grow Green g. the rashes O 93.8
They shall g. not old 64.1
Grown whiskers... g. under glass 592.5
Grow out some of us never g. 555.1
Grub old ones, g. 499.4
Guarantee No one can g. success in war 133.32
Guard Who is to g. the guards? 329.1
Guards Up, G., and at 'em 573.2
Who is to guard the g. themselves? 329.1
Guerre ce n'est pas la g. 71.1
Guilt pens dwell on g. and misery 27.4
Guilty better that ten g. persons escape 65.3
g. of Noel Cowardice 190.3
Guinea round disc of fire somewhat like a g. 67.18
Gulf there is a great g. fixed 62.159
Gulphs whelm'd in deeper g. than he 165.1
Gunga Din better man than I am, G. 341.5
Gunpowder G., Printing, and the Protestant Religion 109.2
Guns G. aren't lawful 433.4
G. will make us powerful 260.1

H

Habit H. is a great deadener 47.6

honour peereth in the meanest h. 498.253
Habitation to airy nothing A local h. 498.207
Habits h. that carry them far apart 150.1
Hae Scots, wha h. 93.15
Haggards H. ride no more 526.2
Ha-ha funny h. 280.1
Hail h. and farewell 114.3
H. to thee, blithe Spirit 500.13
Hair part my h. behind 214.11
Hairs given me over in my gray h. 593.1
Half H. a league onward 539.2
h. a loaf is better than a whole 129.23
One h.... cannot understand... the other 27.1
Too civil by h. 502.8
Half-a-dozen six of one and h. of the other 383.2
Half-truths all truths are h. 580.1
Hampden Some village-H. 268.9
Hand bite the h. that fed them 91.12
His h. will be against every man 62.6
h., the head, and the heart 484.3
Let not thy left h. know 62.125
little onward lend they guiding h. 401.28
sweeten this little h. 498.174
This h. hath offended 168.1
what thy right h. doeth 62.125
Hand-bag A h. 584.9
Handful for a h. of silver he left us 83.9
Handle h. of the big front door 257.16
Hands Into thy h. I commend my spirit 62.50
Licence my roving h. 199.6
mischief... for idle h. to do 568.1
right h. of fellowship 62.193
Handsome with my mourning, very h. 438.3
Handywork firmament sheweth his h. 62.45
Hang I will not h. myself today 129.1
We must indeed all h. together 239.3
wretches h. that jury-men may dine 452.28
Hanged Men are not h. for stealing 274.1
when a man knows he is to be h. 323.31
Hanging h. a man who does not object 499.60
h. prevents a bad marriage 498.268
H. and wiving goes by destiny 498.192
Happened most of which had never h. 133.34
Happening h. to somebody else 472.2
Happens Nothing h. 47.2
Happiest I am h. when I am idle 566.3
Happiness greatest h. of the greatest number 58.1
greatest h. of the whole 448.2
h. fails, existence remains... experiment 488.4
H. in marriage 27.9
H. is a mystery like religion 129.11
H. is a wine of the rarest vintage 511.2
H. is like coke 310.17
In solitude what h. 401.25
life, liberty, and the pursuit of h. 320.1
lifetime of h. 499.37
recall a time of h. when in misery 176.2
result h. 191.8
something curiously boring about somebody else's h. 310.13
We have no more right to consume h. 499.11
Happy Call no man h. until he dies 516.1
duty of being h. 529.3
Few people can be h. unless they hate 485.5
h. families resemble each other 547.1
H. the Man 205.14
If you want to be h., be 547.2
I've had a h. life 281.9
I were but little h. 498.210
No society can be... h. 510.1
policeman's lot is not a h. one 257.19
to have been h. 68.1
We are never so h.... as we imagine 471.11
Harder h. they fall 230.1
Hardy Kiss me, H. 415.2
Hare First catch your h. 259.1
Harm No people do so much h. 169.1
Haste Men love in h. 98.19
Hasten H. slowly 532.1
Hatched chickens before they are h. 6.4

Hatchet did it with my little h. 567.2
Hate enough religion to make us h. 535.16
Few people can be happy unless they h. 485.5
I h. and love 114.2
I h. everyone equally 226.3
I love or I h. 445.1
worst sin... is not to h. 499.15
Hated I never h. a man enough 246.1
Hates Anybody who h. children and dogs 226.2
Hatred h. is... the longest pleasure 98.19
Haunted e'er beneath a waning moon was h. 144.20
Have My fathers can h. it 543.5
To h. and to hold 149.15
Haves H. and the have-nots 116.3
Havoc Cry 'H.' and let slip the dogs 498.114
Hay dance an antic h. 381.1
Head heap coals of fire upon his h. 62.75
If you can keep your h. 341.6
Lay your sleeping h. 25.6
My h. is bloody but unbowed 285.1
no matter which way the h. lies 462.3
Off with his h. 111.8
ought to have his h. examined 263.3
shorter by a h. 215.1
Uneasy lies the h. that wears a crown 498.88
you incessantly stand on your h. 111.4
Head-in-Air Little Johnny H. 299.2
Headmasters H. have powers 133.27
Headpiece h. filled with straw 214.5
Heads Dean and Canons lay their h. together 512.3
H. I win 171.1
Head-waiter diplomat... is nothing but a h. 555.2
Heal Physician, h. thyself 62.153
Healthy h. and wealthy and dead 546.1
Nobody is h. in London 27.2
Hear ear begins to h. 77.3
time will come when you will h. me 195.1
truth which men prefer not to h. 7.1
Heard I have already h. it 468.1
You ain't h. nothin' yet 324.1
Heart Absence makes the h. grow fonder 43.1
Because my h. is pure 539.25
Blessed are the pure in h. 62.119
'Calais' lying in my h. 387.1
hand, the head, and the h. 484.3
h. and stomach of a King 215.2
h. has its reasons 435.1
hid in the h. of love 601.13
holiness of the h.'s affections 332.33
Hope deferred maketh the h. sick 62.69
I am sick at h. 498.39
intellect is always fooled by the h. 471.2
Irishman's h. is... his imagination 499.26
look in thy h. and write. 506.1
mighty h. is lying still 595.12
My h. aches 332.22
my h.'s abhorrence 83.14
My h.'s in the Highlands 93.13
Nature never did betray the h. 595.24
not to get your h.'s desire 499.45
Once a woman has given you her h. 556.1
rag-and-bone shop of the h. 601.2
Sighs... language of the h. 497.1
So the h. be right 462.3
strings... in the human h. 191.1
What comes from the h. 144.27
With rue my h. is laden 304.5
Hearth cricket on the h. 401.4
Hearts h. are dry as summer dust 595.1
Kind h. are more than coronets 539.15
One equal temper of heroic h. 539.27
Queen of H. 111.13
Heat fear no more the h. o' th' sun 498.38
Heaven all H. in a rage 67.2
All this and h. too 288.2
go to H. without being naturally qualified 499.43
H. in Hell's despair 67.9
H. in a wild flower 67.1
H. lies about us in our infancy 595.5
Hell I suffer seems a H. 401.21
make a H. of Hell, a Hell of H. 401.17
man is as H. made him 116.1

more things in h. and earth 498.52
new h. and a new earth 62.218
Parting is all we know of h. 192.2
steep and thorny way to h. 498.46
to be young was very H. 595.14
what's a h. for 83.2
Heavens h. declare the glory of God 62.45
Hedgehogs If you start throwing h. under me 344.2
Hell all we need of h. 192.2
Better to reign in H. 401.18
Heaven of H., a H. of Heaven 401.17
h. a fury like a woman 151.4
H. in Heaven's despite 67.10
H. is a city much like London— 500.11
H. is oneself 214.17
h. of horses 233.1
Italy...h. for women 94.3
it would be h. on earth 499.37
war is...all h. 503.1
way down to H. is easy 560.3
Which way I fly is H.; myself am H. 401.21
wishful thinking in H. 358.2
Help gods h. them that h. themselves 6.2
Since there's no h. 203.2
very present h. in trouble 62.52
Herd H. of such, Who think too little 205.6
Here h. today and gone tomorrow 53.2
Heresies new truths begin as h. 312.1
Hero Every h. becomes a bore 218.11
No man is a h. to his valet 159.1
to his very valet seem'd a h. 98.1
Herod It out-h.'s H. 498.65
Heroes fit country for h. to live in 364.1
Hero-worship H. is strongest 518.7
Hewers H. of wood 62.30
Hidden Nature is often h. 30.31
Hide Robes and furr'd gowns h. all 498.147
talent which is death to h. 401.32
High civil fury first grew h. 96.1
Highlands My heart's in the H. 93.13
Hill h. will not come to Mahomet 30.14
they call you...from the h. 20.8
Hills lift up mine eyes unto the h. 62.60
Himself back shop where he can be h. 403.2
Egotist...more interested in h. 63.4
He fell in love with h. 455.1
Hippocrene blushful H. 332.24
Hire labourer is worthy of his h. 62.155
Hissed you have h. all my mystery lectures 520.1
History deal of h. to produce...literature 317.1
for h. must be false 563.3
H...is a nightmare from which I am trying to awake 326.4
H. is more or less bunk 234.1
H. is philosophy teaching by examples 194.1
H. is the essence of innumerable biographies 109.3
h....is the h. of class struggles 386.4
h. of the human spirit 20.18
h. of the world is but the biography 109.6
Love...h. of a woman's life 523.2
more h. than they can consume locally 486.1
no h.; only biography 218.4
people...never have learned anything from h. 282.1
War makes...good h. 277.2
Hitch H. your wagon to a star 218.12
Hither Come h., come h. 498.21
Hitler H. has missed the bus 118.3
H. You do your worst 133.17
one purpose, the destruction of H. 133.35
tipster who...reached H.'s level of accuracy 538.1
Hodgepodge English h....of all other speeches 519.5
Hog not the whole h. 398.1
Hold centre cannot h. 601.14
h. your tongue and let me love 199.3
To have and to h. 149.15
Holder office sanctifies the h. 1.1
Hole if you knows of a better h. 33.1
smallest h....man can hide his head in 129.18

What happens to the h. when the cheese is gone? 74.6
Holiness h. of the heart's affections 332.33
put off H. 67.5
Hollow We are the h. men 214.5
within the h. crown 498.237
Holmes 'Elementary', said he 201.5
Home at h. you're just a politician 378.2
Charity begins at h. 82.5
eaten me out of house and h. 498.86
feel...at h. in prison 569.12
H. is heaven 414.2
H. is h. 136.1
H. is the girl's prison 499.55
H. of lost causes 20.16
H.... where... they have to take you in 243.2
till the cow comes h. 45.8
What's the good of a h. 273.1
Home-keeping h. youth 498.278
Homely be never so h. 136.1
h. wits 498.278
Homer author of that poem is either H. 310.25
Homo sapiens naked ape... H. 406.1
Honest fine thing to be h. 133.44
I am as h. as any man living 498.213
Though I am not naturally h. 498.285
To be h., as this world goes 498.54
Honey flowing with milk and h. 62.10
h. still for tea 78.2
They took some h., and plenty of money 354.5
Honey bee hive for the h. 601.10
Honey-dew he on h. hath fed 144.21
Honour His h. rooted in dishonour 539.6
H. all men 62.208
H. pricks me on 498.80
h. sinks where commerce long prevails 262.6
H. thy father and thy mother 62.17
Let us h. if we can 25.1
peace I hope with h. 195.5
prophet is not without h. 62.136
So h. peereth in the meanest habit 498.253
What is h.? A word. 498.80
Honour'd custom more h. in the breach 498.49
Hoof out pops the cloven h. 592.2
Hope Abandon h., all ye who enter here 176.1
faith, h., charity 62.188
H. deferred maketh the heart sick 62.69
H. is the power of being cheerful 129.12
H. springs eternal 452.17
I do not h. to turn 214.1
Land of H. and Glory 57.1
no other medicine but only h. 498.182
unconquerable h. 20.11
what was dead was H. 584.2
Hoped Faith is the substance of things h. for 62.204
Hopefully To travel h. is a better thing 529.4
Hopes enough for fifty h. and fears 83.3
Horde Society is now one polish'd h. 98.20
Horizontal we value none But the h. one 25.1
Horn Triton blow his wreathèd h. 595.10
Hornie Auld H., Satan, Nick 93.1
Horrid are they all h.? 27.5
Horror h.! The h. 154.2
I have a h. of sunsets 458.6
Horrors I have supp'd full with h. 498.176
Horse Behold a pale h. 62.215
my kingdom for a h. 498.241
Horses England... hell for h. 94.3
England... hell of h. 233.1
swap h. in mid-stream 360.7
Hospital world, I count it not an inn, but an h. 82.7
Host h., of golden daffodils 595.2
h. with someone indistinct 214.15
Hostages h. to fortune 30.10
Hotels he keeps six h. 499.5
I prefer temperance h. 566.1
Hounds I said the h. of spring 546.4
Hour h. is ill Which severs those 500.4
I also had my h. 129.3
In the h. of death 149.8

Midnight brought on the dusky h. 401.24
one bare h. to live 381.3
their finest h. 133.13
Time and the h. runs through 498.160
Hours h. will take care of themselves 128.6
Three h. a day 550.2
Housbondes H. at chirche-dore 127.10
House being called a woman in my own h. 569.22
h. is a machine for living in 157.1
If a h. be divided against itself 62.147
man's h. is his castle 143.1
not covet thy neighbour's h. 62.22
Household stables... centre of the h. 499.24
House of Lords Every man has a H. in his own head 364.2
Houses H. are built to live in 30.35
plague o' both your h. 498.248
Hue native h. of resolution 498.63
Human Adam was but h. 553.5
All that is h. must retrograde 255.4
H. kind cannot bear 214.3
h. nature... more of the fool 30.13
H. on my faithless arm 25.6
h. race to which... my readers belong 129.16
I got disappointed in h. nature 198.1
importance of the h. factor 125.2
Mercy has a h. heart 67.17
To err is h. 452.15
Humanity Oh wearisome condition of h. 271.1
still, sad music of h. 595.23
Humble h. and meek are thirsting for blood 426.3
It is difficult to be h. 196.1
Humour deficient in a sense of h. 144.26
Freudian... low... sort of h. 267.3
Total absence of h. 145.1
Hump woman... without a positive h. 541.5
Hunger best sauce... is h. 116.2
talk religion to a man with bodily h. 499.33
Hungry If thine enemy be h. 62.75
she makes h. Where most she satisfies 498.9
Hunter Man is the h. 539.23
Miss J. H. Dunn 60.3
Hurricanoes You cataracts and h. 498.137
Hurry old man in a h. 132.1
Hurt Those have most power to h. 45.5
wish to h. 76.1
Husband Being a h. is a whole-time job 56.2
light wife doth make a heavy h. 498.198
My h. is dead 385.6
Husbandry borrowing dulls the edge of h. 498.48
Hush breathless h. in the Close tonight 416.1
Hut Love in a h. 332.13
Hyphenated h. Americanism 476.2
Hypocrisy Conservative government is an organized h. 195.3
H. is the homage paid by vice to virtue 471.3
Hypocrite h. in his pleasures 106.4
No man is a h. in his pleasures 323.35
We ought to see far enough into a h. 129.10
Hysterica H. passio 498.135

I

I I am for people 121.1
I am that I am 62.11
I also had my hour 129.3
Ice i. was all around 144.3
i. was here, the i. was there 144.3
skating over thin i. 218.8
Ice-cream emperor of i. 528.1
Icicles When i. hang by the wall 498.157
Icummen Winter is i. in 454.1
Idea constant repetition... in imprinting an i. 297.2
i. isn't responsible for the people 382.2
Ideals Away with all i. 351.3
Ideas addiction of political groups to the i. 247.3

nice man is a man of nasty i. 535.18
Ides Beware the I. of March 498.106
Idiot tale told by an i. 498.177
Idle I am happiest when I am i. 566.3
Idleness I. is only the refuge of weak minds 128.8
If I. you can keep your head 341.6
much virtue in I. 498.32
Ignorance I. is like a delicate exotic fruit 584.7
I. is Strength 427.3
I know nothing except the fact of my i. 515.3
I. of the law excuses 494.4
one evil, i. 515.2
Where i. is bliss 268.4
Ill Cannot be i.; cannot be good 498.159
woman colour'd i. 498.302
writing or in judging i. 452.7
Illiterate I. him, I say, quite from your memory 502.3
Ills sharp remedy...for all i. 462.2
Illumine What in me is dark, i. 401.15
Illusion Religion is an i. 242.2
visible universe was an i. 69.2
Image created man in his own i. 62.3
Thou shalt not make unto thee any graven i. 62.14
Imagination Art is ruled...by the i. 170.1
his i. for his facts 502.10
Irishman's heart is...i. 499.26
of i. all compact 498.206
to save those that have no i. 499.71
truth of i. 332.33
Imagine never so happy...as we i. 471.11
Imitate I i. the Saviour 310.2
Imitation I. is the sincerest of flattery 148.3
Immortal I have lost the i. part 498.222
make me i. with a kiss 381.2
think they grow i. as they quote 602.1
Immutable Few things are as i. 247.3
Impediment cause, or just i. 149.13
Important little things are the most i. 201.3
Money...most i. thing in the world 499.75
Impossible complete sorrow is as i. 547.3
Difficult...I wish it were i. 323.37
In two words: i. 263.1
when you have excluded the i. 201.1
Improbable an i. fiction 498.275
Impropriety I. is the soul of wit 388.5
Impulse i. from a vernal wood 595.19
Inch every i. a king 498.145
Incident curious i. of the dog 201.9
Inclination man ought to read just as i. leads 323.15
Include I. me out 263.2
Income Annual i. twenty pounds 191.8
live beyond its i. 97.5
sorrows...in which a good i. is of no avail 511.3
Incomes people live beyond their i. 486.2
Incompetence Employee Tends to Rise to his Level of I. 441.1
Incompetent Democracy...election by the i. 499.49
Inconvenient He found it i. to be poor 165.2
Incorruptible seagreen I. 109.10
Increase another man's price i. 589.3
from fairest creatures we desire i. 498.287
Increased influence of the Crown has i. 207.1
Indecency I.'s Conspiracy of Silence 499.58
prejudicial as a public i. 116.4
Indecent sent down for i. behaviour 569.1
Independent something about an I. Labour Party 569.15
To be poor and i. 141.1
India I. is a geographical term 133.8
Indian base I., threw a pearl away 498.229
lay out ten to see a dead I. 498.255
only good I. is a dead I. 501.1
Indictment i. against an whole people 91.3

Indifference equanimity bordering on i. 257.21
Indifferent worst sin...to be i. 499.15
Indignation puritan pours righteous i. 129.25
Indiscretion lover without i. 277.3
Indispensables She was one of those i. 310.16
Indistinguishable in America the successful writer or picture-painter is i. 359.1
Individual No i. could resent 535.3
psychic development of the i. 242.1
Individualism American system of rugged i. 301.1
Art is the most intense mode of i. 584.24
Individuals worth of the i. composing it 396.3
Industry Captains of i. 109.13
i. will supply their deficiency 466.1
Ineffable mystic sees the i. 388.4
Inefficiency efficiency and i. 499.28
Inelegance a continual state of i. 27.12
Inevitability i. of gradualness 570.1
Inexactitude terminological i. 133.1
Infancy Heaven lies about us in our i. 595.5
Infant mixed i. 52.2
Inferiority man...is always conscious of an i. 323.30
Inferiors I. revolt in order that they may be equal 17.3
Infinite everything would appear...i. 67.26
Infinitive When I split an i. 120.3
Infinity I. in the palm of your hand 67.1
Infirmities friend should bear his friend's i. 498.121
Infirmity last i. of noble mind 401.11
Influence How to...I. People 110.1
i. of the Crown has increased 207.1
Influenza call it i. if ye like 56.1
Infortune worst kinde of i. is this 127.17
Inglorious mute i. Milton 268.9
Ingratitude I hate i. more in a man 498.277
I., thou marble-hearted fiend 498.132
man's i. 498.25
Inherit meek shall i. the earth 62.51
they shall i. the earth 62.118
Inhumanity Man's i. to man 93.10
Injury i. is much sooner forgotten 128.3
Recompense i. with justice 150.10
Injustice fear of suffering i. 471.14
Innisfree go to I. 601.10
Innocence ceremony of i. 601.14
Innocent one i. suffer 65.3
Innocently few ways in which a man can be more i. employed 323.23
Innovator time is the greatest i. 30.24
Insanity lay interest in ecclesiastical matters is often a prelude to i. 569.7
Insipid Happiness...seems i. 511.2
Insomnia Amor vincit i. 244.2
Inspiration Genius is one per cent i. 209.1
Institution more than a game. It's an i. 307.2
Institutions working of great i. 488.1
Insult sooner forgotten than an i. 128.3
Intellect by the feelings, not by the i. 518.8
his i. is not replenished 498.154
i. is...fooled by the heart 471.2
put on I. 67.5
Intellectual artist who's an i. 229.1
I had thoughts once of being an i. 491.1
I. disgrace 25.5
thirdly, i. ability 21.1
word I. suggests 25.7
Intelligence I. is quickness to apprehend 580.2
Intelligent i. are to the intelligentsia 35.2
Intelligentsia intelligent are to the i. 35.2
Intensity excellence of every art is its i. 332.35
worst are full of passionate i. 601.14
Intent prick the sides of my i. 498.165
Interest How can I take an i. in my work? 31.1
lay i. in ecclesiastical matters 569.7
Interested always been i. in people 388.10
Intérieur Vive l'i. 495.3
Intoxication best of life is...i. 98.13
momentary i. with pain 76.1

Introduce let me i. you to that leg of mutton 111.31
Introduction buy back my i. to you 385.13
Intrudes society, where none i. 98.10
Invent it would be necessary to i. Him 561.5
Investment There is no finer i. 133.22
Inviolable i. shade 20.11
Invisible no i. means of support 238.1
Inwards he looked i., and found her 205.17
Ireland I. is the old sow 326.1
Irishman I.'s heart is nothing but his imagination 499.26
Iron i. curtain has descended across the Continent 133.23
rule them with a rod of i. 62.214
wink and hold out mine i. 498.92
Irons two i. in the fire 45.2
Irresponsible better to be i. and right 133.25
Island No man is an I. 199.12
Isle this sceptred i. 498.235
Isles i. of Greece 98.15
Italian I speak I. to women 124.1
Italy man who has not been in I. 323.30
I. a paradise for horses 94.3
Itch i. of literature 369.1
Iteration i. of nuptials 151.7
Itself Love seeketh not i. to please 67.9

J

Jackson J. standing like a stone wall 50.1
Jam rule is, j. tomorrow and j. yesterday 111.23
James I wisest fool in Christendom 286.2
Jealous Art is a j. mistress 218.1
Jealousy j. is cruel as the grave 62.89
j.; It is the green-ey'd monster 498.224
Jelly Out vile j. 498.142
Jerusalem holy city, new J. 62.219
Till we have built J. 67.7
Jest fellow of infinite j. 498.73
j.'s prosperity lies in the ear 498.156
Life is a j. 251.3
Jesting j. Pilate 30.2
Jests his memory for his j. 502.10
Jesus Christ J. the same yesterday 62.205
Jew Hath not a J. eyes? 498.193
I'm not really a J.; just Jew-ish 398.1
Jewel j. of gold in a swine's snout 62.68
Jewellery Don't ever wear artistic j. 145.4
j. wrecks a woman's reputation 145.4
Jewish total solution of the J. question 260.2
Jo John Anderson my j. 93.9
Joan greasy J. doth keel the pot 498.157
Job Being a husband is a whole-time j. 56.2
we will finish the j. 133.16
John Beneath this slab J. Brown is stowed 414.3
but for the grace of God goes J. Bradford 73.1
J. Anderson my jo 93.9
Matthew, Mark, Luke and J. 5.1
Johnny Little J. Head-in-Air 299.2
Join will you...j. the dance? 111.11
Joined What God hath j. together 499.22
What therefore God hath j. together 62.149
Joke good deed to forget a poor j. 72.1
to get a j.... into a Scotch understanding 512.2
Journalism j. what will be grasped at once 153.5
Journey One of the pleasantest things in the world is going a j. 281.4
Joy as impossible as complete j. 547.3
j. cometh in the morning 62.49
let j. be unconfined 98.8
Silence is the perfectest herald of j. 498.210
thing of beauty is a j. for ever 332.4
Joys Hence, vain deluding J. 401.2
j. of parents are secret 30.8
Judge J. not, that ye be not judged 62.130
j. of a man by his foes 154.4

Judged Judge not, that ye be not j. 62.130
Judgement day of j. 149.8
Don't wait for the Last J. 106.5
green in j. 498.7
No nation is fit to sit in j. 591.1
no one complains of his j. 471.1
Judging in j. ill 452.7
Judgment after this the j. 62.203
I expect a j. 191.3
Judgments 'Tis with our j. as our watches 452.8
Julia Whenas in silks my J. goes 291.4
Jumblies far and few, Are the lands where the J. live 354.4
Jump We'd j. the life to come 498.164
Jury Trial by j. itself... will be a delusion 186.1
Jury-men wretches hang that j. may dine 452.28
Just rain on the j. and on the unjust 62.124
Justice J. should not only be done 292.1
Let j. be done 224.1
love of j. in most men 471.14
Recompense injury with j. 150.10
Revenge is a kind of wild j. 30.6
Justified No man is j. in doing evil 476.3
Justify j. the ways of God to men 401.15

K

Keep K. up appearances 131.3
Keeper k. stands up 304.4
my brother's k. 62.5
Keepest what company thou k. 116.5
Ken when a new planet swims into his k. 332.29
Kent K., sir—everybody knows K. 191.24
Kew I am His Highness' dog at K. 452.24
Key turn the k. deftly 332.31
Kick k. against the pricks 62.174
Kid leopard shall lie down with the k. 62.96
Kiddies k. have crumpled the serviettes 60.1
Kill churchmen fain would k. their church 539.20
good to k. an admiral 561.2
k. a wife with kindness 498.252
k. the patient 30.27
k. us for their sport 498.144
men are prepared to k. one another 499.34
they k. you a new way 472.1
Thou shalt not k. 62.18
Time: that which man is... trying to k. 518.1
Killeth letter k. 62.190
Killing More ways of k. a cat 340.1
Patriots never talk of... k. 485.6
Kills each man k. the thing he loves 584.1
Who k. a man k. a reasonable creature 401.35
Kin more than k., and less than kind 498.40
Kind more than kin, and less than k. 498.40
Kindness cup o' k. yet 93.3
full o' th' milk of human k. 498.162
kill a wife with k. 498.252
little... unremembered acts of k. 595.20
recompense k. with k. 150.10
Woman Killed with K. 293.1
Kinds We need two k. of acquaintances 511.9
King as diligently as I have served the k. 593.1
conscience of the K. 498.60
every inch a k. 498.145
Every subject's duty is the K.'s 498.98
God save our Gracious K. 108.1
half the zeal I serv'd my K. 498.104
heart and stomach of a K. 215.2
Here lies our sovereign lord the K. 473.1
I think the K. is but a man 498.97
k. can do no wrong 65.2
k. is a thing 494.2
k. never dies 65.1
k. of shreds and patches 498.69

Ozymandias, k. of kings 500.10
such divinity doth hedge a k. 498.72
wash the balm from an anointed k. 498.236
Kingdom my k. for a horse 498.241
of such is the k. of God 62.150
Kings Conquering k. their titles take 119.1
K. are earth's gods 498.230
politeness of k. 367.1
sad stories of the death of k. 498.237
teeming womb of royal k. 498.235
This royal throne of k. 498.235
Kipling Rudyards cease from k. 526.2
Kiss come let us k. and part 203.2
coward does it with a k. 584.1
K. me, Hardy 415.2
K. till the cow comes home 45.8
Let him k. me with the kisses 62.87
make me immortal with a k. 381.2
Then come k. me, sweet and twenty 498.270
Kissed I held him in my arms and k. him 385.6
Kissing President spends most of his time k. 551.2
what fool first invented k.? 535.14
when the k. had to stop 83.18
Kitchen way of all flesh...k. 572.2
Knaves world is made up...of fools and k. 85.1
Knew I k. him, Horatio 498.73
Knife last twist of the k. 214.13
War even to the k. 98.5
Knight verray parfit gentil k. 127.2
Knight at arms what can ail thee, K.? 332.11
Know all our knowledge is, ourselves to k. 452.19
all Ye k. on earth 332.18
I k. myself 229.2
I k. nothing except...my ignorance 515.3
I k. what I like 51.10
K. then thyself 452.18
Mad, bad, and dangerous to k. 347.1
they k. not what they do 62.160
To k. all makes one tolerant 523.1
What we k. of the past 314.1
You k.... what you are 310.26
Knowing woman...if she have the misfortune of k. anything 27.6
Knowledge all k. to be my province 30.42
all our k. is, ourselves to know 452.19
he that increaseth k. increaseth sorrow 62.81
K. is proportionate to being 310.26
k. of a lifetime 577.5
only one good, k. 515.2
Out-topping k. 20.12
Science is organized k. 518.2
search for k. 485.1
Knows One man that has a mind and k. it 499.2
Kubla Khan In Xanadu did K. 144.19

L

Labour L. is not fit to govern 133.6
Six days shalt thou l. 62.16
true success is to l. 529.4
Labourer l. is worthy of his hire 62.155
Labour Party Independent L. 569.15
Labours Children sweeten l. 30.9
Lad many a lightfoot l. 304.5
Ladders lie down where all the l. start 601.2
Ladies lion among l. 498.204
Lady Dance, dance, dance little l. 163.14
I want to talk like a l. 499.67
L. Bountiful 223.2
l. doth protest too much 498.67
l. of a certain age 98.18
young l. named Bright 87.1
Laid all the young ladies...were l. end to end 433.7
l. on with a trowel 498.18
Laissez *L. faire* 459.1
Laity conspiracies against the l. 499.17
Lake sedge is wither'd from the l. 332.11
Lamb as a l. to the slaughter 62.101
Little L., who made thee? 67.15
Pipe a song about a L. 67.14

wolf also shall dwell with the l. 62.96
Lament Have I not reason to l.? 595.7
Lamps l. are going out all over Europe 272.1
new l. for old ones 15.1
Land England's green and pleasant l. 67.7
fat of the l. 62.7
L. of Hope and Glory 57.1
l. of my fathers 543.5
My native L. 98.4
stranger in a strange l. 62.9
they have the l. and we have the Bibles 252.1
Lands in faery l. forlorn 332.27
l. where the Jumblies live 354.4
Language l. of priorities 61.1
l. performs... without shyness 153.3
Lap-dogs when l. breathe their last 452.27
Lards l. the lean earth as he walks 498.78
Large old Priest writ l. 401.34
Lash'd he l. the vice 535.3
Last Die... l. thing I shall do 432.1
Don't wait for the L. Judgement 106.5
l. day but one 353.1
L. of the Mohicans 156.1
Late So l. into the night 98.26
Latin small L., and less Greek 325.2
Laugh L., and the world laughs with you 583.1
Make 'em l. 464.1
old man who will not l. 488.2
Laughed No man who has once heartily... l. 109.14
When the first baby l. 40.1
Laughing idea of wit... is l. immoderately 512.2
Laughter present l. 498.270
Launch'd face that l. a thousand ships 381.2
Laurel-bough burned is Apollo's l. 381.4
Laurels l. all are cut 304.7
once more, O ye l. 401.9
Law Born under one l. 271.1
Every l. is a contract 494.3
He broke the l. when he was born 499.31
Ignorance of the l. 494.4
l. is a ass 191.22
L. is the true embodiment 257.3
L. of England is a very strange one 178.1
l. of the Medes and Persians 62.106
L. of the Yukon 496.2
l. unto themselves 62.178
rich men rule the l. 262.7
There is no universal l. 351.3
windy side of the l. 498.276
Laws L. grind the poor 262.7
L. were made to be broken 421.2
repeal of bad or obnoxious l. 265.1
Laxative sweet l. of Georgian strains 103.1
Lay L. your sleeping head 25.6
Lays l. it on with a trowel 151.1
Lea standing on this pleasant l. 595.10
Lead little child shall l. them 62.96
Leadeth l. me beside the still waters 62.47
Leaf l., the blossom or the bole 601.1
sear, the yellow l. 498.175
where the dead l. fell, there did it rest 332.10
League half a l., Half a l. onward 539.2
Leap great l. in the dark 298.4
one giant l. for mankind 18.1
Leapt Into the dangerous world I l. 67.11
Learn What we have to l. to do 17.1
Learned He was naturally l. 205.17
people... never have l. anything from history 282.1
Learning beauty and the lust for l. 51.7
L. hath gained most 245.4
L. is but an adjunct 498.155
L. without thought is labour lost 150.3
little l. is a dangerous thing 452.10
on scraps of l. dote 602.1
Learnt I only remember what I've l. 579.2
They have l. nothing 536.2
Leaven little l. leaveneth the whole lump 62.184
Leaves If poetry comes not as naturally as l. 332.37

Though l. are many 601.3
Leaving became him like the l. it 498.161
Lecher small gilded fly does l. 498.146
Lechery drink...an equivocator with l. 498.168
Still wars and l. 498.265
Led l. by the nose with gold 498.286
Left for a handful of silver he l. us 83.9
Let not thy l. hand know 62.125
'tis better to be l. 151.5
Legislators Poets are the unacknowledged l. 500.16
Leisure Men...detest at l. 98.19
Lend men who l. 348.1
Lender Neither a borrower nor a l. be 498.48
Lene As l. was his hors as is a rake 127.6
Lente Festina l. 532.1
Leopard l. his spots 62.102
l. shall lie down with the kid 62.96
Lerne gladly wolde he l. 127.7
Lesbia Let us live, my L. 114.1
Vivamus, mea L. 114.1
Less found it l. exciting 257.1
I love not man the l. 98.10
l. in this than meets the eye 38.1
Lethe go not to L. 332.19
Letter l. killeth 62.190
thou unnecessary l. 498.134
Levellers Your l. wish to level down 323.17
Lever firm place to stand 16.1
Lexicographer L. harmless drudge 323.3
Liar fighting a l. in the quad 520.1
Liars L. ought to have good memories 505.1
Liberal either a little L. 257.4
ineffectual l.'s problem 240.1
most l. L. Englishman 351.1
Liberation Madness...is potential l. 346.4
Liberties Freedom, what l. are taken 253.1
Liberty condition upon which God hath given l. 173.1
Corruption...symptom of constitutional l. 255.3
give me l. or give me death 289.1
l. cannot long exist 91.15
life, l., and the pursuit of happiness 320.1
l. is precious 355.2
L. means responsibility 499.50
l. of the individual must be thus far limited 396.2
L. of the press 328.1
L., too, must be limited 91.14
l., what crimes are committed in your name 474.1
Liberty Hall This is L., gentlemen 262.5
Library l. is thought in cold storage 487.3
vanity of human hopes...a public l. 323.8
Licence L. my roving hands 199.7
rest love not freedom, but l. 401.38
Licht Mehr L. 261.6
Lick ill cook that cannot l. his own fingers 498.250
Lie Ambassador...sent to l. abroad 596.1
Father, I cannot tell a l. 567.2
My love and I would l. 304.2
Nature admits no l. 109.12
old L. 430.2
tell a bigger outback l. 352.1
to l. down in green pastures 62.47
Who loves to l. with me 498.21
Lied good memory is needed after one has l. 158.4
Lies l., damned l., and statistics 553.1
which way the head l. 462.3
Life Anythin' for a quiet l. 191.33
Bankrupt of l. 205.4
believe in the l. to come 47.1
best of l. is but intoxication 98.13
cuts off twenty years of l. 498.111
digestion is the great secret of l. 512.8
doctrine of the strenuous l. 476.1
essential thing in l. 160.1
fourteen months the most idle...of my l. 255.1
give l. a shape 14.1
Human l. is...to be endured 323.9
I fall upon the thorns of l. 500.8
I have measured out my l. 214.9

It's as large as l. 111.27
I've had a happy l. 281.9
I will give thee a crown of l. 62.213
keen observer of l. 25.7
lay down his l. for his friends 62.171
l.... effort to prevent... thinking 310.15
L. exists in the universe 319.1
l. flies 228.4
L. is a jest 251.3
L. is an incurable disease 164.2
l. is... a predicament 488.5
L. is as tedious as a twice-told tale 498.127
l. is fall'n into the sear 498.175
l. is frittered away by detail 545.5
L. is just one damned thing after another 306.1
L. isn't all beer and skittles 307.1
L. is one long process 97.3
l. is short 296.1
L. is the art of drawing sufficient conclusions 97.4
L. is the thing 511.5
L. is too short to do anything for oneself 388.9
l., liberty, and the pursuit of happiness 320.1
L., like a dome of many-coloured glass 500.2
l. of a solitary man 323.10
l. of man, solitary, poor, nasty, brutish 298.2
L.'s but a walking shadow 498.177
L.'s too short for chess 99.1
little l. is rounded with a sleep 498.258
lot of trouble in his l. 133.34
man is tired of London... tired of l. 323.32
meddling with any practical part of l. 4.4
my experience of l. has been drawn from l. 51.8
Nothing in his l. Became him like the leaving 498.161
not perish, but have everlasting l. 62.166
our l.'s Star 595.5
passion and the l.... within 144.18
religion... invade... private l. 390.1
selfish being all my l. 27.11
spirit giveth l. 62.190
strange disease of modern l. 20.10
take my l. 223.3
this l. Is nobler 498.36
this long disease, my l. 452.2
Thou shalt give l. for l. 62.23
Three passions... have governed my l. 485.1
total of such moments is my l. 153.8
two tragedies in l. 499.45
useless l. is an early death 261.4
web of our l. is of a mingled yarn 498.2
We'd jump the l. to come 498.164
well-written L. 109.4
We see into the l. of things 595.22
what a queer thing L. is 592.3
Who saw l. steadily 20.6
Life-blood l. of a master spirit 401.36
Life-insurance I detest l. agents 353.3
Lifetime knowledge of a l. 577.5
l. of happiness 499.37
Lift l. up mine eyes unto the hills 62.60
Light Apparelled in celestial l. 595.4
By the l. of the moon 98.27
drainless shower Of l. is poesy 332.32
five-pound note as one got a l. for a cigarette 317.3
I am the l. of the world 62.168
Let there be l. 62.2
L. that Failed 341.11
Lolita, l. of my life 412.1
On the l. fantastic toe 401.6
people... have seen a great l. 62.94
Put out the l. 498.228
rage, against the dying of the l. 543.1
speed was far faster than l. 87.1
sweetness and l. 535.1
When I consider how my l. is spent 401.32
with a l. behind her 257.20
Lightened burthen of the mystery... is l. 595.21
Lightfoot many a l. lad 304.5
Lighthouse sitivation at the l. 191.33
Lightly Angels... take themselves l. 129.22

Like I know what I l. 51.10
I shall not look upon his l. 498.45
I will…finally l. it 468.1
L. doth quit l. 498.186
my work when I don't l. it 31.1
nothing l. the sun 498.300
People who l. this sort of thing 360.9
You should say you do not l. it 577.4
Liked I've never l. them 388.10
Some l. little boys too little 569.17
Likely Not bloody l. 499.68
Nothing is l. about masterpieces 530.1
Lilac l. is in bloom 78.1
Lilacs l. out of the dead land 214.16
Lilies Consider the l. of the field 62.128
L. that fester 498.296
Lily paint the l. 498.128
Limb perils…of wind and l. 96.4
Limited liberty of the individual must be…l. 396.2
Liberty too must be l. 91.14
Limousine One perfect l. 433.3
Line cancel half a l. 228.8
should carry its justification in every l. 154.5
Linguistics Essay in Sociological L. 478.1
Lion l. among ladies 498.204
nation had the l.'s heart 133.42
Lip stiff upper l. 112.1
Liquefaction l. of her clothes 291.4
Liquidation l. of the British Empire 133.21
Liquor they sell worse kinds of l. 566.1
List I've got a little l. 257.9
Literary viewing them as a l. performance 582.6
Literature American professors like their l.…dead 359.2
great deal of history to produce a little l. 317.1
itch of l. 369.1
L. and butterflies are the two sweetest passions 412.3
L. is simply language charged with meaning 454.2
L.…something that will be read twice 153.5
Little it was a very l. one 383.1
l. of what you fancy 362.1
l. things are infinitely the most important 201.3
Littleness l. of those that should carry them out 74.4
Liv'd I have l. today 205.14
Live anything but l. for it 148.1
Come l. with me 199.2
Come l. with me 381.7
country for heroes to l. in 364.1
good men eat…that they may l. 515.4
Houses are built to l. in 30.35
In him we l., and move 62.176
in Rome, l. as the Romans 12.1
Let us l., my Lesbia 114.1
l. beyond its income 97.5
L. that thou mayest desire to l. again 419.4
Man shall not l. by bread alone 62.117
not l. to eat 402.1
not suffer a witch to l. 62.24
one bare hour to l. 381.3
people l. beyond their incomes 486.2
we l. but to make sport 27.10
we that l. to please 323.7
You might as well l. 433.4
Lived Never to have l. is best 601.11
She…has never l. 251.2
slimy things l. on 144.8
Lives he who l. more l. than one 584.4
l. of quiet desperation 545.1
Liveth my redeemer l. 62.41
Living faith…l. up to it 541.3
house is a machine for l. in 157.1
l. need charity 19.1
Livingstone Dr L., I presume 522.1
Loaf half a l. is better than a whole l. 129.23
Loathe I l. the country 151.6
Logic l. of our times 182.1
Logik un-to l. hadde longe y-go 127.5
Loitering Alone and palely l. 332.11
Lolita L., light of my life 412.1
London Hell is a city much like L. 500.11
L.…Clearing-house of the World 117.1

L....the great wen? 141.2
Nobody is healthy in L. 27.2
when a man is tired of L. 323.32
Lonely She left l. for ever 20.5
Lonesome one, that on a l. road 144.12
Long Art is l. 296.1
Not that the story need be l. 545.7
You have sat too l. here 13.1
Longing l. for love 485.1
Longitude l. with no platitude 244.1
Look Cassius has a lean and hungry l. 498.107
frightened l. in its eyes 508.1
If you seek my monument, l. around you 597.1
I have learned to l. on nature 595.23
Looking somebody may be l. 392.1
Looks woman as old as she l. 146.1
Lord blessed be the name of the L. 62.38
fear of the L. 62.58
I replied My L. 290.2
L. among wits 323.11
L. High Everything Else 257.7
L. is my shepherd 62.46
Praise the L. and pass the ammunition. 236.1
Lorn lone l. creetur, ' 191.6
Lose l. his own soul 62.148
l. the substance 6.1
nothing to l. but our aitches 427.5
nothing to l. but their chains 386.5
tails you l. 171.1
To l. one parent...a misfortune 584.8
Losers In war...all are l. 118.1
Lost All is not l. 401.16
better to have loved and l. 539.11
by which the printers have l. 245.4
Home of l. causes 20.16
never to have l. at all 97.7
'Tis better to have fought and l. 140.5
woman that deliberates is l. 4.2
Lot policeman's l. is not a happy one 257.19
Lousy only one fault. It was kind of l. 546.6
Lov'd I never writ, nor no man ever l. 498.298
Of one that l. not wisely, but too well 498.229
Love Absence is to l. 95.1
alike are the groans of l. to...dying 370.1
All mankind l. a lover 218.5
And l. comes in at the eye 601.5
ashamed of having been in l. 471.13
caution in l. is...fatal 485.3
Come live with me, and be my l. 381.7
comfort in the strength of l. 595.8
corner in the thing I l. 498.225
Familiar acts are beautiful through l. 500.12
folly...l. did make thee run into 498.20
God is l. 62.210
Greater l. hath no man 62.171
He fell in l. with himself 455.1
help...of the woman I l. 211.1
he told men to l. their neighbour 74.2
hid in the heart of l. 601.13
hold your tongue and let me l. 199.3
I do not l. thee, Doctor Fell 79.1
If music be the food of l. 498.266
I hate and l. 114.2
I l. or I hate 445.1
I'm tired of l. 55.5
In l.... the amateur status 267.2
I think my l. as rare 498.301
let us prove...the sports of l. 325.6
live with me, and be my l. 199.2
longing for l. 485.1
l. and murder will out 151.2
l. a place the less 27.7
L. bade me welcome 290.6
L. built on beauty 199.4
L. ceases to be a pleasure 53.1
L. conquers all 560.4
L. has pitched his mansion 601.4
l. in a golden bowl 67.3
L. in a hut 332.13
L. in a palace 332.13
L. is a boy 96.3
l. is blind 498.191
L. is like the measles 321.1
L. is my religion 332.39
L. is not l. Which alters 498.298
L. is strong as death 62.89

L. is the whole history of a woman's life 523.2
L. looks not with the eyes 498.202
l. of justice in most men 471.14
l. of money is the root of all evil 62.202
L. seeketh not itself to please 67.9
L. seeketh only Self to please 67.10
L. sought is good 498.274
L., the human form divine 67.17
l. thy neighbour as thyself 62.26
L. your enemies 62.123
man is in l. he endures more 419.1
Man's l. is of man's life 98.12
Many waters cannot quench l. 62.90
Men l. in haste 98.19
My l. and I would lie 304.2
My l. is like a red red rose 93.14
not enough to make us l. 535.16
office and affairs of l. 498.209
One can l.... vulgarity 310.27
oyster may be crossed in l. 502.1
passing the l. of women 62.36
perfect l. casteth out fear 62.211
rebuke is better than secret l. 62.77
She never told her l. 498.272
That ye l. one another 62.170
There can be no peace of mind in l. 458.1
Those have most power to hurt us that we l. 45.5
thy l. is better than wine 62.87
Thy l. to me was wonderful 62.36
To be wise and l. 498.263
To business that we l. we rise betime 498.12
true l. never did run smooth 498.201
Try thinking of l. 244.2
turns to thoughts of l. 539.17
unremembered acts of... l. 595.20
vanity and l.... universal characteristics 128.9
violence masquerading as l. 346.3
War is like l. 74.7
weak man, who marries for l. 323.27
What is l.? 'Tis not hereafter 498.270
worms have eaten them, but not for l. 498.31

Loved And the l. one all together 83.10
better to have l. and lost 97.7
For God so l. the world 62.166
I have l. Three whole days together 531.1
l., to have thought, to have done 20.3
never to have been l. 151.5
She who has never l. has never lived 251.2
'Tis better to have l. and lost 539.11

Loveliest L. of trees, the cherry 304.1

Lover All mankind love a l. 218.5
l. without indiscretion is no l. 277.3
lunatic, the l., and the poet 498.206

Lovers l. cannot see The pretty follies 498.191
l. fled away into the storm 332.6

Loves each man kills the thing he l. 584.1
Every man l. what he is good at 497.3
I have reigned with your l. 215.3
Two l. I have, of comfort and despair 498.302

Lovesome garden is a l. thing 80.1

Loveth He prayeth best who l. best 144.15

Loving most l. mere folly 498.26
night was made for l. 98.27

Low Caesar! dost thou lie so l.? 498.112
He that is l. 90.7

Lower l. one's vitality 51.4

Lubricates dinner l. business 493.1

Luck l. to give the roar 133.42

Lucre filthy l. 62.199

Luminous Dong with a l. Nose 354.2

Lump leaveneth the whole l. 62.184

Lunatic l., the lover, and the poet 498.206
word is... like a l. asylum 364.3

Lungs don't keep using your l. all the time 353.2

Lust Beauty and the l. for learning 51.7
l. in action 498.299
Nonconformity and l. stalking hand in hand 569.5

Luxuries Give us the l. of life 408.1

Luxury Every l. was lavished on you 426.4

Lyf l. so short 127.16

Lying mighty heart is l. still 595.12
One of you is l. 433.6

M

Macduff M. was from his mother's womb 498.179
Machine house is a m. for living in 157.1
not a man, you're a m. 499.7
One m. can do the work of fifty ordinary men 306.2
Machine-gun m. riddling her hostess 310.14
Mad he first makes m. 221.1
let me not be m. 498.133
M. about the boy 163.15
M., bad, and dangerous to know 347.1
soon as he ceased to be m. he became merely stupid 458.3
We all are born m. 47.5
Madding Far from the m. crowd 268.10
Made Annihilating all that's m. 384.5
Little Lamb, who m. thee? 67.15
we're all m. the same 163.6
What man has m. of man 595.7
Madman m. is not the man who has lost his reason 129.17
Madness devil's m.—War 496.3
M. in great ones 498.64
M. need not be all breakdown 346.4
m., yet there is method in't 498.55
Wits are sure to M. near alli'd 205.3
Maestro You can't teach the old m. a new tune 336.2
Magnifique c'est m., mais 71.1
Mahomet If the hill will not come to M. 30.14
Maids Three little m. from school 257.10
Majesty Her M.'s Opposition 32.2
This earth of m. 498.235
Major-General very model of a modern M. 257.17
Majority Fools are in a terrible…m. 313.1
One on God's side is a m. 444.1
Make Scotsman on the m. 40.5
Maladies m. we must not seek to cure 458.3
Malice m. never was his aim 535.3
Malt M. does more than Milton 304.6
Mammon cannot serve God and m. 62.127
Man Ambassador is an honest m. 596.1
another m.'s price increase 589.3
apparel oft proclaims the m. 498.47
Arms and the m. I sing 560.1
'A was a m., take him for all in all 498.45
big m. has no time 229.3
bold m. that first eat an oyster 535.11
Brutus is an honourable m. 498.117
Child is father of the M. 595.13
condition of m. is a condition of war 298.1
created m. in his own image 62.3
disguised as a complete M. 310.3
dog…went mad and bit the m. 262.1
Enclosing every thin m.…. fat m. 569.24
Every m. is as Heaven made him 116.1
Every m. is wanted 218.7
for m. or beast 226.1
God made the woman for the m. 539.5
Go West, young m. 269.1
hanging a m. who does not object 499.60
Happy the m. 205.14
hate ingratitude more in a m. 498.277
I care not whether a m. is Good 67.5
If a m. be gracious and courteous 30.16
I love not M. the less 98.10
In wit a m. 452.6
It matters not how a m. dies 323.19
King is but a m. 498.97
life of a solitary m. 323.10
M.…. always to be blest 452.17
M., being reasonable, must get drunk 98.13
m. can die but once 498.90
M. delights not me 498.57
M. doth not live by bread only 62.27
M. has his will 300.1
m. has made of m. 595.7
m. hath penance done 144.11
M. is a bungler 499.44

M. is a noble animal 82.9
M. is...a political animal 17.2
m. is...a religious animal 91.9
m. is as old as he's feeling 146.1
m. is...a wild animal 179.1
m. is in love he endures more 419.1
m. is only as old as the woman 385.22
M. is something that is to be surpassed 419.5
M. is the hunter 539.23
m. knows he is to be hanged 323.31
m. made the town 165.3
m. meets his Waterloo 444.2
m. must serve his time to every trade 98.24
Manners maketh m. 587.1
M. proposes 333.1
m. right fair 498.302
m.'s a m. for a' that 93.7
M.'s first disobedience 401.14
m. should never put on his best trousers 313.3
M.'s inhumanity to m. 93.10
M.'s life is cheap as beast's 498.136
M.'s love is of m.'s life a thing apart 98.12
m. so various 205.7
M.... still bears the stamp of his...origin 180.1
m.'s worth something 83.4
m. that hath no music in himself 498.196
M. that is born of a woman 62.39
m. that is young in years 30.32
M. was born free 481.1
m. who could make so vile a pun 187.1
m. who...had the largest...soul 205.16
m. who has...laughed 109.14
m. who has no office to go to 499.76
m. who has not been in Italy 323.30
m. who has not passed through the inferno of his passions 327.2
m. who listens to Reason is lost 499.54
m. who makes no mistakes 443.1
m. whose god is in the skies 499.47
m. whose second thoughts are good 40.6
m. who's untrue to his wife 25.7
Marriage is the best state for a m. 323.26
mean m. is always full of distress 150.8
No m.... ever wrote, except for money 323.29
No m. is a hypocrite in his pleasures 106.4
No m. is an Island 199.12
No m. is good enough to govern another 360.1
no m. who has wrestled with a...card table 546.2
no m. worth having 556.2
not a m., you're a machine 499.7
not m. for the sabbath 62.146
No young m. believes he shall ever die 281.3
old m. in a dry month 214.4
old m. who will not laugh 488.2
one m. pick'd out of ten thousand 498.54
one small step for m. 18.1
Painting is a blind m.'s profession. 445.2
play the m. 350.1
proper study of Mankind is M. 452.18
real danger...is m. himself 327.3
say to all the world 'This was a m.' 498.124
silliest woman can manage a clever m. 341.10
single sentence...for modern m. 106.2
Style is the m. himself 86.1
superior m. is distressed by his want of ability 150.11
superior m. is satisfied 150.8
teach you more of m. 595.19
This is the state of m. 498.103
'Tis strange what a m. may do 541.4
To the m.-in-the-street, who 25.7
uneducated m. to read books of quotations 133.28
weak m.... marries for love 323.27
what a m. is to a gent 35.2
What a piece of work is a m. 498.57
what a very singularly deep young m. 257.14
What is m. 62.43
when a m. bites a dog 175.1

When a stupid m. is doing something 499.10
whether he is a Wise M. or a Fool 67.5
Whoso would be a m. 218.9
Women who love the same m. 51.5
you asked this m. to die 25.2
You cannot make a m. by standing a sheep 51.9
you'll be a M., my son 341.7
young m. feels his pockets 304.8
young m. not yet 30.12
young m. who has not wept 488.2
You're a better m. than I am 341.5
Management British m. doesn't seem to understand 125.2
Mandalay On the road to M. 341.8
Mandrake Get with child a m. root 199.9
Man Friday I takes my m. with me 184.2
Manhood m. a struggle 195.7
Mankind all M.'s epitome 205.7
Example is the school of m. 91.11
giant leap for m. 18.1
M. is a club 129.24
M. is not a tribe of animals 129.24
proper study of m. is books 310.6
proper study of M. is Man 452.18
Spectator of m. 4.4
Manner to the m. born 498.49
Manners as a nation...we've no m. 499.73
in England people have...m. 395.1
man...by his m. 519.3
M. are especially the need of the plain 569.25
M. maketh man 587.1
Mansion Love has pitched his m. 601.4
Many m. are called 62.140
m. change and pass 500.2
So m. men, so m. opinions 540.2
so much owed by so m. 133.15
Map Roll up that m. 447.2
Maps Geography is about M. 59.2
Marathon mountains look on M. 98.16
Marble he...left it m. 100.1
Not m., nor the gilded monuments 498.292
March Beware the ides of M. 498.106
Napoleon's armies used to m. on their stomachs 495.3
Marche droghte of M. 127.1
Mare Though patience be a tired m. 498.93
Mariner It is an ancient M. 144.1
Mark ever-fixed m. 498.298
We all leave an indelible m. 222.1
Marriage comedies are ended by a m. 98.14
hanging prevents a bad m. 498.268
Happiness in m. 27.9
It takes two to make a m. 487.1
Let me not to the m. of true minds 498.298
M., ...a community...making in all two. 63.6
M. is like a cage 403.4
M. is the best state for a man 323.26
M.... maximum of temptation 499.52
Married if ever we had been m. 251.1
not being legally m. 499.19
parents were not m. 499.31
virtue...Trade Unionism of the m. 499.41
Marry Every woman should m. 195.9
when a man should m. 30.12
woman...may m. whom she likes 541.5
Mars seat of M. 498.235
Martyrdom M. is the only way in which a man can become famous 499.77
Mask He had a m. like Castlereagh 500.6
Mass m. of men lead lives 545.1
Paris is well worth a m. 286.1
Masses I will back the m. against the classes 258.2
Master I am the m. of my fate; 285.2
M. Mistress of my passion 498.289
Masterpiece m. of Nature 218.3
Masterpieces Nothing is likely about m. 530.1
Masters Assistant m. came and went 569.17
No man can serve two m. 62.126
people are the m. 91.5
Masturbation m. of war 461.1
Mates moves, and m., and slays 228.7

Mathematics Angling...like the m. 565.1
M. possesses not only truth, but supreme beauty 485.4
pregnancy...resort to m. 392.2
Mating only in the m. season 399.1
Matrimony in m. to begin with a little aversion 502.4
m....friendship recognised by the police 529.1
Matter poultry m. 385.3
proverb is much m. decorated 245.3
Matters Nothing m. very much 36.2
Matthew M., Mark, Luke and John, 5.1
Maud Come into the garden, M. 539.19
May as fresh as is the month of M. 127.3
darling buds of M. 498.288
wish a snow in M.'s...shows 498.153
Maybe I'll give you a definite m. 263.5
Me between m. and the sun 193.1
I consider the world as made for m. 513.2
My thought is m. 489.3
think only this of m. 78.3
Meadow There was a time when m., grove 595.4
Mean He who meanly admires m. things is a Snob 541.1
It all depends what you m. by... 322.1
it means just what I choose it to m. 111.25
tears, I know not what they m. 539.22
Meaner motives m. than your own 40.7
Meaning Literature is...language charged with m. 454.2
Means die beyond my m. 584.27
m. just what I choose it to mean 111.25
no invisible m. of support 238.1
Meant more is m. than meets the ear 401.5
Measles Love is like the m. 321.1
Measure M. still for M. 498.186
Shrunk to this little m. 498.112
Measureless caverns m. to man 144.19
Meat man loves the m. in his youth 498.211
one man is appointed to buy the m. 494.2
Out of the eater came forth m. 62.32
Medes law of the M. and Persians 62.106
Medicine miserable have no other m. 498.182
Mediocre Some men are born m. 283.2
Meek Blessed are the m. 62.118
m. shall inherit the earth 62.51
Meet never the twain shall m. 341.1
Meeting as If I was a public m. 558.2
this m. is drunk 191.31
Megalomaniac m....seeks to be feared 485.2
Melancholy M. has her sovran shrine 332.21
M., indeed, should be diverted by every means 323.28
Most musical, most m. 401.3
so sweet as M. 94.1
Melba *M.* dinkum hard-swearing Aussie 279.1
Melodies Heard m. are sweet 332.16
Member club that will accept me as m. 385.19
Memories Liars ought to have good m. 505.1
Memory Everyone complains of his m. 471.1
good m. is needed after one has lied 158.4
Illiterate him...from your m. 502.3
indebted to his m. for his jests 502.10
Men all m. are created equal 320.1
All things to all m. 62.185
All those m. have their price 563.2
Do other m. 191.16
England...purgatory of m. 233.1
give place to better m. 172.3
Great m. are almost always bad m. 1.1
happy breed of m. 498.235
I cannot bear m. and women 499.23
justify the ways of God to m. 401.15
Let us now praise famous m. 62.113
many m., so beautiful 144.8
mass of m. lead lives 545.1
m. about me that are fat 498.107
M. are not hanged for stealing horses 274.1
m....capable of every wickedness 154.6

m. everywhere could be free 360.5
M. fear death 30.3
M. have never been good 41.1
m. may come and m. may go 539.1
M. must endure their going 498.151
M. of few words are the best m. 498.96
M. seldom make passes 433.2
M.'s natures are alike 150.1
m. who borrow, and the m. who lend 348.1
old m. shall dream dreams 62.109
One machine can do the work of fifty ... m. 306.2
Quit yourselves like m. 62.33
rich m. rule the law 262.7
schemes o' mice an' m. 93.12
So far ... from being true that m. are ... equal 323.18
So many m., so many opinions 540.2
Such m. are dangerous 498.107
That all m. are equal 310.21
tide in the affairs of m. 498.122
to form Christian m. 21.2
We are the hollow m. 214.5
Wives are young m.'s mistresses 30.11
young m. shall see visions 62.109
Mene *M., M., Tekel, Upharsin* 62.104
Mens *m. sana in corpore sano* 329.3
Merci La Belle Dame Sans M. 332.12
Mercy For M. has a human heart 67.17
m. I asked, m. I found 102.1
quality of m. is not strain'd 498.194
To M., Pity, Peace, and Love 67.16
Mermaids I have heard the m. singing 214.11
Merry good are always the m. 601.8
I am never m. when I hear sweet music 498.195
Message electric m. came 28.1
Messing m. about in boats 264.1
Metaphysician scientist must be m. 499.8
Method madness, yet there is m. in't 498.55
You know my m. 201.2
Mice schemes o' m. an' men 93.12
Michelangelo Talking of M. 214.8
Microbe M. is so very small 55.6
Mid-day go out in the m. sun 163.9
Middle people who stay in the m. of the road 61.3
Middle classes Bow, bow, ye lower m. 257.2
Midnight cease upon the m. with no pain 332.26
chimes at m. 498.89
M. brought on the dusky hour 401.24
m. never come 381.3
Not to be abed after m. 498.269
soft embalmer of the still m. 332.30
Mid-stream best to swap horses in m. 360.7
Might Britons alone use 'M.' 569.23
m. half slumb'ring 332.32
Mightier pen is m. than the sword 88.1
Mighty How are the m. fallen 62.35
Look on my works, ye M. 500.10
Milk And drunk the m. of Paradise 144.21
flowing with m. and honey 62.10
putting m. into babies 133.22
too full o' th' m. of human kindness 498.162
Mill at the m. with slaves 401.29
Million man who has a m. dollars 24.1
Millionaire I am a M.. That is my religion 499.32
Milton Malt does more than M. can 304.6
mute inglorious M. 268.9
Mimsy All m. were the borogoves 111.17
Mind clear your m. of cant 323.34
diseases of the m. 524.1
education forms the common m. 452.20
exaggerated stress on not changing one's m. 388.1
I eat ... to put food out of my m. 507.1
last infirmity of noble m. 401.11
m. is its own place 401.17
m. that makes the body rich 498.253
never brought to m. 93.2
No m. is thoroughly well organized 144.26
One man that has a m. and knows it 499.2

prodigious quantity of m. 553.3
Reading is to the m. 524.3
sound m. in a sound body 329.3
Mindful thou art m. of him 62.43
Minds great m. in the commonplace 306.3
Little m. are interested in the extraordinary 306.3
marriage of true m. 498.298
quotations beautiful from m. profound 433.1
Superstition is the religion of feeble m. 91.10
Mineral animal or vegetable or m. 111.28
Ministries *The Times* has made many m. 32.1
Minority m. is always right 313.2
Minstrel wandering m. I 257.8
Minute M. Particulars 67.4
sucker born every m. 39.1
unforgiving m. 341.7
Minutes our m. hasten to their end 498.293
take care of the m. 128.6
Mirrors M. and fatherhood are abominable 69.2
Mischief Satan finds some m. still 568.1
To mourn a m. that is past 498.218
Miserable m. have no other medicine 498.182
Misery M. acquaints a man with strange bedfellows 498.256
Misfortune most unhappy kind of m. 68.1
To lose one parent, Mr Worthing, may be regarded as a m. 584.8
Misfortunes In the m. of our best friends 471.5
strength...to endure the m. of others 471.7
real m. and pains of others 91.17
Misgovernment democracy...cheap m. 499.35
Missed who never would be m. 257.9
Mistah Kurtz M.—he dead 154.3
Mistake Woman was God's second m. 419.2
Mistaken think it possible you may be m. 172.1
Mistakes man who makes no m. 443.1
Mistress Art is a jealous m. 218.1
Master M. of my passion 498.289
Mistresses Wives are young men's m. 30.11
Mists Season of m. 332.1
Misunderstood To be great is to be m. 218.10
Mixed m. infant 52.2
Mixed grill not to look like a m. 163.7
Mob best...to do what the m. do 191.26
Mock M. on, m. on, Voltaire, Rousseau 67.8
Mocked God is not m. 62.196
Model very m. of a modern Major-General 257.17
Moderation I stand astonished at my own m. 139.1
M. is a fatal thing 584.16
Modester People ought to be m. 109.15
Modesty Enough for m. 84.2
Mohicans Last of the M. 156.1
Moi *L'État c'est m.* 366.1
Mole Death is still working like a m. 290.5
Moment m. of time 215.4
Mona Lisa older than the rocks 436.1
Monarchs M. must obey 205.13
Money always try to rub up against m. 483.2
Brigands demand your m. or your life 97.8
Business, you know, may bring m. 27.3
He that wants m., means, and content 498.27
How pleasant it is to have m. 140.2
innocently employed than in getting m. 323.23
love of m. is the root of all evil 62.202
M. gives me pleasure 55.5
M. is like a sixth sense 388.3
M. is like muck 30.17
M., it turned out, was exactly like sex 34.2
M.... most important thing 499.75

No man...ever wrote, except for m. 323.29
Put m. in thy purse 498.219
size of sums of m. appears to vary 311.1
some honey, and plenty of m. 354.5
they have more m. 229.4
time is m. 239.1
want of m. is so 97.1
Monster jealousy...green-ey'd m. 498.224
Montgomery In defeat unbeatable 133.43
Month April is the cruellest m. 214.16
Months fourteen m. the most idle and unprofitable 255.1
two m. of every year 98.2
Monument If you seek my m. 597.1
like Patience on a m. 498.272
Monuments Not marble, nor the gilded m. 498.292
Moon by the light of the m. 98.27
moving M. went up the sky 144.9
nothing left remarkable beneath the...m. 498.15
th'inconstant m. 498.244
Moral as soon as one is unhappy one becomes m. 458.2
Englishman thinks he is m. 499.40
Everything's got a m. 111.9
Let us be m. 191.15
m. attribute of a Scotsman 40.4
worst government is the most m. 392.4
Morality I don't believe in m. 499.20
M. consists in suspecting 499.19
m. should have this fact for its basis 499.75
No m. can be founded on authority 29.1
Morals basing m. on myth 487.4
happiness...foundation of m. 58.1
More M. than somewhat 483.1
m. than the wisest man 148.4
Oliver Twist has asked for m. 191.20
take m. than nothing 111.7
Mores O tempora! O m.! 135.4
Morn From m. To noon he fell 401.19
He rose the morrow m. 144.16
Morning I awoke one m. 98.29
joy cometh in the m. 62.49
M. in the Bowl of Night 228.1
Mrs Claypool's cheque...in the m. 385.16
Mortals what fools these m. be 498.205
Most M. may err as grosly 205.10
Mother m. of parliaments 75.2
M. of the Free 57.1
never called me m. 594.1
Mothers There should be no m., only women 499.72
Motion No m. has she now 595.16
Motives m. meaner than your own 40.7
Mountains England's m. green 67.6
m. look on Marathon 98.16
Mourn countless thousands m. 93.10
To m. a mischief that is past 498.218
Mourning with my m., very handsome 438.3
Mouse-trap If a man...make a better m. than his neighbour 218.15
Moustache man outside with a big black m. 385.8
Mouth impossible for an Englishman to open his m. 499.66
of the m. of God 62.117
Out of the m. of babes 62.42
Wine comes in at the m. 601.5
Move But it does m. 248.1
Those m. easiest who have learn'd 452.13
Moves m., and mates, and slays 228.7
novel...one m. through 554.2
Moving M. Finger writes 228.8
people under suspicion are better m. 330.2
Much m.... said on both sides 4.6
righteous over m. 62.83
So little done, so m. to do 467.1
so m. owed by so many to so few 133.15
Muck Money is like m. 30.17
sing 'em m. 389.1
Multitudes I contain m. 582.5
Pestilence-stricken m. 500.7
Mum M.'s the word 147.1
Mundi Sic transit gloria m. 333.2
Murder I met M. on the way 500.6
love and m. will out 151.2

M. considered as one of the Fine Arts 188.1
M. most foul 498.51
m. shrieks out 572.1
M. will out 127.15
So it was m. 385.6
Murmur live m. of a summer's day 20.9
Murmuring m. of innumerable bees 539.24
Muscular His Christianity was m. 195.8
Music Architecture...is frozen m. 490.1
art aspires towards...m. 436.2
how potent cheap m. is 163.3
How sour sweet m. is 498.238
If m. be the food of love 498.266
making m. throatily and palpitatingly sexual 310.1
man that hath no m. in himself 498.196
more or less lascivious m. 392.5
M. and women I cannot but give way to 438.2
M. has charms to soothe 151.3
M. that gentlier on the spirit lies 539.18
My m. is best understood by children and animals 530.2
never merry when I hear sweet m. 498.195
silence sank like m. 144.13
still, sad m. of humanity 595.23
Musical Most m., most melancholy 401.3
Must Genius does what it m. 394.1
Mutton Alice m.; m. Alice 111.31
Myriad-minded Our m. Shakespeare 144.23
Myself as well said as if I had said it m. 535.12
coming down let me shift for m. 404.1
deliver me from m. 82.6
I celebrate m., and sing m. 582.2
I have always disliked m. 153.8
I know m. 229.2
I like to go by m. 281.4
I've over-educated m. 163.8
not only witty in m. 498.83
Mystery burthen of the m. 595.21
Happiness is a m. like religion 129.11
hissed all my m. lectures 520.1
Mystic m. sees the ineffable 388.4
Myth basing morals on m. 487.4

N

Naked N. came I out of my mother's womb 62.38
Poor n. wretches 498.140
Name family n. of Wagstaff 385.9
Good n. in man and woman 498.223
good n. is rather to be chosen than great riches 62.74
Groucho is not my real n. 385.20
I remember your n. perfectly 520.3
lash'd the vice, but spared the n. 535.3
local habitation and a n. 498.207
one whose n. was writ in water 332.40
rose by any other n. 498.243
take the n. of the Lord thy God in vain 62.15
What's in a n. 498.243
Naming Today we have n. of parts 465.1
Napoleon N. of crime 201.6
Narcissist megalomaniac differs from the n. 485.2
Nasty Something n. in the woodshed 256.1
Nation England is a n. of shopkeepers 413.2
n. had the lion's heart 133.42
n. is a society united by a delusion 314.6
n. is not in danger of financial disaster 391.1
n. of amateurs 477.2
n. shall not lift up sword against n. 62.92
No n. is fit to sit in judgement 591.1
No n. was ever ruined by trade 239.2
project unfit for a n. of shopkeepers 510.2
We are a n. of governesses 499.79
Nations Commonwealth of N. 477.1
The day of small n. has long passed away 117.2
great n. have always acted like gangsters 345.1
small n. like prostitutes 345.1

Privileged and the People formed Two N. 195.11
Native My n. Land—Good Night 98.4
white man...looks into the eyes of a n. 356.1
Natives Britons were only n. 495.2
Natural It is n. to die 30.4
N. Selection 180.2
'twas N. to please 205.2
Naturally Though I am not n. honest 498.285
Nature Allow not n. more than n. needs 498.136
but N. more 98.10
Consistency is contrary to n. 310.8
fortress built by N. 498.235
Friend...masterpiece of N. 218.3
God and N. then at strife 539.12
I got disappointed in human n. 198.1
I have learned To look on n. 595.23
Let N. be your Teacher 595.18
Little we see in N. that is ours 595.9
N. admits no lie 109.12
N. is but a name for an effect 165.7
N. is creeping up 577.6
N. is often hidden 30.31
n. is the art of God 82.2
N. is usually wrong 577.2
N. never did betray The heart 595.24
N. remains 582.7
n. to advantage dress'd 452.12
N., to be commanded 30.41
o'erstep not the modesty of n. 498.66
spectacles of books to read n. 205.17
to write and read comes by n. 498.212
Natures Men's n. are alike 150.1
Naught N. so sweet as melancholy 94.1
Nauseate I n. walking 151.6
Navy Ruler of the Queen's N. 257.16
Nearest I am n. to the gods 515.1
Necessities we will dispense with its n. 408.1
Necessity N. is the plea for...infringement of...freedom 447.1
no virtue like n. 498.234
Thy n. is greater than mine 506.3
Neck go to the bottom with my principles round my n. 35.1
Some n. 133.19
Necking Whoever named it n. 385.21
Need reason not the n. 498.136
Needs to each according to his n. 386.2
Negation Capitalist production begets...its own n. 386.1
Negative N. Capability 332.36
Negligent Celerity...admir'd...by the n. 498.11
Neiges les n. d'antan 559.1
Neighbour better mouse-trap than his n. 218.15
love thy n. as thyself 62.26
not covet thy n.'s house 62.22
told men to love their n. 74.2
Neighbours make sport for our n. 27.10
Nelly let not poor N. starve 123.3
Network N. Any thing reticulated or decussated 323.4
Neurotics Everything great in the world is done by n. 458.7
Never N., n., n., n. 498.152
n. to have been loved 151.5
N. to have lived is best 601.11
n. to have loved at all 539.11
What n.... hardly ever 257.15
Nevermore Quoth the Raven, 'N.' 450.1
New fresh woods and pastures n. 401.13
He that will not apply n. remedies 30.24
n. deal for the American people 475.1
n. heaven and a n. earth 62.218
N. roads: n. ruts 129.26
no n. thing under the sun 62.80
New-found-land my n. 199.7
News And it's only n. until he's read it 569.20
man bites a dog, that is n. 175.1
N. is what a chap...wants to read 569.20
n. that's fit to print 424.1
Newspaper good n. is a nation talking to itself 397.1
I read the n. avidly 61.4
Newspapers N. always excite curiosity 348.4
Nice n. man is a man of nasty ideas 535.18
Nick Satan, N., or Clootie 93.1

Night as a watch in the n. 62.54
black bat, n., has flown 539.19
Do not go gentle into that good n. 543.1
ignorant armies clash by n. 20.2
It ain't a fit n. out 226.1
Morning in the Bowl of N. 228.1
n. was made for loving 98.27
outsoared the shadow of our n. 500.1
perils...of this n. 149.6
returned home the previous n. 87.1
So late into the n. 98.26
sound of revelry by n. 98.7
Weeping may endure for a n. 62.49
Nightingales n. are singing 214.15
Nightmare History...is a n. 326.4
Nights Chequer-board of N. and Days 228.7
Nihilist part-time n. 106.6
Nile allegory on the banks of the N. 502.7
my serpent of old N. 498.6
Nip I'll n. him in the bud 470.1
No rebel...man who says n. 106.7
Noblesse *N. oblige* 357.1
Noblest n. Roman of them all 498.123
two n. of things 535.1
Nobody In heaven an angel is n. 499.57
N., and that's my complaint 385.12
silly game where n. wins 245.2
Noise dreadful n. of waters in my ears 498.240
loud n. at one end 343.1
Noises Like n. in a swound 144.3
Nonconformist man must be a n. 218.9
Nonconformity N. and lust stalking hand in hand 569.5
Non-U U and N. 478.1
Noon dark, amid the blaze of n. 401.30
from n. to dewy eve 401.19
Nooses N. give 433.4
Norfolk Very flat, N. 163.4
Nose Dong with a luminous N. 354.2
Entuned in hir n. ful semely 127.4
led by the n. with gold 498.286
Not as the serpent used to say, why n. 499.9
how n. to do it 191.14
Note make a n. of 191.12
Nothing behind them...there is n. 489.2
book's a book, although there's n. 98.23
from n. to a state of extreme poverty 385.11
he may have n. to say 323.24
House of Lords...Did n. in particular 257.5
m. who sees absolutely n. at all 584.20
n. a-year, paid quarterly 533.2
N. can be created out of n. 371.1
n. either good or bad 498.56
N. happens 47.2
n. if not critical 498.220
n. is certain but death and taxes 239.5
N. is ever done in this world 499.34
N. long 205.7
N. matters very much 36.2
N. to do but work 339.1
n. to do with the case 257.12
N. will come of n. 498.130
Signifying n. 498.177
take more than n. 111.7
They have learnt n., and forgotten n. 536.2
those who were up to n. 163.1
we brought n. into this world 62.201
When you have n. to say, say n. 148.2
world where n. is had 140.1
You ain't heard n. yet 324.1
Nought N.'s had, all's spent 498.169
Nourisher Chief n. in life's feast 498.167
Novel good n. tells us the truth 129.14
Great Australian N. 579.4
n. cannot be too bad to be worth publishing 499.64
n. is a static thing 554.2
n. tells a story 237.3
scrofulous French n. 83.17
When I want to read a n. 195.13
Novels characters in one of my n. 229.6
more entertaining than half the n. 388.8
my n. are an accumulation of detail 579.3
Now We are all Socialists n. 276.1
Nude To keep one from going n. 339.1
Nuisance exchange of one n. for another n. 216.1

Number if I called the wrong n., why did you answer 546.5
Numbers divinity in odd n. 498.200
Numbness drowsy n. pains My sense 332.22
Nun upbringing a n. would envy 426.1
Nuptials prone to any iteration of n. 151.7
Nurse sucks the n. asleep 498.17
Nurseries n. of all vice 225.4
Nut-brown spicy n. ale 401.7
Nuts Brazil, where the n. come from 542.1

O

Oaths O. are but words 96.5
Oats O. A grain, which in England is generally given to horses 323.5
Obey great Anna! whom three realms o. 452.26
  Monarchs must o. 205.13
Obeyed Nature…must be o. 30.41
Object hanging a man who does not o. 499.60
  o. of art 14.1
  o. will be, if possible to form Christian men 21.2
Oblige Noblesse o. 357.1
Oblivion alms for o. 498.264
  rest…commend to cold o. 500.3
Observance More honour'd in the breach than the o. 498.49
  o. of trifles 201.2
Occupations worse o. in the world than feeling a woman's pulse 527.2
Occur Accidents will o. 191.10
Odds o. is gone 498.15
Odi O. et amo 114.2
Odious comparisons are o. 199.5
Odorous Comparisons are o. 498.214
O'er Returning were as tedious as go o. 498.172
O'er-leaps Vaulting ambition, which o. itself 498.165
Off O. with his head 111.8
Offence dire o. from am'rous causes springs 452.25
Offend If thine eye o. thee 62.139
Offended This hand hath o. 168.1
Offer nothing to o.…except my own confusion 336.4
Office man who has no o. to go to 499.76
  o. of a wall 498.235
  o. sanctifies the holder 1.1
Often Do you come here o. 399.1
Oh O.! Sophonisba! 544.2
Old few who can grow o. with a good grace 524.2
  for o. lang syne 93.3
  I grow o.…I grow o. 214.10
  I love everything that's o. 262.4
  I was born o. 548.1
  I will never be an o. man 42.2
  man…as o. as the woman he feels 385.22
  o. acquaintance be forgot 93.2
  o. familiar faces 348.6
  O. men forget 498.99
  redress the balance of the O. 107.1
  They shall grow not o. 64.1
  they think he is growing o. 315.1
  You are o., Father William 111.4
Old age I prefer o. to the alternative 130.1
  o. a regret 195.7
  o. is…older than I am 42.2
Older she is o. than the rocks 436.1
Oliver Twist O. has asked for more 191.20
Olympic Games most important thing in the O. 160.1
Omega Alpha and O. 62.212
Omnipotence final proof of God's o. 190.5
On O. with the dance 98.8
Once journalism…be grasped at o. 153.5
  O. more unto the breach, dear friends 498.95
  Yet o. more, O ye laurels 401.9
One All for o. and o. for all 206.1
  O. on God's side is a majority 444.1
  O. remains 500.2

root is o. 601.3
Oneself Hell is o. 214.17
To love o. is the beginning of a lifelong romance 584.5
One up How to be o. 453.2
Only O. connect 237.1
Onward Half a league o. 539.2
little o. lend thy guiding hand 401.28
Open all questions are o. 54.3
O. Sesame 15.2
Opera Bed...is the poor man's o. 310.12
Operatic sunsets, they're so...o. 458.6
Operation o. to get a joke well into a Scotch understanding 512.2
Opinion better to have no o. of God 30.19
of his own o. still 96.7
O. is ultimately determined by the feelings 518.8
whole climate of o. 25.3
Opinions proper o. for the time of year 25.8
So many men, so many o. 540.2
Opium Religion...is the o. of the people 386.3
Opponent Never ascribe to an o. motives meaner than your own 40.7
Opportunist rather be an o. and float 35.1
Oppose duty...to o. 132.3
Opposition duty of an o. 132.3
Her Majesty's O. 32.2
Oppression fanatics...no limit to o. 392.4
Oracle I am Sir O. 498.187
Orange-tree Oh that I were an o. 290.3
Order old o. changeth 539.8
speech copious without o. 323.1
upon the o. of your going 498.171
words in the best o. 144.25
Orgies o. are vile 414.2
Orgy you need an o. 414.2
Origin indelible stamp of his lowly o. 180.1
Original thought is often o. 300.2
Originality All good things which exist are the fruits of o. 396.1
Orthodoxy O. not only no longer means being right 129.7
Oscar You will, O., you will 577.7
Others anything...one can pay o. to do 388.9
By persuading o. we convince ourselves 328.2
corner...for o.' uses 498.225
delight in...misfortunes...of o. 91.17
do not do to o. 150.12
Do not do unto o. as you would they 499.46
some more than o. 163.6
strength enough to endure the misfortunes of o. 471.7
to encourage the o. 561.2
who discommendeth o. 82.1
Otherwise some are o. 513.1
Ours Little we see in Nature that is o. 595.9
Ourselves all our knowledge is, o. to know 452.19
By persuading others we convince o. 328.2
remedies oft in o. do lie 498.1
we but praise o. in other men 452.14
Out Include me o. 263.2
love and murder will o. 151.2
Mordre will o. 127.15
O., damned spot 498.173
Outlive o. this powerful rhyme 498.292
Outlook religious o. on life 327.1
Outside wait till I get you o. 385.14
Outsoared o. the shadow of our night 500.1
Outward I may not hope from o. forms 144.18
Overcome And what is else not to be o. 401.16
o. evil with good 62.182
Over-educated I've o. myself in all the things 163.8
Overflow spontaneous o. of powerful feelings 595.25
Owe We o. God a death 498.90
Owl O. and the Pussy-Cat went to sea 354.5

Own He who can call to-day his o. 205.14
his o. received him not 62.162
mine o. Executioner 199.11
Oxenford Clerk...of O. 127.5
Oxford City with her dreaming spires 20.13
Home of lost causes 20.16
Oyster bold man that first eat an o. 535.11
o. may be crossed in love 502.1
world's mine o. 498.199
Oysters Poverty and o. 191.28
Ozymandias O., king of kings 500.10

P

Pace this petty p. from day to day 498.177
Paddle p. his own canoe 383.3
Pagan I'd rather be A P. 595.10
Pageant insubstantial p. faded 498.258
Pain draw thy breath in p. 498.75
gentleman...never inflicts p. 417.1
momentary intoxication with p. 76.1
Pleasure is...intermission of p. 494.5
what p. it was to drown 498.240
Pained p. at how little he was p. by 569.13
Pains I can sympathize with people's p. 310.13
Paint as fresh as p. 509.1
to p. the lily 498.128
Painted women...not so young as...p. 51.1
Painting great difference between p. a face 245.1
P. is a blind man's profession 445.2
Pair Blest p. of Sirens 401.1
Pajamas shot an elephant in my p. 385.2
Palladium Liberty of the press is the P. of...rights 328.1
Palm To win the p., the oak 384.4
Palms p. before my feet 129.3
Pants p. of my blue serge suit 385.4
Papacy P. is...the Ghost of the deceased Roman Empire 298.3
Paper isn't worth the p. it's written on 263.6
reactionaries are p. tigers 379.1
Papers fornicated and read the p. 106.2
Paper work keep the p. down to a minimum 426.5
Paradise drunk the milk of p. 144.21
England is a p. for women 94.3
England is the p. of women 233.1
p. for a sect 332.8
Wilderness is P. enow 228.3
Paragon p. of animals 498.57
Parent To lose one p....a misfortune 584.8
Parents his p. were not married 499.31
joys of p. are secret 30.8
what p. were created for 414.4
Paris P. is well worth a mass 286.1
Parish all the world as my p. 575.1
Parliaments England...mother of p. 75.2
Parody devil's walking p. 129.2
Part I have forgot my p. 498.35
let us kiss and p. 203.2
read p. of it all the way 263.9
till death us do p. 149.15
Particular angel is nobody in p. 499.57
did nothing in p. 257.5
London p....A fog 191.2
Particulars Minute P. 67.4
Parting P. is all we know of heaven 192.2
P. is such sweet sorrow 498.245
Partisanship P. is our great curse 469.1
Parts one man in his time plays many p. 498.23
Today we have naming of p. 465.1
Part-time p. nihilist 106.6
Party True patriotism is of no p. 513.3
Pass but let it p., let it p. 546.4
many change and p. 500.2
p. for forty-three 257.20
p. the ammunition 236.1
They shall not p. 440.1
Passageways smell of steaks in p. 214.12
Passed He p. by on the other side 62.156
That p. the time 47.3

We have all p. a lot of water 263.8
Passes Men seldom make p. 433.2
Passeth p. all understanding 62.198
Passio Hysterica p. 498.135
Passion Master Mistress of my p. 498.289
p. and the life, whose fountains are within 144.18
ruling p. conquers reason still 452.23
Passions coquette...rouses p. 499.81
devil to have all the p. 499.39
Literature and butterflies...two sweetest p. 412.3
man who has not passed through the inferno of his p. 327.2
man who is master of his p. 153.11
Three p.... have governed my life 485.1
Women...have...but two p. 128.9
Past remembrance of things p. 498.291
something...absurd about the p. 51.2
Study the p. 150.2
Those who cannot remember the p. 488.3
Time present and time p. 214.2
what's p. help Should be p. grief 498.281
What we know of the p. is 314.1
Pastoral Cold P. 332.17
Pastures fresh woods and p. new 401.13
lie down in green p. 62.47
Patches king of shreds and p. 498.69
thing of shreds and p. 257.8
Path primrose p. of dalliance 498.46
world will make a...p. to his door 218.15
Patience like P. on a monument, Smiling at grief 498.272
P., a minor form of despair 63.7
Though p. be a tired mare 498.93
Patient Fury of a P. Man 205.11
kill the p. 30.27
Like a p. etherized upon a table 214.7
Patrie Allons, enfants, de la p. 480.1
Patriotism p. is not enough 115.1
P. is the last refuge of a scoundrel 323.25
True p. is of no party 513.3
Patriots P.... never talk of killing 485.6
Patronize p. everybody without distinction of class 499.29
Pattern Art is the imposing of a p. 580.3
p. of excelling nature 498.228
Pay wonders what's to p. 304.8
Peace hereafter for ever hold his p. 149.14
inglorious arts of p. 384.6
In the arts of p. 499.44
in what p. a Christian can die 4.9
Let him who desires p., prepare for war 557.1
never was a good war or a bad p. 239.4
no p. of mind in love 458.1
no p., saith the Lord, unto the wicked 62.99
P.... a period of cheating 63.8
p. for our time 118.2
p. has broken out 74.8
p. I hope with honour 195.5
p. in our time 149.4
P. is poor reading 277.2
p. of God, which passeth 62.198
P., the human dress 67.17
p. with honour 118.2
Prince of P. 62.95
those who could make a good p. 133.29
War is P. 427.3
When there was p., he was for p. 25.8
Peace-maker If is the only p. 498.32
Peach dare to eat a p. 214.11
Peaches poetry in p. 266.1
Peak Silent, upon a p. in Darien 332.29
Pearl base Indian, threw a p. away 498.229
One p. of great price 62.135
Pearls cast ye your p. before swine 62.131
He who would search for P. 205.15
p. that were his eyes 498.254
Peculiar Funny p. 280.1
Peel *P.* caught the Whigs bathing 195.2
p. me a grape 576.4
Peers Fears, prejudices, misconceptions—those are the p. 364.2
Pen how much more cruel the p. 94.2
less brilliant p. than mine 51.3

nothing can cure it but the scratching of a p. 369.1
p. is mightier than the sword 88.1
Penance man hath p. done 144.11
Pens Let other p. dwell on guilt 27.4
People always been interested in p. 388.10
good of the p. 135.2
government of the p. by the p. 360.6
I am for p. 121.1
indictment against an whole p. 91.3
Let my p. go 62.12
mass of every p. must be barbarous 323.21
p.... are attracted by God 314.4
P. are either charming or tedious 584.12
p. are the masters 91.5
p. may be made to follow a course of action 150.9
P. must not be forced to adopt me as their favourite author 499.78
p. perish 62.78
P. seldom read a book which is given to them 323.22
p.'s government, made for the p., made by the p. 571.2
p. under suspicion are better moving 330.2
p. who... just miss the prizes 76.2
P. who like this sort of thing 360.9
p. whose company is coveted 376.1
p. who stay in the middle of the road 61.3
Religion... opium of the p. 386.3
talk as other p. do 323.34
Perception doors of p. were cleansed 67.26
Perfection friend who loved p. 511.11
pursuit of an unobtainable p. 511.1
pursuit of p. 20.14
Performance desire should... outlive p. 498.87
it takes away the p. 498.168
viewing them as a literary p. 582.6
Performing p. flea 423.2
Perfumes All the p. of Arabia 498.174
Perhaps I am going in search of a great p. 460.3
Perils all p. and dangers of this night 149.6
Perish everything else in our language should p. 375.1
no vision... people p. 62.78
though the world p. 224.1
weak shall p. 496.2
Periwig new p. 438.3
Perón If I had not been born P. 439.1
Perpetually damn'd p. 381.3
Persians law of the Medes and P. 62.106
Person idea of an agreeable p. 195.10
only thing that can exist is an uninterested p. 129.9
to the cheek of a young p. 191.23
To us he is no more a p. 25.3
Persons never more than two p. present in... reading 578.1
ninety and nine just p. 62.157
no respecter of p. 62.175
two aspicious p. 498.215
Persuade Beauty... doth... p. the eyes of men 498.304
Perversion War is... universal p. 461.1
Pervert p. climbs into the minds 76.1
Pestilence He who... acts not, breeds p. 67.22
Pestilence-stricken P. multitudes 500.7
Peter Shock-headed P. 299.4
Philistines Barbarians, P., Populace 20.15
Philosopher never yet p. That could endure the toothache 498.217
some p. has said it 135.1
Philosophy Axioms in p. are not axioms 332.38
dreamt of in your p. 498.52
History is p.... by examples 194.1
mere touch of cold p. 332.14
new P. calls all in doubt 199.1
Phone why did you answer the p. 546.5
Physic Take p., pomp 498.141
Physician P., heal thyself 62.153
Pianist Please do not shoot the p. 584.25
Piano pounding of an old p. 511.1
Pick man... would not scruple to p. a pocket 187.1

Picture easier to replace...than a good p. 499.18
Pictures book without p. 111.1
Piece p. of cod passes all understanding 373.2
p. of divinity in us 82.8
thou bleeding p. of earth 498.113
What a p. of work is a man 498.57
Whoever thinks a faultless p. to see 452.11
Pies I could eat one of Bellamy's veal p. 447.3
Pigs And whether p. have wings 111.22
Pilate jesting P. 30.2
Pillar triple p. of the world 498.4
Pious p. frauds of friendship 225.1
Pipe Blow your p. there 83.12
Piping Helpless, naked, p. loud 67.11
P. down the valleys wild 67.13
Pit bottomless p. 62.217
Whoso diggeth a p. 62.76
Pitchfork clothes...thrown on her with a p. 535.10
Pity P. a human face 67.17
p. beyond all telling 601.13
p. for the suffering of mankind 485.1
Poetry is in the p. 430.1
seas of p. lie 25.5
'Tis p. She's a whore 235.1
Place firm p. to stand 16.1
grave's a fine and private p. 384.3
Home is the p. where 243.2
mind is its own p. 401.17
Never the time and the p. 83.10
p. of excrement 601.4
running...to keep in the same p. 111.18
this is an awful p. 492.1
Upon the p. beneath 498.194
you shall now give p. to better men 172.3
Placid animals...so p. and self-contain'd 582.3
Plague p. o' both your houses! 498.248
Plagues of all p. with which mankind are curst 184.3
Plain best p. set 30.33
Manners are...need of the p. 569.25
Planet When a new p. swims into his ken 332.29
Plans finest p. have always been spoiled 74.4
Platitude longitude with no p. 244.1
To stroke a p. until it purrs 382.1
Plato P. is dear to me 17.4
Play behold the Englishman...p. tip-and-run 227.1
Better than a p. 123.4
good p. needs no epilogue 498.33
know what to say about a p. 499.21
little victims p. 268.3
p., I remember, pleas'd not the million 498.58
p. is a dynamic thing 554.2
p.'s the thing 498.60
p. the man 350.1
p. up! and p. the game 416.2
tale which holdeth children from p. 506.2
Player poor p., That struts and frets his hour 498.177
Players men and women merely p. 498.23
Playing fields won on the p. of Eton 573.3
Playwright Congreve...only sophisticated p. 554.1
Pleasant How p. it is to have money 140.2
Please death after life does...p. 519.1
I...do what I p. 241.1
Love seeketh not itself to p. 67.9
must p. to live 323.7
Natural to p. 205.2
They...say what they p. 241.1
Pleased man is in general better p. when he has a good dinner 323.39
Pleasing art of p. consists in 281.6
Pleasure Debauchee...One who has...pursued p. 63.3
dissipation without p. 255.2
for...p. I'd sooner go to my dentist 569.16
gave p. to the spectators 375.3
greatest p....to do a good action 348.5
great source of p. is variety 323.38

hatred is by far the longest p. 98.19
Love ceases to be a p. 53.1
Money gives me p. 55.5
No profit grows where is no p. 498.251
p. in the pathless woods 98.10
P. is...intermission of pain 494.5
Youth is full of p. 498.303
Pleasure-dome stately p. decree 144.19
Pleasures No man is a hypocrite in his p. 323.35
One half...cannot understand the p. 27.1
purest of human p. 30.36
Plenty but just had p. 93.5
Plods plowman homeward p. his weary way 268.5
Plot p. thickens 85.2
Ploughing Is my team p. 304.3
Plowman p. homeward plods his weary way 268.5
Plowshares beat their swords into p. 62.92
Pluck eye offend thee, p. it out 62.139
Plural in the p. and they bounce 373.1
Plus P. ça change, p. c'est la même chose 331.1
Pocket pound...in your p. 589.2
smile I could feel in my hip p. 120.2
Pockets young man feels his p. 304.8
Poems p....for the love of Man and in praise of God 543.4
Poesy drainless shower of light is p. 332.32
Poet lunatic, the lover, and the p. 498.206
No p., no artist of any sort, has his complete meaning alone 214.19
p. and the dreamer are distinct 332.9
p.'s eye, in a fine frenzy 498.207
To be a p. is a condition 267.4
Poetry If p. comes not as naturally as leaves 332.37
Mr Shaw...never written any p. 129.20
no man ever talked p. 191.30
P. is a comforting piece of fiction 392.5
P. is in the pity 430.1
P. is the spontaneous overflow of powerful feelings 595.25
P. is the supreme fiction 528.2
P. lifts the veil from the hidden beauty 500.15
p. reminds him of the richness 335.4
P.'s unnatural 191.30
p. = the best words in the best order 144.25
there is p. in peaches 266.1
truest p. is the most feigning 498.30
wretched men Are cradled into p. by wrong 500.5
Poets P. are the unacknowledged legislators 500.16
Pole Beloved from p. to p. 144.10
Police friendship recognised by the p. 529.1
Reading...among p. officers 426.5
Policeman p.'s lot is not a happy one 257.19
Policemen repressed sadists...become p. 153.4
Polite every time you are p. to a proletarian 569.21
Politeness Punctuality is the p. of kings 367.1
Political addiction of p. groups to ideas 247.3
formation of the p. will of the nation 297.5
Political Economy Dismal Science 109.11
Politician at home you're just a p. 378.2
Coffee, which makes the p. wise 452.29
like a scurvy p. 498.148
Politicians P. neither love nor hate 205.5
race of p. put together 535.5
Polygamy P. was made a Sin 205.1
Pommie every...P....his fare home 334.1
Pomp Pride, p., and circumstance 498.227
Take physic, p. 498.141
Pompous p. in the grave 82.9
Poms All the faces...bloody P. 125.1
Pooh-Bah P. (Lord High Everything Else) 257.7
Poor decent means p. 437.1
great men have their p. relations 191.4

grind the faces of the p. 62.93
I live by robbing the p. 499.42
inconvenient to be p. 165.2
Laws grind the p. 262.7
p. always with you 62.144
P. Little Rich Girl 163.12
p. shall never cease 62.28
short and simple annals of the p. 268.6
To be p. and independent 141.1
What fun it would be to be p. 14.2
Populace Barbarians, Philistines, P. 20.15
Populi *vox p., vox dei* 10.1
Porcupines I shall throw two p. under you 344.2
Pornography P. is the attempt to insult sex 351.2
p. of war 461.1
Position only one p. for an artist 543.6
Possessing too dear for my p. 498.295
Possessions p. for a moment of time 215.4
Post p. of honour is a private station 4.3
Posterity doing something for p. 4.8
Think of your p. 2.1
Pot greasy Joan doth keel the p. 498.157
Potent how p. cheap music is 163.3
Poultry p. matter 385.3
Pound p. here in Britain, in your pocket 589.2
Pounds two hundred p. a year 96.6
Poured he had been p. into his clothes 592.4
Pouvait *si vieillesse p.* 219.1
Poverty crime so shameful as p. 223.1
from nothing to ... extreme p. 385.11
greatest of evils ... is p. 499.30
P. and oysters 191.28
P. is an anomaly to rich people 32.3
P. is no disgrace to a man 512.1
Power balance of p. 563.1
greater the p. 91.16
P. tends to corrupt 1.1
When p. narrows the areas of man's concern 335.4
Powerful Guns will make us p. 260.1
Powerless p. to be born 20.7
Powers Headmasters have p. 133.27
we lay waste our p. 595.9
Practical meddling with any p. part of life 4.4
Praise bury Caesar, not to p. him 498.116
Damn with faint p. 452.3
highest p. of God ... denial 458.5
I will p. any man that will p. me 498.10
Let us now p. famous men 62.113
People ... only want p. 388.2
P. is the best diet 512.6
P. the Lord 236.1
we but p. ourselves in other men 452.14
Praising advantage of ... p. ... oneself 97.6
Pram sombre enemy of good art than the p. 153.7
Prayeth He p. well 144.14
Preachers P. say, Do as I say 494.1
Precisely thinking too p. on th' event 498.70
Predicament life is ... a p. 488.5
Prefabricated better word than p. 133.40
Prefer I p. Reading 511.5
Pregnancy It is now quite lawful for a Catholic woman to avoid p. 392.2
Prejudice I am free of all p. 226.3
We all decry p. 518.5
Prejudices it p. a man so 512.7
Prelude p. to insanity 569.7
Premise fundamental p. of a revolution 549.1
Presbyter P. is but old Priest writ large 401.34
Present P. mirth hath p. laughter 498.270
Time p. and time past 214.2
President P. spends ... time kissing people 551.2
rather be right than be P. 137.1
Presume Dr Livingstone, I p.? 522.1
Pretty p. can get away with anything 569.25
Prevention P. is better than cure 437.2
Price All those men have their p. 563.2
pearl of great p. 62.135
Prick If you p. us, do we not bleed? 498.193

p. the sides of my intent 498.165
Pricks Honour p. me on 498.80
kick against the p. 62.174
Pride Is P., the never-failing vice of fools 452.9
P. goeth before destruction 62.71
p. that licks the dust 452.5
Priest Presbyter is but old P. writ large 401.34
this turbulent p. 287.1
Priest-craft e'r P. did begin 205.1
Priests I always like to associate with a lot of p. 55.7
Prince P. of Peace 62.95
Princes Put not your trust in p. 62.63
Principle p.... can always be sacrificed to expediency 388.6
p. seems the same 133.38
What is p. against the flattery 502.9
Principles my p. round my neck 35.1
Print news that's fit to p. 424.1
pleasant, sure, to see one's name in p. 98.23
Printers those books by which the p. have lost 245.4
Printing Gunpowder, P., and the Protestant Religion 109.2
mass... must be barbarous... no p. 323.21
Priorities language of p. is 61.1
Prison comparatively at home in p. 569.12
Home is... girl's p. 499.55
Stone walls do not a p. make 368.1
Prison-house Shades of the p. begin to close 595.5
Prize Men p. the thing ungain'd 498.261
Not all that tempts your wand'ring eyes... is lawful p. 268.2
Prizes people who... just miss the p. 76.2
Problem ineffectual liberal's p. 240.1
three-pipe p. 201.7
Procrastination P. is the thief of time 602.3
Prodigal P. of Ease 205.4
Producing consume happiness without p. 499.11
Professions All p. are conspiracies 499.17
one of the p. which are full 545.2
Professors American p. like their literature clear and cold and pure and very dead 359.2
Profit No p. grows where is no pleasure 498.251
what shall it p. a man 62.148
Progress All p. is based 97.5
p. depends on the unreasonable man 499.53
p. is simply a comparative 129.8
What we call p. is 216.1
Progression Without Contraries is no p. 67.19
Proletarian every time you are polite to a p. 569.21
Promise p. made is a debt unpaid 496.1
Promising gods... first call p. 153.6
Pronounce p. foreign names as he chooses 133.41
Proof p. of God's omnipotence 190.5
Proper P. words in p. places 535.6
Property P. has its duties 204.1
P. is theft 457.1
Prophet p. is not without honour 62.136
Prophets Beware of false p. 62.132
Proportion strangeness in the p. 30.34
Proposes Man p. 333.1
Prose anything except bad p. 133.2
p. = words in their best order 144.25
talking p. for over forty years 402.2
what is the p. for God 266.3
Prospect noblest p. a Scotchman ever sees 323.14
Prosper Treason doth never p. 278.1
Prosperitee him that stood in greet p. 127.14
man to have ben in p. 127.17
Prosperity P. doth best discover vice 30.7
Prostitutes small nations like p. 345.1
Protest lady doth p. too much 498.67
Protestant Gunpowder, Printing, and the P. Religion 109.2
Protestantism chief contribution of P. to human thought 392.3

Proteus P. rising from the sea 595.10
Proud Death be not p. 199.8
p. me no prouds 498.249
too p. to fight 591.2
when you have attained the state you will not be p. 196.1
Prove p. anything by figures 109.1
Proved p. upon our pulses 332.38
Proverb p. is much matter 245.3
Providence P. will...end...acts of God 190.6
Province all knowledge to be my p. 30.42
Provincial he was worse than p.... parochial 317.2
Provincialism rather be taken in adultery than p. 310.4
Psyche Your mournful P. 332.20
Psychiatrist Anybody who goes to see a p. 263.3
century of the p.'s couch 377.1
Psychic p. development of the individual 242.1
Psychopathologist p. the unspeakable 388.4
Psychotic label p. is affixed 346.1
Public as if I was a p. meeting 558.2
more... ungrateful animal than the p. 281.5
reasons for a man's not speaking in p. 323.24
strike against p. safety 155.2
Public school enjoy a p. 153.2
Public schools P. are the nurseries of all vice 225.4
Publish I'll p., right or wrong 98.22
P. and be damned 573.4
Publisher Barabbas was a p. 104.3
Publishers those with irrational fear of life become p. 153.4
Publishing novel to be too good to be worth p. 499.64
Pulse worse occupations... than feeling a woman's p. 527.2
Pulses proved upon our p. 332.38
Pun man who could make so vile a p. 187.1
Punctuality P. is the politeness of kings 367.1
Punishment let the p. fit the crime 257.11
Pure All those who are not racially p. 297.1
Because my heart is p. 539.25
Blessed are the p. in heart 62.119
p. as the driven slush 38.2
Purgatory p. of men 233.1
Puritan P. hated bear-baiting 375.3
p.'s a person who pours righteous indignation 129.25
Purple-stained And p. mouth 332.24
Purpose time to every p. 62.82
Purse consumption of the p. 498.85
Put money in thy p. 498.219
Pursued p. by a bear 498.282
Pursuit p. of an unobtainable perfection 511.1
p. of perfection 20.14
Pussy-Cat Owl and the P. 354.5
Pygmies wars of the p. will begin 133.37

Q

Qualified If you go to Heaven without being...q. 499.43
Qualities only two q. in the world 499.28
Quality q. of mercy is not strain'd 498.194
Quantity prodigious q. of mind 553.3
Queen I would not be a q. For all the world 498.102
Q. of Hearts 111.13
Queen Anne Q.'s dead 147.2
Queer All the world is q. 429.1
drink to the q. old Dean 520.2
thou art a little q. 429.1
Question q.... which I have not been able to answer 242.5
that is the q. 498.61
what is the q. 525.3
Questions all q. are open 54.3
Queue Englishman... forms an orderly q. of one 395.2

Quiet Anythin' for a q. life 191.33
Quietness unravish'd bride of q. 332.15
Quintessence this q. of dust 498.57
Quit Q. yourselves like men 62.33
Quod q. erat demonstrandum 220.2
Quoque Tu q. 428.2
Quotation q. is a national vice 569.19
Quotations good thing... to read books of q. 133.28
q. beautiful from minds profound 433.1
Quote think they grow immortal as they q. 602.1

R

Race Slow and steady wins the r. 363.1
Races human species... composed of two distinct r. 348.1
Rachel R. weeping for her children 62.114
Racially those who are not r. pure 297.1
Rack Leave not a r. behind 498.258
Radiance white r. of Eternity 500.2
Radical r. is a man 475.2
Rag-and-bone foul r. shop of the heart 601.2
Rage all Heaven in a r. 67.2
R., r., against the dying of the light 543.1
Rags no scandal like r. 223.1
Rain droppeth as the gentle r. 498.194
r. on the just and on the unjust 62.124
Rainy when it is not r. 98.2
Raise My God shall r. me up 462.1
Rake every woman is at heart a r. 452.21
lene... as is a r. 127.6
Rapidly but not so r. 47.3
Rapture first fine careless r. 83.7
r. on the lonely shore 98.10
Rare O r. Ben Jonson 325.7
Rarely R., r., comest thou 500.14
Rashes Green grow the r. O 93.8
Rat Mr Speaker, I smell a r. 470.1
Rationed liberty... must be r. 355.2
Rats R.! They fought the dogs 83.11
Raven Quoth the R., 'Nevermore' 450.1
Reach man's r. should exceed his grasp 83.2
Reactionaries r. are paper tigers 379.1
Read classic... nobody wants to r. 553.6
His books were r. 55.4
I never r. a book before reviewing it 512.7
only news until he's r. it 569.20
r. just as inclination leads 323.15
R., mark, learn and inwardly digest 149.9
sooner r. a time-table... than nothing 388.8
When I want to r. a novel 195.13
Readers human race, to which so many of my r. belong 129.16
not all books... are as dull as their r. 545.4
Reading few books... are worth r. 499.80
If a book is worth r. 484.1
I prefer R. 511.5
Peace is poor r. 277.2
R. isn't an occupation we encourage among police officers 426.5
R. is to the mind 524.3
R. maketh a full man 30.39
two persons... in the act of r. 578.1
When I am not walking I am r. 348.3
Ready made critics all are r. 98.24
Why not 'r.' 133.40
Real whether Zelda and I are r. 229.6
Reality art... r. in our minds 376.2
Cannot bear very much r. 214.3
Realms travell'd in the r. of gold 332.28
Reap they shall r. in joy 62.61
they shall r. the whirlwind 62.108
whatsoever a man soweth that shall he also r. 62.196
Reason he who destroys a good book kills r. 401.35
madman... has lost his r. 129.17
man... is R.'s slave 153.11
man who listens to R. is lost 499.54
no r. to bring religion into it 423.1
Only r. can convince us 54.3
right deed for the wrong r. 214.18
R. is itself a matter of faith 129.19

r. not the need 498.136
r. of this thusness 566.2
ruling passion conquers r. 452.23
Their's not to r. why 539.3
woman's r. 498.279
Reasonable r. man adapts himself to the world 499.53
Reasons heart has its r. 435.1
two r. for drinking 437.2
Rebel What is a r. 106.7
Rebuke Open r. is better than secret love 62.77
Recall r.... happiness... in misery 176.2
Receive more blessed to give than to r. 62.177
Received his own r. him not 62.162
Reckon'd beggary in the love that can be r. 498.5
Recoils back on itself r. 401.26
Recollected emotion r. in tranquility 595.25
Recompense R. injury with justice 150.10
Red Coral is far more r. 498.300
keep the R. Flag flying 152.1
R. Badge of Courage 167.1
To get very r. in the face 59.1
Redeemer my r. liveth 62.41
Reed r. shaken by the wind 62.133
References Always verify your r. 482.1
Reflection It is a sad r. but a true one 323.16
Refuge God is our r. 62.52
only r. of weak minds 128.8
Refuse never r. a drink 392.6
Regardless r. of their doom 268.3
Regiment led his r. from behind 257.1
Monstrous R. of Women 342.1
Regret old age a r. 195.7
Reign Better to r. in Hell 401.18
Reigned I have r. with your loves 215.3
Relations great men have their poor r. 191.4
Relaxes Bless r. 67.24
Relief For this r. much thanks 498.39
Religion Fascism is a r. 411.1
I am a Millionaire. That is my r. 499.32
just enough r. to make us hate 535.16
Love is my r. 332.39
Men will wrangle for r. 148.1
no reason to bring r. into it 423.1
One r. is as true as another 94.4
r. for gentlemen 123.2
r. is allowed to invade the sphere of private life 390.1
R. is an illusion 242.2
R. is by no means a proper subject 128.12
R.... is the opium of the people 386.3
r. of feeble minds 91.10
r. of Socialism 61.1
r.... yours is Success 40.3
talk r. to a man with bodily hunger in his eyes 499.33
There is only one r. 499.65
Religious first, r. and moral principles 21.1
not r.-good 277.4
r. animal 91.9
r. outlook on life 327.1
Remains Form r. 595.15
One r. 500.2
what r.? Nature r. 582.7
Remarkable nothing left r. Beneath the visiting moon 498.15
Remedies He that will not apply new r. 30.24
Our r. oft in ourselves do lie 498.1
Remedy Force is not a r. 75.3
r. is worse than the disease 30.18
Tis a sharp r., but a sure one 462.2
Remember I only r. what I've learnt 579.2
third I can't r. 534.1
Those who cannot r. the past 488.3
We will r. them 64.1
Remembrance r. of things past 498.291
Render R. unto Caesar 62.141
Repair m. should keep his friendship in... r. 323.12
Repay I will r., saith the Lord 62.181
Repeal method to... r. bad... laws 265.1
Repentance persons, which need no r. 62.157
Winter Garment of R. 228.2
Repenteth one sinner that r. 62.157

Repetition constant r.. .imprinting an idea 297.2
Replenished His intellect is not r. 498.154
Reply Their's not to make r. 539.3
Reprehend If I r. any thing in this world 502.6
Reproduce butlers and lady's maids do not r. 574.1
Reputation it wrecks a woman's r. 145.4
R., r., r.! O, I have lost my r. 498.222
spotless r. 498.232
Requests thou wilt grant their r. 149.5
Requires all the Human Frame r. 55.3
Resemble happy families r. one another 547.1
Resent no individual could r. 535.3
Resist r. everything except temptation 584.13
Resisting fond of r. temptation 48.1
Resolution native hue of r. 498.63
Respectable more r. he is 499.36
R. means rich 437.1
Respecter no r. of persons 62.175
Responsibility In dreams begins r. 601.12
Liberty means r. 499.50
no sense of r. at the other 343.1
Responsible idea isn't r. for the people 382.2
r. and the irresponsible classes 351.1
Rest get rid of the r. of her 556.1
Give his brain a r. 507.2
leave the r. to the Gods 158.2
One needs more r. if one doesn't sleep 569.9
r.... commend To cold oblivion 500.3
r. is silence 498.76
Reticulated Any thing r. or decussated 323.4
Retrograde All that is human must r. 255.4
Return unto dust shalt thou r. 62.4
Returning R. were as tedious as go o'er 498.172
Reveal words... half r. and half conceal 539.10
Revelry sound of r. by night 98.7
Revels Our r. now are ended 498.258
Revenge if you wrong us, shall we not r. 498.193
R., at first though sweet 401.26
R. is a ... wild justice 30.6
Reviewing I never read a book before r. it 512.7
Revolution fundamental premise of a r. 549.1
Revolutions All modern r. have ended 106.8
state of mind which creates r. 17.3
Revolver I reach for my r. 260.3
Reward r. of a thing well done 218.6
Rhyme outlive this powerful r. 498.292
Rich as well off as if he were r. 24.1
no sin but to be r. 498.125
Poor Little R. Girl 163.12
Poverty is an anomaly to r. people 32.3
Respectable means r. 437.1
r. are different from us 229.4
r. are the scum of the earth 129.6
seems it r. to die 332.26
wretchedness of being r. 511.4
Richer for r. for poorer 149.15
R. than all his tribe 498.229
Riches good name... than great r. 62.74
Infinite r. in a little room 381.5
R. are for spending 30.28
Richesses l'embarras des r. 11.1
Rid glad to get r. of it 385.10
never get r. of the rest 556.1
only way to get r. of a temptation 584.19
Ride Haggards r. no more 526.2
Ridiculous fine sense of the r. 9.2
sublime and the r. 431.1
Right All's r. with the world 83.13
better to be irresponsible and r. 133.25
I am not and never have been, a man of the r. 407.1
I had rather be r. than be President 137.1
minority is always r. 313.2
My speciality is being r. 499.74
no r. to strike against public safety 155.2
orthodoxy no longer means... r. 129.7
our country, r. or wrong 183.1
publish, r. or wrong 98.22

r. divine of kings to govern wrong 452.1
so the heart be r. 462.3
Those who believe that they are exclusively in the r. 310.22
Ulster will be r. 132.2
very important to be r. 133.44
Righteous Be not r. over much 62.83
Ring R. down the curtain 460.2
Ripe Cherry R. 105.2
Cherry r. 291.1
we r. and r. 498.22
Ripeness R. is all 498.151
Ripp'd mother's womb untimely r. 498.179
Rise Early to r. and early to bed 546.1
One man's wage r. is another man's 589.3
River Alph, the sacred r. ran 144.19
Fame is like a r. 30.40
Old man r. 275.1
Ol' man r. 275.1
Rivers By the r. of Babylon 62.62
Road Golden R. to Samarkand 231.1
On the r. to Mandalay 341.8
people who stay in the middle of the r. 61.3
r. of excess 67.21
Roads New r.: new ruts 129.26
Roar I had the luck to give the r. 133.42
Robb'd He that is r., not wanting what is stol'n 498.226
Robbing I live by r. the poor 499.42
Robes R. and furr'd gowns hide all 498.147
Robespierre seagreen Incorruptible 109.10
Robin r. redbreast in a cage 67.2
Rocks older than the r. among which she sits 436.1
With r., and stones, and trees 595.16
Rod He that spareth his r. hateth his son 62.70
rule them with a r. of iron 62.214
spare the r. 96.3
thy r. and thy staff they comfort me 62.48
Rode r. madly off in all directions 353.4
Roland Childe R. to the Dark Tower came 83.5
Rolf Harris Did you know that R. was Australian 222.2
Rolled bottoms of my trousers r. 214.10
Rollin' he keeps on r. along 275.1
Roman noblest R. of them all 498.123
Papacy... Ghost of the... R. Empire 298.3
Romance love oneself... a lifelong r. 584.5
Romans Friends, R., countrymen, lend me your ears 498.116
Rome I lov'd R. more 498.115
R. found it brick and left it marble 100.1
When in R. 12.1
when R. falls—the World 98.9
Romeo R.! wherefore art thou R. 498.242
Room always r. at the top 571.1
before my little r. 78.1
Infinite riches in a little r. 381.5
who sneaked into my r. at three o'clock 385.12
Root love of money is the r. of all evil 62.202
r. is one 601.3
Rose At Christmas I no more desire a r. 498.153
One perfect r. 433.3
r. By any other name 498.243
R. is a r. is a r. is a r. 525.2
Roses days of wine and r. 200.3
Flung r., r. riotously 200.2
Send two dozen r. to Room 424 385.17
Rot lie in cold obstruction, and to r. 498.184
we r. and r. 498.22
Rotten r. in the state of Denmark 498.50
Rough-hew R. them how we will 498.74
Roving we'll go no more a r. 98.26
Rowed All r. fast 142.1
Rub there's the r. 498.61
try to r. up against money 483.2
Rubies wisdom is better than r. 62.65
Rudyards When the R. cease from kipling 526.2
Rue With r. my heart is laden 304.5

Ruined r. by trade 239.2
Rule R. Britannia 544.1
r. them with a rod of iron 62.214
Ruler I am the R. of the Queen's Navee 257.16
Rules energetic without r. 323.1
there are no golden r. 499.48
Ruling r. passion conquers reason 452.23
Rumble R. thy bellyful 498.138
Rumours Wars and r. of wars 62.142
Running it takes all the r.... to keep in the same place 111.18
Rush For fools r. in 452.16
Rushes Green grow the r. O 93.8
Russia R. has two generals 418.1
Russians our decadence and the R.' 546.7
Rust r. of the whole week 4.5
Rustling r. in unpaid-for silk 498.36
Ruts New roads: new r. 129.26
Rye Coming through the r. 93.4

S

Sabbath never broke the S. 205.8
s. was made for man 62.146
seventh day is the s. 62.16
Sacred human body is s. 582.1
Sacred Heart Convent of the S. 214.15
Sadder s. and a wiser man 144.16
Sadists repressed s. are supposed to become policemen 153.4
Safe world must be made s. for democracy 591.3
Safest Just when we are s. 83.3
Safety s. is in our speed 218.8
Sages Than all the s. can 595.19
Said great deal to be s. For being dead 59.4
I wish I had s. that 577.7
they do not know what they have s. 133.4
well s., as if I had said it myself 535.12
Saint never a s. took pity on My soul 144.7
Sakes king... men have made for their own s. 494.2
Salad My s. days 498.7
Sally There's none like pretty S. 108.2
Salmon choice between smoked s. and tinned s. 589.1
Salt Ye are the s. of the earth 62.120
Salute those about to die s. you 532.2
Salvation Work out your own s. 62.197
Samarkand Golden Road to S. 231.1
Same he is much the s. 28.1
principle seems the s. 133.38
Their tastes may not be the s. 499.46
we're all made the s. 163.6
Sana mens s. in corpore sano 329.3
Sand Such quantities of s. 111.21
throw the s. against the wind 67.8
World in a grain of s. 67.1
Sans S. teeth, s. eyes, s. taste, s. every thing 498.24
Sappho Where burning S. loved 98.15
Sat we s. down, yea, we wept 62.62
You have s. too long here 13.1
Satan Get thee behind me, S. 62.138
S. exalted sat, by merit raised 401.20
S. finds some mischief 568.1
S., Nick, or Clootie 93.1
Satisfied superior man is s. 150.8
Sauce best s. in the world 116.2
Saul S. hath slain his thousands 62.34
Savage s. place! as holy and enchanted 144.20
soothe a s. breast 151.3
young man who has not wept is a s. 488.2
Savait Si jeunesse s. 219.1
Save he need not exist in order to s. us 190.5
s. those that have no imagination 499.71
Saviour I imitate the S. 310.2
Savour if the salt have lost his s. 62.120
Saw I came, I s., I conquered 101.2
Say hardly anybody has got anything to s. 174.1
Preachers say, Do as I s. 494.1
S. it with flowers 425.1
They are to s. what they please 241.1

they do not know what they are going to s. 133.4
what people s. of us is true 511.6
When you have nothing to s. 148.2
Saying they do not know what they are s. 133.4
Says desire for preventing the thing one s. 458.4
Scandal It is a public s. that gives offence 402.3
There's no s. like rags 223.1
Scape who shall s. whipping 498.59
Scapegoat Let him go for a s. 62.25
Scarlet His sins were s. 55.4
sins be as s. 62.91
Scene Upon that memorable s. 384.7
Sceptred this s. isle 498.235
Schemes best laid s. o' mice an' men 93.12
Schizophrenia S. cannot be understood 346.2
Scholars great men have not commonly been great s. 300.3
School Anyone who has been to an English public s. 569.12
Example is the s. of mankind 91.11
fleshly s. of Poetry 84.1
If every day in the life of a s. 353.1
Three little maids from s. 257.10
Schoolmaster you'll be becoming a s. sir 569.1
Schools hundred s. of thought contend 379.2
We class s., you see, into four grades 569.2
Science S. is organized knowledge 518.2
Scientist genuine s. must be ... a metaphysician 499.8
Scissor-man great, long, red-legged s. 299.3
Scope this man's art, and that man's s. 498.290
Scorned fury like a woman s. 151.4
Scotch get a joke well into a S. understanding 512.2
Scotchman noblest prospect which a S. ever sees 323.14
Scotland I ... come from S., but I cannot help it 323.13
Scots S., wha hae wi' Wallace bled 93.15
Scotsman grandest moral attribute of a S. 40.4
S. on the make 40.5
Scoundrel General Good is the plea of the s. 67.4
man over forty is a s. 499.56
Patriotism ... last refuge of a s. 323.25
Scratching s. of a pen 369.1
Scripture devil can cite S. 498.189
Scrofulous s. French novel 83.17
Scum rich are the s. of the earth 129.6
s. of the earth 573.1
Sea Alone on a wide wide s. 144.7
Down to a sunless s. 144.19
fishes live in the s. 498.231
go down to the s. in ships 62.57
I'm never, never sick at s. 257.15
Into that silent s. 144.5
kings of the s. 20.5
Out of the s. came he 144.2
O . . . and the Pussy-Cat went to s. 354.5
precious stone set in the silver s. 498.235
Proteus rising from the s. 595.10
s. is calm to-night 20.1
s.! the s. 599.1
snotgreen s.. The scrotumtightening s. 326.2
there was no more s. 62.218
They went to s. in a sieve 354.3
why the s. is boiling hot 111.22
Sea-change doth suffer a s. 498.254
Seagreen s. Incorruptible 109.10
Seal And when he had opened the seventh s. 62.216
slumber did my spirit s. 595.16
Sear My way of life Is fall'n into the s., the yellow leaf 498.175
Search in s. of a great perhaps 460.3
s. for knowledge 485.1
Seas s. of pity lie 25.5
Season Only in the mating s. 399.1
To every thing there is a s. 62.82
Second best s.'s a gay goodnight 601.11
Secret digestion ... s. of life 512.8

joys of parents are s. 30.8
to sin in s. 402.3
when it ceases to be a s. 53.1
Sect attached to that great s. 500.3
paradise for a s. 332.8
Sedge s. is wither'd from the lake 332.11
See change we think we s. 243.1
Come up and s. me sometime 576.1
s.... into a hypocrite 129.10
seem to s. things thou dost not 498.148
they shall s. God 62.119
Seeing Is not the Giant's-Causeway worth s. 323.33
Seek To strive, to s.... and not to yield 539.27
Seen Blessed are they that have not s. 62.173
Justice should... be s. to be done 292.1
most beautiful woman I've ever s. 385.1
Sees fool s. not the same tree 67.23
man who s. absolutely nothing 584.20
What, when drunk, one s. in other women 554.3
Seize S. the day 303.1
Selection term of Natural S. 180.2
Self nothing, not God, is greater to one than one's s. 582.4
to thine own s. be true 498.48
Self-adjusting No man... who has wrestled with a s. card table 546.2
Self-indulgence essay on s. 569.3
Self-interest S. speaks all sorts of tongues 471.10
Selfish I have been a s. being 27.11
Self-love S. is the greatest of all flatterers 471.6
S. seems so often unrequited 455.1
true s. and social are the same 452.19
Self-sufficient know how to be s. 403.1
Semed he s. bisier than he was 127.8
Sensational something s. to read in the train 584.10
Sensations life of s. rather than of thoughts 332.34
Sense drowsy numbness pains my s. 332.22
fine s. of the ridiculous 9.2
Money is like a sixth s. 388.3
sound must seem an echo to the s. 452.13
Take care of the s. 111.10
Sensibly things they behave s. about 499.12
Sensitive more s. one is to great art 51.4
Sentence S. first—verdict afterwards 111.15
structure of the British s. 133.26
Serious War is much too s.... to be left to military men 536.5
Serpent as the s. used to say, why not 499.9
my s. of old Nile 498.6
Servant You are *not* his most humble s. 323.34
Serv'd s. my God with half the zeal I s. my King 498.104
Serve No man can s. two masters 62.126
They also s. who only stand and wait 401.33
Served I must have things daintily s. 60.1
Youth will be s. 70.1
Serviettes kiddies have crumpled the s. 60.1
Sesame Open S. 15.2
Sessions s. of sweet silent thought 498.291
Set all, except their sun, is s. 98.15
best plain s. 30.33
Sets dominions, on which the sun never s. 421.1
Setting had elsewhere its s. 595.5
Seven his acts being s. ages 498.23
Sex farmyard world of s. 266.2
Money... was exactly like s. 34.2
Pornography is the attempt to insult s. 351.2
professed tyrant to their s. 498.208
Sexes this absurd division into s. 569.14
Sexual music throatily s. 310.1
Shade inviolable s. 20.11
sport with Amaryllis in the s. 401.10
Shadow lose the substance by grasping at the s. 6.1
Shak'd when degree is s. 498.262
Shakespeare myriad-minded S. 144.23
S. he was naturally learned 205.17

S. is . . . really very good 267.5
S. man who . . . had the largest . . . soul 205.16
S. Out-topping knowledge 20.12
S. small Latin and less Greek 325.2
S. . . . Warble his . . . wood-notes wild 401.8
When I read S. I am struck 351.5
Shame expense of spirit in a waste of s. 498.299
Shape to give life a s. 14.1
Shapes divinity that s. our ends 498.74
Shaw disciple of Bernard S. 499.20
Mr S. . . . has never written any poetry 129.20
She s. is my country still 131.1
S. who has never loved 251.2
Shed tears, prepare to s. them 498.119
Sheep All we like s. have gone astray 62.100
divideth his s. from the goats 62.143
hungry s. look up, and are not fed 401.12
in s.'s clothing 62.132
like lost s. 149.1
make a man by standing a s. 51.9
one is of an old half-witted s. 526.1
shepherd giveth his life for the s. 62.169
Shepherd Go, for they call you, S., from the hill 20.8
good s. giveth his life for the sheep 62.169
Lord is my s. 62.46
Sherry I am very fond of . . . s. 129.4
Shibboleth Say now S. 62.31
Shielding s. men from . . . folly 518.3
Shift coming down let me s. for myself 404.1
let futurity s. for itself 513.2
Shine eyes s. like the pants of my . . . suit 385.4
Few are qualified to s. in company 535.17
Shining sun s. ten days a year 334.1
Ships face that launch'd a thousand s. 381.2
go down to the sea in s. 62.57
S., towers, domes, theatres 595.11
something wrong with our bloody s. 44.1
Shit s. in the streets 334.1
Shock-headed S. Peter 299.4
Shocks s. That flesh is heir to 498.61
Shoes s. and ships and sealing wax 111.22
Shoot Please do not s. the pianist 584.25
Shop man must keep a little back s. 403.2
Shopkeepers altogether unfit for a nation of s. 510.2
England is a nation of s. 413.2
Shore adieu! my native s. 98.3
rapture on the lonely s. 98.10
waves make towards the pebbled s. 498.293
Short it will take a long while to make it s. 545.7
life is s. 296.1
Life is too s. to do anything . . . one can pay others to do 388.9
lyf so s. 127.16
Shorter s. by a head 215.1
Should nae better than he s. be 93.6
no better than you s. be 45.1
Show I have that within which passes s. 498.41
Show off I often wish they would s. a little more 376.1
Shreds thing of s. and patches 257.8
Shrieks murder s. out 572.1
Shrine Melancholy has her . . . s. 332.21
Shrink all the boards did s. 144.6
Shuffled s. off this mortal coil 498.61
Shyness language performs . . . without s. 153.3
Sick I am s. at heart 498.39
I'm never, never s. at sea 257.15
Sidcup If only I could get down to S. 446.1
Side He passed by on the other s. 62.156
on the wrong s. of thirty 535.9
Time is on our s. 258.1
windy s. of the law 498.276
Sides Do not . . . write on both s. of the paper 495.4

man who sees both s. of a question 584.20
said on both s. 4.6
We...assume that everything has two s. 469.1
Sieve They went to sea in a s. 354.3
Signs S. are the natural language of the heart 497.1
Sight s. of you is good for sore eyes 535.8
s. to dream of 144.17
thousand years in thy s. 62.54
Sights few more impressive s. in the world 40.5
Significant s. form 54.1
Signifying S. nothing 498.177
Silence foster-child of s. and slow time 332.15
Friendliest to sleep and s. 401.24
rest is s. 498.76
S. is as full of potential wisdom 310.19
S. is the best tactic 471.15
S. is the perfectest herald of joy 498.210
s. sank Like music 144.13
was s. in heaven 62.216
With s. and tears 98.28
Silk rustling in unpaid-for s. 498.36
s., too often hides eczema 106.1
Silks Whenas in s. my Julia goes 291.4
Silver for a handful of s. 83.9
Silvia Who is S.? What is she 498.280
Simplicity In...s. a child 452.6
Simplify S., s. 545.5
Simultaneously two contradictory beliefs...s. 427.4
Sin beauty is only s. deep 486.3
He that is without s. among 62.167
it is no s. to s. in secret 402.3
no s. but to be rich 498.125
no s. except stupidity 584.23
private s. is not so prejudicial 116.4
wages of s. is death 62.180
worst s. towards our fellow creatures is not to hate 499.15
Sincerest Imitation...s. of flattery 148.3
Sincerity hypocrite...even his s. 129.10
s. is a dangerous thing 584.21
Sing Arms and the man I s. 560.1
s. 'em muck 389.1
Welsh...just s. 569.6
Singed s. the Spanish king's beard 202.1
Singing nightingales are s. near 214.15
Single s. man...must be in want of a wife 27.8
Sinn'd More s. against than sinning 498.139
Sinner one s. that repenteth 62.157
Sinning more sinn'd against than s. 498.139
Sins Charity shall cover the multitude of s. 62.209
from Expensive S. refrain 205.8
His s. were scarlet 55.4
Other s. only speak 572.1
Though your s. be as scarlet 62.91
Sir I am S. Oracle 498.187
Sirens Blest pair of S. 401.1
Sit I will s. down now 195.1
men s. and hear each other groan 332.25
not fit that you should s. here 172.3
So I did s. and eat 290.7
Six s. of one and half-a-dozen of the other 383.2
Six hundred Rode the s. 539.2
Skating s. over thin ice 218.8
Skies man whose god is in the s. 499.47
Skill greater want of s. 452.7
Skin Ethiopian change his s. 62.102
s. of my teeth 62.40
Skinning When you are s. your customers 344.1
Skins beauty of their s. 539.23
Skittles Life isn't all beer and s. 307.1
Sky evening is spread out against the s. 214.7
moon went up the s. 144.9
Slaughter as a lamb to the s. 62.101
Slave man...is Reason's s. 153.11
Slavery Freedom is S. 427.3
Slaves at the mill with s. 401.29
Britons never will be s. 544.1
Slays moves, and mates, and s. 228.7
Sleave ravell'd s. of care 498.167
Sleep an after-dinner's s. 498.183
How do people go to s. 433.1
One needs more rest if one doesn't s. 569.9

our little life Is rounded with a s. 498.258
S. after toil 519.1
s.! it is a gentle thing 144.10
S. that knits up the ravell'd sleave 498.167
To s., perchance to dream 498.61
we must s. 498.13
youth would s. out the rest 498.283
Sleeping All this fuss about s. together 569.16
Slimy thousand thousand s. things 144.8
Slings s. and arrows of outrageous fortune 498.61
Slip he gave us all the s. 83.19
Slipping Time is s. underneath 228.6
Slough s. was Despond 90.2
Slow I am s. of study 498.203
S. and steady wins the race 363.1
too swift arrives as tardy as too s. 498.247
Slowly Hasten s. 532.1
Sluggard Go to the ant, thou s. 62.64
'Tis the voice of the s. 568.2
Slug-horn s. to my lips I set 83.5
Slumber I must s. again 568.2
s. did my spirit seal 595.16
Slumbers Golden s. kiss your eyes 185.1
Slumb'ring might half s. 332.32
Slush pure as the driven s. 38.2
Small Microbe is so very s. 55.6
souls of women are so s. 96.8
still s. voice 62.37
virtue's still far too s. 145.3
Small-endians Big-endians and s. 535.4
Small-talking Where in this s. world 244.1
Smell I once more s. the dew and rain 290.4
I s. a rat 470.1
rose... would s. as sweet 498.243
Smile s. I could feel in my hip pocket 120.2
Smite whosoever shall s. thee on thy right cheek 62.122
Smoking *s.* custom loathsome to the eye 318.1
Smooth course of true love never did run s. 498.201
Smyler s. with the knyf 127.11
Snail s.'s on the thorn 83.13
Snapper-up s. of unconsidered trifles 498.284
Snark For the S. *was* a Boojum 111.16
Sneaked who s. into my room 385.12
Sneer teach the rest to s. 452.3
Sneezed Not to be s. at 147.3
Snob He who meanly admires... is a S. 541.1
impossible... not to be sometimes a S. 541.2
Snotgreen s. sea 326.2
Snow as white as s. 62.91
wish a s. in May's new-fangled shows 498.153
Snows s. of yesteryear 559.1
Soap S. and education... are more deadly 553.2
Sober as s. as a Judge 225.2
one sees in Garbo s. 554.3
Sociable I am a s. worker 52.3
Society is no comfort to one not s. 498.37
Social true self-love and s. are the same 452.19
Socialism religion of S. 61.1
Socialists We are all S. now 276.1
Society nation is a s. united by a delusion 314.6
No s. can surely be flourishing and happy 510.1
S. is no comfort To one not sociable 498.37
S. is now one polish'd horde 98.20
s., where none intrudes 98.10
Socket Burn to the s. 595.1
Softly Tread s. because 601.9
Soldier I never expect a s. to think 499.16
in the s. is flat blasphemy 498.181
You can always tell an old s. 499.4
Soliciting supernatural s. 498.159
Solitude In s. alone can he know true freedom 403.2
In s. What happiness 401.25

Which is the bliss of s. 595.3
Whosoever is delighted in s. 30.26
Solution total s. of the Jewish question 260.2
Solvency S. is a matter of temperament 511.7
Some s. more than others 163.6
You can fool s. of the people all the time 360.8
Somer In a s. season 349.1
Something Everybody was up to s. 163.1
simplifying s. by destroying nearly everything 129.5
S. nasty in the woodshed 256.1
Time for a little s. 400.1
Sometime Come up and see me s. 576.1
Somewhat More than s. 483.1
Son gave his only begotten S. 62.166
He that spareth his rod hateth his s. 62.70
wise s. maketh a glad father 62.67
you'll be a Man, my s. 341.7
Song learn in suffering what they teach in s. 500.5
run softly, till I end my S. 519.4
Who loves not wine, woman and s. 372.1
Songs Where are the s. of Spring 332.2
Sonne when soft was the s. 349.1
Sons S. of Belial had a Glorious Time 205.9
Soon day returns too s. 98.27
Sophonisba Oh! S.! S.! oh 544.2
Sorrow down, thou climbing s. 498.135
increaseth knowledge increaseth s. 62.81
Parting is such sweet s. 498.245
Pure and complete s. is as impossible 547.3
S. is tranquillity remembered in emotion 433.5
There is no greater s. 176.2
Sorrows few s.... in which a good income is of no avail 511.3
When s. come, they come not single spies 498.71
Sort like this s. of thing 360.9
Sought Love s. is good 498.274
Soul Artists are not engineers of the s. 335.5
become a living s. 595.22
Dull would he be of s. 595.11
Give not thy s. unto a woman 62.110
half conceal the S. within 539.10
I am the captain of my s. 285.2
largest and most comprehensive s. 205.16
lose his own s. 62.148
My s. in agony 144.7
No coward s. is mine 77.1
seal the hushed casket of my s. 332.31
s. is not more than the body 582.4
s. like season'd timber 290.9
subject's s. is his own 498.98
Souls s. of women are so small 96.8
Two s. dwell, alas! in my breast 261.2
Sound deeper than did ever plummet s. 498.259
full of s. and fury 498.177
s. mind in a s. body 329.3
s. must seem an echo to the sense 452.13
Sounds s. will take care of themselves 111.10
Soup S. of the evening, beautiful S. 111.12
Take the s. away 299.1
Sour How s. sweet music is 498.238
Sourest sweetest things turn s. 498.296
South beaker full of the warm S. 332.24
Sow Ireland is the old s. 326.1
like a s. that hath overwhelm'd all her litter 498.83
they that s. in tears 62.61
Soweth whatsoever a man s., that shall he also reap 62.196
Sown They have s. the wind 62.108
Space In the United States there is more s. where nobody is 525.1
Spade if you don't call me s. 535.15
Spaniards time to win this game, and to thrash the S. 202.2
Spanish I speak S. to God 124.1
singed the S. king's beard 202.1
Spare S. all I have 223.3
s. the rod 96.3
Spareth He that s. his rod 62.70

Speak I only s. right on 498.120
Let him now s. 149.14
Other sins only s. 572.1
s. when you're spoken to 111.30
When I think, I must s. 498.28
Speciality My s. is being right 499.74
Species s. of person called a 'Modern Churchman' 569.10
Spectacle Life is not a s. 488.5
Spectator S. of mankind 4.4
Spectators pleasure to the s. 375.3
Speech freedom of s. and expression 475.3
real reason...we...champion free s. 174.1
S. was given to man to disguise his thoughts 536.3
Speechless *The Times* is s. 133.3
Speed Be wise with s. 602.2
safety is in our s. 218.8
s. was faster than light 87.1
Spending Getting and s. 595.9
Riches are for s. 30.28
Spent Nought's had, all's s. 498.169
When I consider how my light is s. 401.32
Spice Variety's the very s. of life 165.5
Spies sorrows...come not single s. 498.71
Spin they toil not, neither do they s. 62.128
Spires dreaming s. 20.13
Spirit Give me the s. 498.91
Hail to thee, blithe S. 500.13
haughty s. before a fall 62.71
history of the human s. 20.18
Into thy hands I commend my s. 62.50
life-blood of a master s. 401.36
Music that gentlier on the s. lies 539.18
present in s. 62.183
slumber did my s. seal 595.16
s. giveth life 62.190
s. indeed is willing 62.145
S. of Delight 500.14
s. that always denies 261.3
Th' expense of s. in a waste of shame 498.299
Splendour s. falls on castle walls 539.21
Split when I s. an infinitive...it stays s. 120.3
Spoil s. the child 96.3
Spoiled finest plans have always been s. 74.4
Spoke English as she is S. 552.1
s. among your wheels 45.4
Spoken Speak when you're s. to 111.30
Spoons measured out my life with coffee s. 214.9
Sport kill us for their s. 498.144
s. with Amaryllis 401.10
s. would be as tedious as to work 498.77
to make s. for our neighbours 27.10
Spot Out, damned s. 498.173
Spotless s. reputation 498.232
Spots leopard his s. 62.102
Sprang I s. to the stirrup 83.8
Spread not good except it be s. 30.17
Spring flowers that bloom in the s. 257.12
If Winter comes, can S. be far behind 500.9
In the S. a young man's fancy 539.17
I said the hounds of s. 546.4
lived light in the s. 20.3
S....did happen in Cambridge 412.2
S., sweet laxative 103.1
They call it easing the S. 465.2
Where are the songs of S. 332.2
year's at the s. 83.13
Spur Fame is the s. 401.11
Spurs Let the boy win his s. 210.1
Spurts They move forward in s. 153.9
St Paul's I am designing S. 59.3
Stables s. are the real centre of the household 499.24
Staff I'll break my s. 498.259
Stage All the world's a s. 498.23
Attic s. 20.6
Don't put your daughter on the s. 163.10
If this were play'd upon a s. 498.275
On the s. he was natural, simple, affecting 262.3
this great s. of fools 498.149
Stain contagion of the world's slow s. 500.1

Stand firm place to s. 16.1
no time to s. and stare 181.1
s. a little less 193.1
s. not upon the order of... going 498.171
that house cannot s. 62.147
They also serve who only s. and wait 401.33
Standard raise the scarlet s. high 152.1
Stands S. the Church clock 78.2
Star Bright s., would I were steadfast 332.3
Go, and catch a falling s. 199.9
Hitch your wagon to a s. 218.12
our life's S. 595.5
s. or two beside 144.9
Sunset and evening s. 539.4
Stare no time to stand and s. 181.1
Stars Stone that puts the S. to Flight 228.1
Starting-point s. for further desires 458.1
Starve artist will let his wife s. 499.38
Let not poor Nelly s. 123.3
State I am the S. 366.1
object in the construction of the s. 448.2
reinforcement of the power of the S. 106.8
s. in the proper sense of the word 355.1
worth of a S. 396.3
Stately Homes S. of England 163.2
S. of England ope their doors 103.1
Statesman abroad you're a s. 378.2
Statesmen s.... estranged from reality 346.1
Static class people as s. and dynamic 569.14
novel is a s. thing 554.2
Station honour is a private s. 4.3
Statistics lies, damned lies, and s. 553.1
Statue no s. has ever been put up to a critic 504.1
Steadfast would I were s. as thou art 332.3
Steaks smell of s. in passageways 214.12
Steal Thou shalt not s. 62.20
Stealing hanged for s. horses 274.1
Steals Who s. my purse s. trash 498.223
Stealth do a good action by s. 348.5
Steamer tossing about in a s. from Harwich 257.6
Steel When the foeman bares his s. 257.18
Steeples Till you have drench'd our s. 498.137
Step one small s. for man 18.1
s. from the sublime to the ridiculous 413.1
Stepp'd in blood s. in so far 498.172
Stick kind of burr; I shall s. 498.185
Stiff s. upper lip 112.1
Still of his own opinion s. 96.7
Stillness talent is formed in s. 261.5
Sting death, where is thy s. 62.189
Stirrup Betwixt the s. and the ground 102.1
I sprang to the s. 83.8
Stolen not wanting what is s. 498.226
S. sweets are best 134.2
Stomach army marches on its s. 413.3
little wine for thy s.'s sake 62.200
Stomachs Napoleon's armies used to march on their s. 495.3
Stone head s. of the corner 62.59
Jackson standing like a s. wall 50.1
let him first cast a s. at her 62.167
precious s. set in the silver sea 498.235
s. which the builders refused 62.59
virtue is like a rich s. 30.33
Stoops When lovely woman s. to folly 262.10
Stop come to the end: then s. 111.14
time... must have a s. 498.81
when the kissing had to s. 83.18
Stoppeth he s. one of three 144.1
Stops buck s. here 551.1
Storage library is thought in cold s. 487.3
Storm lovers fled away into the s. 332.6
Story Not that the s. need be long 545.7
novel tells a s. 237.3
snowy summits old in s. 539.21
Straight branch that might have grown full s. 381.4
Strain'd quality of mercy is not s. 498.194
Strange truth is always s. 98.21

Strangeness s. in the proportion 30.34
Stranger s. in a strange land 62.9
S. than fiction 98.21
Strangers better s. 498.29
Straw Headpiece filled with s. 214.5
Straws Errors, like S. 205.15
Strayed s. from thy ways 149.1
Streets shit in the s. 334.1
Strength Ignorance is S. 427.3
My s. is as the s. of ten 539.25
We are not now that s. 539.27
Strenuous doctrine of the s. life 476.1
Strife God and Nature then at s. 539.12
Strike no right to s. against the public safety 155.2
themselves must s. the blow 98.6
String chewing little bits of S. 55.2
Strings 'There are s.', said Mr Tappertit, 'in the human heart' 191.1
Strive Thou shalt not kill; but needst not s. 140.4
To s., to seek, to find, and not to yield 539.27
Stroke none so fast as s. 142.1
Strong out of the s. came forth sweetness 62.32
s. shall thrive 496.2
Stronger ballot is s. than the bullet 360.2
Strongest Hero-worship is s. 518.7
Struck Certain women should be s. regularly 163.5
I s. the board 290.1
Structure essential s. of the normal British sentence 133.26
Struggle manhood a s. 195.7
Struggles history of class s. 386.4
Strumpet s.'s fool 498.4
Struts player that s. and frets 498.177
Studies S. serve for delight 30.37
Study I am slow of s. 498.203
much s. is a weariness of the flesh 62.85
proper s. of Mankind 452.18
s. what you most affect 498.251
Stuff Ambition should be made of sterner s. 498.118
such s. as dreams are made on 498.258
Stuffed We are the s. men 214.5
Stumble they s. that run fast 498.246
Stupidity no sin except s. 584.23
Style s. is the man himself 86.1
s.... often hides eczema 106.1
true definition of a s. 535.6
Subject Every s.'s duty is the King's 498.98
Sublime step from the s. to the ridiculous 413.1
s. and the ridiculous 431.1
Substance lose the s. by grasping at the shadow 6.1
Substitute no s. for talent 310.18
Succeed If at first you don't s. 294.1
those who ne'er s. 192.1
To s.... appear successful. 471.12
Succeeds Nothing s. like excess 584.16
Success not in mortals to command s. 4.1
religion... yours is S. 40.3
S. is counted sweetest 192.1
true s. is to labour 529.4
two to make a marriage a s. 487.1
Successful we do everything we can to appear s. 471.12
Such nothing against apes... As s. 507.4
Sucker s. born every minute 39.1
Suckle To s. fools 498.221
Suckled s. in a creed outworn 595.10
Sucklings babes and s. 62.42
Sucks s. the nurse asleep 498.17
Suffer S. the little children to come unto me 62.150
ye s. fools gladly 62.191
Suffering pity for the s. of mankind 485.1
unless it has all been s. 27.7
Sufficient Is trifle s. for sweet? 60.2
S. unto the day 62.129
Sultry common where the climate's s. 98.11
Sum *Cogito, ergo s.* 189.1
Summer after many a s. dies the swan 539.26
All on a s. day 111.13
Made glorious s. 498.239
S. afternoon... most beautiful words 317.4
S. has set in 144.24
s.'s day 401.19

Summits Man can climb to the highest s. 499.14
snowy s. old in story 539.21
Summum *S. bonum* 135.3
Sun all, except their s. is set 98.15
aweary of the s. 498.178
between me and the s. 193.1
Busy old fool, unruly S. 199.10
Fear no more the heat o' th' s. 498.38
go out in the mid-day s. 163.9
no new thing under the s. 62.80
nothing like the s. 498.300
on which the s. never sets 421.1
S. came up upon the left 144.2
s. has gone in 511.10
s. shining ten days a year 334.1
this s. of York 498.239
To have enjoy'd the s. 20.3
Sunburn S. is very becoming 163.7
Sunday S. clears away the rust 4.5
Sunless Down to a s. sea 144.19
Sunset S. and evening star 539.4
s.-touch 83.3
Sunsets I have a horror of s. 458.6
Supercilious s. knowledge in accounts 502.5
Superlative we have not settled the s. 129.8
Superman I teach you the S. 419.5
Supernatural This s. soliciting 498.159
Superstition S. is the religion of feeble minds 91.10
Superstitions new truths...end as s. 312.1
Supp'd I have s. full with horrors 498.176
Support atheist...no invisible means of s. 238.1
Suppression capitalism...machine for the s. 355.1
Surmise with a wild s. 332.29
Surpassed Man is...to be s. 419.5
Surrender we shall never s. 133.12
Survival Friendship...has no s. value 358.1
S. of the Fittest 180.3
S. of the fittest 518.4
without victory there is no s. 133.11
Survive only the Fit s. 496.2
Suspended laws of God will be s. 499.25
Suspension willing s. of disbelief 144.22
Suspicion people under s. are better moving 330.2
Suspicions S. among thoughts 30.30
Swains all our s. commend her 498.280
Swan after many a summer dies the s. 539.26
Sweet S. of Avon 325.4
Swap s. horses in mid-stream 360.7
Swear s. not by the moon 498.244
Sweat blood, toil, tears and s. 133.10
Sweats Falstaff s. to death 498.78
Sweet Heard melodies are s. 332.16
if today be s. 228.6
Is trifle sufficient for s. 60.2
Revenge, at first though s. 401.26
rose...would smell as s. 498.243
so s. as melancholy 94.1
Stolen waters are s. 62.66
S. day, so cool, so calm 290.8
Sweetest s. things turn sourest 498.296
Success is counted s. 192.1
Sweetness out of the strong...s. 62.32
pursuit of s. and light 20.14
s. and light 535.1
waste its s. on the desert air 268.8
Sweets Stolen s. are best 134.2
Swift Too s. arrives as tardy as too slow 498.247
Swimming s. under water 229.5
Swine cast ye your pearls before s. 62.131
jewel...in a s.'s snout 62.68
Sword brave man with a s. 584.1
more cruel...the pen than the s. 94.2
pen is mightier than the s. 88.1
s. sleep in my hand 67.7
Swords beat their s. into plowshares 62.92
Swound Like noises in a s. 144.3
Symmetry thy fearful s. 67.12
Sympathetic To be s. without discrimination 227.2
Sympathy failed to inspire s. in men 51.6
machine-gun riddling her hostess with s. 310.14

Syne For auld lang s. 93.3
System Christianity accepted...a metaphysical s. 310.10
Systems Our little s. have their day 539.9

T

Table crumbs...from the rich man's t. 62.158
patient etherized upon a t. 214.7
Tactic Silence is the best t. 471.15
Tails t. you lose 171.1
Take T. care of the sense 111.10
They have to t. you in 243.2
Taken Lord hath t. away 62.38
Taking not winning but t. part 160.1
Tale Life is as tedious as a twice-told t. 498.127
our dead bodies must tell the t. 492.2
t. Told by an idiot 498.177
t. to tell of the hardihood, endurance, and courage of my companions 492.2
t. which holdeth children from play 506.2
thereby hangs a t. 498.22
Talent T. does what it can 394.1
t. is formed in stillness 261.5
that one t. which is death to hide 401.32
There is no substitute for t. 310.18
Talents If you have great t., industry will improve them 466.1
Talk Herd...who t. too much 205.6
I dont want to t. grammar 499.67
t. as other people do 323.34
when I hear anyone t. of Culture 260.3
Talked He t. on for ever 281.1
one thing in the world worse than being t. about 584.18
Talking always t. about being a gentleman 533.1
good newspaper...nation t. to itself 397.1
T. of Michelangelo 214.8
Tarts she made some t. 111.13
Task long day's t. is done 498.13
Taste Drink deep or t. not 452.10
Things sweet to t. prove...sour 498.233
Tasted Some books are to be t. 30.38
t. two whole worms 520.1
Tastes Their t. may not be the same 499.46
Taught I forget what I was t. 579.2
Taxes nothing is certain but death and t. 239.5
Tea Dinner, Lunch and T. 55.3
honey still for t. 78.2
sometimes counsel take—and sometimes T. 452.26
Take some more t. 111.7
When I makes t. I makes t. 326.3
Teach t. you more of man 595.19
Teacher Let Nature be your T. 595.18
Teaches He who cannot, t. 499.51
Team Is my t. ploughing 304.3
Tears blood, toil, t. and sweat 133.10
God shall wipe away all t. 62.220
If you have t., prepare to shed them 498.119
mine own t. Do scald 498.150
T., idle t. 539.22
They that sow in t. 62.61
too deep for t. 595.6
With silence and t. 98.28
Teche gladly wolde he lerne and gladly t. 127.7
Tedious People are either charming or t. 584.12
Teeth skin of my t. 62.40
take the bull between the t. 263.7
Teetotaller I'm only a beer t. 499.13
Tell do not t. them so 128.1
Father, I cannot t. a lie 567.2
Telling I am t. you 577.1
pity beyond all t. 601.13
Temperament artistic t. is a disease 129.15
Solvency is a matter of t. 511.7
Temperance I prefer t. hotels 566.1
Tempests That looks on t. 498.298
Temple in the very t. of delight 332.21
Temples Ships, towers, domes, theatres, and t. lie 595.11
tempora *O t.! O mores* 135.4
Temporary force alone is but t. 91.2

Tempt things that are bad for me do not t. me 499.3
Temptation I never resist t. 499.3
last t. 214.18
Marriage is popular because it combines the maximum of t. 499.52
only way to get rid of a t. 584.19
over-fond of resisting t. 48.1
resist everything except t. 584.13
Ten as the strength of t. 539.25
Ten-sixty-six T. And All That 495.1
Terminological t. inexactitude 133.1
Terribles Les enfants t. 250.1
Text great t. in Galatians 83.16
Thames Sweet T.! run softly 519.4
Thank T. me no thankings 498.249
Thanks For this relief much t. 498.39
That Goodbye to All T. 267.1
1066 And All T. 495.1
Theatre Farce is the essential t. 166.1
Theft Property is t. 457.1
Themselves law unto t. 62.178
Theory t. is all grey 261.1
Thick Through t. and thin 96.4
Thickens plot t. 85.2
Thief Procrastination... t. of time 602.3
Time... t. of youth 401.31
Thin Enclosing every t. man, there's a fat man 569.24
Through thick and t. 96.4
Thing beauty... no such t. 445.1
It is a far, far, better t. that I do 191.34
Life is the t. 511.5
play's the t. 498.60
Things former t. are passed away 62.220
good t.... are the fruits of originality 396.1
Shape of T. to Come 574.2
T. are entirely what they appear to be 489.2
T. fall apart 601.14
To talk of many t. 111.22
We see into the life of t. 595.22
Think apparatus with which we t. 63.2
Books t. for me 348.3
comedy to those who t. 564.2
Herd... who t. too little 205.6
I cannot sit and t. 348.3
I exist by what I t. 489.3
I just can't t. of your face 520.3
I'm not so t. as you drunk I am 521.1
I never t. of the future 212.1
I t. him so, because I t. him so 498.279
I t., therefore I am 189.1
never expect a soldier to t. 499.16
T. of your posterity 2.1
t. only this of me 78.3
Thinking It ain't t. about it 550.1
one prolonged effort to prevent oneself t. 310.15
There is wishful t. in Hell 358.2
t.makes it so 498.56
try t. of love 244.2
Thirsty when you are t., to cure it 437.2
Thirty on the wrong side of t. 535.9
This All t. and heaven too 288.2
Thorn t. in the flesh 62.192
Thorns I fall upon the t. of life 500.8
Thou Book of Verse—and T. 228.3
Thought green t. in a green shade 384.5
Learning without t. is labour lost 150.3
My t. is *me* 489.3
pale cast of t. 498.63
residual fraction is t. 488.1
sessions of sweet silent t. 498.291
silent form, dost tease us out of t. 332.17
T. does not become a young woman 502.2
t. in cold storage 487.3
t. is often original 300.2
t. without learning is perilous 150.3
What oft was t. 452.12
You should have t. of all this before you were born 507.3
Thoughts man whose second t. are good 40.6
sensations rather than of t. 332.34
Speech... to disguise... t. 536.3
Suspicions amongst t. 30.30
t.... too deep for tears 595.6
Thousand I could be a good woman if I had five t. 541.6
Thousands Saul hath slain his t. 62.34
t. at his bidding speed 401.33
Where t. equally were meant 535.3
Three he stoppeth one of t. 144.1

In married life t. is company 584.6
t. fundamental truths 54.3
T. little maids from school 257.10
t. things I always forget 534.1
we galloped all t. 83.8
Three-pipe t. problem 201.7
Threescore t. years and ten 62.55
Thrice circle round him t. 144.21
thou shalt deny me t. 62.151
Thrive strong shall t. 496.2
Throne barge... like a burnished t. 498.8
High on a t. of royal state 401.20
royal t. of kings 498.235
Through part of it all the way t. 263.9
Throw do not t. this book about 55.1
t. away the dearest thing he ow'd 498.161
Thrown t. on her with a pitchfork 535.10
Thrush That's the wise t. 83.7
Thrust greatness t. upon them 498.273
Thus Why is this t. 566.2
Thusness reason of this t. 566.2
Thyself Be so true to t. 30.23
Know then t. 452.18
love thy neighbour as t. 62.26
Tide blood-dimmed t. is loosed 601.14
lived in the t. of times 498.113
t. in the affairs of men 498.122
t. in the affairs of women 98.17
t. is full 20.1
Tiger T.! T.! burning bright 67.12
Tigers reactionaries are paper t. 379.1
Timber soul like season'd t. 290.9
Time And t.... Must have a stop 498.81
big man has no t. 229.3
chronicle of wasted t. 498.297
Even such is T. 462.1
Had we but world enough, and t. 384.1
I haven't had t. to work 336.3
inaudible and noiseless foot of T. 498.3
moment of t. 215.4
Never the t. and the place 83.10
no t. to stand and stare 181.1
not of an age, but for all t. 325.3
peace for our t. 118.2
peace in our t., O Lord 149.4
Procrastination... thief of t. 602.3
That passed the t. 47.3
There was a t. when meadow, grove 595.4
this bank and shoal of t. 498.164
those feet in ancient t. 67.6
T. and the hour runs through 498.160
t. as a tool not as a couch 335.2
T. for a little something 400.1
t. has come,' the Walrus said 111.22
T. hath, my lord, a wallet at his back 498.264
t. is flying 560.5
t. is money 239.1
T. is on our side 258.1
T. is slipping underneath our Feet 228.6
t. is the greatest innovator 30.24
T. present and t. past 214.2
T.'s winged chariot 384.2
T.: that which man is always trying to kill 518.1
T., the subtle thief of youth 401.31
t. to every purpose 62.82
t. will come when you will hear me 195.1
To choose t. is to save t. 30.25
Work expands... to fill the t. 434.1
Times lived in the tide of t. 498.113
logic of our t. 182.1
The T. has made many ministries 32.1
The T. is speechless 133.3
Time-table I would sooner read a t. 388.8
Tim'rous Wee, ... t. beastie 93.11
Tinned I'd have it t. 589.1
Tip-and-run watch him play t. 227.1
Tipping Do they allow t. on the boat? 385.15
Tipster racing t. who only reached Hitler's level of accuracy 538.1
Tired I'm t. of Love 55.5
Life... process of getting t. 97.3
when a man is t. of London 323.32
To-day here t., and gone tomorrow 53.2
He who can call t. his own 205.14
if t. be sweet 228.6
I have lived t. 205.14
Toe light fantastic t. 401.6
Together And the loved one all t. 83.10

We must...all hang t. 239.3
Toil Ambition mock their useful t. 268.6
they t. not, neither do they spin 62.128
Tolerant To know all makes one t. 523.1
Tolls for whom the bell t. 199.13
To-morrow for t. we shall die 62.97
here today and gone t. 53.2
T., and t., and t. 498.177
T. do thy worst 205.14
Tom-tit little t. sang Willow 257.13
Tone t. of the company you are in 128.4
Tongue him whose strenuous t. Can burst Joy's grape 332.21
hold your t. and let me love 199.3
sharp t. is the only...tool 315.2
Tongues Self-interest speaks all sorts of t. 471.10
Tool sharp tongue is the only edged t. 315.2
time as a t., not as a couch 335.2
Tools Give us the t. 133.16
Too much Not t. zeal 536.4
Tooth t. for a t. 62.121
t. for t. 62.23
Toothache philosopher that could endure the t. 498.217
Top always room at the t. 571.1
Torrent character in the world's t. 261.5
Total t. eclipse 401.30
t. solution of the Jewish question 260.2
Totter t. into vogue 564.1
Touch mere t. of cold philosophy 332.14
sunset t. 83.3
t. of earthly years 595.16
Toves slithy t. did gyre 111.17
Towels never darken my t. again 385.7
Tower Childe Roland to the Dark T. 83.5
Towers cloud-capp'd t. 498.258
Town man made the t. 165.3
next t. drain 520.1
Trade man must serve his time to every t. 98.24
no nation was ever ruined by t. 239.2
Trade Unionism virtue...of the married 499.41
Tradition It's t.. We don't want t. 234.1
Tragedie go litel myn t. 127.18
T. is to seyn a certeyn storie 127.14
Tragedies t. are finish'd by a death 98.14
two t. in life 499.45
Tragedy Farce brutalized becomes t. 166.1
food a t. 455.2
We participate in a t. 310.7
world is...a t. to those who feel 564.2
Train something sensational to read in the t. 584.10
Tranquillity emotion recollected in t. 595.25
Sorrow is t. remembered in emotion 433.5
Transit Sic t. gloria mundi 333.2
Trappings the t. and the suits of woe 498.41
Trash Who steals my purse steals t. 498.223
Travel To t. hopefully is a better thing than to arrive 529.4
T., in the younger sort 30.20
Traveller from whose bourn no t. returns 498.62
Tread frightful fiend...behind him t. 144.12
where angels fear to t. 452.16
you t. on my dreams 601.9
Treason T. doth never prosper 278.1
T. was no Crime 205.9
Treasure Preserve it as your chiefest t. 55.1
purest t. mortal times afford 498.232
Tree billboard lovely as a t. 414.5
chestnut t.... great rooted blossomer 601.1
same t. that a wise man sees 67.23
spare the beechen t. 104.1
that forbidden t. 401.14
t. of life is green 261.1
t.'s inclined 452.20
Under the greenwood t. 498.21
Trees Loveliest of t., the cherry 304.1
With rocks, and stones, and t. 595.16
Trial T. by jury...a delusion 186.1
t. of which you can have nō conception 499.76
Tribe Mankind is not a t. 129.24

Richer than all his t. 498.229
Trick When in doubt, win the t. 305.1
Tried conservatism...adherence to the old and t. 360.4
I take the one I've never t. 576.7
Trifle Is t. sufficient for sweet 60.2
Trifles observance of t. 201.2
snapper-up of unconsidered t. 498.284
Trinity I the T. illustrate 83.15
Tristesse Bonjour t. 217.1
Triton hear old T. blow his wreathèd horn 595.10
Triumph We t. without glory 158.1
Trot I don't t. it out and about 145.3
Trouble Genius...capacity of taking t. 109.5
lot of t. in his life 133.34
very present help in t. 62.52
Troubles take arms against a sea of t. 498.61
Trousers bottoms of my t. rolled 214.10
I shall wear white flannel t. 214.11
man should never put on his best t. 313.3
Trowel laid on with a t. 498.18
lays it on with a t. 151.1
True Be so t. to thyself 30.23
faith unfaithful kept him falsely t. 539.6
No man worth having is t. to his wife 556.2
One religion is as t. as another 94.4
to thine own self be t. 498.48
truism is... none the less t. 487.2
what people say of us is t. 511.6
what we believe is not necessarily t. 54.3
Truism t. is on that account none the less true 487.2
Trust I don't t. him. We're friends 74.3
Put not your t. in princes 62.63
Truth all we shall know for t. 601.5
Beauty is t., t. beauty 332.18
dearer still is t. 17.4
few enthusiasts...speak the t. 36.1
it cannot compel anyone to tell the t. 178.1
It takes two to speak the t. 545.6
T. comes out in wine 449.1
t. is always strange 98.21
t. of imagination 332.33
t. that makes men free 7.1
t. universally acknowledged 27.8
whatever remains, however improbable, must be the t. 201.1
What is t. 30.2
What is t. 62.172
who ever knew T. put to the worse 401.37
wither into the t. 601.3
Truths new t. begin as heresies 312.1
no whole t. 580.1
those three fundamental t. 54.3
t. begin as blasphemies 499.1
t. being in and out of favour 243.1
Try axe's edge did t. 384.7
T., t. again 294.1
Tu Et t., Brute 101.4
Et t., Brute 498.110
T. quoque 428.2
T.-whit, T.-who 498.157
Tune You can't teach the old maestro a new t. 336.2
Tunes devil should have all the good t. 295.1
Turbulent this t. priest 287.1
Turn I do not hope to t. 214.1
Turtle voice of the t. is heard 62.88
Twain never the t. shall meet 341.1
Tweedledee Tweedledum said T. Had spoiled his nice new rattle 111.19
Tweedledum T. and Tweedledee Agreed to have a battle 111.19
Twentieth T. Century Blues 163.11
Twenty sweet and t. 498.270
Twenty-nine t. distinct damnations 83.16
Twice Literature... will be read t. 153.5
t. as natural 111.27
Twig as the t. is bent 452.20
Twilight T. grey 401.23
Twinkle T. t. little bat 111.6
Twist last t. of the knife 214.13
Two It takes t. to speak the truth 545.6
t. things that will be believed of any man 537.1
Tyrannize man should t. over his bank balance 337.1

Tyranny Ecclesiastic t.'s the worst 184.3
Tyrant professed t. to their sex 498.208

U

U U and Non-U 478.1
Ulster U. will fight; U. will be right 132.2
Umble We are so very u. 191.9
Unbelievable bombs are u. 579.1
Un-birthday u. present 111.24
Uncertainty I have known u. 69.1
Uncomfortable when he is only u. 499.40
Unconfined let joy be u. 98.8
Unconquerable u. hope 20.11
Unconscionable most u. time dying 123.1
Unconscious It'll do him good to lie there u. 507.2
Under chunder... watch u. 308.1
Underdogs find an Englishman among the u. 569.18
Underestimated effect of boredom is... u. 314.3
Underrate no duty we so much u. 529.3
Understand It's all they can u. 389.1
makes me u. anti-clerical things 55.7
people... may not be made to u. 150.9
Understanding passeth all u. 62.198
piece of cod passes all u. 373.2
well into a Scotch u. 512.2
Understood Schizophrenia cannot be u. 346.2
Undone estate o' th' world were now u. 498.178
left u. those things 149.2
Uneasy U. lies the head that wears a crown 498.88
Uneatable unspeakable in full pursuit of the u. 584.14
Unforgiving fill the u. minute 341.7
Ungain'd Men prize the thing u. more 498.261
Unhappy I don't believe one can ever be u. for long 569.4
most u. kind of misfortune 68.1
u. family is u. in its own way 547.1
u. one becomes moral 458.2
Uninteresting no... u. subject 129.9
Unite Workers of the world, u. 386.5
United States U. has to move very fast 335.3
U. of Europe 133.24
Universal There is no u. law 351.3
Universe I accept the u. 109.16
I don't pretend to understand the U. 109.15
Life exists in the u. 319.1
visible u. was an illusion 69.2
University true U. of these days 109.7
Unjust rain on the just and on the u. 62.124
Unkind Thou art not so u. 498.25
Unkindness I tax not you, you elements, with u. 498.138
Unlike Life... u. anything else 592.3
Unnatural so u. as the commonplace 201.4
Unpaid promise... debt u. 496.1
Unprofitable How weary, stale, flat, and u. 498.42
Unrequited Self-love seems so often u. 455.1
Unrest u. which men miscall delight 500.1
Unsettle They only u. him 592.1
Unspeakable psychopathologist the u. 388.4
u. in full pursuit of the uneatable 584.14
Unstable U. as water 62.8
Unwatched Madness... must not u. go 498.64
Up U., Guards, and at 'em 573.2
Upbringing u. a nun would envy 426.1
Upper u. classes Have still the u. hand 163.2
Upright position for an artist... u. 543.6
Use what is the u. of a book 111.1
Useless All Art is quite u. 584.17
most beautiful things... are the most u. 484.2
Uses all the u. of this world 498.42

Usual Business as u. 133.5
Utterly All changed...u. 601.6

V

Vae victis *V.* 361.1
Vain name of the Lord...in v. 62.15
No great man lives in v. 109.6
V. are the thousand creeds 77.2
vale *ave atque v.* 114.3
Valet No man is a hero to his v. 159.1
to his very v. seem'd a hero 98.1
Valiant v. never taste of death but once 498.109
Valley All in the v. of Death 539.2
v. of the shadow of death 62.48
Valleys Piping down the v. wild 67.13
Valour better part of v. is discretion 498.82
Value Friendship...has no survival v. 358.1
Vanity name of V. Fair 90.4
v. and love...universal characteristics 128.9
v. of human hopes 323.8
v. of vanities; all is v. 62.79
Vanquished redress of the grievances of the v. 133.30
Woe to the v. 361.1
Varies quality of moral behaviour v. 310.11
Variety custom stale her infinite v. 498.9
great source of pleasure is v. 323.38
V.'s the very spice of life 165.5
Various man so v., that he seem'd to be 205.7
Vary money appears to v. 311.1
Veal Bellamy's v. pies 447.3
Vegetable animal or v. or mineral 111.28
Veil Poetry lifts the v. 500.15
Velasquez Why drag in V. 577.3
Vengeance V. is mine 62.181
Verbal v. contract isn't worth the paper 263.6
Verbosity inebriated with...his own v. 195.6
Verdi strains of V. will come back to you tonight 385.16
Verdict Sentence first—v. afterwards 111.15
Verify Always v. your references 482.1
Veritas *In vino v.* 449.1
Verse Curst be the v. 452.4
Verses No one will ever get at my v. 582.6
Versing I once more... relish v. 290.4
Versions hundred v. of it 499.65
Vertical v. man 25.1
Vice He lash'd the v., but spared the name 535.3
homage paid by v. to virtue 471.3
no v. but beggary 498.125
Pride...v. of fools 452.9
Prosperity doth best discover v. 30.7
public schools are the nurseries of all v. 225.4
quotation is a national v. 569.19
When v. prevails 4.3
Vices small v. do appear 498.147
Victim v. must be found 257.9
Victims little v. play 268.3
v. who respect their executioners 489.1
Victis *Vae v.* 361.1
Victorious Send him v. 108.1
Victory Before Alamein we never had a v. 133.36
grave, where is thy v. 62.189
in v. unbearable 133.43
In war it is not right that matters, but v. 297.4
V. at all costs 133.11
without v. there is no survival 133.11
Vidders be very careful o' v. 191.27
Vieillesse *si v. pouvait* 219.1
View lends enchantment to the v. 104.2
Vigilance condition upon which God hath given liberty...is eternal v. 173.1
Villains God should go before such v. 498.216
Vino *In v. veritas* 449.1
Vintage O, for a draught of v. 332.23
Violence v. masquerading as love 346.3
Vipers generation of v. 62.116
Virginia Woolf Afraid of V.? 9.1

Virtue adversity doth best discover v. 30.7
Fine words...seldom associated with v. 150.4
forbearance ceases to be a v. 91.7
homage paid by vice to v. 471.3
much v. in If 498.32
My v.'s still far too small 145.3
no v. like necessity 498.234
to practise five things...constitutes perfect v. 150.7
V. is like a rich stone 30.33
v.... Trade Unionism of the married 499.41
Virtues ape-like v. without which 153.2
greater v. to sustain good fortune 471.8
v. We write in water 498.105
world to hide v. in 498.267
Vision Where there is no v. 62.78
Visions young men shall see v. 62.109
Vitality busyness...is a symptom of deficient v. 529.2
lower one's v. 51.4
Vogue totter into v. 564.1
Voice still small v. 62.37
v. of the people is the v. of God 10.1
v. of the turtle is heard 62.88
Voices Two v. are there 526.1
Vox populi, vox dei 10.1
Vulgar Funny without being v. 257.22
Vulgarity One can love a certain kind of v. 310.27
Vulgarizing Death...we haven't succeeded in completely v. 310.9

W

Wabe gyre and gimble in the w. 111.17
Wages ta'en thy w. 498.38
w. of sin is death 62.180
Wagon Hitch your w. to a star 218.12
Wagstaff disgrace to our family name of W. 385.9
Wait They also serve who only stand and w. 401.33
W. and see 23.1
Waiting We're w. for Godot 47.4
Waked You have w. me too soon 568.2
Walking I'm w. backwards till Christmas 399.3
I nauseate w. 151.6
I were w. with destiny 133.31
When I am not w., I am reading 348.3
Walks She w. in beauty 98.25
Wall office of a w. 498.235
There is Jackson standing like a stone w. 50.1
Wallace Scots wha hae wi' W. bled 93.15
Wallet Time hath...a w. at his back 498.264
Walls splendour falls on castle w. 539.21
Stone w. do not a prison make 368.1
Walrus W. and the Carpenter 111.21
Wandered I w. lonely as a cloud 595.2
Wandering w. minstrel I 257.8
Want freedom from w. 475.3
I shall not w. 62.46
w. of money is so 97.1
What does a woman w. 242.5
Wanted Every man is w. 218.7
it will not be w. these ten years 447.2
Wanting art found w. 62.105
Wants Having the fewest w. 515.1
one does just exactly what one w. 569.4
War cold w. 42.1
defeat without a w. 133.9
him who desires peace, prepare for w. 557.1
in every w. they kill you 472.1
In starting and waging a w. it is not right that matters, but victory 297.4
In w.... there are no winners 118.1
let slip the dogs of w. 498.114
My subject is W., and the pity of W. 430.1
neither shall they learn w. any more 62.92
never was a good w. 239.4
No one can guarantee success in w. 133.32
that devil's madness—W. 496.3
Those who can win a w. well 133.29
W. even to the knife 98.5

W. is, after all, the universal perversion 461.1
w. is...all hell 503.1
W. is like love 74.7
W. is much too serious a thing to be left to military men 536.5
W. is Peace 427.3
W. makes rattling good history 277.2
w. of the giants is over 133.37
w. which...left nothing to be desired 74.5
We are not at w. with Egypt 208.2
What they could do with round here is a good w. 74.1
when there was w., he went 25.8
Warble W. his...wood-notes wild 401.8
Wards key deftly in the oiled w. 332.31
Waring What's become of W. 83.19
Warned my Friends, be w. by me 55.3
Wars end to the beginnings of all w. 475.5
Still w. and lechery 498.265
W. and rumours of w. 62.142
W. are not won by evacuations 133.33
Washing painting a face and not w. 245.1
Waste we lay w. our powers 595.9
Watch as a w. in the night 62.54
why not carry a w. 548.2
Watches 'Tis with our judgments as our w. 452.8
Water better deeds Shall be in w. writ 45.6
drawers of w. 62.30
I came like W. 228.5
name was writ in w. 332.40
Unstable as w. 62.8
virtues we write in w. 498.105
We have all passed a lot of w. 263.8
when I makes w. I makes w. 326.3
w. still keeps falling over 133.38
W., w., every where 144.6
Watering a-w. the last year's crop 213.1
Waterloo Every man meets his W. 444.2
W. was won on the playing fields of Eton 573.3
Waters Cast thy bread upon the w. 62.84
do business in great w. 62.57
dreadful noise of w. in my ears 498.240
leadeth me beside the still w. 62.47
Stolen w. are sweet 62.66
w. cannot quench love 62.90
Wave Folk dance like a w. of the sea 601.7
lift me as a w. 500.8
Waves Britannia rule the w. 544.1
w. make towards the pebbled shore 498.293
Way catch the nearest w. 498.162
going the w. of all flesh 572.2
I met Murder on the w. 500.6
in every war they kill you a new w. 472.1
plowman homeward plods his weary w. 268.5
There was a sure w. to see it lost 92.1
Through Eden took their solitary w. 401.27
War...always finds a w. 74.7
w. down to Hell is easy 560.3
w. of all flesh 151.9
w. of all flesh 497.2
w. to dusty death 498.177
woman has her w. 300.1
Ways consider her w. 62.64
strayed from thy w. 149.1
We put it down a w. 191.32
w. are for the dark 498.16
Which...w. have not got 465.2
Weak concessions of the w. 91.1
flesh is w. 62.145
only refuge of w. minds 128.8
surely the w. shall perish 496.2
Wealth Outshone the w. of Ormus and of Ind 401.20
W. is not without its advantages 247.1
W. maketh many friends 62.72
W.... must be advertised 247.2
Weapon art is not a w. 335.5
Weapons books are w. 475.4
Wear City now doth, like a garment, w. 595.11
I...chose my wife...for...qualities as would w. well 262.8
Weariness much study is a w. 62.85
w., the fever, and the fret 332.25

Weary Age shall not w. them 64.1
Weather Englishmen...first talk is of the w. 323.6
I like the w. 98.2
winter and rough w. 498.21
Web w. of our life is of a mingled yarn 498.2
Wee W., ... tim'rous beastie 93.11
Weeds Lilies that fester smell far worse than w. 498.296
Worthless as wither'd w. 77.2
Week greatest w. in the history of the world 420.1
Weep Fair daffodils, we w. to see 291.3
W., and you w. alone 583.1
Weeping W. may endure for a night 62.49
Weighed w. in the balances 62.105
Welcome Advice is seldom w. 128.7
Love bade me w. 290.6
Well lov'd not wisely, but too w. 498.229
nothing...and did it very w. 257.5
reward of a thing w. done 218.6
We never do anything w. 281.7
worth doing w. 128.2
Well off as w. as if he were rich 24.1
Well-written w. Life is almost as rare 109.4
Welsh W....just sing 569.6
Wen fate of the great w. 141.2
Wench w. is dead 381.6
Went as cooks go she w. 486.4
Wept They w. like anything to see 111.21
we sat down, yea, we w. 62.62
young man who has not w. 488.2
Wert Bird thou never w. 500.13
West East is East, and W. is W. 341.1
Go W., young man 269.1
Go w., young man 517.1
West Wind O Wild W. 500.7
Wet joly whistle wel y-w. 127.13
Whale Very like a w. 498.68
What W. is truth? 30.2
Wheel bound upon a w. of fire 498.150
Wheels spoke among your w. 45.4
When had forgotten to say 'W.!' 592.4
w. a man should marry 30.12
Where to die, and go we know not w. 498.184
Wherefore For every why he had a w. 96.2
There is occasions and causes why and w. 498.100
w. art thou Romeo 498.242
Whiff w. of grapeshot 109.9
Whigs caught the W. bathing 195.2
Whim strangest w. 129.1
Whimper not with a bang but a w. 214.6
Whipping who shall scape w. 498.59
Whirlwind reap the w. 62.108
Whiskers Oh my fur and w. 111.3
w.... grown under glass 592.5
Whistle So was hir joly w. wel y-wet 127.13
W. and she'll come to you 45.9
White w. as snow 62.91
White House no whitewash at the W. 420.3
White man When a w. in Africa 356.1
When the w. came we had the land 252.1
W.'s Burden 341.9
Whites until you see the w. of their eyes 456.1
Whitewash no w. at the White House 420.3
Who W. is Silvia? 498.280
Whole greatest happiness of the w. 448.2
Whom for w. the bell tolls 199.13
Whore 'Tis Pity She's a w. 235.1
Whoreson w. zed 498.134
Whoso W. would be a man 218.9
Why For every w. 96.2
occasions and causes w. and wherefore 498.100
Their's not to reason w. 539.3
they knew not w. 96.1
Wicked no peace... unto the w. 62.99
Wickedness men alone are quite capable of every w. 154.6
w. of a woman 62.112
Widnes men become attached even to W. 538.2
Wife artist will let his w. starve 499.38

chose my w. for ... qualities as would wear well 262.8
light w. doth make a heavy husband 498.198
man who's untrue to his w. 25.7
No man worth having is true to his w. 556.2
single man ... must be in want of a w. 27.8
Wilderness one crying in the w. 62.115
W. is Paradise enow 228.3
w. of this world 90.1
Wild-fowl more fearful w. than your lion 498.204
Will complies against his w. 96.7
formation of the political w. of the nation 297.5
Man has his w. 300.1
You w., Oscar, you w. 577.7
William You are old, Father W. 111.4
Willin Barkis is w.'. 191.7
Willing spirit indeed is w. 62.145
Willow W., titwillow, titwillow 257.13
Win Heads I w. 171.1
Let the boy w. his spurs 210.1
Those who can w. a war 133.29
Wind Blow, blow, thou winter w. 498.25
Fair stood the w. for France 203.1
gone with the w. 200.2
like W. I go 228.5
of w. and limb 96.4
reed shaken with the w. 62.133
sown the w. 62.108
throw the sand against the w. 67.8
what w. is to fire 95.1
w. bloweth where it listeth 62.165
w. of change is blowing 378.3
words but w. 96.5
Wine days of w. and roses 200.3
Flask of W. 228.3
for its poisonous w. 332.19
good w. needs no bush 498.33
Happiness is a w. 511.2
love is better than w. 62.87
new w. into old bottles 62.154
Truth comes out in w. 449.1
use a little w. for thy stomach's sake 62.200
Who loves not w., woman and song 372.1
W. comes in at the mouth 601.5
w. is in, the wit is out 49.1
w. was a farce 455.2
Wing Bird is on the W. 228.2
Wings whether pigs have w. 111.22
w. like a dove 62.53
Wink I will w. and hold out mine iron 498.92
Winners In war ... there are no w. 118.1
Winning Gamesmanship ... Art of W. Games 453.1
not w. but taking part 160.1
Wins silly game where nobody w. 245.2
steady w. the race 363.1
Winter furious w.'s rages 498.38
If W. comes, can Spring be far behind? 500.9
w. and rough weather 498.21
W. is icummen in 454.1
w. of our discontent 498.239
Wisdom beginning of w. 62.58
in much w. is much grief 62.81
palace of W. 67.21
Silence is full of potential w. 310.19
W. be put in a silver rod 67.3
w. is better than rubies 62.65
Wise Be w. with speed 602.2
Coffee, which makes the politician w. 452.29
more of the fool than of the w. 30.13
Nor ever did a w. one 473.1
Some folk are w. 513.1
'Tis folly to be w. 268.4
To be w. and love 498.263
Wisely lov'd not w., but too well 498.229
Wiseman Mr Worldly W. 90.3
Wiser Be w. than other people 128.1
sadder and a w. man 144.16
Wish Conscience is ... rejection of a w. 242.3
w. to hurt 76.1
Wished consummation devoutly to be w. 498.61
Wishful w. thinking in Hell 358.2
Wit Brevity is the soul of w. 498.53

cause that w. is in other men 498.83
idea of w.... is laughing immoderately 512.2
I have neither w., nor words, nor worth 498.120
Impropriety is the soul of w. 388.5
In w. a man 452.6
True w. is nature to advantage 452.12
wine is in, the w. is out 49.1
w. among Lords 323.11
W. that can creep 452.5
Witch suffer a w. to live 62.24
With He that is not w. me is against me 62.134
Wither Age cannot w. her 498.9
w. into the truth 601.3
Wither'd w. is the garland of the war 498.15
Within that w. which passes show 498.41
when the fight begins w. himself 83.4
Witness Thou shalt not bear false w. 62.21
Wits Great W.... to Madness near alli'd 205.3
homely w. 498.278
Witty I am not only w. in myself 498.83
Wives W. are young men's mistresses 30.11
Wiving Hanging and w. goes by destiny 498.192
Woe suits of w. 498.41
W. to the vanquished 361.1
Wolf w. also shall dwell with the lamb 62.96
Wolfe I wish he would *bite*...my generals 254.1
Wolf's-bane neither twist W. 332.19
Wolves inwardly they are ravening w. 62.132
Woman being called a w. in my own house 569.22
body of a weak and feeble w. 215.2
every w. is at heart a rake 452.21
Every w. is infallibly to be gained 128.10
Every w. should marry 195.9
fair w. which is without discretion 62.68
Frailty, thy name is w. 498.43
Give not thy soul unto a w. 62.110
God made the w. for the man 539.5
good w. if I had five thousand 541.6
hell a fury like a w. scorned 151.4
help and support of the w. I love 211.1
I am a w.? When I think, I must speak 498.28
Love...history of a w.'s life 523.2
Man that is born of a w. 62.39
most beautiful w. I've ever seen 385.1
needs a very clever w. to manage a fool 341.10
never trust a w. who tells one her real age 584.15
nor w. neither 498.57
No w. should ever be quite accurate about her age 584.11
Once a w. has given you her heart 556.1
One is not born a w. 46.1
one of w. born 498.179
silliest w. can manage a clever man 341.10
such beauty as a w.'s eye 498.155
Thought does not become a... w. 502.2
What does a w. want 242.5
When lovely w. stoops to folly 262.10
Who loves not wine, w. and song 372.1
wickedness of a w. 62.112
w. as old as she looks 146.1
w. colour'd ill 498.302
w. has her way 300.1
W. is always fickle 560.2
w. is his game 539.23
w. is only a w. 341.2
w. killed with kindness 293.1
w.... knowing anything 27.6
W.'s at best a contradiction 452.22
w. seldom asks advice 4.7
w.'s reason 498.279
w.'s whole existence 98.12
w. that deliberates is lost 4.2
W. was God's *second* mistake 419.2
w. who is really kind to dogs 51.6
W. will be the last thing civilized by Man 393.1
w.... without a positive hump 541.5

w. yet think him an angel 541.4
wrecks a w.'s reputation 145.4
Womb mother's w. Untimely ripp'd 498.179
Naked...out of my mother's w. 62.38
teeming w. of royal kings 498.235
Women England...paradise for w. 94.3
experience of w. 201.8
fickleness of the w. I love 499.63
Monstrous Regiment of W. 342.1
Music and w. I cannot but give way to 438.2
no mothers, only w. 499.72
passing the love of w. 62.36
souls of w. are so small 96.8
tide in the affairs of w. 98.17
w. are glad to have been asked 428.1
W. are much more like each other 128.9
w. come and go 214.8
w.... not so young as... painted 51.1
w. require both 97.8
w. should be struck... like gongs 163.5
W. who love the same man 51.5
Womman worthy w. al hir lyve 127.10
Wonder common w. of all men 82.3
Wood Hewers of w. 62.30
impulse from a vernal w. 595.19
Woodman w. spare the beechen tree 104.1
Wood-notes Warble his native w. wild 401.8
Woods fresh w., and pastures new 401.13
pleasure in the pathless w. 98.10
We'll to the w. no more 304.7
w. decay, the w. decay and fall 539.26
Woodshed Something nasty in the w. 256.1
Word better w. than pre-fabricated 133.40
by every w. that proceedeth 62.117
every w. that proceedeth out of the mouth of the Lord 62.27
Greeks had a W. for It 8.1
In the beginning was the W. 62.161
in the captain's but a choleric w. 498.181
Mum's the w. 147.1
Suit the action to the w. 498.66
What is honour? A w. 498.80
when I use a w. 111.25
W. was made flesh 62.163
Words best w. in the best order 144.25
Fine w. and an insinuating appearance 150.4
For w., like Nature, half reveal 539.10
In two w.: im - possible 263.1
Men of few w. are the best 498.96
neither wit, nor w., nor worth 498.120
w. but wind 96.5
W. may be false and full of art 497.1
Wore w. enough for modesty 84.2
Work How can I take an interest in my w. 31.1
I haven't had time to w. in weeks 336.3
I like w.; it fascinates me 321.2
To sport would be as tedious as to w. 498.77
W. expands so as to fill the time available 434.1
W. is accomplished 441.2
W. is much more fun than fun 163.16
W. is the curse of the drinking classes 584.28
W. out your own salvation 62.197
w. that aspires to... art 154.5
Worked I w. my way up...to... poverty 385.11
Worker sociable w. 52.3
Workers W. of the world, unite 386.5
Workhouse Home is... woman's w. 499.55
Working w. of great institutions 488.1
Works all his w. 149.11
Faith without w. 62.206
Look on my w., ye Mighty 500.10
World All's right with the w. 83.13
all the uses of this w. 498.42
all the w. as my parish 575.1
All the w. is queer 429.1
All the w.'s a stage 498.23
brave new w. That has such people in't 498.260
citizen of the w. 30.16
estate o' th' w. were now undone 498.178

excellent foppery of the w. 498.131
fill the w. with fools 518.3
gain the whole w. 62.148
God so loved the w. 62.166
good deed in a naughty w. 498.197
greatest week in the history of the w. 420.1
Had we but w. enough, and time 384.1
I am…a citizen of the w. 515.5
I am the light of the w. 62.168
I called the New W. into existence 107.1
I consider the w. as made for me 513.2
Into the dangerous w. I leapt 67.11
Laugh, and the w. laughs 583.1
One had as good be out of the w. 134.1
queen for all the w. 498.102
reasonable man adapts himself to the w. 499.53
say to all the w. 'This was a man' 498.124
This is the way the w. ends 214.6
this little w. 498.235
This w. nis but a thurghfare 127.12
though the w. perish 224.1
triple pillar of the w. 498.4
we brought nothing into this w. 62.201
where in this small-talking w. 244.1
wilderness of this w. 90.1
w., I count it…but an hospital 82.7
W. in a grain of sand 67.1
w. is a comedy to those who think 564.2
w. is becoming like a lunatic asylum 364.3
w. is charged with the grandeur of God 302.3
w. is made of people who 76.2
w. is made up for the most part of fools 85.1
w. is too much with us 595.9
w. must be made safe for at least fifty years 133.39
w. must be made safe for democracy 591.3
w.'s mine oyster 498.199
w., the flesh, and the devil 149.7
w. to hide virtues in 498.267
w. was all before them 401.27
w. where nothing is had for nothing 140.1
w. will make a…path to his door 218.15
w. without end 149.3
w. would go round…faster 111.5
Worldly Mr. W. Wiseman 90.3
Worlds best of possible w. 561.1
So many w. 539.13
Wandering between two w. 20.7
Worm concealment, like a w. i' th' bud 498.272
Worms w. have eaten them, but not for love 498.31
you have tasted two whole w. 520.1
Wormwood w. and the gall 62.103
Worse Defend the bad against the w. 182.1
for better for w. 149.15
one thing…w. than being talked about 584.18
Truth put to the w. 401.37
Worship freedom of every person to w. God 475.3
Worst we can say This is the w. 498.143
w. Are full of passionate intensity 601.14
w. kinde of infortune is 127.17
Worth man's w. something 83.4
Whatever is w. doing 128.2
w. of a State 396.3
Worthington daughter on the stage, Mrs W. 163.10
Wrapping To perceive Christmas through its w. 578.2
Wrath flee from the w. to come 62.116
Wren Sir Christopher W. Said 59.3
w. goes to't 498.146
Wrestling I wretch lay w. with (my God!) my God 302.2
Wretchedness w. of being rich 511.4
Wretches feel what w. feel 498.141
Poor naked w. 498.140
w. hang that jury-men may dine 452.28
Writ I never w., nor no man ever lov'd 498.298
Write as much as a man ought to w. 550.2
bad book is…a labour to w. 310.20

Better to w. for yourself 153.10
Do not...w. on both sides of the paper at once 495.4
look in they heart and w. 506.1
w. and read comes by nature 498.212
Writer successful w....is indistinguishable 359.1
Writes Moving Finger w. 228.8
Writing All good w. is swimming under water 229.5
ease in w. comes from art 452.13
in w....ill 452.7
w. an exact man 30.39
Wrong anxious to do the w. thing correctly 486.6
cradled into poetry by w. 500.5
Nature is usually w. 577.2
our country, right or w. 183.1
right deed for the w. reason 214.18
right divine...to govern w. 452.1
something w. with our bloody ships 44.1
That the king can do no w. 65.2
their authors could not endure being w. 106.3
When people agree with me...I must be w. 584.22

X,Y,Z

Xanadu In X. did Kubla Khan 144.19
Yarn web of our life is of a mingled y. 498.2
Yawns grave y. for him 548.3
Year all the y. were playing holidays 498.77
nothing a-y. 533.2
That time of y. thou mayst in me behold 498.294
two months of every y. 98.2
y.'s at the spring 83.13
Years After long y. 98.28
he that cuts off twenty y. of life 498.111
thousand y. in thy sight 62.54
threescore y. and ten 62.55
touch of earthly y. 595.16
world must be made safe for...fifty y. 133.39
y. of discretion 149.12
Yesterday Jesus Christ the same y. 62.205
Yesterdays And all our y. 498.177
Yesteryear snows of y. 559.1
Yet but not y. 26.1
young man not y. 30.12
Yield temptation...y. to it 584.19
To strive, to seek...and not to y. 539.27
Yorick Alas, poor Y. 498.73
York this sun of Y. 498.239
You Y. also 428.2
Young be y. was very Heaven 595.14
country of y. men 218.14
Go west, y. man 517.1
I am sixty years y. 548.1
man's friends begin to compliment him about looking y. 315.1
man that is y. in years 30.32
Most women are not so y. as they are painted 51.1
Younger I...get y. every day 548.1
Yourself Better to write for y. 153.10
no friends not equal to y. 150.5
What you do not want done to y. 150.12
Youth age and y. cannot live together 498.303
Home-keeping y. 498.278
lying days of my y. 601.3
man loves the meat in his y. 498.211
Thou has nor y. nor age 498.183
Time...thief of y. 401.31
Y. is a blunder 195.7
Y. is full of pleasure 498.303
Y.'s a stuff will not endure 498.270
Y. will be served 70.1
y. would sleep out the rest 498.283
Youthe Withouten other companye in y. 127.10
Yukon Law of the Y. 496.2
Zeal Not too much z. 536.4
Zed whoreson z. 498.134